Japan's Sea Lane Security, 1940–2004

This is the first major English language study to comprehensively explore the broad and longstanding connections between Japan's national security and the safety of its sea lanes. Tracing issues from pre- and post-1945 eras, the book explores how Japan's concerns with sea lane protection have developed across such diverse fields as military strategy, diplomacy, trade policy, energy security and law enforcement.

Drawing upon case study material and primary research including interviews with officials and security analysts, the book presents a chronological analysis of Japan's sea lane security. From the late nineteenth century onwards Japan has depended upon seaborne imports of food, energy and industrial commodities for its prosperity and survival. The book investigates how, despite radical changes to Japan's economic and political structures, this remains a defining feature of the country's political economy. Graham argues that there is a basic continuity in Japan's defence and foreign policy, borne out in policymakers' ingrained perceptions of Japan as a resource-poor nation in a hostile international environment.

Although Japan's security policies have undergone relatively rapid changes a defence policy review in December 2004 concluded that 'securing Japan's sea lanes is crucial to Japan's prosperity and development'. *Japan's Sea Lane Security, 1940–2004* reveals a neglected but important aspect of Japan's military and economic security, investigating why officials and analysts continue to portray the defence of Japan's sea lanes as 'a matter of life and death'.

Euan Graham is a senior research officer for the North Asia and Pacific Research Group at the Foreign and Commonwealth Office in London.

The Nissan Institute/Routledge Japanese Studies Series

Other titles in the series:

The Myth of Japanese Uniqueness
Peter Dale

The Emperor's Adviser
Saionji Kinmochi and pre-war Japanese politics
Lesley Connors

A History of Japanese Economic Thought
Tessa Morris-Suzuki

The Establishment of the Japanese Constitutional System
Junji Banno, translated by J. A. A. Stockwin

Industrial Relations in Japan
The peripheral workforce
Norma Chalmers

Banking Policy in Japan
American efforts at reform during the occupation
William M. Tsutsui

Educational Reform in Japan
Leonard Schoppa

How the Japanese Learn to Work
Second edition
Ronald P. Dore and Mari Sako

Japanese Economic Development
Theory and practice: second edition
Penelope Francks

Japan and Protection
The growth of protectionist sentiment and the Japanese response
Syed Javed Maswood

The Soil, by Nagatsuka Takashi
A portrait of rural life in Meiji Japan
Translated and with an introduction by Ann Waswo

Biotechnology in Japan
Malcolm Brock

Britain's Educational Reform
A comparison with Japan
Michael Howarth

Language and the Modern State
The reform of written Japanese
Nanette Twine

Industrial Harmony in Modern Japan
The intervention of a tradition
W. Dean Kinzley

Japanese Science Fiction
A view of a changing society
Robert Matthew

The Japanese Numbers Game
The use and understanding of numbers in modern Japan
Thomas Crump

Ideology and Practice in Modern Japan
Edited by Roger Goodman and Kirsten Refsing

Technology and Industrial Development in Pre-war Japan
Mitsubishi Nagasaki shipyard, 1884–1934
Yukiko Fukasaku

Japan's Early Parliaments, 1890–1905
Structure, issues and trends
Andrew Fraser, R. H. P. Mason and Philip Mitchell

Japan's Foreign Aid Challenge
Policy reform and aid leadership
Alan Rix

Emperor Hirohito and Shôwa Japan
A political biography
Stephen S. Large

Japan: Beyond the End of History
David Williams

Ceremony and Ritual in Japan
Religious practices in an industrialized society
Edited by Jan van Bremen and D. P. Martinez

Understanding Japanese Society
Second edition
Joy Hendry

The Fantastic in Modern Japanese Literature
The subversion of modernity
Susan J. Napier

Militarization and Demilitarization in Contemporary Japan
Glenn D. Hook

Growing a Japanese Science City
Communication in scientific research
James W. Dearing

Architecture and Authority in Japan
William H. Coaldrake

Women's *Gidayû* and the Japanese Theatre Tradition
A. Kimi Coaldrake

Democracy in Post-war Japan
Maruyama Masao and the search for autonomy
Rikki Kersten

Treacherous Women of Imperial Japan
Patriarchal fictions, patricidal fantasies
Hélène Bowen Raddeker

Japanese–German Business Relations
Competition and rivalry in the inter-war period
Akira Kudô

Japan, Race and Equality
The racial equality proposal of 1919
Naoko Shimazu

Japan, Internationalism and the UN
Ronald Dore

Life in a Japanese Women's College
Learning to be ladylike
Brian J. McVeigh

On The Margins of Japanese Society
Volunteers and the welfare of the urban underclass
Carolyn S. Stevens

The Dynamics of Japan's Relations with Africa
South Africa, Tanzania and Nigeria
Kweku Ampiah

The Right to Life in Japan
Noel Williams

The Nature of the Japanese State
Rationality and rituality
Brian J. McVeigh

Society and the State in Inter-war Japan
Edited by Elise K. Tipton

Japanese–Soviet/Russian Relations since 1945
A difficult peace
Kimie Hara

Interpreting History in Sino-Japanese Relations
A case study in political decision making
Caroline Rose

Endô Shûsaku
A literature of reconciliation
Mark B. Williams

Green Politics in Japan
Lam Peng-Er

The Japanese High School
Silence and resistance
Shoko Yoneyama

Engineers in Japan and Britain
Education, training and employment
Kevin McCormick

The Politics of Agriculture in Japan
Aurelia George Mulgan

Opposition Politics in Japan
Strategies under a one-party dominant regime
Stephen Johnson

The Changing Face of Japanese Retail
Working in a chain store
Louella Matsunaga

Japan and East Asian Regionalism
Edited by S. Javed Maswood

Globalizing Japan
Ethnography of the Japanese presence in America, Asia and Europe
Edited by Harumi Befu and Sylvie Guichard-Anguis

Japan at Play
The ludic and logic of power
Edited by Joy Hendry and Massimo Raveri

The Making of Urban Japan
Cities and planning from Edo to the twenty first century
André Sorensen

Public Policy and Economic Competition in Japan
Change and continuity in antimonopoly policy, 1973–1995
Michael L. Beeman

Modern Japan
A social and political history
Elise K. Tipton

Men and Masculinities in Contemporary Japan
Dislocating the Salaryman Doxa
Edited by James E. Roberson and Nobue Suzuki

The Voluntary and Non-Profit Sector in Japan
The challenge of change
Edited by Stephen P. Osborne

Japan's Security Relations with China
From balancing to bandwagoning
Reinhard Drifte

Understanding Japanese Society
Third edition
Joy Hendry

Japanese Electoral Politics
Creating a new party system
Edited by Steven R. Reed

The Japanese-Soviet Neutrality Pact
A diplomatic history, 1941–1945
Boris Slavinsky translated by Geoffrey Jukes

Academic Nationalism in China and Japan
Framed by concepts of nature, culture and the universal
Margaret Sleeboom

The Race to Commercialize Biotechnology
Molecules, markets and the state in the United States and Japan
Steve W. Collins

Institutions, Incentives and Electoral Participation in Japan
Cross-level and cross-national perspectives
Yusaka Horiuchi

Japan's Interventionist State
The role of the MAFF
Aurelia George Mulgan

Japan's Sea Lane Security, 1940–2004
A matter of life and death?
Euan Graham

Japan's Sea Lane Security, 1940–2004

A matter of life and death?

Euan Graham

Routledge
Taylor & Francis Group
LONDON AND NEW YORK

First published 2006
by Routledge
2 Park Square, Milton Park, Abingdon, Oxon OX14 4RN

Simultaneously published in the USA and Canada
by Routledge
270 Madison Ave, New York, NY 10016

Routledge is an imprint of the Taylor & Francis Group

Typeset in Times New Roman by
Newgen Imaging Systems (P) Ltd, Chennai, India
Printed and bound in Great Britain by
Antony Rowe Ltd, Chippenham, Wiltshire

British Library Cataloguing in Publication Data
A catalogue record for this book is available
from the British Library

Library of Congress Cataloging in Publication Data
Graham, Euan.
Japan's sea lane security, 1940–2004: a matter of life and death / Euan Graham.
p. cm. – (Nissan Institute/Routledge Japanese studies series)
Includes bibliographical references and index.
1. Merchant marine–Japan. 2. Trade routes–Japan. 3. Freedom of the seas–Japan. 4. Sea power–Japan. I. Title. II. Series.

HE891.F73 2005
359′.03′0952–dc22 2005001984

ISBN10: 0–415–35640–7
ISBN13: 9–78–0–415–35640–4

Contents

Figures

Maps

Tables

Series editor's preface

The Nissan/Routledge Japanese Studies Series was launched in 1986 and is now approaching its seventieth volume. It seeks to foster an informed and balanced, but not uncritical, understanding of Japan. One aim of the series is to show the depth and variety of Japanese institutions, practices and ideas. Another is, by using comparisons, to see what lessons, positive or negative, can be drawn for other countries. The tendency in commentaries on Japan to resort to out-dated, ill-informed or sensational stereotypes still remains, and needs to be combated.

Whereas in the 1990s the Japanese economy struggled through a lengthy period of recession and structural adjustment, punctuated by some serious episodes of mismanagement, the new millennium has seen a limited but significant economic recovery. If – in a famous phrase – the 1990s were the 'lost decade', there is a good case for arguing that the first decade of the twenty-first century is a decade of new directions, and of revived confidence. In politics, the fluid party manoeuvrings and frequent changes of leadership that were such a marked feature of the *fin de siècle* have given way to relative stability, greater political balance and fortified leadership capacities. There is a strong case for saying that true political maturity will only arrive when single-party dominance is replaced by party alternation in power. This still seems some way off, but is a goal that it is now at least realistic to contemplate.

In the present decade, Japanese foreign policy has been dominated by two major issues. The first is the perceived threat from North Korea, and the difficulties of dealing with that maverick state. The second issue, however, is that of how Japan should deal with an economically resurgent China. It is difficult to escape the conclusion that Japan and China have been finding it increasingly difficult to deal with each other. A number of bilateral problems divided them, with the Koizumi Government in Tokyo deliberately cleaving closer to the United States under President Bush. The Taiwan issue now presents a worrying aspect, with Japan becoming perceptibly more concerned with the difficult scenarios that it presents. Deteriorating relations between Japan and China are understandable on certain levels, but are nevertheless surprising in view of the major economic interactions between the two of them. Japanese trade with and investment in China has been indeed a major factor in the economic recovery of Japan.

Historically and in contemporary circumstances, Japanese economic prosperity (and even survival) are heavily reliant on the free passage of goods to and from Japan by sea. Sea lane security has long been a primary preoccupation of Japanese governments, businesses and the public. Notoriously, Japan lacks its own sources of raw materials (oil most conspicuously), which need to be shipped through a number of potentially vulnerable and overcrowded 'chokepoints', such as the Straits of Malacca. Surprisingly, there has never been a comprehensive study of Japanese sea lane security before in English. Dr Euan Graham ably fills this gap with the present carefully researched and enlightening volume. The reader will find here much that throws light on Japanese thinking about security and foreign relations, given the underlying sense of insecurity engendered by chronic supply vulnerability, as well as the need to maintain a free flow of exports.

J. A. A. Stockwin

Preface

The end of 2004 is an opportune juncture to take stock of Japan's sea lane security. Rising concerns about marine terrorism, piracy, Chinese and North Korean maritime activities have reinvigorated interest in sea lane security not only in Japan, but regionally and globally. Japan's security policy itself is undergoing a general transformation towards the adoption of a 'normal' security posture and the renewed salience of maritime and sea lane security within this process was confirmed in a review of defence capability completed in December. A brief survey of Japan's maritime activities near the time of writing illustrates how far the parameters of its maritime security environment have shifted since the end of the Cold War. In the last quarter of 2004, a Japanese Maritime Self Defense Force (MSDF) flotilla in the Indian Ocean was providing fuel to United States, United Kingdom and other vessels, as part Japan's ongoing support for counter-terrorism operations in Afghanistan since November 2001. The MSDF was simultaneously providing logistic support to a Japanese ground contingent deployed to Iraq earlier in 2004. In October, Japan Coast Guard and MSDF units participated in Asia's first Proliferation Security Initiative drill, near Tokyo Bay hosted by Japan. In the following month, the Japanese government ordered maritime security operations for only the second time in the post-1945 era after a Chinese nuclear submarine encroached into Japan's territorial waters. Such a dynamic maritime environment presents Japanese decision-makers with both a more diffuse and pressing set of policy concerns than was the case in the 1980s when Tokyo and Washington prepared to defend Japan's sea lanes against the slim possibility of a high-intensity maritime conflict with the Soviet Union in the western Pacific.

Several Japanese books on sea lanes were published in the 1980s, when 'sea lane defence' last topped the agenda of US–Japan Alliance relations, following Prime Minister Suzuki Zenkō's May 1981 statement that Japan would undertake to defend several hundred miles of surrounding waters and the sea lanes to a distance of 1,000 nautical miles. These texts tended to concentrate on Japan's prospective role in defence cooperation with the United States, in the context of Japan's dependence on imported strategic commodities.[1] In the English-language literature dedicated to Japan's post-war defence and security, James Auer's 1973 history of the *Postwar Rearmament of Japanese Maritime Forces, 1945–71*, and Peter

Woolley's more recent *Japan's Navy: Politics and Paradox, 1971–2000*, provide a wealth of information on the Maritime Self Defense Force (MSDF) – Japan's *de facto* navy – including the special attention paid in Japan to defending sea lanes.[2] Linton Wells' 1975 doctoral thesis explores Japan's maritime strategic interests broadly, but on a more compressed time-scale.[3] The importance attached to securing a stable supply of natural resources within Japan's foreign and economic policies has been highlighted in Chapman, Drifte and Gow's 1983 study of *Japan's Quest for Comprehensive Security*, and in more sensational terms by Friedman and Lebard, in *The Coming War with Japan*.[4] Yet surprisingly, there has been no dedicated English-language attempt to relate Japan's sea lane security to the broader, historical context of its defence policy, alliance relations and national strategy. This book aims to fill that gap, arguing that the sea lane issue demonstrates a long-term continuity in Japan's 'strategic geography' from the pre-war period to the present. This continuity transcends Japan's post-1945 experiment in constitutional pacifism and is borne out in policy-makers' ingrained perceptions of their country as a resource-poor island nation in a hostile international environment, whose prosperity and survival depend upon seaborne imports of food, energy and industrial commodities. As a companion theme, submerged below declaratory policy but constantly accompanying it, I am also interested in accounting for the instrumental use of sea lane security by decision-makers on both sides of the Pacific as a rationale to justify contentious aspects of Japan's defence and alliance policy throughout the post-1945 period.

This book is based on a doctoral thesis awarded in 2003 by the Australian National University. Primary research material is drawn from Japanese and English-language primary and secondary sources. I conducted interviews with officials and security analysts in Japan, Australia, Indonesia and the United Kingdom between 1999 and 2004. Primary field work in Japan was carried out with the support of a Japanese Government Ministry of Education Scholarship from October 1997 to March 1999, while based at Aoyama Gakuin University and Keio University. I revisited Tokyo in February 2002 and June 2004, conducting further interviews and documentary research. The views expressed here and any factual errors are entirely my own. They bear no relation to UK government policy or my position as a Foreign and Commonwealth Office Research Analyst.

Acknowledgements

There are many people to thank, who were involved in the eight years it took to write this book, counting its origins as a doctoral thesis at the Australian National University. Professor Desmond Ball, of the Strategic and Defence Studies Centre, chaired the academic supervisory panel. Fieldwork in Japan was carried out with the support of a Japanese Ministry of Education research scholarship from October 1997 to March 1999, under the supervision of Professor Watanabe Akio, President of the Research Institute for Peace and Security (RIPS), whose assistance in arranging interviews in Japan was especially helpful. Dr Chris W. Hughes, Dr Richard Tanter and Dr Stanley Weeks provided valuable comment and encouragement on turning a thesis into a book.

Dr Karl Claxton's friendship and detailed support were indispensable to improving the quality of research and writing. I also owe a special debt to Ann Snow and to my parents, Kenneth and Sheila for their help as patient, diligent proof-readers and for their moral support. Valuable assistance was provided by Dr Nikki Baker, of the Australian Defence Force Academy, Dr Jennifer Amyx of the University of Pennsylvania and Mr Paul Riseborough. I would also like to acknowledge the comradeship of Mr John McFarlane, former Executive Director of the Australian member committee of the Council for Security Cooperation in the Asia Pacific. Professor Sakanaka Tomohisa of RIPS, Dr Katahara Eichi of Kobe University, Professor Soeya Yoshihide of Keio University and Mr Yoshizaki Tomonori of the National Institute for Defence Studies all helpfully volunteered their time and insights towards dispelling the fog around Japanese defence policy decision-making.

Admirals Sakonjo Naotoshi, also of RIPS, Hirama Yoichi formerly of the National Defense Academy at Yokosuka, Kawamura Sumihiko, of the Okazaki Institute, and Akimoto Kazumine, of the Ship and Ocean Foundation, provided essential information and background regarding the Maritime Self Defense Force's outlook on Japan's maritime security. I am grateful to the ICC-International Maritime Bureau for granting permission to use copyright material, as I am to the Maritime Institute for Malaysia and the Department of Marine Affairs and Fisheries, Republic of Indonesia.

Abbreviations and acronyms

AEW	Airborne Early Warning
APEC	Asia Pacific Economic Cooperation
APERC	Asia Pacific Energy Research Centre
ARF	ASEAN Regional Forum
ASDF	Air Self Defense Force
ASEAN	Association of Southeast Asian Nations
ASF	Asian Ship Owners' Forum
ASL	Archipelagic sea lane
ASW	Anti-submarine warfare
AWACS	Airborne Warning and Control System
BMD	Ballistic Missile Defence
COLREG	Convention on the International Regulations for Preventing Collisions at Sea
CSCAP	Council for Security Cooperation in the Asia Pacific
DD	Destroyer
DDG	Guided-missile destroyer
DDH	Helicopter-equipped destroyer
DE	Destroyer escort
DoD	Department of Defense
DSP	Democratic Socialist Party
DWT	Deadweight tons
EEZ	Exclusive economic zone
EU	European Union
FTA	Free Trade Area
FY	Financial year (1 April–31 March)
GAM	Gerakan Aceh Merdeka (Free Aceh Movement)
GDP	Gross Domestic Product
GNP	Gross National Product
GRT	Gross registered tons
GSDF	Ground Self Defense Force
IMB	International Maritime Bureau
IMCO	Inter-governmental Maritime Consultative Organisation
IMO	International Maritime Organisation

ISM	International Safety Management code
ISPS	International Ship and Port Facility Security code
JCG	Japan Coast Guard
JCP	Japan Communist Party
JDA	Japan Defense Agency
JSA	Japan Shipowners' Association
JSP	Japan Socialist Party
LDP	Liberal Democratic Party
LNG	Liquefied natural gas
LPG	Liquefied petroleum gas
LTTE	Liberation Tigers of Tamil Eelam
MARPOL	International Convention for the Prevention of Pollution from Ships
METI	Ministry of Economy, Trade and Industry
MITI	Ministry of International Trade and Industry
MoF	Ministry of Finance
MOFA	Ministry of Foreign Affairs
MoT	Ministry of Transport
MOX	Mixed-oxide
MSA	Maritime Safety Agency (former name of the Japan Coast Guard)
MSDF	Maritime Self Defense Force
MTCR	Missile Technology Control Regime
MTDP	Mid-Term Defense Program
MTDPE	Mid-Term Defense Program Estimate
NATO	North Atlantic Treaty Organization
NCS	Naval Control of Shipping
NDC	National Defense Council
NDPO	National Defense Program Outline
NGO	Non-governmental organization
NPRF	National Police Reserve Force
NSR	Northern Sea Route
NYK	Nippon Yūsen Kaisha
ODA	Overseas Development Assistance
OPK	Ocean Peace-Keeping
OSPAR	Oil Spill Preparedness and Response
OTH	Over-the-horizon
PKO	Peace-keeping operations
PLAN	People's Liberation Army Navy
PSI	Proliferation Security Initiative
RIMPAC	Rim of the Pacific Exercise
RMSI	Regional Maritime Security Initiative
SAM	Surface-to-air missile
SDF	Self Defense Forces
SLBM	Submarine-launched ballistic missile
SLOC	Sea lines (or lanes) of communication

SOLAS	International Convention for the Safety of Life at Sea
SOSUS	Sound surveillance sonar system
SSBN	Nuclear-powered ballistic missile submarine
SSK	Conventionally-powered attack submarine
SSM	Surface-to-surface missile
SSN	Nuclear-powered attack submarine
SUA	Suppression of Unlawful Acts at Sea
SURTASS	Surveillance Towed Array Sensor System
TEU	20-foot equivalent unit
TSS	Traffic Separation Scheme
ULCC	Ultra-large crude carrier
UNCLOS	United Nations Convention for the Law of the Sea
UNGA	United Nations General Assembly
UNSC	United Nations Security Council
VLCC	Very large crude carrier
VTOL	Vertical take-off and landing
WMD	Weapons of mass destruction
WTO	World Trade Organisation

Introduction

This is the first major study in English to examine sea lines of communication (SLOC) as a security concern for Japan, tracing the issue from industrialization in the late nineteenth century to 2004. It does so in a comprehensive way, identifying significant imperatives defining policy continuity despite points of departure in Japan's overall security stance. Japanese officials and analysts have repeatedly portrayed the security of Japan's sea lanes as 'a matter of life and death'.[1] A review of defence policy concluded in December 2004 that 'securing the sea lanes is crucial to [Japan's] prosperity and development'.[2] Indeed, as an island nation Japan has an obvious strategic interest in maintaining the safety of maritime merchant traffic. First, since industrialization in the late nineteenth century, Japan has been reliant on shipping to transport the vast majority of bulk materials, liquid fuels and manufactured goods in and out of the country. Second, despite having the world's second-largest industrial economy and a population approaching 127 million, it possesses limited mineral resources and arable land. Import dependence is marked across a range of strategic commodities including oil (99 per cent), liquefied natural gas (LNG) (96 per cent), iron ore (100 per cent) and copper (96 per cent). Many of its basic energy, raw material and food requirements must be met through imports, for which shipping is the only commercially viable mode of transportation.

A combination of archipelagic geography, poor resource allocation and the large distances separating Japan from its primary suppliers of energy, raw materials and food has accentuated the importance of shipping to its security, despite a comparatively modest trade-to-GDP weighting. Japan depends particularly on sea lanes connecting it with the oil terminals in the Gulf, from which it draws nearly all its oil, and other shipping routes connecting it with the mineral resources of the Indian Ocean basin, Australasia, Southeast Asia and North America. 'Self-help' economic policy measures such as stockpiling, austerity controls, substitution and building a diverse supply portfolio have the capacity to reduce the disruption caused by a halt to seaborne imports. However, any prolonged interruption of Japan's maritime transportation networks would undermine both industrial production and the government's ability to provide for the basic welfare of the population. Furthermore, in the event that Japan was threatened with military aggression, trans-Pacific SLOC would be vital to military reinforcement from the United States, which has retained substantial forces in Japan since 1945.

I consider here Japan's efforts to minimize its exposure to the threat of seaborne supply disruptions within a 'comprehensive security' context, connecting disparate policy fields including diplomacy, trade relations, industrial policy, energy policy and law enforcement. However, the core concern is military security and the impact that the vulnerability of Japan's sea lanes, as perceived by its decision-makers, has had upon strategy and defence policy.

Specifically, I set out to answer two questions:

- How has Japan's vulnerability to the disruption of its sea lanes defined its perceived security imperatives and choices in defence and alliance policy since 1940, particularly in terms of decision-makers' responses to changing strategic circumstances?
- How has Japan's vulnerability to SLOC disruption been used instrumentally, as a rationale to legitimize politically or constitutionally problematic military activities in the post-war period?

Two wider concerns inform these questions. The first is the influence which Japan's 'strategic geography' has had on decision-makers over a relatively long period. Strategic geography, for the purposes of this book, is defined as the influence on a nation's defence and foreign policy, as well as its threat perceptions, resulting from its geographic location relative to the global distribution of resources and military capabilities.

Japan's security is usually approached in terms of the discontinuity between the pre- and post-1945 policy-making environment, often thought of as a cultural shift, as constitutional defence constraints and the orientation of national priorities towards mercantile goals replaced military government and an imperial security paradigm. The legacy of the pre-1945 period is normally approached in terms of Japan's ability 'to face the issue of war responsibility' as the key political question confronting its post-war security policy, leading to its designation as a 'handicapped' state.[3] In my view, a disjunction between Japan's pre- and post-war political systems, security institutions and structures has obscured the fact that significant continuity has been maintained, in the way that 'strategic geography' has shaped threat perceptions and strategic policy references of Japan's decision-makers. Such continuity is also likely to straddle advances in military technology and the post-Cold War re-definition of security threats from state-led to non-state paradigms, which received impetus from the terrorist attacks of 11 September 2001 and Japan's own experience with the Aum Shinrikyō cult in the mid-1990s.

The second concern pertains to Japan's security policy decision-making process. The various individual and institutional domestic actors shaping post-war policy include the prime minister, cabinet, the Liberal Democratic Party (LDP) and opposition parties, the Ministry of Foreign Affairs (MOFA), the Japan Defense Agency (JDA) and the uniformed members of the Self Defense Forces (SDF). In addition to domestic actors, the United States has had a highly influential role in shaping

Japan's security affairs since 1945, both at the level of formal alliance linkages and through the close personal ties between the United States and Japanese armed forces, 'navy-to-navy' relations in particular. The dynamics of this post-war decision-making process are analysed in Chapter 4, which dissects policy at the levels of Japan's strategic interaction within the international system, domestic politics and alliance linkages. It is widely assumed that for most of the post-war period the US–Japan Alliance has functioned as a 'prism', filtering interaction between the systemic pressures and domestic constraints that define the parameters of Japan's security policy. However, I argue in later chapters that strategic pressures, especially concerning China and North Korea, have led Japanese policy-makers latterly to adopt increasingly 'realist' – that is systemic, balance of power-based – perceptions of potential security threats within Japan's regional security environment.

A historical narrative approach is chosen as the method most suited to demonstrating that a long-term continuity in Japan's 'strategic geography' has guided Japanese security policy-makers' perceptions and responses, in spite of the post-war redefinition of the country's political institutions, structural economic change and fluidity in the international systemic environment.

In short, Chapters 1 and 2 are broad in scope and serve as an empirical and contextual anchor for the six, broadly chronological chapters that follow, exploring Japan's SLOC security from 1940 to 2004. Chapter 3 examines the pre-1945 era; Chapter 4, the 1945–77 period, and Chapter 5, the late Cold War period from the late 1970s to 1990. Chapter 6 detours slightly from this chronology, to critique Japan's sea lane diplomacy in Southeast Asia from the early 1970s to 2004. Chapters 7 and 8 pick up the thread from Chapter 5, providing an overview of Japan's security and defence policy in the post-Cold War era. Consecutive case studies then examine Japan's responses to non-state, maritime security threats from terrorism and piracy, and state-level, sea lane concerns regarding China and North Korea.

In greater detail, Chapter 1 profiles Japan's import dependence; the core factor underpinning the perception of SLOC security as a strategic policy concern for Japan. It analyses the features of the global distribution of resources and the structure of Japan's industrial economy that have brought about exceptionally high levels of dependence on imported fuels, raw materials and food, and generated a corresponding requirement to export manufactured goods in order to fund imports. As well as profiling the extent of Japan's import dependence in key sectors, the chapter analyses the potential for self-help measures, such as stockpiling, resource substitution and diversification, to militate against perceptions of economic vulnerability and any temptation to compensate for this through increased military preparedness. The chapter suggests that despite considerable investment in such measures and long-term trends that point to declining import requirements, seaborne trade will for the foreseeable future continue to be perceived within Japan as vital not only for maintaining wealth, but to sustaining basic economic activity and human survival. The major sea lanes and chokepoints used to convey Japan's overseas trade are also identified and profiled, together with an analysis of re-routing options and estimates of the additional shipping costs they would generate.

Chapter 2 defines the concept of SLOC by tracing its origins with reference to classical theories of sea power developed around the turn of the twentieth century and the importance these placed on the control of maritime communications. The chapter examines how such concepts were challenged by advances in military technology and all-out conflict during the Atlantic and Pacific anti-shipping offensives of the two world wars. Next, the evolution of SLOC security is examined during the Cold War, concerning Western plans to defend Atlantic and Pacific SLOC from Soviet interdiction. The chapter then explores the widening definition of SLOC security applied since the end of the Cold War, which incorporates economic, military, law enforcement, diplomatic, non-state and environmental concerns. Although a rigorous conceptual exploration of sea lines of communication is attempted, for the purposes of this book 'sea lane' and 'SLOC' are interchangeable terms, except where 'sea lane' is used in a narrow, navigational context, as in Chapter 6.

Chapter 3 reveals how Japan's opening up by foreign naval powers from the 1850s and rapid industrialization brought about a new dependence on maritime transportation. It shows that the drive to secure a captive resource base in Asia, in order to lessen the leverage of Western powers (particularly that of the United States over its oil supplies) helped to determine the grand strategy of Japan's imperial expansion. The objective of controlling Southeast Asia's natural resources partly as a solution to Western energy sanctions, ultimately motivated Japan to attack the United States and Great Britain in December 1941. However, the strategic vulnerability of seaborne imports in transit was not adequately appreciated until exposed by the Allied anti-shipping campaign of 1943–45. The chapter argues that the pre-1945 period is still relevant to understanding Japan's contemporary SLOC security as the only case study of a full fledged attempt to cut off its seaborne supply routes. Post-war Allied and Japanese official assessments revealed that the wartime blockade was an instrumental factor in the defeat, a fact now largely forgotten outside Japan. In Japan, the traumatic memory of the 'war of the maru', involving the destruction of Japan's merchant fleet without adequate protection from the Imperial Navy, continues to resonate popularly in terms of perceived vulnerability to supply disruptions and institutionally within the Maritime Self Defense Force (MSDF) through the priority accorded to sea lane defence.

Chapter 4 locates Japan's sea lane security from 1945 to 1977 in the context of sweeping changes to Japan's strategic and domestic circumstances arising from the defeat, occupation, the onset of the Cold War and the radical effect these had upon the approach of post-war governments to security and defence. An overarching analysis is developed, identifying the major drivers and constraints of Japan's post-war defence and security policy-making environment at three levels: systemic/strategic, alliance linkages and domestic politics. The chapter shows that despite radical policy departures from the pre-war period, Japan's maritime geography and resource distribution ensured that basic continuity was maintained in policy-makers' perceptions of the country's potential vulnerability to a disruption of maritime transportation. Indeed, this concern mounted with rapid economic growth, as Japan lost access to traditional, proximate markets and supply bases in Northeast Asia, and became increasingly reliant on Middle Eastern oil shipped via the narrow and congested Straits of Malacca. The chapter argues that notwithstanding constitutional constraints on defence capability and responses to political pressures within the US–Japan Alliance, Japanese policy-makers' own perceptions of the vulnerability of Japan's sea lanes helped to shape their decisions at the level of alliance and defence policy. The chapter also considers the influence over Japan's defence policy exercised at a transnational level, via navy-to-navy links between the MSDF and the US Navy.

Chapter 5 analyses the decision-making process that propelled sea lane defence to the forefront of Japan's defence policy and alliance relations during the 1980s. Building from the analysis of Japan's post-1945 security outlined in the preceding chapter, it argues that Japan's involvement in sea lane defence was, *a priori*, a reaction to pressure from Washington's post-Vietnam determination to move more of the burden of defence to regional allies. However, the chapter demonstrates that Japan's increasing integration as a military partner in US global strategy also reflected Japanese policy-makers' independent concerns about the build-up of Soviet maritime forces in the Soviet Far East and a perceived decline in the relative power of the United States. Existing concerns about the vulnerability of Japanese shipping routes, honed by the memory of the wartime blockade, the oil crises of the 1970s and attacks on Japanese tankers in the Gulf during the 1980–88 Iran–Iraq War, lent weight to the concept of sea lane defence as a rationale to persuade politicians, the business elite and a sceptical public and opposition of the need to develop closer alliance defence cooperation and to modernize the SDF's capabilities. The elastic spatial definition of sea lanes also gave supporters of an extra-territorial defence role for the MSDF and Air Self Defense Force (ASDF) the flexibility to expand the geographical boundaries of Japan's self-defence zone without directly confronting the proscriptions against overseas dispatch and collective self-defence, which have constrained where, how and with whom the SDF can operate.

Chapter 6 critiques the effectiveness of Japan's diplomatic efforts to maintain navigational access and safety in geographically remote sea lanes. It focuses on Southeast Asia, reflecting the fact that nearly half of Japan's imports and exports are shipped via chokepoint waterways in the region, including nearly all its oil. The chapter examines official and private-level Japanese initiatives since the early 1970s and concentrates on efforts to preserve freedom of navigation in the Straits of Malacca and Indonesia's archipelagic waters as well as the more recent shipments of Japan's re-processed nuclear waste through the region. It argues that Japan's mixed formal and informal approach has been largely successful at balancing its interests in upholding navigational safety standards and maintaining legally unencumbered access to regional sea lanes on one hand, while accommodating concerns of the coastal states about sovereignty, environmental risk and cost-sharing on the other.

Chapters 7 and 8 evaluate how Japan's sea lane security has evolved since the collapse of the Soviet Union in 1991 abruptly ended the rationale for sea lane defence, based on a potential Soviet threat to Japan's SLOC linked to scenarios for superpower conflict. Chapter 7 is divided into two sections. The first provides an overview of Japan's changing post-Cold War defence and security policies, including official reviews of defence policy conducted in 1995 and 2004 and their impact on the MSDF's force structure. It argues that despite a modest downsizing of the SDF's frontline capabilities since the end of the Cold War, 'realist' perceptions of Japan's security environment on the part of policy-makers and analysts have grown. This reflects awareness of a more diffuse set of state and non-state-level security concerns as well as strategic uncertainty. This shift, which has hastened under Prime Minister Koizumi Junichirō's administration, is then explored in terms of specific threats and potential challenges posed to Japan's sea lanes. The second section introduces the first of two case studies in Japan's post-Cold War SLOC security, dealing with non-state threats posed by maritime terrorism-at-sea and piracy, and builds on the general profile of these factors given in Chapter 2. The chapter also identifies ways in which such concerns have been employed as pretexts for the exploration of new security roles for the SDF and the Japan Coast Guard (JCG), and the pursuit of security cooperation with the United States and various states along Asia's coastal periphery.

Chapter 8 explores potential conventional military threats to Japan's SLOC in the post-Cold War era, focussing on China and North Korea. China is seen in Japan as the most important state-level variable bearing on Japan's SLOC, reflecting its status as a party to sovereignty disputes in the South China Sea and Taiwan Strait, its geographically dominant position along East Asia's coastal periphery, its growing economic and political influence, and ongoing military and naval modernization programme. This chapter analyses perceptions among security policy-makers (in China as well as Japan) in as far as these relate specifically to sea lanes and draws conclusions about how they are informing the strategic dynamic of Sino-Japanese relations. The chapter reveals that underlying much of the contemporary interest in sea lane issues in Japan is an emerging realist view and fear of China. Although still disputed within policymaking circles, this foresees two possible threats. First, that China could disrupt Japan's seaborne imports collaterally as a result of the spillover of a maritime conflict in the East or South China Seas. Second, at some point after 2020, China may be sufficiently emboldened by the modernization of its naval, air and missile capabilities to threaten obstruction of Japan's seaborne imports for strategic leverage and to satisfy its resource needs in competition with those of Japan. It is also argued that concerns about the security of sea lanes are used to justify aspects of the MSDF and ASDF's force structure, operational concepts and the adoption of new security legislation designed to expand the spatial and functional scope of Japan's security ambit. The limited but more immediate and multifaceted maritime security threats that North Korea presents are considered mainly in the latter regard, especially concerning measures to prevent maritime incursions by 'suspicious vessels' and Japan's participation in the Proliferation Security Initiative (PSI) since May 2003.

Briefly, I conclude that the strategic imperative of SLOC security has remained essentially consistent over time for Japan despite its shifting threat perceptions. However, material strategic calculations alone are insufficient to explain policy responses linked with sea lane security in the post-war period. Political advantages associated with the instrumental use of SLOC security have led decision-makers at various levels, in both Japan and the United States, to employ such concerns to justify contentious aspects of defence and alliance policy. The Conclusion ends with a discussion of future trends in Japan's SLOC security.

1 Japan's maritime trade and trade routes

An empirical analysis

Introduction

The extent to which SLOC have historically been perceived by Japanese policy-makers as core security concerns in a large part reflects the economic importance to Japan in maintaining inward-bound shipments of fuels, metal ores, other raw materials and food, as well as outward-bound exports of manufactured goods. This chapter provides an empirical analysis of Japan's economic geography, consumption patterns and dependence on imported resources, and major trading partners. It shows that overseas trade, although accounting for a relatively small proportion of national output, is vital to Japan's survival, as a reflection of its poor resource endowment. The assessment offered, establishes that the basic imperative of Japan's SLOC security is its vulnerability to supply disruption. The data set out here will serve as an empirical basis for comparison with the perceptions of Japanese policy-makers, explored in later chapters, about the locations of such vulnerabilities – geographically and sectorally.

After a brief geographic overview in the following section, the defining features of Japan's economy are outlined in the section 'Economic overview', including its poor natural resource allocation and resultant dependence on overseas sources for a wide range of essential industrial and energy commodities, as well as food to meet its nutritional needs. Efforts to build oil and mineral stockpiles are assessed together with other austerity measures that are potentially available to mitigate the impact of a blockade or other systemic disruption to Japan's resource in-flows. Imports are categorized into raw materials, mineral fuels, foodstuffs and manufactured goods. These are sourced by region and by country in the case of key commodities such as oil. Japan's principal export markets are profiled only briefly, reflecting the greater strategic importance of imports.

In the section 'Maritime transportation and Japan', the infrastructure underpinning Japan's trade and the maritime geography of its main trade routes is explored. The size and composition of Japan's merchant fleet is analysed, before consideration is given to the prevailing trade routes linking Japan to its major resource suppliers and export markets. Three basic 'streams' connect Japan, first with Europe, the Middle East and Southeast Asia; second with Australasia and the South Pacific; and third, with North and South America. Special attention is paid to those areas where Japanese trade is most concentrated and potentially vulnerable to disruption, at 'chokepoint' straits and seas in Southeast Asia and the Middle East. Estimates are compared of the likely costs arising from the closure of chokepoints and the availability of alternative diversionary routes.

Geographic overview

Japan is an archipelago composed of four major islands, Hokkaidō, Honshū, Shikoku and Kyūshū and over 3,000 lesser islands (Map 1.1).

Two prominent island chains (*shotō*) extend along southwesterly (*nansei*) and southerly (*nampō*) axes. The *nansei shotō*, incorporating the Ryūkyū islands (including Okinawa) runs parallel to the Nansei trench, towards Taiwan. The islands comprising the *nampō shotō* follow the Izu-Ogasawara trench, extending

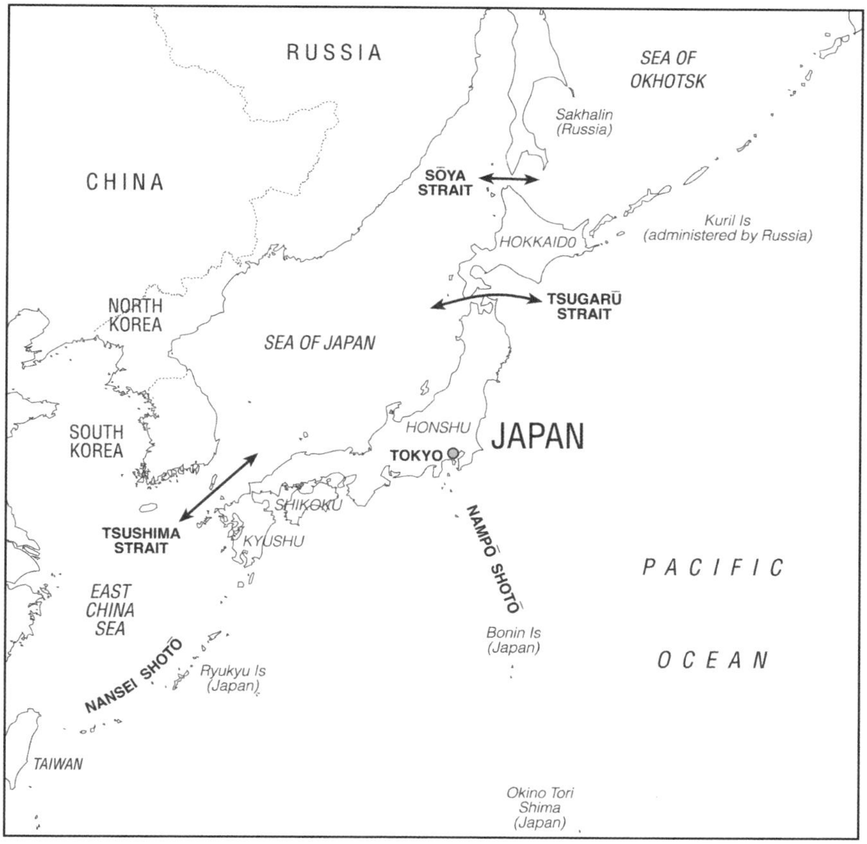

Map 1.1 Japan and surrounding straits.

almost due south from Tokyo as far as Io Jima in the Bonin Islands. The remote outcrop of Okino Tori Shima (Parece Vela) marks the southernmost extent of Japanese territory; at 20° latitude, 136° longitude it is 1,740 km from Tokyo. Although at nearly 30,000 km, Japan's coastline is one-third longer than that of the United States, no inland point is more than 150 km from the sea. Japan is bisected by central mountain ranges that have restricted human settlement to around one quarter of national territory. Only 11 per cent of surface land area is used for cultivation.

With nearly 127 million people, Japan has the seventh largest population in the world and a population density, at 335 persons per km^2, exceeding that of India. The population is predominantly urbanized and concentrated in a coastal conglomeration which runs uninterrupted from the Kantō Plain (including Tokyo) to Hiroshima. Over 43 per cent of the population live in Tokyo, Osaka and Nagoya.[1] Although the birth rate fell to a record low of 1.33 in 2001, demographic trends suggest the population will peak at 128 million in 2006, owing largely to the fact that, at 80 years of age, Japan now has the longest average life-expectancy in the world: the ratio of those aged 65 and above is expected to rise from 17 per cent in 2000 to over one-third of the population by 2050. However, without large-scale immigration (which is politically and socially problematic), the population is likely to dip below current levels in 2013, decreasing sharply thereafter, to around 100 million by 2050.[2]

Economic overview

During the 1950s and 1960s, Japan's economic miracle was based on a model of value-added production, whereby manufactured goods produced from imported raw materials were exported, generating a surplus that could be re-invested in expanded production and access to foreign technology.[3] The success of the Japanese 'state capitalist' developmental model has been attributed to a high degree of coordination amongst a triumvirate composed of industrialists, bureaucrats and politicians from the LDP, which held power continuously from 1955 to 1993, resulting in policies that ensured capital allocation to targeted industrial sectors, effective export promotion and high levels of regulation protecting the domestic market.

While the expansion of foreign trade was essential to Japan's rapid post-war development, trade constitutes a surprisingly small fraction of the economy. The ratio of Japan's exports and imports to Gross Domestic Product (GDP) was 11 and 7 per cent respectively in 1986, since when the weighting of trade to GDP has risen only gradually.[4] With the exception of the immediate aftermath to the 1973–74 oil crisis, Japan has maintained a trade surplus since 1965. In 1998, since when trade levels have remained broadly unchanged, Japan's total import bill amounted to \$319 billion, compared to export receipts of \$440 billion. Since 1960, Japan has made the transition from exporting primary industrial goods, such as textiles, iron and steel, to much greater reliance on medium technology goods including automobiles, electronic goods and chemicals, and increasingly towards high-technology goods and services. However, Japan's developmental model is now acknowledged to have brought with it economic dysfunction. Relationship-based borrower–creditor arrangements and the influence of vested interests entrenched within the political system encouraged investment in delinquent assets, augmented high levels of bad debt in the banking system, contributing to chronic over-capacity and, in turn, deflation.[5]

After heavy industries such as shipbuilding powered Japan's economic expansion in the 1960s, the contribution of manufacturing to GDP dropped from over one-third to less than one-quarter between 1970 and 1995.[6] During the 1980s, spurred by the mounting cost of domestic production, 'sunset industries' began relocating overseas, to Southeast Asia in particular. This initial 'hollowing out' is being followed by further relocation of the remaining industrial base to China, where labour costs are 5 per cent of the average in Japan and land prices are also fractional. The allure of China's low-factor costs is such that high-technology firms whose Japan-based plants remain competitive are reported to be relocating there.[7]

These structural shifts combined with stagnant economic growth over the last decade have constrained Japan's raw material imports. However, this does not alter the continued importance of heavy industry to the domestic economy and its associated commodity and energy resource import requirements. For example, although crude steel production peaked at 120,000 tons in 1973, in the mid-1990s, Japan still produced over 100,000 tons of steel per year; more than it turned out in 1970 and 15 times more than it did in 1940.[8] As Japan is almost totally dependent on overseas sources of supply for iron ore, this requires around 120 million tons to be imported annually.[9]

The move to high-end services and the production of information-technology goods that require fewer resource-inputs than 'old economy' staples such as steel, ship-building and cars means that Japan's prosperity is not as directly linked to imports of mineral ores as it was during the industrial expansion of the 1960s and 1970s. This trend appears likely to continue for the foreseeable future, with little prospect of a return to the high growth of the 1980s and the likelihood that manufacturers will seek to relocate production offshore in order to remain competitive.[10]

Resource dependence

Basic dependence on foreign imports of minerals and fossil fuels remains a defining feature of Japan's economy at the beginning of the twenty-first century. Japan is naturally lacking across a range of non-ferrous ores and metals required in heavy industry, such as iron ore, bauxite, manganese, nickel and titanium. Apart from very limited coal, oil and gas reserves – proven oil reserves of 59 million barrels amount to a little over ten days' consumption – Japan is largely dependent on seaborne imports for mineral fuels, minerals and many basic foodstuffs (Table 1.1).[11]

Worldwide, Japan is the fourth-largest consumer of energy and as an importer of energy is second only to the United States. Because of its unfavourable

Table 1.1 Japan's import dependence for fuels, minerals and foodstuffs

Crude oil	99.7%	Cobalt	100%
Iron ore	99.8%	Zinc	92%
Bauxite	100%	Titanium	100%
Manganese	100%	Cotton	100%
Wool	100%	Wheat	93%
Copper ore	99.9%	Timber	80%
Nickel	100%	Fish/shellfish	44%

Source: Foreign Press Center, Japan, *Facts and Figures of Japan*, 1997 edition, Tokyo: Foreign Press Center, Japan, 1997, pp. 40–2.

resource endowment, Japan imports over 80 per cent of its primary energy needs, a figure approached only by South Korea among major economies within the Organisation for Economic Cooperation and Development (OECD). In 1997, Japan's total mineral fuel import bill amounted to around $60 billion, of which crude oil accounted for $35 billion (roughly equal to the defence budget), LNG $10 billion, petroleum products $7 billion and coal $7 billion. Following the first oil crisis, which saw oil prices quadruple between 1973 and 1975, the government devoted great effort towards improving energy efficiency and invested heavily in alternative energy sources, especially nuclear power. The Ministry of International Trade and Industry (MITI, now renamed the Ministry of Economy, Trade and Industry – METI) drew up an energy programme to improve the nation's energy security through a raft of measures directed at domestic demand and international supply.[12] These included:

- conserving energy;
- fully exploiting domestic sources;
- developing alternatives to petroleum;
- developing closer cooperation with producer states;
- diversifying energy sources away from the Middle East;
- siting energy production in the most efficient locations;
- stockpiling coal and oil (a statutory requirement under the 1975 Petroleum Stockpiling Law obliges private oil refiners to stock a minimum 70 days' worth of consumption).

As a result of government and private initiatives, Japan was transformed into one of the most energy-efficient of the major economies, enabling it to absorb a second wave of oil price rises six years later with relative ease.[13] Overall, energy intensity in the industrial sector improved by 38 per cent between 1973 and 1999. Heavy investment in alternatives to petroleum resulted in greater use of coal and LNG, and launched Japan into the top tier of nuclear-energy states. As of July 2001, 51 nuclear power plants were in operation in Japan, surpassed only by the United States and France.[14] However, mounting safety concerns, technical problems with proposed fast-breeder reactors, and public opposition since the 1999 criticality accident at

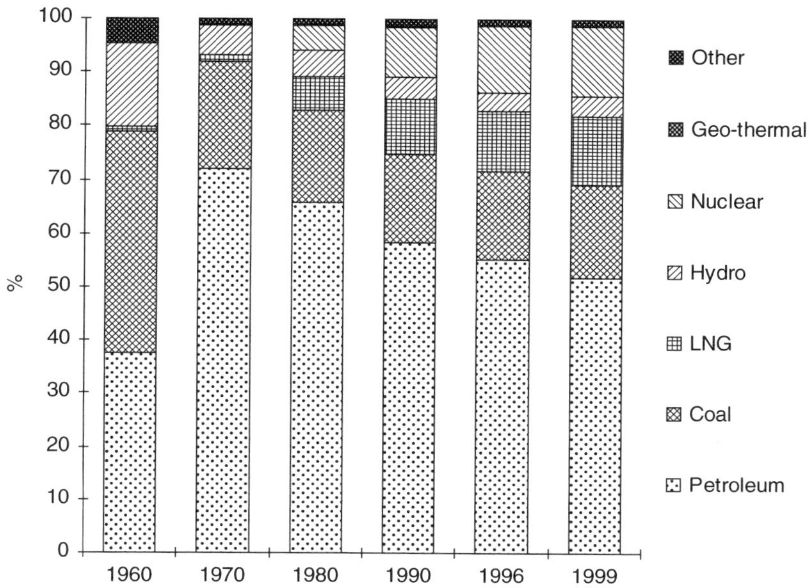

Figure 1.1 Breakdown of Japan's primary energy supply, 1960–99.

Source: METI and Statistics Bureau and Statistics Center, Ministry of Public Management, Home Affairs, Posts and Telecommunications. Online. Available www.stat.go.jp/english/data/handbook/c07cont.htm (accessed 20 June 2002).

Tokaimura and further fatalities at Mihama in 2004 could work against plans for further expansion of the nuclear sector.[15] Since 2000, energy policy has been directed toward the '3Es' of energy security, economic growth and environmental protection. A 1994 advisory report drawn up by the METI set a target of cutting growth in energy consumption to under 1 per cent up to 2010, and oil's share in energy production from 56 to 48 per cent (Figure 1.1).[16] Japan's commitment under the 1997 Kyoto Protocol to cut its carbon emissions by 6 per cent constitutes an additional policy pressure to diversify energy production away from oil and coal. However, demand for energy in transportation, where scope for fuel substitution is limited, and the residential sector has nearly doubled since 1973, in contrast to trends within the industrial sector.[17]

As of 2002, Japan's petroleum accounted for 49.7 per cent of the total energy mix; coal 18.9 per cent; nuclear power 13.7 per cent; natural gas 12.7 per cent; hydroelectric 3.7 per cent; renewables (including geothermal) 1.3 per cent.[18]

Imports

According to the former MSDF Chief of Staff, Yoshida Manabu, any calculation as to the minimum level of imports required under emergency conditions is approximate. However, against the scenario of a naval and air blockade or some other calamity befalling the international trading system, Japan's austerity import requirements are estimated at around one-third of normal requirements, in order to sustain essential economic activity and support the population.[19] Writing in 1976, David Shilling argued that scope exists for Japan to reduce its import volume by up to 70–80 per cent without curbing consumption levels, by halting exports and switching productive capacity to meet domestic demand.[20] Shipping requirements could be cut from 1,850 arrivals per month to just 400. If consumption were reduced, this could be lowered to just 280 per month, or 15 per cent of 1975 levels. Although this analysis is now almost 30 years old, demographic projections of a declining population combined with the likelihood of a declining industrial base suggest that Shilling's estimate still bears scrutiny in Japan's contemporary economic and security environment.

Imports can be categorized into raw materials, foodstuffs, mineral fuels and manufactures. While the ratio of Japan's imports to exports, by value, is roughly 3:4, when measured by volume the ratio is reversed to around 7:1, due to the large quantity of solid and liquid bulk commodities, led by crude oil, coal and iron ore. In 2002, Japan's seaborne trade totalled 939 million tons, with exports of 154 million tons and imports of 785 million tons.[21] Measured by value, seaborne trade accounted for 68.2 per cent – a proportion that has declined steadily from around 87 per cent of the total in 1985, due mainly to the growth of air freight. However, in terms of volume, 99.7 per cent of Japan's trade was still carried by ship in 2002. Although economists tend to focus exclusively on the value of trade, the logistics of maintaining in-flows of raw materials in such volumes is a significant security factor (Figure 1.2).

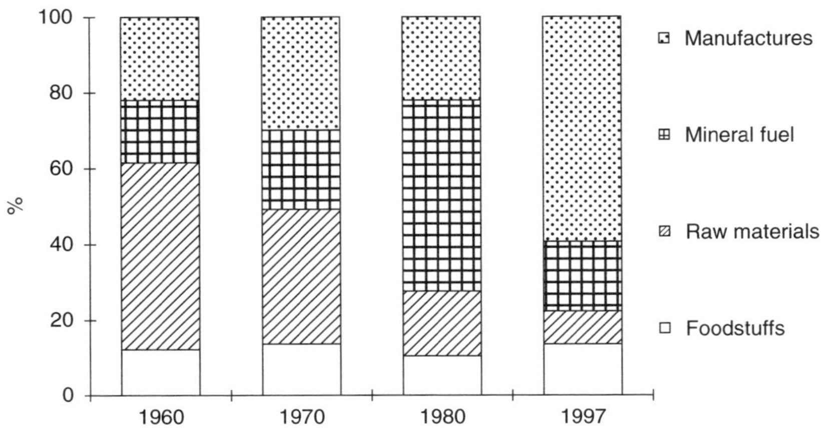

Figure 1.2 Breakdown of Japan's imports; percentage value by sector.

Source: Adapted from METI/*Asahi Shimbun*, *Japan Almanac 1999*, Tokyo: Asahi Shimbunsha, 1998, p. 116.

Table 1.2 Seaborne trade volumes for Japan and the world, 1998 (million tons)

Commodity	*Global volume*	*% global trade volume*	*Japanese volume*	*% Japanese trade volume*	*Japan's % of global trade volume*
Oil	1,550	30.6	217	26	14.0
Coal	465	9.2	131	16	28.3
Iron ore	420	8.3	121	14.5	28
Oil products	395	7.8	31	3.5	7.8
Grains	190	3.7	32	4	16.7
Others	2,050	40.4	299	36	14.6
Total	5,070	100	831	100	16.4

Source: Japan Shipowners' Association.

Seaborne trade worldwide totalled just over 5 billion tons in 1998, of which crude oil constituted 31 per cent, coal 9 per cent and iron ore 8 per cent. Together with petroleum products and grains, these made up more than half the total of seaborne trade, worldwide, Japan's share of the total was 16.4 per cent (Table 1.2). This represents a slight decrease from 1994, when Japan accounted for 18.5 per cent of global tonnage transported by ship; or 21.4 per cent in ton-miles, the standard efficiency measure for the movement of goods by sea.[22] Measured in ton-miles, Japan's trade accounts for slightly higher values for most commodities, except for petroleum products.

There are two important trends in Japan's imports over the last 40 years. First, the percentage value of raw materials declined from almost half in 1960 to under 10 per cent by 1998. Second, the major increase has been in manufactures, which now account for nearly 60 per cent of the import bill. The value share of mineral fuel imported in 1997, while slightly up on 1960, was sharply down from 1980, when it made up half of the import bill as a result of price hikes during the second oil crisis. Among the four import sectors, the value of foodstuffs has remained the most stable.

Raw materials

By value, the most important of Japan's raw material imports in 1997 was timber (2.6 per cent of total import value), followed by iron ore (1 per cent). In 1995, raw materials imported in substantial quantities included: iron ore (120 million tons), timber (89 million tons), copper and nickel (3.8 million tons each). After oil and coal, iron ore occupies the largest volume of any imported commodity, accounting for around 16 per cent of seaborne imports. Non-ferrous metals totalled 3.7 per cent. Japan must import other important non-ferrous metals such as manganese, zinc, chrome, titanium and cobalt, but in much smaller quantities, making them easier to stockpile. In 2000, a METI stockpiling target of 43,183 tons for manganese had already been exceeded and targets for nickel (19,505 tons), chrome (94,853 tons), tungsten (579 tons), cobalt (251 tons) and molybdenum (1,771 tons) were

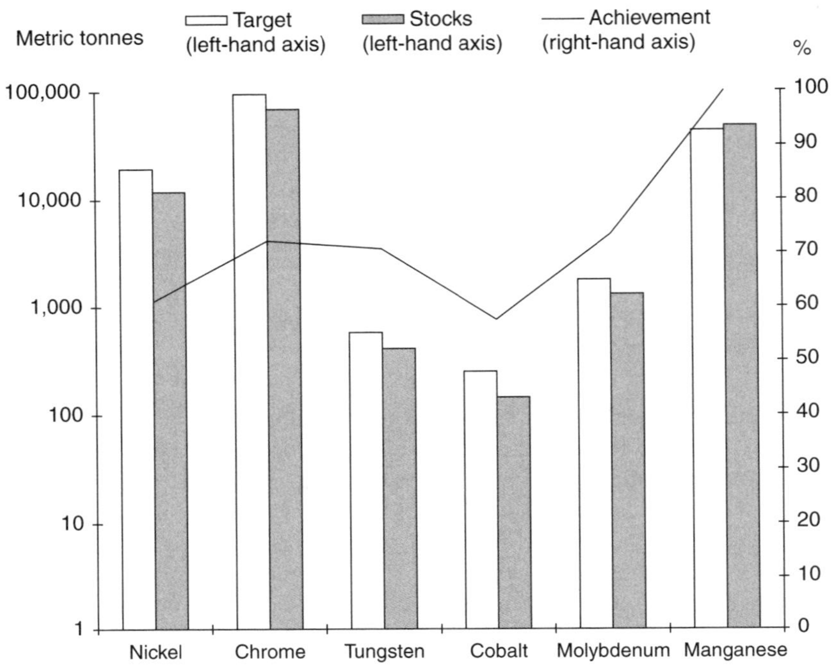

Figure 1.3 Japan's non-ferrous metal stockpiles (2000).

Source: Mining and Mineral Agency/METI.

respectively 61, 72.3, 70.8, 57.6 and 73.4 per cent completed (Figure 1.3). METI aimed to achieve its non-ferrous metal stockpile objectives by 2005.[23]

Mineral fuels

OIL

Relative dependence on crude oil for energy production in Japan peaked at 77 per cent in 1973, declining to 52 per cent in 1999.[24] Despite efficiency gains, demand for oil maintained pace with economic growth in the 1980s, until crude imports overtook 1975 levels again in 1990.[25] However, economic stagnation and the shift to alternative fuels has caused demand to fall since oil consumption peaked at nearly 5.9 million barrels per day in 1996. Monthly imports in early 2002 were down by around 13 per cent year-on-year, by which time oil's share in total energy had fallen to around 50 per cent.[26] As of June 2002, Japan's crude oil stockpiles totalled 91 million kl, respectively divided between those held by the state-owned Japan National Oil Corporation (48 million) and private oil firms (43 million).[27] This represents around 150 days of domestic consumption (Figure 1.4).[28]

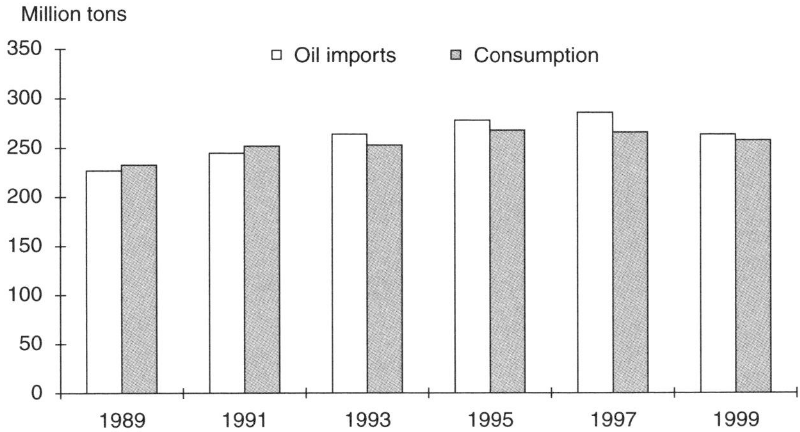

Figure 1.4 Japan's oil imports and consumption (million tons).

Source: Adapted from BP Amoco Statistical Review of World Energy: 'Oil Consumption 1989–1999', 'Trade Movements 1989–1999'. Online. Available www.bp.com/worldenergy/oil/index.htm (accessed 6 May 2002).

Notes

Crude oil and oil products; oil products typically make up between 10 and 20 per cent of the total. In 1999, Japan imported 215 million tons of crude and 49 million tons of oil products (Agency of Natural Resources and Energy figures cited in Foreign Press Center, Japan, *Facts and Figures of Japan*, 1997 edition; 'Imports of Oil 1985–1994', p. 59).

LNG AND COAL

Japan imports over 25 per cent of all coal traded globally and is easily the world's largest importer of steam coal, which is used in power generation and cement production, as well as of coking coal. In 1999, coal made up 17.4 per cent of primary energy, compared to 41 per cent in 1960.[29] Reliance on imports sharply escalated over the same period, from around 14 per cent to around 97 per cent in 1997. Imports grew from 8,595 tons in 1960 to 149 million tons in 2000. Domestic coal production ceased in January 2002. LNG is a major fuel, particularly in power generation: total imports in 2000 amounted to 54 million tons.[30] Although the share of natural gas in energy production in 2002 was still below that of coal, at 12.7 per cent, this figure was in line with METI forecasts from the early 1980s, for LNG use by 2010.[31]

Foodstuffs

The relatively stable proportion of foodstuffs among Japan's overall imports since 1960 has masked a steady decline in the self-sufficiency rate for staple food groups. By the late 1980s, Japan was importing half of its calorific intake, as rising affluence whetted Japanese appetites for non-traditional foods, such as

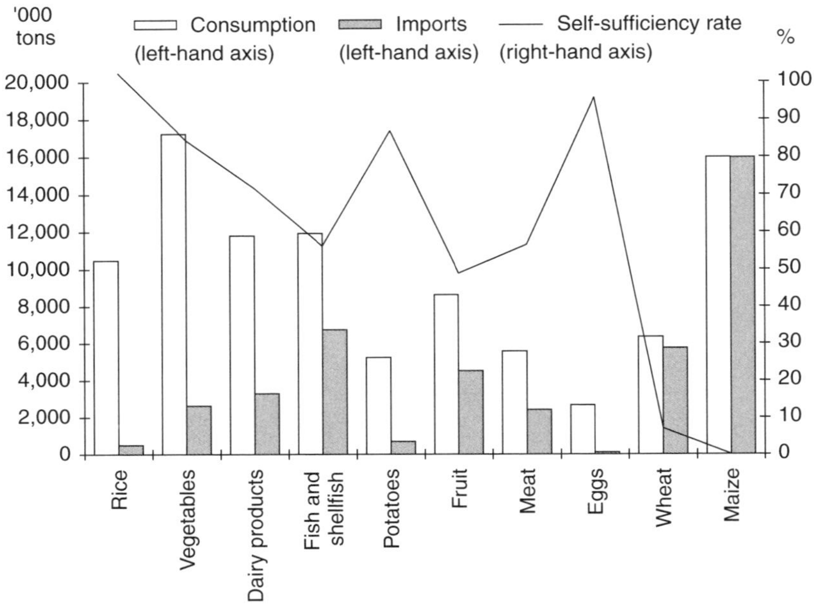

Figure 1.5 Food imports and self-sufficiency rates (1,000 tons), 1995.

Source: Ministry of Agriculture, Forestry, and Fisheries.

red meat, wheat and corn. The major exception is rice, in which Japan is self-sufficient, partly for domestic, political as well as food security reasons, through the concentrated use of pesticides, fertilizers and tariff protection.[32] For other cereals and soya beans, import dependency is over 90 per cent (Figure 1.5). Overall, Japan's cereal self-sufficiency rate is just 30 per cent, which compares to surpluses in the United States, United Kingdom, France and Germany. Measured in terms of the calorie-supply, Japan's food self-sufficiency dwindled from 79 per cent in 1960 to 42 per cent in 1996.[33]

Japanese diets, although more meat-rich than they used to be, still rely heavily on marine products for protein intake, accounting for 40 per cent of the average daily supply of protein in 1996. Japan is the largest importer of marine products in the world. In 1995, it imported almost one-third of the global marine catch, accounting for 5 per cent of its total imports by value. Japan's own fishery production has been gradually declining since 1989, when China overtook it as the leading global producer. Japan is currently placed fourth in the world.

Manufactured products

The sharp increase in Japan's import of foreign manufactures in recent years is due to the expansion of machinery and equipment as well as consumer goods, which have gained more liberal access to the Japanese market. Major imported manufactured items include computers and semi-conductors, textiles and chemicals. In addition, many firms are now 're-importing' products manufactured in China and Southeast Asia for final assembly in Japan.[34]

Import partners

In 1997, Japan sourced 37 per cent of its imports from Asia, 25 per cent from North America, 15 per cent from the European Union and 11 per cent from the Middle East, a shift favouring trade flows from Asia and to a lesser extent, Europe. Although North America has managed to maintain its share, other regions have declined in overall importance (Table 1.3).

In 1995, Japan imported $75 billion worth of US goods, followed by China ($36 billion), South Korea ($17 billion), Australia ($15 billion), Taiwan and Germany ($14 billion each). Since China acceded to the World Trade Organisation (WTO) in December 2001, two-way trade has grown rapidly.[35] In 2003, Japan imported goods worth $75 billion from China, up 22 per cent from the previous year.[36] China overtook the United States as Japan's leading trade partner in 2004.

This general pattern yields an incomplete picture, as dependence on particular suppliers in key commodity sectors remains strong. In the wake of the oil crises, Japan made efforts to diversify its sources of supply in minerals as well as energy, opening up new resource bases in the Indian Ocean and Latin America. India and Brazil became major new suppliers, reducing Japan's dependence on Australia.[37] Agreements to supply Japan with a wide variety of primary commodities were

Table 1.3 Japan's import partners by region (percentage market share)

	1960	*1970*	*1980*	*1997*
Asia	21.1	17.6	25.8	37
W. Asia	9.4	12	31.3	—
N. America	39.1	34.4	20.7	25.3
EU/E. Europe	—	—	—	14.7
M. East	—	—	—	11.3
Oceania	9	9.6	6	5.3
Latin America	6.9	7.3	4.1	3.4
Ex-USSR	—	—	—	1.5
Africa	3.6	5.8	3.2	1.4
W. Europe	8.8	10.2	7.4	—
Comecon	2.1	3.1	1.5	—

Source: Adapted from METI/*Asahi Shimbun*, *Japan Almanac 1999*, Tokyo: Asahi Shimbunsha, 1998, p. 116.

Notes

Pre-1995 figures, for Southeast Asia and 'Communist Asia' have been combined to enable comparison with METI's post-1995 'Asia' category. METI officially re-designated 'West Asia' as Middle East in 1995.

concluded with countries in East Africa and South Asia, raising the profile of the Indian Ocean as a resource base. It is generally recognized, both internationally and within Japan, that commodity supplies are more likely to be disrupted at source than in transit.[38] The record of attempts by the Organization of Petroleum Exporting Countries (OPEC) to maintain the price of oil at the historically high rates of the late 1970s demonstrates that supplier countries' market leverage is limited; price, as in all markets, being a function of demand as well as supply. However, the restriction of supply at source, whether for commercial and/or political reasons, would involve fewer political costs than any military effort to interrupt the supply of commodities in transit. To protect itself from supply disruption at source, Japan's efforts to diversify its resource supply base have been relatively successful, with the crucial exception of oil.

Japan's success in lessening dependence on the Middle East for petroleum since the oil crises has been reversed, since the late 1980s, although intra-regionally the United Arab Emirates and Saudi Arabia each supply roughly one-quarter of Japan's oil. In 1970, 85 per cent of Japan's crude was sourced from the Middle East, falling to 68 per cent in 1987. However, by December 1998, Japan was importing 82 per cent of its oil from the Gulf region.[39] Overall in 2000, this rose to 87 per cent, peaking at 91.7 per cent in December 2001.[40] In 1997, the United Arab Emirates supplied 28 per cent of Japan's crude oil, Saudi Arabia 25 per cent and Iran 10 per cent.[41] In 2003, the top five suppliers were United Arab Emirates (23 per cent), Saudi Arabia (23 per cent), Iran (16 per cent), Qatar (9 per cent) and Kuwait 7 per cent.[42] Indonesia (4.8 per cent) and China (2.2 per cent) retained their long-held positions as Japan's largest non-Middle Eastern oil suppliers. The prospect of access to Russian energy as a means of reducing Japan's dependence on the Middle East, first raised seriously in the 1970s, was revived during Prime Minister Koizumi Junichirō's visit to Russia in January 2003.[43] Intense Japanese lobbying, backed by promises of project finance worth up to $10 billion, appeared more likely to secure a proposed pipeline that would transport Siberian oil 4,000 km to a Sea of Japan terminal at Nakhodka than a rival Chinese-backed pipeline route to Daqing.[44] Japan has also made efforts to invest in exploration in the Caspian to lessen its dependence on Arabian oil. Mitsui acquired a 15 per cent stake in Azerbaijan's Kur Dashi oil field in 2001, reported to contain reserves of 0.5–1.0 billion barrels. In early 2004, a Japanese consortium signed a major deal with Iran to develop the Azadegan oil field, with estimated reserves of 26 billion barrels and the capacity to meet around 10 per cent of Japan's total crude imports through to the contract's expiry in 2016.[45] However, international tensions over Iran's suspected nuclear weapons programme could yet hamper the Azadegan deal, whereas attacks on oil pipelines in Iraq underline the downside of political risk in pursuing new upstream development in the Middle East. Moreover, within the next decade new Japanese exploration will have to be offset as Malaysia and Indonesia become net importers and dwindling light oil imports from China dry up altogether.

Japan's major LNG suppliers are located in Southeast Asia and Australia. Indonesia (37 per cent), Malaysia (20 per cent) and Australia (15 per cent) were the largest providers in 1997.[46] In 2000, Malaysia, Indonesia and Australia together accounted for nearly 67 per cent of Japan's LNG imports, although in that year a new contract was signed with Oman towards maintaining a diversified supply portfolio.[47] In 2004, Tokyo Electric Power Corp. agreed a long-term contract to buy 2.3 million tons of LNG per year from Russia's Sakhalin-2 project from 2007. Increased access to Russian LNG (and oil) could bring significant commercial and SLOC security benefits for Japan. LNG shipments from Sakhalin would take around two days to transport from Sakhalin, compared with one week from Indonesia, and shipping costs make up 20–25 per cent of the cost of LNG.[48] Japan imports half its coal from Australia (steam and coking coal in roughly equal proportions) and the remainder from North America, China and Indonesia. In 1995, of the total of 120 million tons of iron ore imported 59 million tons were from Australia, 28 million tons from Brazil and 18 million from India.[49] With regard to non-ferrous metals, Japan has built up a diverse network of suppliers to minimize its dependence on single-suppliers as far as possible. For example, Japan imports no more than one-fifth of its bauxite/aluminium and nickel from any one country. In the mid-1990s, among suppliers who dominate non-ferrous metal imports, Chile provided 44 per cent of Japan's copper, Russia supplied 62 per cent of palladium, while China met 68 per cent of Japan's zinc needs – though China has since emerged as a major consumer of metallic ores. The United States was and remains Japan's most important supplier of foodstuffs accounting for almost one-third of the $51 billion Japan spent on imported food in 1995, including most of its soya beans.[50]

Exports

In a security context, commercial exports are of lesser strategic importance during armed conflicts than imports, assuming that imports can be financed for the duration. Manufactured goods account for almost all Japan's exports (96 per cent in 1997). Three regions account for the bulk of Japan's markets (Table 1.4). In 1997, Asia accounted for 42 per cent of Japan's export market; North America

Table 1.4 Japan's export markets by region (percentage of overall export value)

	1960	*1970*	*1980*	*1997*
Asia	32.2	28.5	28.1	42
W. Asia	3.5	2.8	10.1	—
N. America	29.7	33.7	26	29.3
EU/E. Europe	—	—	—	16.5
Latin America	7.5	6.1	6.9	5
Middle East	—	—	—	2.9
Oceania	4.9	4.2	3.4	2.4
Africa	8.7	7.4	6.2	1.3
Ex-USSR	—	—	—	0.6
W. Europe	11.7	15	16.5	—
Comecon	1.6	2.3	2.8	—

Source: Adapted from METI/*Asahi Shimbun*, *Japan Almanac 1999*, Tokyo: Asahi Shimbunsha, 1998, p. 116.

29 per cent and the EU 16 per cent.[51] The United States has traditionally been Japan's biggest customer for passenger cars, integrated circuits, computers, automotive parts, machine tools and cameras, absorbing $121 billion-worth of Japanese products in 1995; more than South Korea, Taiwan, Hong Kong and China combined.[52] While the United States remains Japan's largest bilateral export partner, the situation is changing rapidly owing principally to exponential growth in Japan's exports to China since the latter's WTO accession, increasing by 43 per cent in 2003 to $57 billion.[53]

Maritime transportation and Japan

Shipping performs the function of a 'conveyor belt' for Japan's economy, drawing in energy, raw materials and food from around the world and distributing manufactured products to overseas markets. Although one quarter of Japan's trade by value is now carried by air, maritime transport accounted for 99.74 per cent of Japan's total trade volume of over 800 million tons in 1996. Japan's major ports are clustered around its central Pacific coast and the Inland Sea (*seto naikai*). Compared with South Korea or the Russian Far East, this gives Japan better protection against any attempt to block access to the Sea of Japan, which shares some of the characteristics of a chokepoint, being ringed by several narrow straits. Presently, the five largest ports in terms of cargo handled are, in descending order, Chiba, Kobe, Nagoya, Yokohama and Mizushima.

Coastal shipping has traditionally played an important role in Japan's domestic transportation network. During the *sakoku* period of 'national seclusion' (1639–1854), when international trade and travel were strictly limited and controlled by the Shogunate, the economic importance of shipping was still such that a law restricting ship construction to under 1,000 *koku* (49 gross tons) was revised to allow larger ships to ply trade along Japan's coasts. While this dependence on shipping for domestic commerce has been diminished by the expansion of road and rail infrastructure, coastal shipping still accounts for 42 per cent of the volume of goods transported domestically, with average costs one-fifth those of land haulage.[54] After 1945, Japan's emergence as a global mercantile power was dependent on the development of a large, Japanese-owned merchant fleet. Prime Minister Ikeda Hayato's goal of doubling national income during the 1960s was accompanied by an unprecedented expansion of the merchant fleet in order to boost trade. During 1963–67, oil tanker tonnage expanded at an average of 22 per cent per year, and non-tanker tonnage by 12 per cent. As a result of this construction boom, Japan was able to meet increased import demand for oil, which rose at an average annual rate of 18 per cent. Imported dry cargo grew by 19 per cent and dry cargo exports expanded by 12.5 per cent.[55]

Merchant fleet

In 2001, according to the United Nations, Japan's merchant fleet totalled 14.6 million gross registered tons (GRT).[56] After contracting from a peak of

40 million GRT in 1984, gross tonnage has stabilized since the mid-1990s in the range of 13–14 million GRT.[57] The total fleet is divided into oil tankers (3.3 million GRT), bulk carriers (3.1 million), general cargo ships (2.0 million), container ships (0.6 million) and other types (5.6 million).[58]

As of 1999, Japan operated around 214 petroleum tankers, divided between smaller specialized tankers and very large crude carriers (VLCCs), super tankers that range from 160,000 to over 300,000 deadweight tons (DWT).[59] The recent trend has been towards building smaller double-hulled VLCCs of around 230,000 DWT, purpose built to comply with under-keel clearance draft restrictions that apply to vessels transiting the Straits of Malacca. Some Japanese shipping companies have negotiated for a further allowance of 0.5 m.[60] Breaking down the remainder of the ocean-going fleet by vessel type, in 1999, there were 146 bulk carriers, 49 general purpose cargo ships, 13 chemical tankers, 16 combination bulk carriers, 4 combination ore/oil carriers, 25 container ships, 45 LNG carriers (including 23 Japanese-flagged), 22 refrigerated cargo ships, 48 roll-on/roll-off ferries, nine passenger ships and 60 vehicle carriers.

In terms of DWT, as of 2002, Japan's merchant fleet measured 102 million DWT, comprising nearly 2,000 vessels above 2,000 GRT. Japan remains a major global shipping power measured by vessels controlled by Japanese companies, accounting for 13.6 per cent of the world merchant fleet, second only to Greece.[61] However, 1,221 vessels counted as part of the Japanese fleet in 2002 were simply chartered and 657 were foreign-chartered vessels under Japanese control. Only 110 merchant ships (or 6 per cent) were Japanese flagged, down from 1,508 (or 50 per cent) in 1970.

Among the recommendations of the *Report on Comprehensive National Security*, commissioned by Prime Minister Ohira Masayoshi in April 1979, were that the Japanese government should 'Examine alternative marine routes in case a situation occurs in which existing routes, such as the Malacca and Lombok straits, are blocked to traffic (and) secure a constant volume of marine transport capacity'.[62] Regarding the latter, Japan has since followed the international trend towards open registry ('flags of convenience') provided by Panama, Liberia and the Bahamas, as a means of cutting costs. This phenomenon was aggravated by the sharp appreciation of the yen after 1985, which saw Japanese shipping giants such as Nippon Yūsen Kaisha (NYK) and Mitsui O.S.K. Lines accumulate debts of up to $1 billion on their trans-pacific cargo routes. The estimated costs of maintaining a Japanese-flagged, all-Japanese manned merchant ship, are four times those of a ship crewed by Southeast Asians.[63] As well as resorting to foreign registry as a means to cut overheads, Japanese shipping firms have made massive cuts in their Japanese workforce to the point that foreign seafarers typically make up 90 per cent of crews, and there are no modernized, Japanese-flagged vessels with an all-Japanese crew left in operation. In 2002, the merchant fleet carried 66 per cent of the country's imports and 29 per cent of exports. When foreign charters were excluded from this total, just 10 per cent of imports and 1 per cent of exports were carried in Japanese hulls.[64] The extent of the decline of the Japanese-flagged fleet is clear from the fact that in 1974,

Japanese-flagged vessels carried 44 per cent of imports and 27 per cent of exports.[65]

Assuming that a sufficient quantity of Japanese-flagged, chartered or foreign-registered vessels continued to service Japan's import needs in the event of a major security crisis, substantial scope would appear to exist for shipping to divert around most localized obstructions at chokepoints located in Middle-Eastern or Southeast Asian waters, albeit generating higher transportation costs. Higher costs would also provide a profit incentive for shipping companies to add capacity to routes servicing Japan. But their willingness (and that of seamen's unions) to sail in the face of increased risk or the withdrawal of insurance cover is by no means assured, as is explored in Chapters 2 and 5. Moreover, the absence in post-war Japan of any Naval Control of Shipping (NCS) legislation, owing to political sensitivities over the influence of the military, denies the Japanese government any legal instrument to compel Japanese-flagged merchant ships to sail.

Shipping routes

Japan's most important regular shipping routes fall into three broad streams. First, and economically most important, is the southwest stream (composed of several interlinking sea lanes) connecting Japan with Europe, the Middle East and Southeast Asia. Second, a southern stream connects Japan with Australasia and the South Pacific. Third, the trans-pacific 'Great Circle' route connects Japan with the Americas.[66]

Peacetime patterns of trade and import dependence are not synonymous with the exigencies of wartime. But for economies as dependent upon imported energy resources and raw materials as Japan's they are still likely to be strategically relevant in the event of a sustained conflict, even assuming scope exists to switch to alternative sources of supply and shipping routes. Oil remains the most strategic commodity of all. Notwithstanding Japan's impressive stockpiles and attempts at diversifying its supply base, shipping routes to the Gulf would probably assume particular importance in any medium- to long-term security crisis. However, several alternative routes exist within this south western 'stream', as is explored below. Maintaining supplies of mineral fuels and metallic ores from Australia and Southeast Asia would also be important. The disruption of food imports would have a less acute security impact, reflecting the much greater substitution options available. However, it is significant that the 'disruption of sea lanes' was mentioned among 'conceivable threats to Japan's food security' in the 1979 *Report on Comprehensive National Security*.[67]

Of Japan's three maritime transportation streams, the trans-pacific Great Circle and central Pacific routes traverse mostly open ocean or sparsely populated coastal areas. Since the end of the Cold War these have been largely free of geopolitical tensions. However, the two other major streams are geographically encumbered by several chokepoints, in the Middle East and Southeast Asia, where shipping is concentrated into narrow waterways close to areas where political instability and regional conflict are prevalent.

Those used for transporting significant proportions of Japanese commerce include the straits of Malacca, Lombok and Makassar and, to a lesser extent Sunda, all of which fall wholly or partly within Indonesian archipelagic waters. Although 1,800 nm from north to south, the South China Sea can itself be considered a chokepoint, reflecting the partial constriction of its southern, eastern and northern egress points. The Sea of Japan and the Taiwan Strait can also be regarded as chokepoints though the latter is only a significant route for Japan's trade with Taiwan and Chinese mainland ports opposite. In the Middle East, the Suez Canal is an artificial chokepoint, but the most important is the Strait of Hormuz.

Southeast Asian chokepoints

In 1993, Japan imported 385 million tons worth $102 billion through Southeast Asia's major SLOC, representing 42 per cent of total import value, or 4 per cent of GDP. It also exported 33.5 million tons worth over $153 billion, representing 42.5 per cent of total exports, or 6 per cent of GDP. Only Australia rivals Japan's level of dependence on Southeast Asian SLOC. Comparable figures for Australia, on much lower volumes, were 39.5 per cent of export value and 53 per cent of import value.[68] China, for example, relied on Southeast Asian chokepoints for 22 per cent of export value and just 10 per cent of import value in 1993, although its dependence on these SLOCs for trade and imported energy has since grown considerably (Tables 1.5 and 1.6).

Table 1.5 Japan's imports through Southeast Asian chokepoints (1993)

SLOC	*% import value*	*Value ($ billion)*	*Million tons*
Malacca	29	71.5	240
Sunda	0.5	1	9
Lombok	2.5	5.5	69.5
South China Sea	40	96	305
Combined total	42	101.5	385

Table 1.6 Japan's exports through Southeast Asian chokepoints (1993)

SLOC	*% export value*	*Value ($ billion)*	*Million tons*
Malacca	27.5	99.5	12
Sunda	0.1	0.5	0.1
Lombok	2.5	9	3
South China Sea	41.5	150	32
Combined total	42.5	153.5	33.5

Source: J. Noer with D. Gregory, *Chokepoints: Maritime Economic Concerns in Southeast Asia*, Washington, DC: National Defense University Press/Center for Naval Analyses, 1996, appendix A, p. 67.

STRAITS OF MALACCA

The Straits of Malacca (composed of the Malacca Strait, the Phillip Channel and the Singapore Strait) are the most important waterways for Japanese trade outside of Japan's territorial waters, leading to the straits' description as 'the most crucial to the economic life of Japan'.[69] The straits connect the Indian Ocean (via the Andaman Sea) to the Pacific (via the South China Sea). From their northernmost and widest extremity, between Thailand and the Indonesian island of Sumatra, to their egress into the South China Sea east of Singapore, the straits extend for over 500 miles, with widths varying from 200 to just 3 miles.

At its narrowest point, the commanding width of the navigable channel is only 500 m, with a commanding depth of 23 m.[70] In certain shipping lanes within the straits, draft is as little as 16 m.[71] (For details of the Traffic Separation Scheme (TSS) in operation there, see Map 6.2.) Despite these canal-like parameters (Suez is 21 m deep and 300 m across) the Straits of Malacca are the busiest international waterways in the region and second only to the Dover Strait in the world. The value of total trade passing in both directions has been put as high as $500 billion.[72] Traffic through the straits is also forecast to grow by 5 per cent annually through to 2010, prompting speculation that the waterway is approaching capacity.[73] Estimates of the straits' overall usage vary between 30,000 and 100,000 ships per year, depending on the date of the estimate and whether cross-straits traffic is included. The likely figure for inter-regional traffic through the straits is around 50,000 transits per year, yielding a daily average of around 137 ships.[74] One Japanese estimate based on International Maritime Organisation (IMO) data from 2000 puts the number of ships of 300 tons or greater passing daily through the straits at 182.[75] In 1993, a daily average of around 30 tankers passed through the straits in both directions, with crude oil estimated to account for 58 per cent of cargo tonnage.[76] According to more recent data, in 2000, a total of 17,579 tankers of all sizes carried petroleum products through the straits, yielding a daily average of 48 transits.

The daily volume of petroleum estimated to pass though the Straits of Malacca is 10.3 million barrels, a total surpassed only by the Straits of Hormuz.[77] VLCCs from the Gulf typically carry around 2 million barrels, implying that as few as six fully laden VLCCs could technically carry all of the oil normally passing through the straits, but the large number of terminals to be serviced in Northeast Asia requires tankers in greater numbers and of specialized designs.[78] In addition, over 3,000 LNG carriers passed through the straits in 2000. About 72 per cent of laden tankers passing from the Gulf to Northeast Asian destinations are thought to use the straits. As a result of an Under-keel Clearance scheme introduced in the straits since 1981, loaded VLCCs exceeding 230,000 DWT and ultra-large crude carriers (ULCCs) are diverted through the Lombok Strait.[79]

Japan remains the largest user. In 1993, with combined west and eastbound trade estimated by Noer and Gregory at $170 billion, Japanese cargoes accounted for 37 per cent of all inter-regional tonnage passing through the straits in either direction.[80] Around $100 billion of this, or 27.5 per cent of Japan's total exports, travelled through the Straits of Malacca in 1993, amounting to 12.2 million tons

(Table 1.5). Japan controlled 28 per cent of tonnage transiting the straits in that year, four times as much as any other user, although a diminishing proportion of such vessels is Japanese-flagged.[81] While China's rapidly rising oil imports are likely to erode Japan's position as the number one tanker user over time, Japan has until recently accounted for around 70 per cent of all the oil shipped through the strait, followed by South Korea, China and Taiwan. Japan, in turn, relies on the straits for a similar proportion of its oil, with most of the remainder being routed via the Lombok Strait.[82] In spite of the high volume of oil bound for Japan via the straits, surprisingly few VLCC transits are required: of 2,148 tankers monitored through the strait from the Middle East during 1995, 969 were bound for Japan, while a 1994 estimate puts the number of fully laden large tankers bound for Japan slightly lower at around 700 per year, or around two per day.[83] Such a figure is basically consistent with Japan's daily consumption of 5.44 million barrels of oil in 2001, although the import of specialist fuels requires a larger number of smaller, specialist tankers to meet Japan's petroleum product needs.

SUNDA STRAIT

After the Straits of Malacca, the Sunda Strait, separating Java and Sumatra, is the second most direct route for shipping passing from the northern Indian Ocean to the South China Sea, involving an additional 630 nm, or about two days' steaming. Sunda is about 50 nm long and passage to the South China Sea is gained through the Gaspar or Karimata Straits. For cargoes bound from the Cape of Good Hope and other southern Indian Ocean destinations, the Sunda Strait is the most direct route for traffic to and from Northeast Asia, although trade volumes are miniscule compared with the Straits of Malacca. In 1993, Japan received 9 million tons of imports through the strait, mostly coal, coke and iron ore from Africa. About one-quarter of two-way tonnage through the strait was bound to or from Japan in 1993. Although the strait is relatively wide at about twelve miles across, draft is limited to 18 m in places and strong currents hamper navigation to a greater degree than in the Straits of Malacca. Ships exiting the strait must also negotiate hazardous offshore oil installations in the Java Sea.[84] As a result, most ships displacing in excess of 100,000 DWT use either Malacca or Lombok. If used as an alternative to the Straits of Malacca, Sunda would add around 8.5 per cent to the cost of a one-way voyage.[85] (Until 1992, when the United States closed its bases in the Philippines, Sunda also connected US bases there with Diego Garcia, in the Indian Ocean.[86])

LOMBOK–MAKASSAR

The Lombok Strait separates Bali and Lombok and connects to the Makassar Strait to the north. Lombok–Makassar is the second most important strait in Southeast Asia for Japan's trade, with half of the total tonnage observed in the waterway in 1993 bound to or from Japanese ports.[87] Combined passage through the two straits is 660 nm. Both offer a minimum width of 11 miles and unlimited draft. For this reason, Lombok–Makassar is the favoured deep-water alternative to the Straits of Malacca. According to Chia, the volume of oil shipped to Japan from the Middle East is evenly split between Lombok and Straits of Malacca (the larger size of vessels meaning fewer are required).[88] However, Noer and Gregory estimate that only 5.5 million tons of crude was shipped through the strait in 1993 (in 8 VLCC transits and 29 smaller tankers).[89] Iron ore and coke shipments from Australia account for most of the cargo moved through the Lombok Strait.

To cover the extra 1,014 nm between Malacca and the Lombok route requires three days steaming and adds 13.5 per cent to shipping costs. Lombok offers potential economies of scale because its deeper draft enables passage of ULCCs above 300,000 DWT. However, tanker operators no longer favour such gargantuan designs, because the draft at most off-loading terminals is insufficient to accommodate them.[90] Despite the efforts of the Indonesian authorities to attract tanker traffic (and associated revenues) by installing mooring buoys and refuelling facilities off Ampenan, the main port in Lombok, the shift away from ULCC designs as uneconomical has reduced the number of tankers transiting the Lombok Strait,[91] and 'in recent years, most oil shipments to the Far East use the relatively maneuverable 250,000 ton VLCC and the shorter route' via Malacca.[92] However, Lombok remains the principal route for bulk carriers sailing from western Australia to Japan.

If the Straits of Malacca were closed most Japanese tankers would have to pass through the Lombok Strait. According to one Japanese estimate, this would require an extra 15 tankers and add approximately $88 million to the annual import bill. Based on an oil import bill of $35 billion in 1997, this amounts to 0.3 per cent of the total.[93] Another source puts the per-ship cost for the entire detour through Lombok at $200,000–300,000.[94] Among Japan's shipping firms, 'K'-line has studied re-routing options in case of a closure of the Straits of Malacca and maintains adequate bunker reserves to make the 2-day diversion via the Sunda strait, in the case of shallow-draft vessels, or otherwise via the Lombok Strait. In a worst-case scenario, the company has looked at a southerly route through the archipelago via Maluku. It has not considered the far longer diversion south about Australia.[95]

SOUTH CHINA SEA

In 1993, commercial transits through the South China Sea totalled 36,000 according to Noer and Gregory's estimate.[96] Although not as enclosed as the Mediterranean, to which it is sometimes compared, the South China Sea shares some of the characteristics of a chokepoint (see Map 1.2). According to Kawamura (1998), owing to the shallowness of the sea surrounding the Spratly Islands, the South China Sea for practical purposes is a 'sea lane where ships move primarily along the continental shelf'.[97] Southern access is through the Malacca, Sunda or Lombok Straits. Eastern access is via the Sulu Sea. Northern access is via the Luzon Strait/Bashi channel and the Taiwan Strait. Shipping normally passes west of the

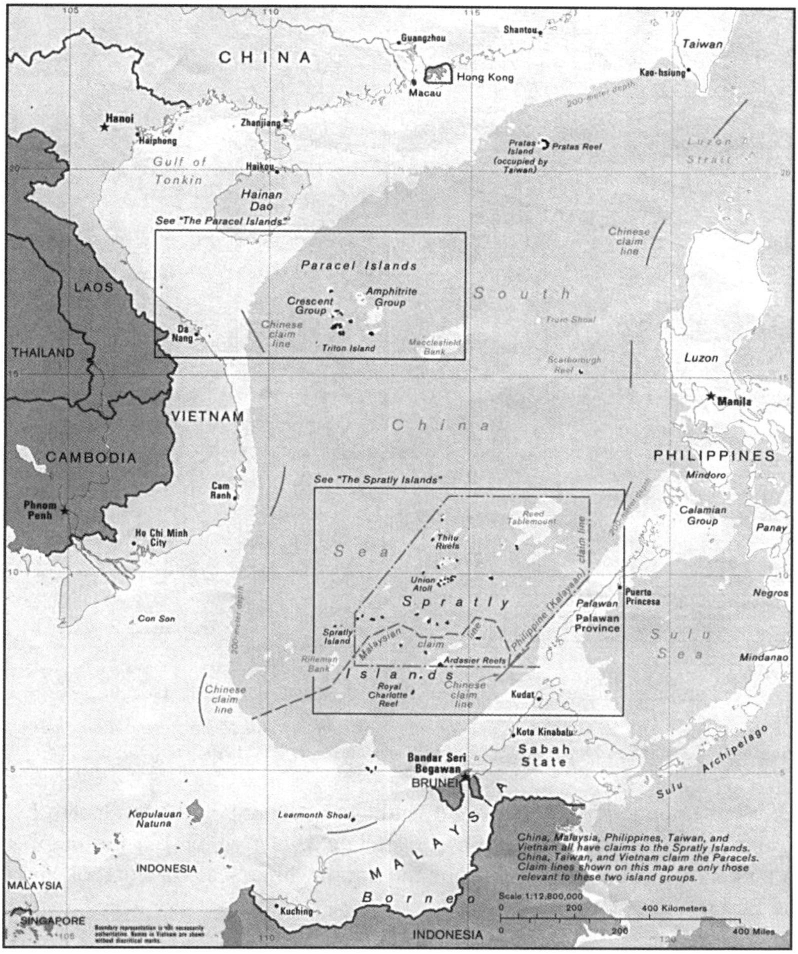

Map 1.2 The South China Sea and island groups.

Source: Courtesy of the General Libraries, the University of Texas at Austin.

Spratlys. The composition of shipping and cargoes bound to and from Japan via the South China Sea is basically the same as the Straits of Malacca and Sunda. During typhoon season, shipping using Lombok–Makassar enters the South China Sea via the Sulu Sea/Basilan Strait, south of Mindanao.

The cost to Japan of a 12-month closure of the South China Sea, diverting oil tankers via the Lombok Strait and east of the Philippines, has been estimated at $200 million. A Japanese estimate puts the cost as basically the same to that imposed by a closure of the Malacca Strait, requiring 15 additional tankers to be added to the route generating an extra $88 million in shipping costs. This is

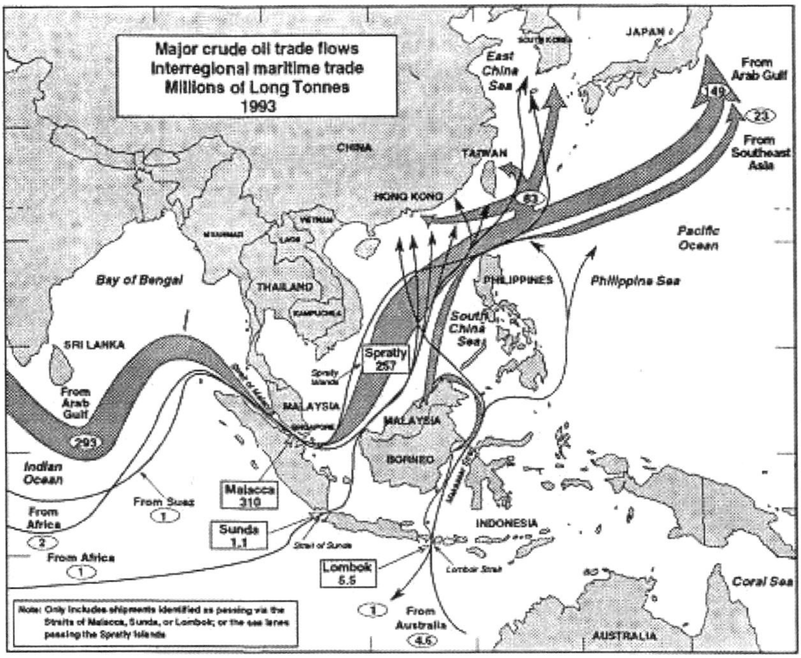

Map 1.3 Oil shipment routes and volumes through Maritime Southeast Asia.

Source: J. H. Noer with D. Gregory, *Chokepoints: Maritime Economic Concerns in Southeast Asia*, Washington, DC: National Defense University Press/Center for Naval Analyses, 1996, p. 18.

roughly corroborated by the reported findings of a joint study conducted by the JDA and the Indonesian authorities in the late 1980s which put the number of extra tankers required to divert around the South China Sea, via Lombok and east of the Philippines, at 18 (Map 1.3).[98]

OMBAI–WETAR

Also within Indonesian waters, the Ombai passage, between Timor and the Alor islands, is wide and deep and for this reason is believed to be the favoured route for American submarines passing between the Pacific and the Indian Ocean. The interconnecting Wetar passage runs between the Arafura Sea and Flores Sea. Ombai–Wetar could be a significant diversionary route for Japanese commercial traffic if other passages were blocked, providing equidistant passage for Australian exports from the north and west to Japan and it is deep enough to take VLCCs.[99] Further east, the Torres Strait poses navigational hazards for vessels over 50,000 tons.[100] For Japan's iron ore shipments forced to divert from north western Australia around Indonesia and Papua New Guinea, transportation costs would rise by 15–20 per cent.[101] In the worst-case scenario involving a full-scale closure of the Indonesian archipelago to international shipping, sea traffic bound from the Middle East and Europe to Japan could divert around Australia, although this would at least double the mileage compared with the Straits of Malacca route.[102] Noer and Gregory estimate that $1.5 billion would be added to Japan's annual oil import bill, compared with Akimoto's calculation of $1.2 billion.[103]

Middle Eastern chokepoints

The voyage between Japan and Gulf oil terminals typically takes 20 days each way. The distance from Yokohama to Aden, via the Straits of Malacca, is 6,535 nm (see Map 1.4). The Strait of Hormuz sits at the mouth of the Gulf, where Japanese tankers were repeatedly attacked during the Iran–Iraq War of 1980–88. A total of 13 million barrels per day is estimated to flow through the strait. Japan has a considerable stake in the freedom of navigation through the Strait of Hormuz, and accounts for around 20 per cent of all tanker tonnage. The strait is strategically unique owing to the lack of alternative tanker routes to access Gulf oil terminals (although there are alternate pipeline routes). Shipping passes through two-mile wide lanes in either direction.

However, the Strait of Hormuz is wide enough, despite overlapping maritime territorial claims by riparian states, for the extension of territorial seas to 12 nm under the United Nations Law of the Sea Convention, not to have changed its international status. Moreover, its importance to global oil supplies automatically qualifies it as an international security concern. Closure of the Suez Canal, which is economically significant to Japan only for the container trade, would require diversion via the Cape of Good Hope, adding ten days' steaming, or 23 per cent to the cost of exports shipped from Yokohama to Rotterdam. LNG carriers receive a discount on the toll tariff to transit the canal.[104] In February 2003, in response to an increased risk of a terrorist attack on the canal, in the lead-up to US military action against Iraq,[105] Japanese firms including Nissan, Sony and Murata Manufacturing were reported to be considering diverting shipments to Europe normally routed through Suez via the Cape route.

Conclusion

This chapter has surveyed Japan's maritime geography and economic structure and concluded that stockpiling, substitution, diversification and other economic contingency measures have not altered the fundamentals of a political economy defined by poor natural resource allocation and a large population relative to domestic food production. Since industrialization, these fundamentals have determined, as a central imperative of Japan's foreign policy, a requirement to import food and essential raw materials. Globalization and the transnationalization of production under the control of multinationals have made maritime trade indispensable to all advanced industrial economies. To a certain degree Japan's economic geography is shared by Taiwan and South Korea. But, Japan's dependence on imported commodities is on a much larger scale and the risks

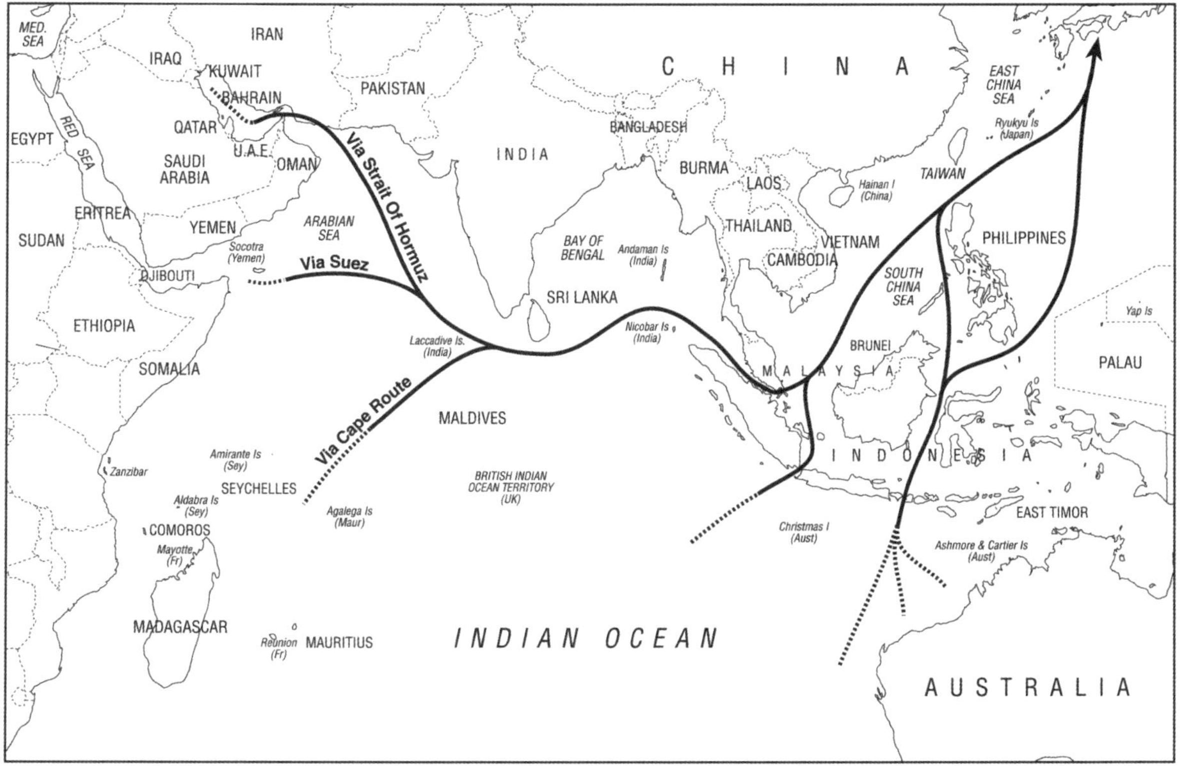

Map 1.4 Indian Ocean and Middle East chokepoints.

attached to supply disruption thus carry a very high premium for Japanese policy-makers.

Stockpiling measures put in place in the 1970s serve to give the country a combined public–private cushion equivalent to five months' oil consumption in the civilian sector under normal conditions; a period that could probably be extended if austerity controls were enacted quickly. However, the comparatively lean energy consumption profile of industry since the oil crisis means that there is limited scope to cut back without affecting production, and dependence on petroleum remains especially high in automotive transport. If Japan were to switch to an austerity footing, import requirements for fuels, raw materials and non-substitutable food items could be cut to around one-third or approximately 262 million tons, based on the 785 million tons of goods imported in 2002. As Shilling suggests, essential imports could be trimmed further if the government decided to forego export earnings. However, the economic costs of doing so could only be sustained a temporary basis (as of late 2002, Japan's foreign exchange reserves were equivalent to import cover of 8.5 months).

The structure of Japan's international seaborne trade has created a peculiar dependence on the south western SLOC connecting Japan with Southeast Asia, the Middle East and Europe, and above all on the Straits of Malacca, Japan's energy 'lifeline'. Australia's role as an energy, minerals and food supplier to Japan also makes the southern SLOC strategically important, while the trans-pacific SLOC to North and South America hold great economic as well as militarily significance for Tokyo. Against the risk of a localized obstruction occurring in chokepoints along these SLOC, considerable scope exists for alternative routing, the security implications of which are taken up in Chapters 2 and 6. Having established the geographic and economic fundamentals of Japan's vulnerability to SLOC disruption, in Chapter 2, the definition of SLOC security and threats to shipping are considered in a historical, strategic context.

2 Sea lines in strategy

Introduction

This chapter explores the historical background to, and definition of, SLOC, as a strategic concept. It examines how SLOC security has evolved over the last century by drawing upon 'classical' theories of sea power, the evidence of the two world wars, the Cold War and the post-Cold War period. I aim mainly to identify general principles as a benchmark to apply in subsequent chapters to Japan's particular SLOC concerns. Japan's pre-1945 SLOC security is the subject of the following chapter. Reference to Japan's historical experience is included here to the extent that it corroborates or contradicts general themes and institutional continuities.

The security of 'sea lines of communication', a military term that has entered the lexicon of mainstream international relations, is still widely assumed to be among the leading national security concerns of maritime commercial and naval powers, such as the United States and Japan. This is despite the fact that the last major conventional confrontation at sea occurred more than 20 years ago, in the Falkland Islands – the only occasion since 1945 that a submarine has sunk another vessel in anger. In spite of widespread reference to the security of SLOC and sea lanes in security studies literature, surprisingly little intellectual rigour has been directed towards a conceptual definition.

This chapter tracks the origins of SLOC, with reference to classical theories of sea power and how these strategic premises were re-evaluated over two world wars and the Cold War. It also traces the re-definition of maritime security in the post-Cold War period, to encompass a broader policy agenda, especially non-state threats to shipping from terrorism and piracy. The analytical focus spans economics, geography, diplomacy, military science and law enforcement – fields that are set in the general context that they are applied to Japan's circumstances. The historical lens is deliberately extended, reflecting the assumption that military threats regardless of probability have the most significant potential to disrupt sea communications on a systemic scale, despite the resurgence of piracy and maritime terrorism. As long as navies like that of Japan still focus on SLOC security as a core rationale, it is necessary to take account of the empirical record of three major strategic offensives against merchant shipping during the two world wars, which continue to cast a disproportionate shadow over doctrine, force structure and institutional memory. The relevance of theories of sea power formulated in the era of navalism and high imperialism may appear of doubtful relevance to the contemporary parameters of maritime security, given the magnitude of technical and political change in the intervening century. However, the works of Mahan and Corbett, as well as later writers such as Castex and Brodie, are still helpful in distilling first principles.

Principles of sea communications

The importance of controlling communications is a central tenet of many classical theories of sea power. In *The Influence of Seapower Upon History, 1660–1783*, the work that from its publication in 1890 established Alfred Thayer Mahan's reputation as the doyen of sea power acolytes, Mahan wrote that 'certain well-worn paths' exist within the 'wide common' of the sea within which ships are concentrated and vulnerable to obstruction.[1] Great Britain's foremost famous naval strategist, Sir Julian Corbett, was a contemporary and a critic of Mahan, whose *Some Principles of Maritime Strategy* was published in 1911. Corbett in particular asserted that 'all problems of Naval Strategy can be reduced to terms of "passage and communication"' – a nautical term dating from the late eighteenth century.[2]

'Sea power' can be broken down into 'command of the sea', denoting a somewhat idealized state in which the freedom of movement on, above or under the sea is unchallenged and the more widely used relative term, 'sea control', the corollary of which is 'sea denial'. Although Corbett's theory of maritime strategy was concerned mainly with the positive uses of command of the sea, he also appreciated that the sea has a negative strategic value in terms of its denial to an enemy, which for continental powers seeking to preserve gains against intervention by maritime powers may of itself be a strategic objective.[3]

SLOC originates from an analogy drawn with overland lines of supply – including the fixed infrastructure of roads and railways – used by armies to connect frontline forces with bases and production centres in the rear. These, in turn, require the control or at least benign neutrality of the surrounding territory. The definition of lines of communication at sea is more relative owing to the very different properties of water. Corbett regarded naval strategy conceptually as a battle over sea communications for the objective of gaining control and ultimately command of the sea. However, he also realized that an analogy drawn between conquest of territory and dominance over sea space has the potential to mislead because 'the sea cannot be the subject of political dominion or ownership'.[4] Definitional problems that confuse military principles of land and sea power are compounded by the overlapping use of such terms as 'chokepoints', 'sea lanes', 'strategic waterways', 'trade routes', 'focal areas', 'approaches' and similar terms that risk conflating the principles of naval strategy with those governing maritime economics.

The most basic, passive, strategic quality of sea space is as a barrier to the movement of peoples and armies. The defensive advantages that separation by water offers against invasion, although latterly eroded with the advent of air power, long-range missiles or indeed 'asymmetric' terrorist attacks, still pertains to the contemporary strategic environment. Since 1945, the logistical and operational difficulties involved in mounting large-scale amphibious warfare have meant that only a select number of states have invested in the capabilities required. As a reflection of the rising costs of military action, among those possessing such capability, very few have done so against opposition; the US landings at Inchon during the 1950–53 Korean War; the Anglo-French landings at Suez in 1956 and the UK re-occupation of the Falkland Islands in 1982 being among a handful of post-war examples.

Although technology continues to erode the barriers posed by distance, and non-state actors are increasingly the focus of threat perceptions, physical geography still exerts a cardinal influence on the strategic, operational and tactical levels of warfare. Australia's post-Vietnam defence doctrine was defined with reference to the 'sea-air' gap separating it from the Indonesian archipelago.[5] Japan's defence white paper contains the premise that 'as Japan is made up of an arch-shaped archipelago, a foreign country has to invade it via sea and air'.[6] Further back in history, the Tsushima Strait, separating Japan from the Korean peninsula by only 40 miles, thwarted successive attempts by the Mongols to invade, even though Japan itself lacked a navy.[7] The Tokugawa Shogunate's policy of maintaining national seclusion for over 200 years would not have been possible had Japan not been an island nation. The strategic advantages of being 'sealed relatively well from external threats' continue to be stressed in a contemporary context, as by Satō Seizaburō who argues that the country's experiment with post-war pacifism is facilitated by geography.[8] Buzan observes in a Japanese context that 'isolationism can sometimes be a workable security policy in a way that it almost never can be for continental states'.[9]

In an active sense, the relative efficiency of waterborne transportation compared with overland means has afforded decisive strategic advantages – in terms of projecting power and conducting trade – to those states with the technology, resources and political foresight to construct ocean-going fleets. Militarily, as Norman Friedman has observed, sea communications have given maritime states advantages comparable to interior lines of communication.[10] Commercially, the advantages of waterborne transportation are such that it costs as much to ship one ton of coal from Australia to Great Britain as it does to transport the same amount 150 miles within Great Britain by rail.[11] Ships carry over 90 per cent of the volume of global trade.

Such paradoxical strategic qualities of the sea, as part-buffer, part-enabler are exemplified in Great Britain's historical experience. The narrow Channel separating the English south coast from Continental Europe helped Great Britain escape domination by successive continental hegemons – sixteenth century Spain, Napoleonic France and Nazi Germany – each unable to project their superior ground strength over water. Conversely, Great Britain's access to the sea and possession of a large naval and merchant fleet paved the way for the establishment – if more by accident than design – of a global trading network and overseas territorial acquisitions. While mercantilism enabled Britain strategically to 'out-flank' European continental powers, its naval superiority also enabled it to capture the overseas trade of weaker mercantile powers such as Portugal and Holland. In the countervailing case of Japan, the Shogunate's two centuries of reliance on the sea as a physical barrier to foreign encroachment was converted overnight into a strategic liability with the arrival of Commodore Perry's 'black ships' in Uraga Bay in 1853. Because Japan's military technology was in stasis during its self-imposed isolation, sudden exposure to superior Western military technology left the Shogunate little choice but to accede to trade treaties on unfavourable terms, signalling its demise.

Sea power, when used to project force on land can confer decisive multiplier effects upon an attacker through manoeuvre and surprise. At one extreme, the Normandy landings in 1944 – which remain the largest-scale example of maritime power projection to date – succeeded because opposing forces were dispersed thinly along Europe's coastal periphery, affording the Allies the initiative to choose the time and place at which to mass their forces. However, the possession of maritime forces can equally give rise to strategic 'over-stretch'. From Athens' campaign against Syracuse during the Peloponnesian Wars to the Anglo-French campaigns in the Crimea (1854–56), and the Dardenelles (1915–16), the problems of operating at the end of an extended seaborne supply chain with poor intelligence have spawned costly military failures. The D-Day landings themselves were made possible only by meticulous planning and preparation reflecting the bitter lessons gleaned by raids such as that of Dieppe, and ultimately the use of overwhelming force. In naval strategy too, 'concentration', has long been stressed as a cardinal principle, on the grounds that the military effectiveness of naval forces generally declines the further they are deployed from their home bases (nuclear submarines being one major exception).[12]

Mahan and Corbett rose to influence before the First World War, in a strategic context dominated by a few, mainly European naval powers. Although sea mines, submarines, aircraft and torpedoes had all been invented, the surface dimension was predominant. The major naval conflict of the era, the 1904–05 Russo-Japanese War, culminating in the epic gun-duel at Tsushima, appeared to confirm the primacy of the battleship, reinforcing what Corbett termed the 'battle faith' of the Royal Navy, as well as that of its Japanese, European and US counterparts.[13] This focus on the decisive battle-fleet encounter he thought, distracted naval planners from the true purpose of naval strategy which is to gain control over maritime communications, rather than to annihilate enemy fleets *per se*.[14] However, the operational debut of new weapons such as torpedoes and sea mines, which had cost Admiral Tōgō Heihachirō's fleet two battleships during the blockade of the Russian Far East squadron at Port Arthur, forewarned that the battleship's supremacy was threatened and that the days of the close blockade were numbered. By 1914, the close blockade was no longer viable against the increased lethality of inshore defences. Instead, the Royal Navy opted for a distant blockade to contain the German fleet during the First World War, though at the expense of ceding it limited freedom of movement within the North Sea.

Mahan advanced the view that 'The necessity of a navy...springs...from the existence of a peaceful shipping and disappears with it, except in the case of a nation which has aggressive tendencies'.[15] However, his belief in – and prescriptions for – achieving sea power were guided more by a deterministic and dogmatic view of naval power as an end in itself rather than linked instrumentally to trade protection. Mahan held that a set of criteria: geographical location; physical conformity (including natural resources and climate); extent of territory; population; national character and political system together constituted 'natural conditions' determining the development of sea power. However, he also differentiated functionally between 'lines of communication' to support foreign military ventures such as Napoleon's offensive in Egypt and 'lines of travel', or trade routes.[16]

Corbett saw overland and maritime lines of communication sharing three common military purposes, as:

1 lines of supply;
2 lines of lateral communication;
3 lines of retreat.

He further subdivided maritime communications into those required by the belligerents' fleets for supply of fuel, stores and ammunition; communications between an army overseas and its home base; trade routes (servicing the resource needs of the belligerents' home bases); and 'lateral' communications interconnecting their overseas bases.[17] Corbett's claim that command of the sea 'means nothing but the control of maritime communications, whether for commercial or military purposes',[18] was revived during the inter-war period by the French Admiral, Raoul Castex, who wrote that 'The mission of maritime forces is simply to dominate lines of communications, and the achievement of that situation is normally described as having sea mastery'.[19] Eric Grove suggests that Corbett's attachment to the abstract appeal of 'lines of communication' may have led him astray intellectually from the premise that it is ships, rather than belts of sea, that have intrinsic strategic value.[20] However, it is notable that a British Admiralty committee advocated the concept of patrolled sea routes, in conjunction with the blockade of enemy ports, as early as 1885, having rejected convoying as an 'impracticable' concept.[21]

Commerce warfare received only peripheral attention from Mahan, who thought that it 'could not be by itself alone decisive'.[22] Similarly, Corbett's recognition that the security of bulk imports and food had become a 'a matter of life and death' for Great Britain did not sway him from his conviction that the *guerre de course* (literally, 'war of the chase') was marginal within naval strategy. The objective of dominating the enemy's communications would be achieved by seeking out the enemy's fleet 'nine times out of ten'.

Corbett also asserted that if maritime communications are shut down and command of the sea established, then the analogy with territorial conquest is close, since economic pressure on one's enemy begins immediately, unlike on land where it only follows a military result.[23] Corbett's apparent failure to grasp the strategic potential of the *guerre de course* may be attributed partly to the then-untested potential of the submarine as a weapon of economic blockade. Since Corbett held that 'No power will incur the odium of sinking a prize with all hands' only six years before the German Navy adopted unrestricted U-boat warfare against Allied merchant ships, it was also the product of an ethos of an established naval power, in which the non-lethal seizure of ships was still regarded as 'more akin to a process of law . . . than to a military operation'.[24]

Corbett saw focal areas and terminals, where concentration is unavoidable, as merchant ships' greatest point of vulnerability, but thought a flotilla guard could adequately defend these.[25] He also rejected the notion that trade routes in the open ocean were 'undefended', believing that Great Britain's merchant fleet was large enough, measured against the threat of attack from surface raiders, to ensure that sufficient imports would reach the home islands without the need of organizing convoys which would dilute limited naval resources.[26]

The world wars

The Central Powers' North Atlantic submarine campaign during the First World War demonstrated that even in the face of a successful Allied blockade of Germany's battle fleet, a 'counter-blockade' could be mounted using submarines. The first Battle of the Atlantic revealed new vulnerabilities for maritime powers in an attrition-based conflict decided ultimately by industrial capacity and economic stamina. By breaking down the conceptual distinction between 'military' and 'commercial' shipping, the conflict eroded taboos against targeting merchant shipping and using 'all means of effective maritime pressure', leading ultimately to 'unrestricted' U-boat warfare, from February 1917.[27]

The first Battle of the Atlantic demonstrated that a potentially decisive sea denial capability, in the submarine arm, could operate independently of forces challenging for sea control. In April 1917, a total of 852,000 tons of Allied shipping, including one-quarter of all merchant ships leaving UK ports, was lost, taking the country's domestic food stocks to within six weeks of exhaustion. The potency of the submarine is appreciated from the small numbers of U-boats committed (a total of 199 were lost during the war), the relatively unsophisticated tactics used (single U-boats operating independently) and the partial blockade, by mine fields, of the main ingress points from Germany's North Sea U-boat pens to the Atlantic. After raids against Germany's submarine bases and despite persisting with the 'proven futility' of area anti-submarine patrols, merchant losses were not properly curtailed until the convoy system was fully operational in August 1917, having been adopted belatedly in May.[28]

Based on his experience during the First World War, Castex (who commanded antisubmarine patrols in the Mediterranean, where Japanese Imperial Navy vessels were operating on the Allied side) believed that acquiring a limited capacity for sea denial might be adequate for a continental power to preserve territorial gains against intervention by maritime powers. He recognized that in the age of total war, economic factors themselves had become 'military', but believed that a distinction could still be drawn between; first, 'peacetime' maritime communications as the foundation of economic wealth; and second, communications during war. The latter could be separated functionally into: (i) those required to sustain a war economy; (ii) those allowing forces to be moved; and (iii) those fulfilling the function of internal communications under certain geographic conditions.[29]

Castex stressed the importance of national geography, population and the distribution of resources – energy, raw materials and food – in deciding the different extent to which a disruption of seaborne trade would affect states. By the 1920s, when most major navies had converted or were converting from coal to oil as their primary bunker fuel it was already clear that oil was in a category of its own among strategic commodities. Given the expectation that in future conflicts, victory would flow ultimately from economic strength, 'accessory concerns' such as navy-transport bureau relations, stockpiling and austerity measures to limit import demand were recognised by Castex as integral to an overall national effort.

Although Castex maintained that the *guerre de course* could not be independently decisive, he saw the potential of the submarine and aeroplane to erode the dominance of surface fleets, and was thus a keen proponent of the submarine.[30] Regarding measures to protect shipping against submarines, he considered convoy to be superior to arming, diverting or independently routing merchant ships, stressing that convoy minimizes losses, returns the initiative to the defence by maximizing the potential for counter-attack and maintains the focus correctly on defending 'the objects themselves rather than the space'. Based on his experience as a practitioner in anti-submarine warfare (ASW), he rejected the concept of patrolled areas as misconceived.[31]

During both world wars, the Battle of the Atlantic was a contest between maritime 'sea control' and continental 'sea denial' powers. On both occasions, a maritime coalition with Great Britain and the United States at its core sought to assert sea control in order to maintain trans-atlantic communications to sustain Great Britain's war effort and to project US military power into Europe (and in the Second World War, North Africa), against a German-led alliance that sought to sever sea communications binding the maritime coalition. Germany's surface fleet, although venturing out in the early phases of both wars, was unable successfully to challenge the UK and US navies for sea control in the Atlantic, leading to its confinement as a 'fleet in being' in the North Sea during the First World War and to its piecemeal destruction in the Second. However, by means of a strategic offensive against merchant shipping led by submarines and aided by mines and shore-based aircraft, Germany nonetheless significantly disrupted the maritime supply chain between the United States and Great Britain and between the latter and the Soviet Union.

In the Second World War, the U-boat threat was eventually stemmed, though at a cost in resources far in excess of those committed by Germany to its submarine campaign, estimated by one source at a ratio of 15:1.[32] The approximately

900 submarines of the *Kriegsmarine* at Admiral Karl von Dönitz's disposal (781 of which were lost) sank 15 million tons of Allied and neutral shipping, or 60 per cent of the total.[33] In addition to the direct losses, this forced the Allies to divert substantial naval assets to the defence of shipping, withholding their use for offensive application, and delayed the flow of men and *materiel* across the Atlantic, pushing back the date of the Normandy invasion from 1943.

Writing in 1943, Bernard Brodie noted that contrary to the evidence of naval conflicts up to the Russo-Japanese war, the German anti-shipping campaigns in the Atlantic in the First and Second World Wars suggested that 'the decision on the seas might go not to the belligerent with a stronger navy, but to the one least vulnerable to interrupted communications'.[34] Brodie concluded that disputed sea control had become the norm in naval warfare, as the submarine acted as an equalizer for lesser naval powers, unable to vie for surface command.[35] Brodie regarded the maintenance of trans-atlantic communications as a *sine qua non* of victory in the Second World War, echoing Winston Churchill's 'only real fear' of losing the Battle of the Atlantic. In total war, Brodie recognized – as had Castex earlier – that the outcome depended as much on the industrial capacity of the United States and Great Britain to compensate for shipping losses as it did on naval strategy.[36]

In the Pacific theatre during the Second World War, the Japanese Imperial Navy attempted to establish sea control in the Western Pacific by forcing a decisive encounter with the US main battle fleet. The rapidity of its military successes in 1941–42 disguised the country's vulnerability to a merchant blockade until US submarines and aircraft were in a position to exploit it, in 1943–44. (Japan's pre-1945 SLOC security is fully discussed in Chapter 3.)

Brodie identified three types of defensive cover for shipping; 'general cover', evasive routing and direct protection.[37] First, general cover refers to the indirect protection conferred through command of the sea, secured by a superior naval force disposed in such a way as either to destroy or neutralize a hostile fleet-in-being. Second, against the threat of sub-surface or air attack, the most basic form of protection for merchant shipping is evasive routing except near to terminals where concentration is unavoidable.[38] Brodie noted that during the early phases of both world wars, merchant raiders enjoyed their greatest success by preying upon lone ships whose inexperienced or uninformed captains adhered to predictable peacetime routes. Third, of strategies aimed at direct protection, convoy presented merchant ships with greater overall security compared to single sailings.

Since the end of the Napoleonic wars, convoy has been discarded by navies at the end of one war as 'dull and unspectacular work' only to be resurrected belatedly in the next, usually to positive effect.[39] During the First World War, convoy was initially resisted as logistically difficult to organize and tactically flawed, presenting a concentrated target limited to the speed of the slowest vessels in the group. However, after its introduction in May 1917 the convoy system had within five months reduced the rate of Allied shipping lost to one-quarter that of April – and to just 1 per cent of shipping under convoy.[40] The United States was an enthusiastic supporter of convoys in the First World War. By the time it entered the Second World War, valuable information on convoying routes and procedure had passed out of the Navy's institutional memory. Only disastrous losses suffered by Allied shipping operating off the US eastern seaboard in the first half of 1942 challenged the prevailing US view that 'The Navy does not like convoys. It is a purely defensive form of warfare . . . in so far as enemy submarine warfare forces us to use the convoy system, we unwittingly play into his hands'.[41]

Once established, convoys were demonstrated during both world wars to offer the most effective protection, proving only marginally easier to detect than single ships, as well as offering the most effective means of counter-attack. Convoy, according to the authoritative post-Second World War account,[42] became a means 'not only of protecting shipping but of locating and destroying U-boats'.[43] Given the shortage of naval vessels available for escort duty, the concentration of merchant shipping in convoy presented the most efficient means to allocate limited resources for their protection. Of the 2,240 merchant ships lost in the Atlantic and Arctic, 63 per cent were either sailing singly or were separated from their convoys.[44]

Many of the lessons from the Second World War were specific to the differing geography and distribution of capabilities in the Atlantic and Pacific theatres. However, a number of general principles pertaining to SLOC security from both world wars can be advanced. In both conflicts a maritime coalition, based on an Anglo-US trans-atlantic axis, was victorious against a predominantly continental alliance. This observation excludes the fact that the Soviet Union/Russia was present as a continental ally on the Allied side to absorb most of Germany's military energy, while Japan, as a key maritime power, was defeated in the Second World War. However, the US–UK experience in the Atlantic in both world wars demonstrated that sea communications were surprisingly robust in the face of sustained military pressure, once measures (convoy in particular) were organized for the defence of shipping. Trans-atlantic SLOC yielded strategic advantages as well as vulnerabilities, allowing maritime (and air) power to be projected throughout Western Europe and North Africa and enabling strategic economies comparable to those which Germany enjoyed internally within occupied Europe. The Japanese experience showed, equally, that if inadequately defended, SLOC could lay open import-dependent belligerents to a blockade of merchant shipping that would eventually sap their industrial capacity to support modern warfare. The Allies' distant blockade of the European Central Powers in 1914–18 showed that, over time, blockade could be effective in degrading the fighting power of even relatively autarkic continental powers.

All attempts during the world wars to institute patrolled lanes proved to be unambiguous and costly failures. In spite of the poor record of such efforts when attempted in 1916–17 off the south-west coast of Ireland, the 'Ship Lane Patrol' when mounted by the US Navy in early 1942, off the US Atlantic seaboard proved singularly unable either to locate enemy submarines or to protect merchant shipping. The introduction of convoy in the Atlantic thus corrected the 'fallacious doctrine' that sea routes or SLOC possessed concrete reality or strategic value independent of the ships themselves.[45]

Germany's submarine offensive in 1940–43, although ultimately unsuccessful, demonstrated the strategic potential of the submarine-led counter-blockade. Germany's anti-shipping campaign and that of the United States in the Pacific achieved results out of all proportion to the resources invested. Indeed, a German victory in the Battle of the Atlantic might well have been secured had more resources been committed to von Dönitz's submarine programme at the outset, denying Great Britain and its allies the time to re-learn half-forgotten strategies such as convoy and bring their cumulative industrial superiority to bear.

During the Second World War in the Pacific, Japan benefited initially from substantial sea control yielded during the US and European retreat from Southeast Asia, as well as an island screen against the Pacific 'proper', extending south through Okinawa, Formosa/Taiwan, to the Philippine and Indonesian and Micronesian archipelagos, allowing it to maintain resource in-flows from East Asia and the South Pacific with only limited impedance until the second half of 1943. However, once the United States had overcome technical, doctrinal and logistical obstacles to employing its submarines effectively, its anti-shipping campaign from late 1943 onwards (latterly assisted by carrier and land-based aviation), proved that targeting maritime economic communications could be independently decisive. Despite possessing submarines and torpedoes technically superior to those of the United States, the Imperial Navy itself failed to exploit the potential for attacking extended US SLOC sustaining MacArthur's and Nimitz's amphibious pincer movements, respectively pushing north from Australia and west from Hawaii – such was the strength of its 'battle faith'.

The Cold War

At the end of the Second World War, at the very moment that US Navy appeared to have secured maritime dominance, the introduction of nuclear weapons rendered questionable future scenarios for sustained, high-intensity naval conflict. The advent of the nuclear age threatened to make the traditional power-projection role of the US Navy obsolete. The US Navy responded to this partly technical, partly bureaucratic challenge (on the part of the Air Force) by arguing for and gaining control over the submarine component of the nuclear 'strategic triad'.[46] It also lobbied successfully to retain a conventional strike capability based around carrier battle groups, which have since formed the core of its post-war force structure. Until the mid- to late 1960s, US naval superiority over the Soviet Union was not questioned. Conventional military conflict between the superpowers, although planned for on the scenario of a Warsaw Pact move on western Europe and other regional flashpoints, took on proxy forms in 'wars of national liberation', in which the United States was rarely challenged at sea. As a result, logistic lines of communication across the Pacific used to sustain US interventions on the Korean Peninsula and in Vietnam were largely unimpeded.

Although the importance of shipping protection in western naval planning diminished after 1945, the lessons learned and institutionally retained from the Second World War continued to intrude into western naval planning during the Cold War. This was evident from the Radford-Collins Naval Control of Shipping Agreement of 1951, which arose from discussions among senior naval officers from the United States, Great Britain, Australia and New Zealand who set out to divide the Pacific into geographical zones of responsibility for the protection of merchant shipping including such activities as convoying, safe routing and the exchange of weather information, ASW, search and rescue, and surveillance (the latter being subject to a further agreement in 1978).[47] Organizations for the NCS, spanning such activities as authorizing sailings, route selection, the organization of convoys, tactical diversions and movement reporting continued to be maintained beyond the Cold War by the United States and allies such as Australia and Singapore, manned largely by naval reservists.[48]

Until the mid-1960s, the Soviet Union restricted its maritime ambitions to developing a 'brown water' navy for coastal operations and acquiring its own strategic missile submarines. From the late 1960s, Western planners perceived a rising potential Soviet threat to US sea control in both the North Atlantic and North Pacific, particularly from Soviet attack submarines 'primarily aimed at interdicting our sea lines of communication' used to re-supply US forward-deployed forces and those of US allies.[49] In response to the build-up of the Soviet Navy and the emergence of new sub-surface and air threats to the blue-water operations of US aircraft carriers and nuclear-powered ballistic missile submarines (SSBNs), initial variants of a 'maritime strategy' stressed the direct defence of US military SLOC.[50]

At the end of the 1970s, a far more ambitious version of the maritime strategy was developed, closely associated with Admirals John F. Lehman and James D. Watkins (appointed Secretary of the Navy and Chief of Naval Operations, respectively, under the Reagan administration) who believed that by using the superiority of the US Navy in mobile strike power to target Soviet SSBNs and other high-value targets, the Soviet Navy would be forced to divert its surface, air and submarine assets into a defensive posture within 'bastion' seas, thereby alleviating pressure upon trans-atlantic and trans-Pacific SLOC. A reactive posture of defending directly against Soviet strengths at sea and 'swinging' naval forces from one theatre to another was replaced by the far more radical concept of 'horizontal escalation', based on utilizing forward-deployed US forces to target vulnerable sectors of Soviet military infrastructure. Beginning in 1981, a review of naval defence policy and burden-sharing conducted by the Reagan administration gave political backing to the acquisition of a '600-ship fleet'. An unprecedented peacetime defence build-up ensued, funded by a 76 per cent increase in military expenditure between 1976 and 1986, the same year that the Maritime Strategy was officially announced by Admiral Watkins and adopted by the Reagan administration.[51]

In North-east Asia, the Maritime Strategy and 'horizontal escalation' meant that US forces would be able to open a new front in the Soviet Far East, in the event that Soviet forces threatened in areas of relative strength such as Western Europe or the Middle East. As geography was key to US calculations of relative strength vis-à-vis the Soviet Union, Japan's role assumed critical importance 'as a springboard from which the United States can launch attacks against the Soviet homeland [and] . . . a shield behind which the US Navy can fight Pacific battles'.[52]

Such scenarios necessarily proceeded from the problematic assumption that a high-intensity conflict that was global in scope could be contained below the threshold of a strategic nuclear exchange. Desmond Ball has argued that the escalatory pressures inherent in the Maritime Strategy could have brought a nuclear response at an early stage of any superpower clash in the Northwest Pacific.[53] (The importance of the Maritime Strategy and horizontal escalation to Japan's involvement in sea lane defence is explored in Chapter 5.)

With the Maritime Strategy increasingly geared towards an offensive force posture, doubts were expressed about the continued relevance of Second World War-type convoys, especially in the Pacific, given the likely prioritisation of trans-atlantic SLOC in any superpower conflict.[54] In the late 1980s, Vice Admiral J. Blouin outlined four concepts towards securing key Pacific SLOC, involving convoy, independent sailings, defended lanes and offensive operations.[55] In this context, the concept of patrolled SLOC was revived as an 'expansion of the convoy concept':

> A protected or defended lane would involve sanitizing a geographical area against the submarine threat, followed by the installation of a barrier or protected perimeter to provide for penetration warning.... Protective forces would be positioned along a transit route. Each unit of the protective force would be assigned an area of responsibility, the size of which depended upon the speed and sensors of the protective platform, perceived threat, environmental conditions and weapons involved.[56] [My ellipsis]

The credibility of patrolled lanes as conceived in the late Cold War was predicated upon the advances made since 1945 in ASW, drawing upon the combined resources of air- and sea-based patrol units and a global, remote surveillance infrastructure, based on a network of sound surveillance sonar system (SOSUS) sea-bed acoustic arrays, land-based high-frequency radio detection nets and dedicated naval reconnaissance satellites providing comprehensive optical, infra-red and signals-intelligence coverage of the oceans.[57] Despite such technical advances, the attachment of Pacific and North Atlantic Treaty Organization (NATO) planners to defending SLOC was criticized in some quarters as duplicating past mistakes made in respect of the abstract concept of patrolled SLOC.[58]

Starting in 1979, with a proposal to establish a private study group to examine SLOC security in the Asia-Pacific region, a series of bi-annual international conferences dedicated to SLOC security were inaugurated in 1982. Co-organized by the United States, Japan, South Korea, Australia, China, Taiwan and a number of the Association of Southeast Asian Nations (ASEAN) member states, SLOC conferences were attended by politicians, defence officials, serving military officers and representatives from shipping firms and other maritime industries. By the end of the Cold War, the conference agenda had evolved into three main objectives, namely:

1 to arrive at a mutual understanding of SLOC defence;
2 to agree upon the methods of SLOC defence and its necessity;
3 to implement practicable cooperation for SLOC defence and burden sharing.[59]

Post-Cold War SLOC security

Since the end of the Cold War, a 'narrow' military-focused paradigm of SLOC security based on great power conflict and the defence of freedom of navigation on the high seas has given way to a comprehensive agenda, incorporating political-legal and non-military issues, such as expanding maritime sovereignty claims under the United Nations Convention for the Law of the Sea (UNCLOS), environmental problems and general issues of shipping safety. The definition of maritime threats has also been expanded to include non-state actors involved in terrorism and piracy. The roles of navies have undergone a corresponding shift to more constabulary tasks and 'operations-other-than-war', such as sanctions enforcement, anti-piracy patrols, counter-terrorism, peace-keeping support, fisheries protection, and 'benign' functions including disaster relief, search-and-rescue and naval diplomacy, with a larger number of exercise partners than was the case during the Cold War. While deterrence is still seen 'as the bottom line of naval policy', the reduced risk of high-level conflict at sea has fed into an expectation that fewer ships are needed to perform a broader range of functions than was the case when Western navies planned for global superpower conflict.[60]

Concerns that were present but sidelined during the Cold War have risen higher on policy-makers' agenda. Efforts by coastal states to extend state controls beyond the three-mile limit of territorial waters formerly adhered to by most Western maritime states prompted the first of three conferences on the UNCLOS, which was held in 1958. However, UNCLOS did not enter into force until after the Cold War had concluded, in November 1994. Concern about threats to shipping from non-state actors long pre-dates the end of the Cold War. In 1985, the hijacking of the *Achille Lauro* cruise ship, although an isolated incident, first brought modern terrorism to sea, while piracy began to attract attention as a resurgent phenomenon in Southeast Asia from the early 1980s.[61] Despite the US declaration of a global 'war on terrorism' since 11 September 2001, counter-terrorism will continue principally to be a campaign of intelligence and law enforcement, in which conventional military power plays a supportive but subordinate role.

In terms of capabilities, the run-down of the former Soviet fleet has left a much-diminished Russian navy and China's fledgling blue-water capability as the only remotely credible local challenges to US military superiority. Buoyed by outlays exceeding the combined defence expenditure of the next 25 powers,[62] the US armed forces have reaped the benefits of multiplier technologies in command, control, communications and intelligence, and computerized battle management that are at least one generation ahead of competitors.[63] The end of the Cold War and the run-down of much of the former Soviet Navy restored US command of the sea in the open ocean to levels unmatched since 1945. Confirmation of this was seen in the doctrinal shift adopted by the US Navy to littoral operations, 'Forward from the Sea'. For the most part, the force structure built up by western navies for open-ocean ASW operations during the Cold War could be adapted to littoral roles with relative ease. A major exception concerns the limited ability of the United States to manoeuvre its large, exclusively nuclear-powered attack submarines (SSN) – designed to hunt Soviet submarines in the open ocean – in shallow seas. Similarly, the bias built into US acoustic monitoring for detecting Soviet SSBNs and SSNs in open, deep-water areas led Eric Grove to predict, in 1993, that in the post-Cold War era, ultra-quiet conventionally-powered attack submarines (SSK) 'may become an important equalizer, the means by which smaller and poorer countries can defend themselves from richer and more powerful assailants'.[64] The submarine procurement patterns of China, Taiwan, Malaysia, Singapore and South Korea as well as established SSK operators such as Japan, appear to have borne out Grove's prediction in East Asia.[65] The potential for SLOC being severely disrupted in the event of regional conflict in the Asia-Pacific, collaterally or by a modern-day blockade or *guerre de course*, is still assumed possible, in the expectation that 'Strong regional powers will acquire submarine forces and develop doctrine to employ them against sea lines of communication'.[66]

The US military remains reliant on sea communications to project power reactively and to sustain its network of overseas bases. In major post-Cold War US strategic planning documents, while no threat to US sea control is foreseen in the Atlantic, the security of SLOC in the Middle East and Western Pacific has been retained among stated core US security interests. The East Asia Strategic Review released in 1995 highlighted the security of sea lanes and a particular need to maintain the 'ability to move forces through the sea lines to support contingencies in the Middle East', reflecting East Asian economies' growing dependence on oil from the Gulf. However, indicative of a shift in US post-Cold War perceptions, the security value of Southeast Asian chokepoint waterways such as the Malacca Strait has been evaluated as much in terms of their economic importance to regional and global trade as their significance as transit routes for military deployments between the Western Pacific and Indian Ocean. According to an unclassified 1993 National Defense University/Center for Naval Analyses study commissioned by the US Navy's Deputy Chief of Naval Operations:

> For many years, the prime concern was military, not economic, as the United States required secure maritime transport via SLOCs in case of war. Now the emphasis has shifted to the economic component of our national security, a policy reaffirmed when the United States announced (in March and May, 1995), that it would not accept disruption of trade in the South China Sea.[67]

Reflecting the uncertainty which prevailed as to the trend of future US security priorities, the same study notes that as the 'Cold War mind-set recedes, the naval mission of protecting shipping could emerge as an explicit national priority'.[68] This, indeed, has been borne out in various US maritime security initiatives since the 11 September attacks. Despite periodic downturns, seaborne trade, as measured in ton-miles, underwent almost a quadruple expansion between 1965 and 2002.[69] The end of the Cold War provided impetus for the emergence of a truly global trading system within the framework of the WTO and the 1990s saw an unprecedented expansion of global trade, much of this emanating from the developing economies of the Asia-Pacific, which had already doubled their share of world trade, from 10 to 20 per cent in 1970–90. Viewed from realist perspectives in international relations, the boost to global trade facilitated by the end of the Cold War has the potential to add to security tensions by increasing competition over finite energy resources and to amplify the vulnerability of key chokepoints to military pressure or terrorist attack. With overall Asian energy demand forecast to rise by around 71 per cent between 1999 and 2020, the risk of a strategic dynamic developing as part of increasing inter-state competition for access to hydrocarbons is seen by certain commentators as potentially focussing conflict on the energy import routes themselves.[70] In April 2002, reflecting increasing anxiety within Asia about oil supply interruptions in transit, a sea lane disruption simulation exercise was launched by the Asia Pacific Energy Research Centre (APERC; a part of Asia Pacific Economic Cooperation – APEC), involving wide-ranging participants drawn from over 20 Asian states.[71] From countervailing neo-liberalist positions, the growth of maritime trade is viewed as a force militating against inter-state maritime conflict by increasing the number of stakeholders in the security of the hard and soft infrastructure underpinning international trade and raising the economic costs of conflict.[72]

Since the end of the Cold War, the internationalization of the maritime transport industry has also increased, to the point where a ship's registry, owner, insurer, crew and cargo are typically contracted among several nationalities. This process, which has occurred as a result of increased liberalization and commercial pressures to drive down ship operators' costs, itself carries strategic consequences. Commentators view dwindling national fleets as undermining state security given doubts about the dependability of international shipping firms during crises and the inability of governments legally to compel them to sail.[73] Other analysts see the internationalization of the shipping industry as complicating the option of blockade for potential aggressors by raising political costs to unacceptable levels. Daniel Coulter contends that defence planners have been slow to adjust from Mahanian security paradigms in response to a revolution in maritime transportation, in which ships, ports and other transportation nodes are increasingly networked.[74]

The strategic quality of a given waterway is a relative calculation of geopolitical and military factors, and all waterways are potentially strategic.[75] However, Coulter assumes that in the absence of credible threats to shipping in the open ocean, SLOC are synonymous with chokepoints, as the only places where ship traffic can systemically be hindered. Although the time-sensitive requirement of military planners to deploy forces in the quickest time possible via the most direct route is essentially unchanged since Mahan's day, the economics of navigational access through chokepoints operates under market-based rules which give the system considerable flexibility to cope with most localized obstructions. Whereas for reactive military deployments, timeliness is the most important criterion of success, the unit of efficiency for commercial cargoes is ton-miles.

Such obstructions can be diverted around without incurring prohibitive add-on costs as long as alternative routes are available, and spare shipping and port-handling capacity exists. As a result of over-investment by heavily subsidized ship-builders in Europe and Asia, large surpluses were built up during the 1990s across the global dry bulk and tanker fleets. Of the 252 million DWT of dry bulk-carrier capacity in service globally in 1995, there was a surplus of nearly 18 million DWT. While the surplus for bulk carriers had declined to around 3 million DWT in 2001, for tankers the surplus rate was above 6 per cent, or 18 million DWT, out of a global tanker fleet of 280 million DWT. Until 2002, a glut existed in relation to container shipping, with around 3,500 container ships estimated to be in service globally, for a combined capacity of around 6 million 20-foot-equivalent units (TEU), almost three times the level of 1990.[76] Owing to efficiency gains from new and larger cargo vessel designs, between 1980 and 1999, freight costs increased by only 7 per cent whereas global trade grew by 12 per cent.[77] From 1999 to 2002, trans-Pacific container freight rates fell by around one-third.

However, from the global glut that prevailed as recently as 2002, the shipping industry has recovered rapidly to the point that it is probably experiencing a cyclical peak unprecedented in 50 years. A ban on single-hulled tankers from EU ports following the loss of the *Prestige* off northern Spain in November 2002 has contributed to demand for double-hulled tankers that currently exceeds supply.[78] Of far greater and more enduring significance is China's rapid economic development and emergence as a global trading power. Since the country's accession to the WTO, the exponential growth of its commodity imports and manufactured exports is the main factor behind a worldwide freight boom, particularly in the dry bulk and container sectors.[79] Since 2002, container traffic across the Pacific has doubled, with Chinese penetration at above 80 per cent in some US manufactured import sectors. In April 2004, Asia's shipowners predicted that trans-Pacific cargo movement would grow by 12–15 per cent in the year ahead, while in 2003 intra-Asian cargo movement expanded by a similar amount to reach over 8 million TEU.[80] Shipping capacity overall is forecast to rise by 14 per cent in 2006, probably sufficient to ensure that enough slack exists within the system to cope with most foreseeable contingencies, though the same does not necessarily follow for port-handling capacity which currently lags behind the global shipbuilding boom.

The shipping boom has at the same time sharply driven up shipping costs by more than 300 per cent since the beginning of 2002.[81] Nevertheless, transportation costs still form a fractional, albeit higher, proportion of the overall import bill. The economic consequences of increased demand for shipping, or a requirement to divert trade via longer routes would hence likely remain manageable for large economies, while the additional profit generated from extra ton-mile requirements would also create a strong incentive for shipping firms to add capacity.[82] As evidence of this, Coulter points to the closure of the Suez Canal, from 1967 to 1975, as having only a marginal effect on global trade, despite the long diversion around the Cape of Good Hope. Only in the case of the Straits of Hormuz is the potential for the closure of a major chokepoint acknowledged by Coulter to have strategic potential, given its monopoly over access to oil terminals in the Gulf. However, the continued passage of tankers through the straits during the 1980–88 Iran–Iraq war, in spite of ships being targeted by both sides and raised insurance premiums, is seen as evidence of the resilience of modern maritime transportation networks and the tanker's surprisingly robust ability 'to get through'. Indeed, while individual tankers are vulnerable, there are weaker links in the oil supply chain: pipelines are fixed, exposed and non-substitutable, while the infrastructure of oil production, refining and storage presents more lucrative targets to potential adversaries, as the Iraqi experience has proved. The loss of a single tanker would not necessarily halt supplies.

Coulter blames the residual influence of Mahan for the persistent confusion between military principles and market principles governing contemporary maritime transportation. As a result, he concludes that chokepoint SLOC are not essential to the free flow of seaborne commerce reflecting the fact that the 'choice of route is a function of market conditions'. Similarly, according to MccGwire's 1975 assessment, 'despite the volume of traffic passing through Malacca and the other straits of the Indonesian archipelago, these waterways are not essential for inter-oceanic trade'.[83]

However, Coulter has also argued that a new Achilles Heel has been created within the global trading system, limiting its ability to withstand shocks. This, he argues, is declining as the up-scaling trend in container shipping funnels world trade via a small number of hub ports concentrated in East Asia.[84] Combined with the relocation of industrial production to China and other low cost-factor destinations and the widespread adoption of just-in-time production techniques, this renders the maritime transportation system vulnerable to the disruption of operations at those few ports capable of handling vessels with a capacity of 5,000 TEU or above, for which no substitute port-handling capacity exists. The top five hub ports in the world are all located in East Asia, led by Hong Kong and Singapore (handling 18 million and 15.5 million TEU respectively in 2001), South Korea's Pusan (8 million), Taiwan's Kaohsiung (7.5 million) and Shanghai (6.3 million).[85] Further large classes of container ship are in prospect with 8,000-TEU vessels and above considered technically and commercially viable.

The capacity of maritime trade, especially the flow of goods between East Asia and the United States, to survive the shocks of the 1995 Kobe earthquake, the 11 September 2001 terrorist attacks and the US West Coast ports stoppage in October 2002 suggests that the system is perhaps more robust than feared. However, Asia's ability to withstand disruption will only truly be tested in the event of a hub-port stoppage, a regional military crisis or a terrorist strike targeted at its ports infrastructure.

The greatest point of vulnerability in the maritime transportation system may in fact be the 'soft' infrastructure of marine insurance: it is uncertain to what extent shipping firms would be able or willing to operate if confronted by a sharp spike in premiums, or the extension of 'exclusion zones' withdrawing insurance cover in the Middle East or Southeast Asia should terrorist or war risk be judged unacceptably high.[86] Since the 12 October 2002 Bali bombing, war-risk status has applied to Indonesian ports, but not to passage through the archipelago.

Sources of potential threat

Some factors which have the potential to disrupt maritime transportation, such as maritime accidents, disasters at sea, or industrial disputes, while important to the flow of shipping are clearly not military SLOC security concerns. Potential challenges and threats to SLOC security that merit the attention of post-Cold War defence planners fall into three categories:

1 maritime sovereignty claims that restrict navigational access to specific waters;
2 terrorism-at-sea and piracy;
3 regional conflicts, which have the potential to disrupt proximate sea transportation routes, either as a result of the collateral effects of wars spilling out onto the maritime plain, or through deliberate obstruction by a sea denial power.

Maritime sovereignty claims

At the end of the Second World War, the vast majority of the world's seas and oceans were regarded as 'high seas', in which states enjoyed equal freedom of navigation rights, based on principles first outlined by the Dutch jurist Hugo Grotius in his *Mare Liberum* of 1609. Currently, two-fifths of the world's seas and oceans are subject to some form of jurisdictional claim. The dramatic post-1945 shift in the legal status of seas and oceans arose out of a basic division between the desire of coastal states (mainly in the de-colonizing world) to assert their sovereignty and enclose surrounding waters, against Western maritime states keen to preserve freedom of navigation for naval and commercial shipping and to maximize their access to marine resources in the water column and seabed.

The end of the Cold War was taken as a cue by some coastal states to re-direct the onus of maritime security away from great power military interests in power projection to the responsibility of littoral states for the management of coastal waters and straits. Malaysia's former maritime ambassador B. A. Hamzah, for example, has described it as an opportunity for littoral states in the Straits of Malacca to escape their perceived historical role as 'gate-keepers' to the great powers.[87]

The UNCLOS was born in 1958 out of a need to mediate a compromise in international law between the interests of coastal and maritime states. The political difficulties and technical complexity involved in reaching an agreement acceptable to all participants led to a second and third convention in 1968 and 1982 (UNCLOS II and III, respectively), and it was only in 1994 that the Convention finally entered into force. UNCLOS incorporated several new concepts into international law, many of which had already been codified within national statutes. These included an extension of territorial seas from 3 to 12 nm, archipelagic status (ultimately granted to 14 nations, including Indonesia, the Philippines and the Solomon Islands) and 200-nm exclusive economic zones (EEZ). Several categories of passage were added to the prevailing regime of high-seas passage (see Appendix). It is claimed that UNCLOS brought 116 straits within the joint or sole jurisdiction of coastal states.[88]

Many newly independent coastal states harboured sensitivities over the prevailing regime of high-seas passage, which was resented as a legal cover for former colonial powers to preserve a strategic presence offshore. Many de-colonizing states, particularly archipelagic nations, such as Indonesia, were acutely sensitive to the risk of foreign intervention and infiltration. This was matched by a strong desire on the part of post-independence elites to assert sovereignty over geographically and ethnically fractured polities. Moreover, many coastal states lacked the capacity necessary to monitor their own coastlines. Tensions between the maritime and coastal states over legal attempts to enclose areas of sea were especially acute in maritime Southeast Asia, where Indonesia sits at a 'geopolitical crossroads'.[89]

UNCLOS has been viewed positively as reinforcing an order-based, institutionalized approach to establishing a common legal framework that both recognises the sovereignty claims of coastal states while upholding principles of freedom of navigation through international straits and offshore areas.[90] In the Asia-Pacific, no state has opposed the principles of freedom of navigation or innocent passage, while North Korea alone has not adopted the Convention.[91] Nor has any state in the region yet introduced tolls for the use of straits. Despite lingering sensitivities over the terms of passage for naval vessels under UNCLOS, particularly concerning the terms of archipelagic sea lanes (ASLs) passage, maritime and coastal states were able to reach agreement on freedom of navigation, probably in mutual recognition of the benefits of maintaining access to maritime commerce.[92]

Relative to the scale of daily flows of global and regional maritime traffic, restrictions introduced to date have had a very modest influence on the navigational freedoms of commercial vessels and aircraft, with the exceptions confined mainly to the transportation of nuclear cargoes and very large oil tankers. However, UNCLOS has failed to assuage the concerns of those who regard it as creating a framework for 'creeping jurisdiction' that could lead to new restrictions on passage or tolls being levied on heavily used waterways.[93] Most freedom of navigation concerns relate to naval vessels and overflight rights. In July 1994, in the lead-up to UNCLOS' passage into international law, the US Department of Defense (DoD) conducted a study to calculate the extra time and fuel required for a carrier battle group deploying from Japan to Bahrain to detour around Australia, based on a scenario of being denied access to the Indonesian Archipelago and the Straits of Malacca.[94]

Terrorism-at-sea and piracy

Among potential maritime security threats posed by non-state actors, terrorism-at-sea and piracy have received most attention since the end of the Cold War. This section looks first at terrorism-at-sea before profiling modern piracy.

The *modus operandi* of maritime terrorism comprises attacks on ships and the more insidious potential threat of vessels themselves being used to deliver concealed weapons of mass destruction (WMD); in containers, hidden within a ship's superstructure or in the form of volatile cargoes. Both terrorist threats have the potential to cause systemic economic dislocation, with the effect of a major attack on a US port or a transhipment hub such as Singapore being felt globally.

The potential for terrorism at sea was first demonstrated by the October 1985 hijacking of the *Achille Lauro* cruise ship by the Palestine Liberation Front. The list of terrorist attacks on shipping since then is remarkably short, even in the post-11 September era. The organizational and resource demands of mounting major terrorist attacks at sea compared with the greater publicity generated by attacks on land has deterred most radical groups from attempting marine operations. However, in October 2000, a new form of suicide 'ramming' attack was unleashed by al-Qaida against the USS *Cole* outside Aden harbour in Yemen, killing 17 sailors. After the foiling of suspected plots to bomb naval targets in Singapore in October 2001 and the Straits of Gibraltar in June 2002, a switch to 'soft targets' was suggested by the 6 October 2002 ramming of the French oil tanker *Limburg*, again off Yemen, which in its execution closely resembled the attack on the *Cole*.[95] After the attack on the *Limburg*, the International Maritime Bureau (IMB) recommended that designated lanes used by tankers be declared 'no-go' areas for unauthorized craft, enforced by intensified naval and police patrols.[96]

As of 2004 there had been no repeat of the attack on the *Limburg* or *Cole*. However, increased sensitivity to the risk of marine terrorism has prompted a succession of anti-terrorist initiatives at the national and international level. The US Container Security Initiative adopted after the 11 September 2001 terrorist attacks on New York and Washington requires designated port authorities to report to US customs the contents of containers destined for US ports 24 hours before a ship's departure. The US Antiterrorism Act 2002 (HR 3983) allows entry into American ports to be refused for suspect vessels and for security assessments to be conducted in foreign ports. The governments of Hong Kong, Singapore and Malaysia are among those to have US customs inspectors stationed at their ports.[97] Most important of all, the Maritime Safety Committee of the IMO announced plans in May 2002 to draw up a convention on countering terrorism-at-sea and to initiate new guidelines for ships and port infrastructure.[98] These were carried forward into the International Ship and Port Facility Security (ISPS) code, a global IMO initiative which requires the mandatory installation of a Ship Security Alert System for all new vessels above 500 GRT and the designation of on-board security officers for each of the approximately 50,000 vessels in the world merchant fleet. The core of the ISPS is the mandatory development and implementation of ship security plans, which must be approved either by flag states or delegated Recognised Security Organisations.[99] Amendments to the 1974 International Convention for the Safety of Life at Sea (SOLAS) further require the embossing of registration numbers on ships' hulls. Both initiatives were adopted by the IMO in December 2002 and came into effect from 1 July

2004. The IMO has been working separately to address the arguably more challenging and pressing issue of port security through a Code of Practice on Security in Ports, adopted in December 2003.

The IMB warned in its 2001 piracy report that terrorists might target shipping while the head of the IMO warned that extra vigilance would be required.[100] The Bali bombing underlined Indonesia's susceptibility to Islamic terrorism and a heightened risk that inter-regional shipping passing through chokepoints such as the Malacca, Sunda and Lombok straits could be targeted. Several hypothetical post-September 11 scenarios have been mooted, such as a terrorist attack on a LNG carrier or similar vessel transiting the Malacca Straits, an act which security analysts claim 'would devastate Southeast Asia's economies and environment and severely disrupt trade as the straits could be closed to shipping for years'.[101] Similar assertions have been made elsewhere, though usually with little offered in the way of substantiating evidence. The US-based Maritime Intelligence Group has alleged that members of Southeast Asian terrorist groups have been trained in suicide ramming techniques by the Liberation Tigers of Tamil Eelam (LTTE), in Sri Lanka. It is also claimed they are developing techniques for targeting shipping in Southeast Asia, using mines and submersibles.[102] Maritime terrorism has risen steadily up the agenda of regional policy-makers. In June 2003 the ASEAN Regional Forum (ARF) adopted a statement warning about 'the potential for terrorist attacks on vulnerable sea shipping [to] threaten the growth of the Asia-Pacific region and disrupt the stability of global commerce'.[103] Similarly, at the at the Third 'Shangri-La' Asia Security Conference in June 2004, Singapore's Defence Minister Tony Tan warned that a terrorist strike on shipping in the Straits of Malacca 'would cripple world trade'. Singapore officials have suggested that a chemical tanker boarded by pirates in the Straits in early 2004 and abandoned after only one hour, may have been a rehearsal for a terrorist 'spectacular'. Yet apart from the recovery of video footage of US warships at anchor in Singapore in 2001 there is little evidence to suggest that the Straits of Malacca are being actively targeted. Merchant ships may begin to look more attractive as targets if the security of land-based infrastructure shows relative improvement.[104] However, large ships such as tankers are difficult to sink or to manoeuvre, while hazardous cargoes with the exception of liquefied petroleum gas (LPG) are usually carried in non-volatile forms.

More 'conventional' acts of terrorism-at-sea have been carried out as part of the spill-over of separatist conflicts, the most organized and audacious being those by the 'Sea Tigers', the LTTE's maritime wing, until a February 2002 cease-fire. In July 1999, an LTTE suicide diver bombed a passenger ferry in Trincomalee port. In addition to terror attacks on local shipping, LTTE maritime actions have extended to robbery targeting international shipping in the busy sea lanes south of the island for revenue-generating purposes, as well as operating its own fleet of ships to smuggle in arms and supplies to the Jaffna Peninsula. Gerakan Aceh Merdeka (GAM) separatist guerrillas, in Indonesia's Aceh province, have specialized in hostage-taking as a means to fund their insurgency. GAM is believed responsible for the hijack of a ship carrying coal in the Malacca Strait on 25 August 2001, the crew of which was subsequently ransomed.[105] Since the breakdown of the December 2002 peace settlement, Acehnese guerrillas have apparently reverted to this means of fund-raising, including a spate of attacks on shipping within a 100-mile radius of Kuala Langsar in mid-2004.[106] The Abu Sayyaf group in the southern Philippines has engaged in similar activities, with much bloodier results.[107] Nine of the 21 crew fatalities reported worldwide to the IMB in 2003 were attributed to pirates in the Philippines.[108]

Though the line between terrorism and piracy is blurred, modern piracy has a more established track record and varied *modus operandi*. In 1983, maritime piracy was raised at the IMO's general meeting, leading to the adoption of Resolution A545 calling for governments to adopt 'measures to prevent acts of piracy and armed robbery against ships'.[109] The IMO subsequently requested that member states inform the Organization of the details concerning any act of piracy or armed robbery against ships under their flag, including the reaction of coastal state authorities. In May 1995, the IMO Maritime Safety Committee instructed the Secretariat to begin drawing up reports to record piracy incidents on a monthly and quarterly basis. This was widened to include annual reporting from 1996.[110]

Modern maritime piracy (different definitions and sub-categories of which are explored below) is a developing world problem, mainly confined to waters off South America, West and East Africa, the Middle East, South and Southeast Asia. According to the IMO, from 1984 to the end of 2003, the total number of actual or attempted incidents of piracy and armed robbery against ships was 3,456.[111] The problem has been most intractable in Southeast Asia, centring on Indonesia since its economic crisis in 1997–98.

In 1998, over 200 incidents were reported worldwide to the IMB, including at least 67 fatalities, 138 vessel boardings, 11 shootings and 15 hijackings.[112] In 1998, the IMB concluded that the incidence of piracy had reached 'alarming' rates around Indonesia, the Straits of Malacca, Bangladesh, India and the Red Sea. The number of piracy incidents reported worldwide to the IMB peaked at 469 in 2000, 119 of which occurred off Indonesia. Although the global incidence of piracy fell to 335 reported incidents in 2001, it rose again to a total of 370 in 2002 and 445 in 2003. Indonesian waters were reconfirmed as the world's most dangerous, host to 121 incidents.

Piracy incidents in the Straits of Malacca reached a record high of 75 in 2000. However, only 8 of these incidents involved actual attacks; 7 to ships under way and 1 involving a ship berthed in the Indonesian side of the straits. Thereafter reported incidents in the Straits dropped to just 16 in 2002 and 28 in 2003, most of which occurred in Indonesian waters.[113]

The IMO defines piracy according to Article 101 of the 1982 UNCLOS declaration as, 'any illegal acts of violence or detention, or any act of depredation directed at private ships or aircraft on (or above) the high sea'. Reflecting its institutional focus on preventing maritime crime, the IMB uses a more inclusive definition, incorporating any 'act of boarding or attempting to board any ship

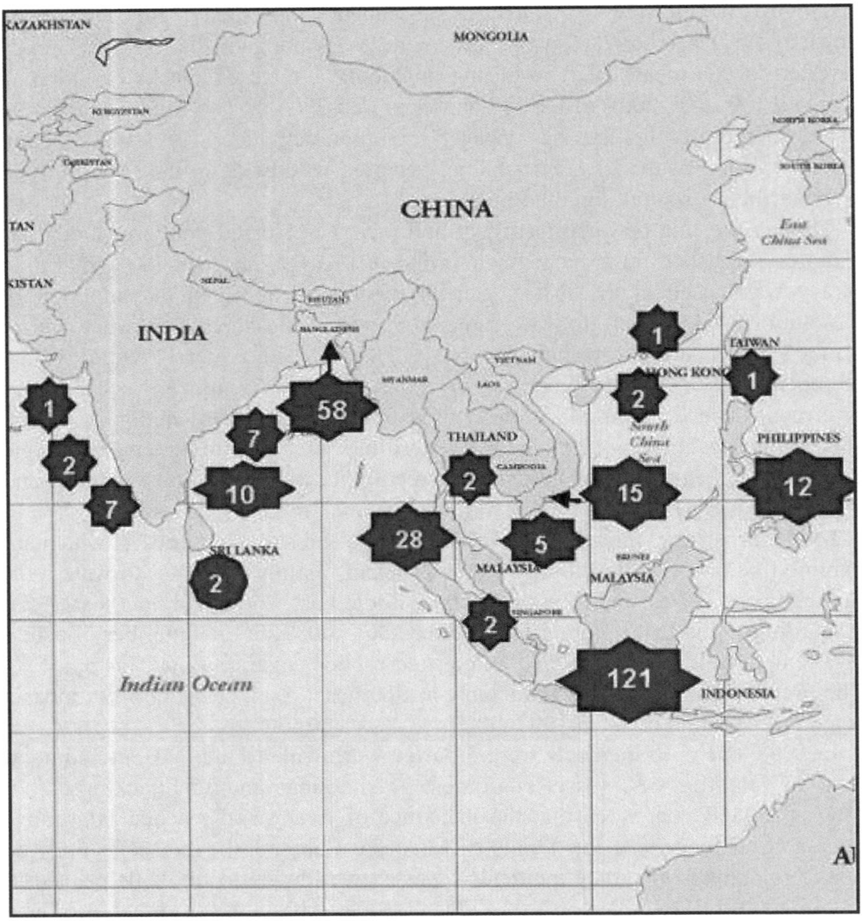

Map 2.1 Piracy and armed robbery-at-sea attacks in Asia, as reported to the IMB in 2003.
Source: International Chamber of Commerce/IMB.

with the intent to commit theft or any other crime and with the intent or capability to use force in the furtherance of that act'.[114] The IMO's high-seas only definition of piracy has been criticized as overly restrictive and anachronistic, since it excludes the vast majority of illegal activities against ships (and aircraft), which almost always take place within territorial and archipelagic waters, and EEZs. Conversely, the IMB's looser definition has been criticized by some shipping associations as exaggerating the scale of the piracy problem, including acts of petty theft committed against ships in port.[115] However, the problem of harmonising the respective IMO and IMB approaches to piracy was largely resolved in

November 2001 when the IMO Assembly adopted its Code of Practice for the Investigation of the Crimes of Piracy and Armed Robbery Against Ships. According to Resolution A922(22):

> Armed Robbery against Ships means any unlawful act of violence or detention or any act of depredation, or threat thereof, other than an act of 'piracy' directed against a ship or against persons or property on board such ship, within a State's jurisdiction over such offences.[116]

This definition covers actual or attempted attacks against ships, whether berthed, at anchor or steaming.[117] In fact, the IMO's annual reports on piracy incidents usually record slightly higher totals of actual or reported incidents, for example 452 to the IMB's 445 in 2003. Many piracy incidents are thought to go unreported by shipping companies, which tend to weigh the slim probability of recovering stolen property and apprehending pirates unfavourably against the risk of raised insurance premiums and the prohibitive cost of charter delays incurred while port-side investigations can be conducted.[118]

Crimes against shipping grouped under the 'piracy' umbrella differ widely in motivation and method. The IMB has identified a typology of modern piracy.[119] First, the practice of illegally boarding vessels under way, at night and from the rear, for the purpose of theft has been the most common type of piracy in Southeast Asia, formerly concentrated around the Phillip Channel between Singapore and Indonesia. The average value of property and cash stolen during boardings has been put at between $5,000 and $15,000, but this does not include the cost of damage, or the indirect and often much higher costs of delays and increased insurance.[120] Such attacks, generally characterized by low levels of violence, occur in territorial waters rather than high seas. The declining size of ships' crews is a factor contributing to the increased vulnerability of merchant ships to hit-and-run attacks, making it harder to maintain deck watches over large vessels.[121]

Second, robberies directed at easily removable property or valuables aboard ships at anchor are reported to be a common feature of piracy as practised in South American and West African waters. Until recently, these were characterized by higher levels of violence than the boardings under-way in Southeast Asia. However, since its economic crisis, a wave of impromptu robberies on ships near Indonesia also falls into this category.

Third, a category of 'military' piracy incorporates the illicit involvement of uniformed personnel in attacks on shipping for material gain and overlaps terrorism-at-sea in cases where shipping is targeted by separatist guerrillas for the purpose of smuggling or fund-raising through extortion, theft and kidnapping. In September 2003, the IMB's Piracy Reporting Centre expressed concern that suspected Acehnese rebels using speed or fishing boats were singling out small gas and oil tankers for attack in the Straits of Malacca, in order to take senior crew members hostage for ransom. In less than one week, three such boardings were attempted against an LPG carrier, a gas tanker and oil tanker including the Malaysian-registered *Penrider*.[122] It is also been alleged that attacks on shipping with covert military involvement have been sanctioned for political as well as commercial reasons. In 1991–93, the intimidation of ships in the East China Sea took on quasi-military overtones during a series of incidents when firearms were used against merchant ships and fishing vessels, frequently without any attempt at boarding. As explored in Chapter 8, Japanese analysts in particular have asserted that Chinese officials for the purpose of reinforcing sovereignty claims tacitly sanctioned the harassment of Japanese and other shipping.

Fourth, ship seizures have occurred when pirates hijack a vessel under way, beyond the range of coastal law enforcement, until appropriated cargo can be offloaded to another vessel alongside or at a friendly port. Such acts imply a high level of organization and potential violence, in the worst cases resulting in the killing or abandonment of the original crew.[123] Several instances of this type of piracy have occurred in East and Southeast Asia, including the *Petro Ranger*, the *Tenyu* and the *Alondra Rainbow*. Incidents of hijacking more than tripled from 8 in 2000 to 25 in 2002, against the trend of an overall reduction in piracy incidents. However, despite an overall rise in the total number of piracy incidents reported in 2003, the number of hijackings declined to 19 – a positive development, which the IMB attributes to stiffer sentencing and increased patrolling by coastal states.[124] In extreme cases, whole vessels have been appropriated for use as ‘phantom ships’ in transnational cargo fraud: examples include the *M.V. Antoinette* and the *M.V. Isla* in the Philippines.

Piracy ‘hotspots’ identified at various times in the Asia-Pacific region over the last decade include the Yellow Sea, the waters north of Taiwan, the Hong Kong–Luzon–Hainan ‘triangle’ (which includes the northern portion of the South China Sea), the Surigao Strait south of Mindanao, and the Straits of Malacca and Sunda. Piracy is an inherently mobile problem, complicating law-enforcement efforts. In 1991–93, after anti-piracy patrols were introduced by Malaysia and Singapore in the Malacca Strait the reported incidence fell from 32 to 5 incidents, while those in the adjacent South China Sea climbed from 6 to 31 between 1992 and 1993, suggesting that local success may merely have had a displacement effect.[125] Nonetheless, the IMB’s Deputy Director has expressed the view that the scale of crimes at sea is small in relation to the incidence of onshore crime and that pirates’ operations are most effectively disrupted by targeting their shore bases. This view extends to regional navies, with Admiral Dato Noor Azman bin Haji Othman of the Royal Malaysian Navy emphasizing the importance of investigating coastal villages given the limited deterrent value of vessel patrols along a long coastline.[126]

Although the total cost of maritime crime in 2000 has been estimated as high as US$25 billion,[127] compared with the prospect of intentional military obstruction of SLOC or terrorism-at-sea intended to cause mass destruction or economic damage, modern piracy cannot be considered as a systemic threat to the security of international shipping lanes, much less to global trade. While not precluding the necessity for, and ability of, international law enforcement cooperation and joint coast guard patrols to counter the spread of maritime piracy, the number of incidents involving vessels under way remains a small proportion of the total.

As a 'fact of life', some measure of lawlessness at sea might best be thought of as an extension of organized and opportunistic crimes committed on land in developing countries, which create add-on costs for businesses but do not generally deter their operations.

Regional conflicts

Regional conflicts since the end of the Cold War, in the Balkans, the Middle East and sub-Saharan Africa, have been mostly civil wars involving little or no maritime element, with Sri Lanka, Aceh and the southern Philippines as exceptions in Asia. Although the 1991 and 2003 Gulf Wars were mainly air-land conflicts, damage done in 1991 to two US vessels from mines, and the prospect of submarines being used to interdict Coalition SLOC in the Gulf caused concern for US military planners.[128] The most serious regional military threat to international shipping in recent times was during the 1980–88 Iran–Iraq War, especially once both sides began systematically targeting tankers and other neutral ships in the Gulf, from 1984. These attacks employed air-launched *Exocet* missiles, shore-based *Silkworm* missiles, fast-attack craft and mines. As a result of continuing attacks, including an Iraqi *Exocet* strike on the USS *Stark*, from July 1987, the United States began escorting convoys of Kuwait tankers re-registered under the US flag in Operation 'Earnest Will'. US military efforts, however, were directed at Tehran, culminating in significant retaliatory actions against Iranian oil installations and naval targets in October 1987 and April 1988.[129]

Despite a generally positive post-Cold War record, several flash-points with potentially serious maritime dimensions are located astride major shipping routes in the Asia-Pacific. Among the most frequently cited is the South China Sea, where it is claimed that 'even low-level, local conflicts could disrupt the SLOCs'.[130] Though not proven, the Spratly and Paracel islands are reported to lie atop major oil and gas deposits, are subject to competing territorial claims among several ASEAN members and are wholly claimed by Vietnam, China and Taiwan (although the latter's claim is in practice limited to occupation of the largest island in the Paracels).[131] On 10 May 1995, US Secretary of State Warren Christopher warned Beijing, after Chinese territorial markers were placed on Mischief Reef, which lies well within the Philippines' 200-nm EEZ, that Washington would view 'with serious concern any restriction on maritime activity in the South China Sea that was not consistent with international law'.[132] According to a 1998 report by Congressman Dana Rorabacher,[133] China's naval activity around the Spratlys 'threatens trade and military sea lanes vital to the United States and our allies'. Under normal conditions, a large volume of inter-regional merchant shipping (in the order of 36,000 ship transits per year) passes through the South China Sea.[134] Overlapping territorial disputes have not triggered a clash between regular naval forces since 1988 and only minor confrontations since. However, the South China Sea is still regarded as potentially volatile, in the context of 'resource nationalism', sovereignty claims inflamed by domestic political pressures and armed forces modernization programmes being undertaken by multiple claimants.

The relatively undeveloped and reactive nature of the existing confidence building and crisis-resolution machinery in the region is also seen as hampering the effectiveness of regional diplomacy, despite ASEAN's success in persuading China to accept a Code of Conduct for the South China Sea in 2002.

Any large-scale resumption of fighting on the Korean Peninsula would almost certainly be a predominantly air-land battle. The naval element would probably be limited to the enforcement of a sanctions blockade, the infiltration of special forces from the North, or clashes in the Yellow Sea, of the type that led to the sinking of a South Korean naval vessel in June 2002 and a similar incident in 1999 (see Chapter 8). However, there would also be a substantial risk of mines being used by the North, affecting sea lanes used by South Korea and Japan.

In the case of an armed conflict between China and Taiwan, unless limited to an air and missile exchange across the Taiwan Strait, the spectrum of cross-strait naval conflict can range from China's seizure of Taiwanese-held islands off the mainland, through various gradations of blockade, to a full-blown invasion of the island. China's planning for a cross-strait conflict and the impact of this and potential maritime conflicts in the South China Sea on the SLOC security interests of the United States and Japan is explored in Chapter 8. However, it suffices to say that compared with the North Atlantic, where the perception of acutely threatened Western SLOC during the Cold War has since given way to a wholly benign naval security environment, in the Western Pacific the view is widely held that 'it is simply too early to conclude that war has lost all its appeal'.[135]

Conclusion

This chapter traced the conceptual origin of SLOC in theories of sea power and observed how its definition as a narrowly conceived concept within naval strategy was remoulded and expanded by the currents of technological and geopolitical change in the twentieth century. I have conveyed how Sir Julian Corbett and others identified the importance of controlling maritime communications for conducting trade and projecting power as the key to maritime strategy. The mono-dimensional definition of sea power on which Mahan and Corbett predicated their assumptions was transformed by the development of the aircraft, the sea mine and – above all – the submarine, which during two world wars gave sea denial powers the revolutionary capability to mount a counter-blockade without having to directly challenge superior naval powers for sea control.

The total nature of these conflicts blurred the combatant/non-combatant distinction between navies, used to project power, and merchant fleets, whose role in transporting food, *materiel* and natural resources essential to sustaining industrial production became equally 'strategic'. Submarine-led offensives against shipping in the Atlantic and Pacific exposed the vulnerability of import-dependent maritime powers, raising the importance of 'commerce raiding' from an ancillary aspect of the war at sea to a potentially decisive factor. Conceptually, the advent of total war thus broke down the distinction between 'economic' and 'military' SLOC.

The experience of the war at sea up to 1945, underlined somewhat ambiguously not only the vulnerability of maritime powers against the unique strategic potential of the submarine, but also the robustness of maritime transportation networks, when properly defended. Convoy, though initially resisted by the Allies in the Second World War as it had been in the First, was critical to overcoming the German submarine threat in the Atlantic on both occasions. Conversely, all attempts to implement SLOC defence as an ASW operational concept ended in failure. Japan's negligence in protecting its shipping in the Pacific (the subject of Chapter 3) accelerated the destruction of its merchant fleet and played a major role in hastening its defeat.

Despite doubts about whether a high-intensity naval conflict could realistically be sustained between nuclear powers given the dangers of nuclear escalation and the one-sided naval nature of most regional conflicts after 1945, the defence of SLOC stayed integral to the planning of the United States and its maritime allies during the Cold War, especially in response to the growth of Soviet naval power from the mid-1960s onwards. However, concepts for SLOC defence underwent a transition within US naval strategy, as 'reactive' plans for the direct defence of high-value cargo were eclipsed by the Maritime Strategy's bold emphasis on 'offence as the best defence'.

The threat of a superpower 'blue water' conflict disappeared with the end of the Cold War. However, the Asia-Pacific region is host to a number of unresolved territorial disputes which, particularly in the context of China's accelerating military modernization programme, have the potential to lead to a high-intensity maritime conflict, across the Taiwan Strait and/or in the South China Sea. There is a widespread consensus that chokepoints remain the most vulnerable segments of SLOC and concerns that conflicts in East Asia could interrupt international shipping flows reflect the proximity of regional 'flash-points' to chokepoint straits where merchant shipping is concentrated. Most such waterways normally used in transit could probably be bypassed, as seen in Chapter 1, at less economic cost than is often widely assumed. However, the scope for diversion narrows as ships approach their terminals and the concentration of the container trade in particular around a small number of hub ports augments this contemporary aspect of SLOC vulnerability above others.

The end of the Cold War has witnessed an expanding definition of SLOC security, as reflected in the broader maritime agenda of the ongoing Asia-Pacific SLOC conferences. This has brought to the fore new threats and challenges potentially impinging upon freedom of navigation for international shipping from piracy and terrorism-at-sea, as well as non-military issues of environmental security and shipping safety. Al-Qaida's capacity to cause mass destruction and economic dislocation, including suicide attacks on the *Cole* and *Limburg*, has eclipsed piracy's more limited concern with financial gain as the most important potential non-state threat confronting shipping and seaborne trade. Since September 11, the United States has moved closer to making the protection of shipping an explicit national security objective, than at any time since the Cold War.

Although the world wars broke down the division between 'military' and 'economic' SLOC, such a distinction is still conceptually useful, especially as contemporary SLOC threats are likely to arise below the threshold of total war. Moreover, as Coulter suggests, the strategic requirements applying to the use of SLOC to project military power reactively differ significantly from the use of SLOC to conduct maritime trade. While the onus on speed for reactive naval deployments inherently limits flexibility in the choice of route, commercial shipping retains a much higher degree of flexibility to divert around localized obstructions in transit. In the remaining chapters, these definitions and concepts are related to the specific circumstances of Japan's SLOC security, from 1940–2004.

3 Japan's pre-1945 SLOC security

Introduction

This chapter, which starts with Japan's opening up to the outside world and ends with its defeat in the Second World War, explores historical precedents for Japan's post-war SLOC security concerns. The underlying contention is that although post-war strategic circumstances have changed, the geographical and economic context is still relevant. Indeed, the waters near Taiwan where Japan's merchant fleet was annihilated by US submarines are once again the focus for Japanese defence planners worried about a potential submarine threat to Japanese shipping, this time from China. The catastrophe suffered by Japan's merchant marine during 1943–45 continues to have psychological resonance in modern Japan and upon popular and elite perceptions of vulnerability. Furthermore, although the MSDF are structured and oriented very differently to the Imperial Navy, continuity between the two institutions is revealed in the history of the pre-1945 era, with a bearing on the post-war priority placed on SLOC security by senior MSDF officers, many of whom formerly served in the Imperial Navy. The chapter is divided into four sections: (1) Maritime economic interests, outlining Japan's foreign trade, merchant marine and economic dependency on sea-borne commerce; (2) Maritime strategic interests, dealing with relevant aspects of the development of the Imperial Navy, 1868–1945; (3) The War of the *Maru*; an account of the Allied anti-shipping campaign in the Pacific War; and (4) The inadequate protection of merchant shipping, which details Japan's defence of maritime transportation and reasons for its shortcomings.

In the century between Commodore Perry's act of gunboat diplomacy in Uraga Bay in 1853, which began Japan's opening up to the world, and 1953, its first full year of independence after the Allied Occupation, few nations' history have been as compressed. At the point of departure Japan was still in self-imposed quarantine, in place since the seventeenth century. Trade was minimal, delegated to Dutch merchants operating through Nagasaki, and the possession of large sailing craft was prohibited by an ordinance dating back to 1635. At the midpoint, 1903, Japan had prevailed in its first modern test of arms against China; was an ally of Great Britain, the pre-eminent sea power of the day; and stood poised to inflict a historic victory over Russia, the world's third-largest naval power and Japan's immediate expansionist rival in Northeast Asia. Japan's metamorphosis from international recluse to great power in just 50 years also marked the high-point in its pre-1945 maritime history. In 1945, the Imperial Navy was already fading into memory, the broken hulks of its battle fleet strewn from Midway Island to the Philippine Sea, its surviving units disestablished in October. Yet by 1953, the nation's post-war leaders were in the process of covertly establishing a new navy, this time under American auspices.

One of the major consequences of two centuries of closure to the outside world was Japan's failure to develop strong maritime traditions, in spite of its geography. Lacking meaningful overseas trading links or sailing ships bigger than inshore fishing and cargo vessels, Japan had to import and model the skills of a seafaring nation when suddenly compelled to end its international isolation. In overcoming the emotional and technological inertia of two centuries of insularity, the generation that lived through the Meiji Era (1868–1912) demonstrated an incredible capacity to absorb and adapt alien systems of thought and action. Japan's transformation from quasi-feudal to proto-modern in 30 years is perhaps unrivalled. Rushing to put in place a modern system of government across fields as disparate as finance, defence and education, the Meiji statesmen were attempting not only to catch up with western organizational concepts and technology from a low base, but did so at a time when Western civil and military science was itself advancing at a revolutionary pace.

The scale of Japan's post-war economic dependence on sea transportation was outlined in Chapter 1. Japan's pre-war maritime interests can be divided into the economic, arising from industrialization, and the strategic, as power began to be projected beyond the shores of the new unitary state. Militarily, from 1894 to 1945, the Imperial Army was continuously engaged on the Northeast Asian mainland and it fell to the Imperial Navy to provide transportation and sea control as prerequisites to the army's continental presence. Economically, sea transportation was indispensable to developing Japan's industrial base. For the civilian economy, exports were the only means to generate the foreign exchange needed to finance imported technology and raw materials (including metallic ores, rubber, high-grade coal and later, oil). Mechanization spread this dependence to the military until modern warfare was no longer possible without a strong industrial base and a secure fuel supply. However, in none of the wars fought prior to 1941 was Japan's vulnerability to commerce warfare sufficiently exposed to prepare it for the disaster suffered by the merchant marine in the Pacific War and the important part this played in the country's defeat.

Maritime economic interests: foreign trade and the merchant marine before 1945

Once launched on the path to industrialization, the Meiji founders' immediate concern was to import the skills and equipment necessary to lay the economic foundations of a modern state. Although this initial need ameliorated with the success of import substitution policies, industrialization and population growth made it necessary to import increasing quantities of raw materials and food. With this general 'problem' in mind, Japan's pre-1945 foreign trade and industry can be divided into two periods: 1859–1914 and 1914–45.

1859–1914

The first phase, from the full opening of Japan's ports in 1859 to around 1880, was mainly concerned with setting up Japanese commerce to compete with western firms trading in Japan. Government investment was also directed into infrastructure and key industries such as shipbuilding and munitions. Most of Japan's trade stayed in foreign hands during the first half of Emperor Meiji's reign. Primary and semi-manufactured goods, such as tea and silk, were exported for foreign exchange to pay for the purchase of foreign plant and know-how. The trend towards increased Japanese ownership was pioneered by the family-run *zaibatsu* conglomerates; Mitsui, established in 1876; Mitsubishi; Sumitomo and Yasuda.[1] Under Meiji, the bottom-up mercantile culture built up organically under the Tokugawa Shogunate met and was co-opted by the top-down, planned capitalism of Meiji bureaucrats, forging the links between commerce and political administration which have since characterized the Japanese developmental model. In the second phase, from 1880 to the Sino-Japanese war of 1894–95, textiles, as Japan's first major commercial manufacturing sector, began to move out of people's homes into small factories. Latecomers on the international scene, Japanese manufacturers found themselves at a disadvantage in competition for overseas markets with western firms able to produce superior-quality products while enjoying the protection of empires and spheres of influence. Once China was commercially opened to Japan as a participant in the treaty port system in 1895, this suited investment in textiles and light manufacturing, but heavy industry required greater protection. By the turn of the century, the Meiji government's efforts to build up indigenous commerce and industry had successfully reduced the need for foreign machinery, chiefly from Great Britain, although Japan's reliance for certain kinds of manufactured goods continued up to the First World War.[2] Exports, still dominated by silk, also began to include a rising proportion of manufactured goods.[3] In the third phase, which lasted up to the First World War, heavy industry began to emerge properly in Japan.[4] Textiles still accounted for half of exports, chiefly to the United States, Korea and China (which doubled as a supplier of raw cotton and consumer of the finished product). Investment in urban power electrification also surged during this time.[5]

However, during the Meiji period, 'scarcely any change took place without indirect, if not direct, connections with wars or preparations for war'.[6] Commerce and conquest became intertwined in several ways. First and foremost, to the Meiji oligarchy the creation of national prosperity was considered only as one half of the national security equation. Military strength and wealth were equated as sources of national power and prestige, encapsulated in the slogan *fukoku kyōhei* ('rich country: strong army'). Industrialization was actively promoted as part of the Meiji oligarchs' drive to acquire modern armaments. Armaments production received a major boost after the Triple Intervention of 1895, when Russia, in concert with France and Germany, compelled Japan to return the Liaotung Peninsula, newly and painfully wrested from China. Determined to avoid a recurrence of this humiliation, Meiji officials added six regular divisions to the army and began constructing a new battle fleet with the aim of making Japan as self-sufficient in military production as possible. Spending on the Navy leapt four-fold, to over 50 million yen, between 1895 and 1898.[7] Second, financing an arms build-up on this scale, much of it purchased overseas, was only possible with a healthy commercial sector to provide a taxation base. Third, obtaining captive markets by force in China and Korea shielded Japan's fledgling industries from western competition and allowed them to prosper. Fourth, territories brought under Japanese control promised to provide a steady stream of raw materials, and labour, needed for industrialization. Among these raw materials only coal was relatively plentiful in Japan, and this was of low-grade quality requiring the importation of higher grades for coking.[8] As more of Northeast Asia came under the Japanese yoke, Korea, Manchuria and China became important sources of coal, iron ore and pig-iron to the home economy. Manchuria began receiving Japanese investment in 1906 and, as the army-run colony of Manchukuo from 1932, would eventually provide 20 per cent of Japan's pig-iron and 8 per cent of its steel.[9] Lastly, an indirect consequence of industrialization was the doubling of Japan's population to 50 million during the Meiji era. Self-sufficiency in food production dropped to 80 per cent and to compensate, Taiwan, ceded by China in 1895, and Korea, annexed in 1910, became important suppliers of rice.[10]

1914–45

The First World War provided a timely fillip, bringing the Japanese economy out of recession in 1915. Japan was able to break into trading concessions formerly monopolized by the European powers, while catering to the huge transportation and shipbuilding needs of the Allies. Though the war was not of great military significance for Japan, the expansion of its trading and shipping interests and the new significance which oil gained during the conflict nudged Japan over a strategic threshold. The functioning of the nation's economy and its military arms would in future be hostage to the security of seaborne transportation and overseas resources.

Since the 1900s, exports had expanded from an annual average of 85 million yen in 1890–94, to 1,800 million yen in 1920–24.[11] Yet because imports outstripped exports in most years except for the wartime boom of 1915–18, Japan actually carried a balance of payments deficit into the 1930s.[12] The end of the war also left Japan with an overcapacity in shipbuilding and other industries. Recession returned in 1920 and was followed by the devastating Kantō earthquake of 1923, which required massive reconstruction in Tokyo and Yokohama. These negatives aside, Japan's economy had by the 1920s attained a mature, generally balanced structure in which the *zaibatsu* held a dominant position. By mid-decade, annual foreign trade was approaching 5 billion yen, or around one-tenth of national wealth.[13] Despite the onset of global depression, by 1930 heavy industry and chemicals had overtaken textiles as the most productive sector of the economy, accounting for nearly one-third of output.[14]

After Japan experienced a severe recession known as the *Shōwa* Slump, from the official designation of Emperor Hirohito's reign (1926–89), the devaluation of the yen in 1932 provided incentive to import cheaper raw materials from East Asia. Exports to the region, where there were relatively few barriers to Japanese products, flourished at the same time. During 1934–36, China, Korea and Taiwan between them absorbed 60 per cent of Japan's exports and accounted for half its imports.[15] Encouraged by generous government subsidies directed toward rearmament, heavy industry pulled Japan out of recession until it accounted for almost 60 per cent of output by 1940.[16] The transition to a wartime economy followed Japan's withdrawal from the Washington and London naval treaties in 1936, and the outbreak of general hostilities in China in July 1937. Increasingly militaristic governments funnelled state resources into war preparations, raising military spending from 9 per cent of Gross National Product (GNP) between 1933 and 1937 to 38 per cent of GNP in 1938–42.[17]

As Tokyo's political ties with Washington soured over Japan's China policy, the reliability of the United States as primary supplier of oil and a host of other mineral resources presented Japan's military and civilian leadership with an acute dilemma. In none of the territories under Japan's control was there an adequate supply of rubber, non-ferrous metals or oil – commodities all critical to a sustained war effort. Japan therefore had to purchase most of its strategic resources on the open market. The combined total of bulk commodity imports in 1941 amounted to about 20 million tons.[18] As access to US resources became politically uncertain, military and business circles began contemplating Southeast Asia as an alternative source of strategic materials. Until the war in Europe changed the balance of power, Japan was reluctant to risk confrontation with the United States and Great Britain by pressuring for a greater commercial allocation of Southeast Asian resources. In October 1939, with the European colonial powers preoccupied with the struggle against Hitler, the Cabinet Planning Board concluded that Japan should 'bring within our economic sphere areas on the East Asian mainland and in the southern region'.[19] The ideal of economic autarky for Japan found expression in the Greater East Asian Co-prosperity Sphere. Overseen by a special ministry created in November 1942, the Greater East Asian Co-prosperity Sphere was partly political in nature, responding to a long-running Japanese foreign policy ambition to exclude European colonialism from Asia. The economic motivation was to incorporate Japan's military conquests into a yen-denominated bloc capable of furnishing its material needs in wartime and beyond.

Merchant fleet

The creation of a merchant fleet, as a necessary adjunct for an aspiring trading nation, was assigned high priority in Meiji development strategy. Modern cargo vessels were essential for coastal as well as foreign trade. Japan constructed its first steamer in 1866, but imported about 90 per cent of its merchant ships up to the Sino-Japanese War of 1894–95. Shortcomings in Japanese designs exposed in the war motivated the Meiji government to invest and intervene heavily in shipbuilding to augment its naval and merchant fleets, the latter doubling in size to 1.5 million tons within a decade. Shipbuilding was further invigorated by the Russo-Japanese War, and while still on a modest scale compared to other industrial powers, by 1913, half of Japan's trade was being carried in Japanese bottoms.[20] Owing to the stimulus to shipbuilding provided by the First World War, Japan possessed the world's third largest merchant navy by 1917 and was unable to keep pace with new orders its shipyards were receiving.[21] A post-war glut in shipping worldwide hit Japanese shipbuilders hard, but the industry eventually recovered in the 1930s with the aid of renewed subsidies and the introduction of a scrap-and-build scheme by the government designed to encourage the modernization of the fleet.[22] In 1935, the merchant fleet consisted of 924 cargo ships, 319 semi-cargo ships, 73 passenger ships and 39 tankers.[23] By 1941, Japan's merchant marine was eclipsed only by Great Britain and the United States.[24] Yet this belied Japan's continuing dependence on foreign bottoms to carry 40 per cent of its trade, most of which were certain to withdraw their services in wartime.[25] Furthermore, the projected shortfall was sure to be aggravated by requisitioning on the part of the Imperial armed forces.

Requisitioning in fact began in the 1930s, dividing the merchant fleet under separate Army, Navy and civilian direction. The General Staff of both services oversaw shipping under their control, while the Shipping Control Board was created within the Ministry of Communications to manage civilian vessels. No central coordinating authority existed. The Navy increased its demands for merchantmen until 1,740,200 tons, approaching one third of the total, had been commandeered by the time of the attack on Pearl Harbor.[26] Some of this included 'shadow' warships classed as ocean liners to circumvent the limitations treaties,[27] but requisitioning of civilian ships and crews on such a scale would nevertheless leave the merchant marine genuinely under-equipped to meet the nation's economic transportation needs in wartime. Army requisitioning was even more draconian, bringing over 2 million tons of merchant shipping under its control by Pearl Harbor. Though some was returned to civilian control, the extended campaigns in the Solomons and Burma retarded the process and the army remained so short of transports during the war that even the 'super-battleship' *Yamato* was pressed into service as a troop ferry.[28]

Prior to the attack on Pearl Harbor, the Cabinet Planning Board determined that 3 million tons of merchant shipping would be required to keep Japan's economy afloat. Added to this, the army's transportation needs were estimated to be 2.3 million tons during the first six months of operations, declining to 1.1 million tons per year thereafter. The Navy's shipping requirements were predicted to remain steady at 1.8 million tons annually.[29] By the outbreak of war, the combined merchant fleet had reached 6.4 million tons, and with further construction, the prospect of captured vessels and a flotilla of wooden craft to draw upon, these demands appeared within its reach on paper at least. Provided that merchant shipping losses could be kept to under 1 million tons per year and ample resources for steel production secured, the director of the Planning Board judged that new construction would enable Japan to maintain the flow of materials to Japan at 1941 levels.[30] Other government studies warned that if civilian shipping was reduced to 1.5 million tons, steel production would decline by one-fifth and more than half the output of the secondary sector, composed of bulk commodities such as coal, salt, fertilizer, soy, bricks and cotton, would be lost. The 3 million-ton figure calculated by the Cabinet Planning Board as necessary for economic survival, was in fact over-assessed, described in one view as 'a positive assessment intended to bring war about'.[31] Prewar estimates in general demonstrated insufficient understanding of the pressures that wartime conditions would impose on the sea transportation system. Compounding the dangers and logistical difficulties faced during the Pacific War, Japan's civilian and military transportation were approached as discrete problems. This partly was for bureaucratic reasons, but for a relatively few cases, the front lines were too far removed from natural resources to combine economic and military supply missions efficiently. Military supply ships generally returned to Japan carrying ballast, leaving civilian ships to bear the unsupported burden of supplying the home economy.[32]

Maritime strategic interests: the Imperial Navy, 1868–1945

Before turning to the war against Japanese shipping in the Pacific and the responses of the Imperial Navy and Japanese government, it is worth focussing on the institution of the Navy and relevant aspects of its 77-year history in three phases; Phase 1: birth to maturity, 1868–1905; Phase 2: uncertainty, austerity and expansionism, 1906–36; Phase 3: oil – life-blood for the Navy, 1937–45. This is not a battle history, but intended to highlight the most important influences on the traditions, outlook, threat perceptions and doctrine of the Imperial Navy, including such particular factors as the Navy's role in politics and its dependence on imported oil.

Phase 1: birth to maturity, 1868–1905

The Imperial Navy formally came into existence with the Meiji Restoration in 1868, from a composite force of foreign vessels assembled by the Satsuma clan since the 1850s.[33] The enduring schism between Army and Navy under Meiji owed something to the legacy of clan rivalry between the Satsuma and Choshu households who fought a civil war early in the Meiji era. While Satsuma exerted a lasting influence over the Imperial Navy, Choshu maintained a close association with the new national army.[34] Early development was concerned with building up the fleet and overcoming the shortage of indigenous knowledge by importing modern naval technology, tactics and strategy from the West. This meant reliance on imported vessels, mostly from Great Britain, which as the world's leading naval power established a paternal relationship with the world's newest.[35] The Imperial Navy was ideally placed as an institution to fulfil the Meiji ethos, acting as a conduit for foreign learning and technology, strengthening Japan's defences and enhancing national prestige. Proof of the latter came with the conclusion of the Anglo-Japanese Alliance in 1902, Japan's symbolic accession to the great power club. The alliance, too, was largely naval in character, the product of Great Britain's desire to preserve a favourable balance with Russia. However, the British government was careful to negotiate its terms so that military assistance only applied in cases of attack by more than one country. Though not party to Japan's pre-1914 wars, Great Britain supplied it with naval vessels used to win naval victories over China and Russia, delivering its last battleship, *Kongō*, to the Yokusuka shipyards in November 1913.[36] The horizons of Japan's early naval leaders were necessarily confined and their energies consumed by the challenges of building up a modern navy. This in fact aided the development of a coherent naval strategy limited to exercising local sea control. Only once the Imperial Navy escaped the territorial and technical limitations of its inaugural phase, in 1905, did it set out on the path to strategic over-extension.

Early Imperial Navy officers tended to imbibe the tenets of western naval thinking uncritically, accepting the navalist orthodoxy of Alfred Thayer Mahan that the way to national greatness lay in domination of the seas, the means to which resided in potent battle fleets. Though Mahan wrote for an Anglo-American audience, his works fed through into a preference for offensive naval doctrine in Japan.[37] In later years, after Japan emerged as the naval hegemon in the Western Pacific, Mahan's views helped to shape a deterministic strand of thinking in both Japan and the United States that a naval clash to decide mastery of the Pacific was inevitable. In 1894, Japan entered into its first modern war against China with a mixed fleet of 28 warships totalling 57,000 tons and a force of 24 torpedo boats, incorporating Japanese-designed quick-firing guns and torpedoes. On the strength of prestige accruing from its victory over the Chinese Fleet at the Yalu River, and its role in facilitating landing operations in Liaotung and Korea, the Navy successfully boosted its status and budgetary share to a level comparable with the army. With memories of the 1895 Triple Intervention still fresh, Yamamoto Gombei, then chief of the Naval Affairs Bureau of the Navy Ministry, pushed for the construction of a battle fleet to be built up over ten years comprising 6 battleships, 6 armoured cruisers and 23 destroyers (DD) amounting to 234,000 tons. When complete, the 'six–six' fleet was a quantitative and qualitative leap that elevated Japan into the top flight of naval powers. Yamamoto's rationale for the core of the new fleet – six battleships – was based on his (1896) estimate of the largest opposing naval force that Japan was likely to face, which he surmised to be a '4 + 2' squadron assembled by one major and a lesser naval power in coalition.[38] As long as the Russians were equally determined to reinforce their Pacific Squadron, based in Port Arthur and Vladivostok, the Imperial Navy would lack control of the Japan and Yellow seas, an essential requirement if it was to challenge Russian expansion in Manchuria and Korea.

By 1903, Japan was openly gearing for war with Russia and hurried additions to the fleet took the Imperial Navy into hostilities the following February with a total of 6 battleships, 8 armoured and 16 other cruisers, 20 destroyers and

58 torpedo boats. As in 1894–95, the scope of Imperial Navy operations against Russia was local, involving pre-emptive, small-unit attacks on the enemy's fleet ports, the support of landing operations and a major fleet encounter. Although conducted offensively, the strategic role of the Imperial Navy – to support army operations on land – was defensive, a point realized at the time by Sir Julian Corbett.[39] At Tsushima, in May 1905, Admiral Tōgō Heihachirō scored the most famous annihilating victory in modern naval history against the Csar's Baltic Fleet (renamed the Second Pacific Squadron) at the end of its 7-month voyage from Europe. The totality of Tōgō's victory, presaging Russia's defeat on land, heralded a major shift in the balance of power in East Asia, confirmed the Imperial Navy's strategic, tactical and technological prowess and dealt a shock to those unprepared for the first defeat of a European power by a non-European race. In its wake, Japanese naval theorists such as Akiyama Saneyuki and Satō Tetsutarō found the confidence to ponder a naval strategy tailored to meet Japan's requirements, but which would extend the horizons of the Imperial Navy beyond local defence.

The Imperial Navy's success at Tsushima blinded its leadership to less glamorous aspects of the war that could have yielded important lessons including the failure to develop any strategy for protection of commerce. Having requisitioned 681,000 tons or most of the merchant fleet, to fulfil Army and Navy transportation needs, Japan had to rely on foreign and especially British-flagged shipping for 90 per cent of its trade for the duration of the Russo-Japanese war.[40] In the conflict's early stages, a detachment of Russian cruisers from the Vladivostok squadron successfully broke out of the Sea of Japan through the Tsugaru Strait into the Pacific and began raiding merchantmen plying Japan's eastern coasts. More damaging than the physical destruction caused by these raids was the resulting increase in insurance rates, the suspension of selected shipping services from Great Britain and the effect on public morale until the squadron was finally disabled in August 1904. This first experience of commerce-raiding, though much to the Navy's embarrassment, did not prompt a serious re-evaluation about the defence of merchant shipping.[41] The overriding naval concern in the wars against China and Russia was the protection of military SLOC.

Phase 2: uncertainty, austerity and expansionism, 1906–36

With the Russian naval threat neutralized and Japan's position in Korea firmly established, the nation's immediate security aims had been met and the direction of defence policy was no longer so obviously determined. In April 1907, the Imperial Defence Policy (*teikoku kokubō hōshin*) was inaugurated as an attempt to codify national threat perceptions and force requirements in this new period of strategic uncertainty. In addition to 25 standing army divisions, the '8:8' plan called for a fleet composed of eight battleships and eight cruisers. Great Britain was still Japan's ally, but the other foreign powers featured in the Policy were Russia, Germany and France; the agents of Japan's humiliation in 1895, as well as the United States. The addition of the United States came at the insistence of the Imperial Navy.[42] With Russia discounted as a naval challenger after Tsushima, the Imperial Navy cast a wary eye eastwards to the United States as its long-term rival, concerned at how the opening of the Panama canal and the projected fortification of bases in Guam and the Philippines would affect the naval balance in the Pacific.[43] Japan's suspicions were reciprocated in Washington, and political relations were further aggravated by two recurrent sources of tension over the 'Open Door' to China and Japanese migration to North America. These tensions were contained, but the British, for their part, felt sufficiently apprehensive to renegotiate the Anglo-Japanese alliance in 1911, to exclude the United States from its terms.[44]

As the founder of a Japanese naval doctrine distinct from western tutelage, Akiyama Saneyuki culled from Japan's conflicts with China and Russia a number of precepts and beliefs which according to Mark Peattie did much to shape the pre-war course of the Imperial Navy.[45] At the Naval War College in Tsukiji, Akiyama helped instill a respect for planning, training and logistics and developed an operational concept designed to inflict attrition on an enemy fleet by the launching of forward attacks prior to committing the Combined Fleet.[46] Central to its success would be Japan's ability to acquire 'big ships and big guns' (*taikan kyohōshugi*) capable of overcoming the quantity of any opposing battle line with the quality of its own.[47] Akiyama developed his theories after the Russo-Japanese war, when Tōgō's tactical initiative at Tsushima had paved the way for a strategic victory over a numerically superior foe. Having delivered success in Japan's limited wars against China and Russia, the strategy of seeking a decisive fleet encounter was adapted by Akiyama to meet the hypothetical threat of an American battle fleet advancing across the Pacific. Akiyama's other legacy was the emphasis he placed on non-material factors in achieving victory. Belief in the triumph of spiritual over material elements in war, if not unique to Japan, was culturally deep-rooted and has been ascribed to the martial legacy of the *samurai* class.[48] In the years following Tsushima, the Imperial Navy faced no immediate threat to its control over surrounding waters, and had little need to call upon spiritual or moral reinforcement to compensate for material weakness. The contradictions between rationalist and emotional strains of thinking in the Imperial Navy only surfaced in the 1930s, as it prepared to take on the United States. Akiyama's confidence in the ability of Japan's moral qualities to prevail over the industrial and military potential of the United States only grew as war approached. Reinforced in Japanese society at large by the strengthened role of state Shintoism, this faith took on a canonical appeal at all levels of the Navy.

Satō Tetsutarō, whose works on seapower appeared slightly earlier at the turn of the century, argued Japan's need of an oceanic defence posture extending well beyond the requirements for local defence.[49] In Satō's notion of command of the seas (*seikaiken*), though vaguely defined, lay the seeds of the Imperial Navy's commitment to offence as the best means of defence.[50] His legacy has been more concretely identified in the practice of setting a ratio of capital ships to maintain against a potential enemy.[51] After naval threat perceptions centred on the United States, for planning purposes at least, the powerful Operations Division of the

General Staff determined that the Imperial Navy needed to maintain 70 per cent of the US Navy's first-line strength in heavy cruisers.[52] More broadly, Satō's influence on the Navy is associated with territorial expansionism enshrined in the concept of a 'south advance' (*nanshin*). Since its creation, the Imperial Navy had enjoyed independent access to the emperor, its constitutional status equal with that of the Army, although its political influence was never as strong. The intense rivalry and suspicion which grew between both institutions was one of the most destructive and unresolved features of the governmental system set up under Meiji.[53] Once the Army established a permanent foothold in Korea and Manchuria, the Navy risked losing status, not to mention its budgetary allocation, without a rival strategy of its own. Despite the Navy's generally moderate reputation, its more impulsive officers were inspired by Satō's dream of carving out an area of influence to the south. The obvious problem in the 1900s was that this meant certain collision with the western colonial powers, which among them already controlled most of Southeast Asia and the South Pacific. Logically, the path of least resistance for Japan's imperial ambitions lay in China's vast north-eastern hinterland, with the Army as its chief agent. The concept of a 'south advance' to trump the army's 'north advance' (*hokushin*) received a more concrete imperative once East Indies oil became a coveted commodity, but made little practical sense until the First World War created an opening for Japan in the Pacific.

After joining the Allies in late August 1914, Japan moved against German possessions north of the Equator in China and the Pacific. With Germany virtually powerless to resist, by 1915 Japan had seized the Kaiser's possessions in Shantung, expanded its commercial concessions across north-eastern China and incorporated Germany's island territories from Palau to the Marshalls. However, Japan's virtually bloodless extension into the Pacific did not fundamentally shift the centre of gravity of expansionism away from the Imperial Army in Northeast Asia, where by 1917, 50,000 troops were deployed in Shantung and Manchuria, substantial forces in Korea and a further 75,000 about to be sent to Siberia.[54] Japan's gains in the Pacific were recognized as League Mandates at Versailles in 1919 and supposed to remain unfortified under the terms of the Washington Naval Treaty, ratified in 1923. Though of limited economic worth, Japan's Pacific mandates held a considerable strategic value by excluding a foreign naval presence and acting as outposts to monitor US Pacific Fleet manoeuvres in peacetime. In war, they could be quickly adapted as submarine and sea-plane bases to block communications between the United States and its western Pacific possessions (the Philippines and Guam), and as logistic stepping stones for any advance on Southeast Asia.

The Imperial Navy had a secondary, but potentially instructive, involvement in convoy and anti-submarine operations during the First World War. The Australian Imperial Expeditionary Force destined for Gallipoli was given a Japanese escort across the Indian Ocean in 1915. Then in 1917, at Britain's request, the Imperial Navy sent a destroyer squadron to the Mediterranean to assist in convoying allied shipping against submarines of the Central Powers.[55] Although its arrival had a favourable impact upon allied losses, as in the Russo-Japanese war, experience did not translate into lessons learned. Instead, in the eyes of Japan's naval staffers it was the inconclusive gun duel at Jutland which reconfirmed the primacy of the decisive fleet encounter. Overshadowed by Jutland, the German U-boat offensive against Allied shipping in the Atlantic, which had demonstrated the strategic potential of the submarine and the effectiveness of convoys, received little attention in Japan after the war. The same might be said of the Royal Navy – and with less excuse.[56] However, Japan's experience in the First World War differed from that of its Allies in that it was not a party to any of the major land offensives and untouched by the value shifts wrought among other belligerents. Japan, in fact, had a 'good' war, enhancing its economic and strategic position at the relative expense of the European powers, but it was left curiously out of place in 1919, in a war-weary world receptive to Wilsonian idealism and arms limitation. Having mastered the rules of the imperial game as late-comers, Japan's military elite saw little reason to dim their enthusiasm for expansion.

The 1920s brought economic austerity to Japan and a period which saw Japanese democratic institutions temporarily flourish; factors which kept the military in check. Smaller, recession-pinched budgets forced hard choices on the Navy, sharpened by the spiralling costs of constructing battleships with ever-bigger guns and thicker armour. This did not prevent the Navy from pushing for the construction of an '8:8:8' fleet (to be composed of twin battleship squadrons and a force of eight heavy cruisers). When plans for the fleet were trimmed to an 8:6 configuration, fiscal reality was as much the culprit as were Japan's new treaty obligations. The drafters of the Washington Naval Limitations Treaty, negotiated over 1921–23, conceived it as a stabilizing alternative to military alliances and arms races. With fewer resources than Great Britain or the United States, the Treaty offered Japan an escape from a cycle of competition it could not hope to win, at the psychological price of being fixed into a position of inferiority. Over strong objections from the Navy, the Foreign Ministry (*gaimushō*) settled for a capital ship ratio of 5:5:3 and a mutual agreement to refrain from fortifying Pacific bases. This represented a loss on the 10:10:7 ratio upon which the Imperial Navy had predicated the success of its war plan against the United States. Elements in the Navy objecting to what they construed as a slight to national pride organized themselves into a Fleet Faction to oppose the Treaty.[57] While the Fleet Faction was unable to prevent Japan's accession to the Washington Treaty in 1923 it won a partial victory when the Imperial Defence Policy was revised, in deference to the Navy, designating the United States as Japan's number one enemy ahead of the Soviet Union and China. In a portent of Japan's international isolation, the Anglo-Japanese Alliance was allowed to expire in the same year.

Belief in the dominance of surface battle-fleets held firm in Japan, as it did within the US Navy and Royal Navy, even as improvements in submarines and naval aviation chipped away at the 'capital' status of the battleship, still defined by the throwing distance of its guns. Failing to see a strategic threat to merchant shipping in these new technologies naturally inhibited the ability of Japan's naval planners to develop their own doctrine for commerce protection or commerce warfare. Japanese submarines, of which several classes were developed in the 1920s and 1930s had the range, endurance and armament to equip them for both roles. The J-class submarines were capable of sustained operations off the US west coast, and were armed with torpedoes superior in range, speed and payload to their American counterparts throughout the Pacific war. A British strategist wondered at the time whether a larger submarine force would make Japan's coastal waters and the Yellow Sea impregnable against raiding squadrons.[58] Yet the Imperial Navy's inability to develop a submarine doctrine independent of the surface fleet was not simply a failure of imagination.[59] Underlying the Navy's preoccupation with offensive doctrine was the strategic rationale that Japan could only hope to prevail in a short war with the United States, forcing a negotiated settlement before US industry could bring its greater mobilization capacity to bear. Unable to rebuild its fleet quickly enough the larger power would be obliged to seek terms, as it had in 1905. To those responsible for drawing up the Navy's war plans in the 1920s, a strategy of economic blockade against an enemy with ten times Japan's industrial capacity, copious natural resources, and whose eastern seaboard lay beyond Japan's reach must have seemed illogical. Had Japanese planners developed the doctrine and tactics for interdicting US logistic SLOC across the Pacific, their prospects might well have been more rewarding. While unlikely to have halted US amphibious operations across the Pacific, Japan's capacity to complicate Allied efforts would probably have justified the investment. During the Battle of the Atlantic, reports of the success enjoyed by German U-boats against Allied shipping until 1942 did nothing to jolt the Japanese naval command into rethinking submarine operations, despite all attempts at persuasion by the German naval attaché (and U-boat commander) in Tokyo, Paul Wenneker.[60] As a result, Japan's naval submarine doctrine and design remained welded to the Combined Fleet throughout the Pacific War and the long supply chains used to sustain the US 'island-hopping' campaign went largely unharried.[61]

What did occupy the close attention of Japan's naval staff in the 1920s and 1930s were the anticipated communication routes of the US surface battle fleet across the Pacific. After the American Asiatic squadron in the Philippines and Guam had been neutralized, it was assumed that the US Navy would undertake a massed sally westward to retake Guam and the Philippines. Japanese naval strategy was originally based on luring the American fleet to a line between the Bonin and Mariana Islands where the superior gunnery of the Combined Fleet could inflict a Tsushima-type blow despite its numerical inferiority. It was expected that the bulk of the US Pacific Fleet would advance along one of four lines of approach to the western Pacific. The first of these, the north circular route, was the shortest but discounted owing to its rough weather conditions. The second, South Pacific route was considered overly long. This left the direct route from Hawaii and a south-central path through the Gilbert and Marshall island chains, both of which necessitated the capture of territory that could be converted into forward bases. After the Washington Naval Treaty pegged Japan's naval shipbuilding with the United States and Great Britain at 5:5:3 the war plan was broadened to include attacks on the advancing US fleet forward of the Bonin-Mariana line, by submarines and aircraft operating out of the Pacific Mandates. Provided that a roughly equalized American fleet would obligingly steam into the path of the Combined Fleet it was believed that the Imperial Navy could overcome its quantitative disadvantage and prevail in a short conflict.[62]

The Navy's battle strategy was not without its own critics. In the 1930s, air power advocates sensitive to the impact of evolving technologies and tactics, including the wartime commander of the Combined Fleet, Yamamoto Isoroku, questioned the tethering of Imperial Navy doctrine to the decisive fleet encounter on the grounds that aircraft were eroding the traditional primacy of battleships in naval warfare.[63] In place of battleships, the advent of fully-fledged aircraft carriers from the late 1920s promised to introduce a quantum leap in offensive reach. Others doubted the ability of the Imperial Navy to concentrate sufficient force or to manoeuvre tactically in the open expanses of the Pacific, unlike in the confines of the Tsushima Strait, or Yellow Sea. Continuing to rely on a reactive strategy of drawing the enemy fleet into the superior gun range of the Japanese battle line was, they argued, no longer credible.[64] Nevertheless, the maxim of 'big ships and big guns' continued to dictate procurement into the 1930s, reaching its zenith with the laying down of the leviathan super-battleships *Yamato* and *Musashi*, displacing over 60,000 tons each.[65] Only once Japan withdrew from the treaty regime in 1936 and began to quadruple military spending, did Japan's carrier force come into its own. However, the effect was merely to supplant one offensive orthodoxy with another, obscuring the Navy's weakness in escort vessels.[66] Had the naval limitations regime not been extended to cover destroyers, sub-chasers and lesser vessels in the 1930 London Naval Treaty it is likely they would have continued to be marginalized by budgetary pressures.

From the mid-1930s, developments in the domestic and international political environment brought war closer. The gradual accession of army hardliners to power in Japan from 1930 intensified after 1936.[67] By the mid-1930s, the Fleet Faction had bested moderate elements for control of the Navy and started cooperating with the army to subvert civilian control, culminating in the military-run cabinet of Tōjō Hideki, a serving army general, in 1940.[68] The Imperial Defence Policy was revised for the third and final time in 1936. The revised document identified the United States and Soviet Union as equal threats, as a compromise between Imperial Army and Navy threat perceptions, while China and Great Britain (for the first time) were added as subordinate enemies. The uncertainty and austerity of the 1920s and early 1930s had given way to the clear expectation of war, for which preparations began in earnest. The existence of four major potential adversaries spoke on one level of confusion between the Imperial Army and Navy over Japan's strategic direction.[69] More fundamentally, it revealed the slide in Japan's international relations since the Manchurian Incident in 1931. Responsibility for the deterioration of Japan's diplomatic position up to this point lay largely with the Kwantung Army's expansionist policies in China. However, from the late 1930s, the Imperial Navy's ambition and its thirst for oil caused it to lead the charge into Southeast Asia.

Phase 3: oil – life-blood for the Navy, 1937–45

After the idea of a Mahanian clash with the United States took root in the Imperial Navy in the 1920s, Japan's dependence upon the United States for 80 per cent of its oil, even more in the case of high-octane aviation fuel, loomed large in the minds of naval policy-makers, seeding the idea for the seizure of the oil-rich East Indies. Early on, Japanese ship designers had realized the advantages, in range and speed, to be gained from oil's high calorific value as a bunker fuel, and were replacing coal-fired warships prior to the First World War.[70] The flip-side of this increased military performance for Japan was that of all the powers, it was the most vulnerable to a cut-off of overseas supplies. A single battleship of the Combined Fleet burned over 1,000 tons of oil to maintain its top speed over 24 hours.[71] In 1940, the Navy accounted for one quarter of the national consumption of 100,000 barrels per day.[72] Domestic production had by that time barely reached 10,000 barrels per day, including synthetics.[73] Among independent exporters, the Soviet-controlled half of Sakhalin offered proximity and huge potential but was politically undependable.[74] Great Britain, for its part, consumed most of the oil produced in Persia, Burma and northern Borneo. By far the most promising commercial prospect were the oil fields of the Netherlands East Indies which could potentially yield up to 10 million tons per year, enough in theory to meet Japan's combined military and civilian fuel demands at full production. The colonial government was reluctant, however, to increase Japan's allocation beyond 20,000 barrels per day, or one-fifth of its import requirements.[75] The cheapest and most abundant source left open was the United States.

The Navy fell back on two strategies to lessen its vulnerability; synthetic production and stockpiling. Japan's synthetics programme yielded much more disappointing results than in Germany and despite the hopes placed in Manchurian oil shales as a captive source of petroleum, failed to deliver oil in strategic quantities. Oil stockpiling dated back to 1909 and accelerated in the late 1920s when the conversion of the fleet to oil-fired boilers was completed.[76] The Imperial Navy's potential oil weakness was apparent at the time, leading Hector Bywater to predict, in 1927, that Japan would retain mostly coal-fired warships.[77] In 1931, the Navy had 3 million tons of oil in its stores which, according to its earlier estimates, would meet wartime needs for one year based on the projected fuel consumption of the assembled fleet steaming at 24 knots.[78] General stockpiling was made compulsory under the Oil Industry Law, passed in 1934, bringing all petroleum imports under government control.[79] By 1936, the Navy's stockpile of oil products had progressed to 3.5 million tons. However, so had the Navy General Staff's estimates of their fuel requirements – to 3.5 million tons in bunker per year, plus 440,000 tons of aviation fuel.[80] After 1937, a combination of the Navy's involvement in China operations, intensified training, and the expansion of the fleet siphoned off an unforeseen volume of fuel, retarding the oil stockpiling effort.

Impending war with the United States threatened disaster for the Navy unless alternative oil supplies could be secured in short order. The colonial powers, which had stood in the way of the Navy's 'south advance' ever since Satō

Tetsutarō's day, were left exposed in Southeast Asia by the outbreak of war in Europe. A narrow window opened, framed by military opportunity in Southeast Asia on one side and the prospect of an American oil embargo and runaway arms build-up on the other. It was assumed that any move on the East Indies would necessitate control of the Philippines and Malaya, meaning war with the United States and Great Britain. A further diplomatic squeeze on the beleaguered Dutch East Indies administration in the face of Dutch colonial intransigence, even after Holland was occupied, resulted in an agreement to supply Japan with 72,000 barrels daily for six months, in November 1940. This still fell well short of Japanese expectations. Facing a mounting tide of suspicion in the United States, Japan embarked on an all-out purchasing campaign to procure as much crude as possible on the open market and especially to increase its stocks of American high-octane aviation fuel.[81] In early 1941, the Army High Command commissioned a report from the Economic Mobilization Bureau of the War Ministry outlining two scenarios. Japan could opt immediately for war with Great Britain and the United States, expect shipping losses leading to oil shortages and industrial disruption after two years. The alternative would be to face an economic blockade that would eventually compel it to accede to American demands on China or face ruin. The study concluded that war gave Japan better options, but warned its forecast of two years of self-sufficiency in oil might be shortened if vital sea lanes were blocked.[82]

On 2 July, an Imperial Conference was convened to put the royal imprimatur on the Navy's planned 'south advance', describing it as necessary for 'the security and preservation of the nation'. The setting up of forward bases in southern Indochina, relinquished by Vichy French authorities under threat of Japanese attack, triggered the freezing of Japanese assets in the United States and a total oil embargo on 1 August.[83] The hawkish chief of the Navy General Staff, Admiral Nagano Osami, was appraised of the risks of war with the United States but nonetheless put his view before the emperor that it was better to fight than accept defeat through economic strangulation, thus 'risking war rather than shame'.[84] With its stockpiles being depleted at the rate of 2,900 barrels per hour, the Navy staff committed itself to seeking war at the earliest opportunity.[85] In the early autumn of 1941, Admiral Yamamoto's pioneering advances in carrier operations, developed over the summer and emboldened by the British success at Taranto, injected a radical and tantalizing option for the Imperial High Command: the possibility of a pre-emptive strike on the US Pacific Fleet, which had relocated from its west coast bases to Pearl Harbor in 1940.[86] Insecurity about its fuel supply built up over 15 years had become the leading *casus belli* for the Imperial Navy, pushing it into the enormous gamble of attacking the United States and invading Southeast Asia simultaneously.[87]

The Navy entered the Pacific War with 3.6 million tons of bunker fuel, 490,000 tons of aviation fuel and 1.4 million tons of crude, accounting for a total of around 5.5 million tons of oil products out of a nationally stockpiled total of nearly 8 million tons.[88] The Cabinet Planning Board estimated that it would be able to recoup 850,000 kilolitres from Southeast Asia in 1942, 2.6 million in 1943 and

5.3 million in the third. Thus it was projected that the draw-down of Japan's stockpiles over two years would be offset by imports from the 'southern regions'.[89] Until the 1930s, the Navy's plans for war with the United States had not extended far beyond the waters north of Taiwan and the Northeast Asian littoral. Yet in 1942, the scope of its operations rippled out to encompass Hawaii to the east, the Aleutians to the north, the Coral Sea to the south and the Indian Ocean to the west. Following the Navy's inability to deliver a knock-out blow to the US Pacific Fleet at Pearl Harbor or Midway, its fuel calculations went hopelessly awry. In fact the Imperial Navy fought three major sea battles, Midway, the Philippine Sea/Marianas and Leyte Gulf, as well as several lesser engagements instead of the single decisive encounter anticipated. These three main battles alone consumed over 1 million tons of oil.[90] Unsurprisingly, the Navy's petroleum consumption during the war turned out to be double its pre-war estimates.[91] To put this in perspective, one calculation puts the Navy's petroleum use at 60 per cent of national consumption during the Pacific War.[92]

Considering the determining role of oil in Japan's naval strategy, the question of tanker capacity received belated attention. The Navy operated its own tankers, but began to subsidize civilian construction heavily in the 1930s. In 1934, Japan owned some of the largest tankers then in existence, but the fleet totalled only 39 ships and 120,000 tons. Tonnage tripled to 364,000 in 1940, and because the new additions to the fleet were also faster, efficiency improved fourfold.[93] Nevertheless, the essential modesty of Japan's pre-war tanker fleet is easily appreciated when compared with opposing countries. In 1940, Great Britain boasted 450 tankers of 3,235,000 tons, and the US tanker fleet totalled 2,824,000 tons.[94] A special subsidy for tanker construction in Japan was introduced in 1941 enlarging the fleet to 94 ships representing 575,000 tons.[95] This was still inadequate to meet combined civilian and military demand, and Japan stayed dependent on American, British and Dutch tankers right up to Pearl Harbor. A crash wartime construction effort expanded the tanker fleet to a peak of 834,000 tons at the end of 1943.

On 8 May 1942, Japan suffered an early setback to its hopes for oil production in Southeast Asia when a patrolling US submarine sank the *Taiyō Maru*, carrying a party of Japanese oil experts *en route* to organize production in the captured East Indies oil fields.[96] However, for the first full year of the conflict, the criticality of the oil situation remained latent. In its initial conquests the Imperial Army captured 4 million barrels left by the retreating Allies who had also failed to complete the demolition of Southeast Asian wells. In spite of the loss of the *Taiyō Maru*, Japan was thus able to recover 70 per cent of the East Indies pre-war production rate of 180,000 barrels per day within the first year.[97] Moreover, Allied attacks on Japanese tankers were very slow in developing, sending a mere 4,000 tons to the bottom in the whole of 1942.[98] As 1943 approached, Tōjō and the War Cabinet felt confident that Japan had solved its energy crisis. Of the 136,000 barrels produced daily in Southeast Asia in 1943, 96,000 were locally consumed, much of this by fleet units at Singapore, and the excess sent to Japan.[99] But in shipping the squeeze was already being felt. Three out of every four tankers

Japan owned were shuttling oil from Southeast Asia to Japan. Although an absolute increase in oil imports was achieved, from a daily average of 29,000 barrels in 1942 to 40,000 barrels in 1943, the proportion being exported to Japan declined, from 40 per cent in 1942 to 29 per cent in 1943 suggesting that inadequate transportation capacity, not production, was the limiting factor.[100]

The 8th of May 1942 coincidentally marked the end of the Battle of the Coral Sea, the first setback suffered by the Imperial Navy in the war and an indication that the swift victory its leaders were depending on would be elusive. The first steps to organize protection for the merchant fleet were taken only that spring, while the vital energies of the Imperial Navy were channelled into preparations for the decisive showdown expected at Midway, in June.

The War of the *Maru*

When the US submarine offensive against Japanese shipping finally geared up in 1943, it would become known as the 'war of the *Maru*' after the generic designation for Japanese merchant vessels. The following sections outline the Allied campaign against shipping before analysing Japan's maritime protection efforts in closer detail. A variety of military means were at the disposal of United States and Allied forces in the campaign to destroy Japanese shipping; submarines, surface vessels, mines, coastal artillery, land-based and carrier aviation. It is testimony to the offensive power of the submarine that, as in the Atlantic, it also emerged as the dominant weapon against shipping in the Pacific, sinking 55 per cent of the 8 million tons destroyed by US forces.[101] In the latter stages of the war, carrier aircraft and mine-laying B-29 bombers levied an increasing toll on Japanese shipping. However it was without question the fleet submarine that broke the back of the merchant marine, and with it Japan's war economy.

Despite its ultimate success the submarine campaign against Japanese shipping began hesitantly, beset by technical and doctrinal handicaps. After the fall of the Philippines, the US submarine force was dispersed among three bases; Pearl Harbor, Fremantle and Brisbane, which took time to organize in the chaos that followed the Japanese attack. The US Navy had also to contend with its own Mahanian stalwarts reluctant to abandon outmoded doctrine. As a consequence, commerce warfare against Japan was approached cautiously. For the US submarine force, the pursuit of the Imperial Navy's capital ships was considered the most important of a plethora of missions, limiting their effectiveness against the more lightly protected merchant targets.[102] Many submarine commanders were replaced for lacking aggressiveness in their patrols and the main weapon in the US sub-surface inventory, the magnetic torpedo, was plagued by malfunctions.[103] The total Japanese tonnage sunk in 1942, 725,000 tons, amounted to no more than the combined German tally of Allied shipping in the Atlantic for February and March and fell within the margin of acceptable losses outlined by the Cabinet Planning Board before the war. The flow of strategic materials to the homeland, at around 20 million tons, remained constant on 1941 levels. Japan's merchant fleet saw off the first year of the submarine campaign with a minimal net loss of tonnage while managing to increase the size of its tanker fleet by 111,000 tons to 686,000 tons.[104]

US fleet submarines, operating unmolested out of Australia and Hawaii with the benefit of greater numbers, better tactics and focus built up in the first year of the war, sent 388,000 tons of tankers to the bottom in 1943. Slow to spot the Achilles heel in Japan's war-fighting capability, the US Navy, once aware of it, prosecuted the war against Japanese merchantmen ruthlessly, targeting tankers in particular. 'Wolf-pack' tactics, on the German model, were introduced to interdict Japan's shipping where it was most concentrated, in the Luzon Strait and Empire waters (Figure 3.1).[106] In 1943, over 2 million tons of shipping was destroyed and Japan suffered a 3 million-ton shortfall in bulk commodities on the previous year. Home-based refineries operated at less than one-third capacity.[107] Mounting merchant losses exposed the shortcomings of Japan's limited shipbuilding infrastructure which proved inadequate to meet both naval and cargo vessel construction needs. Concentrating ship-building resources on tankers at the expense of ordinary merchant ships miraculously preserved aggregate tanker tonnage for most of 1944 at around 800,000 tons in the face of appalling losses.[108] However, this did nothing to improve security for those tankers inbound from Southeast Asia. In a more telling statistic, from a peak of 740,000 tons of oil imported to Japan in the second quarter of 1943, the flow fell off in the third quarter of 1944 to just 178,000 tons.[109] In the final 15 months of the war, just 9 per cent of oil shipments from Southeast Asia made it through to Japan.[110]

Figure 3.1 Periscope photograph of a Japanese merchant ship torpedoed by *Seawolf*, late 1942.[105]

Source: Department of the Navy, Naval Historical Center, Washington, DC.

In 1944, the anti-shipping campaign crippled the Japanese war economy. In that year, US submarines alone sank over 600 ships amounting to 2.38 million tons, exceeding their tally for the rest of the war.[111] Japan's merchant fleet which started the year at nearly 5 million tons was halved by the end of December.[112] The successor organization to the Cabinet Planning Board acknowledged at the end of fiscal 1944, 'Damage to shipping, chiefly from enemy submarines, has been far greater that [*sic*] anticipated just prior to the war and has far outstripped the volume of vessels built.'[113] The report also admitted that military production and transportation had been maintained 'at the sacrifice of the civilian sector'. The flow of bulk commodities to Japan slumped to 10 million tons, half that of the total three previous years. US offensive efforts were redoubled by contrast. In February 1944, 52,000 tons of tankers were among 186,000 tons of Japanese shipping decimated in a 2-day air-raid on Truk, the Combined Fleet anchorage in the Caroline Islands.[114] Air attacks and mining directed at Japanese refining facilities at source in Southeast Asia also forced the closure of the Navy oil refinery at Balikpapan. By this stage, aircraft carriers earlier used exclusively against Imperial Navy targets were numerous enough to target merchant ships. Once US forces were re-established in the Philippines in late 1944, the shipping routes from Southeast Asia to the homeland became far more hazardous. Attempts at fighting tanker convoys through to Japan most often resulted in their wholesale destruction, and after the first quarter of 1945 oil imports ceased altogether.[115] For the Imperial Army and Navy the loss of the Southeast Asian shipping lanes threatened not just supplies to the home base, but the flow of arms and ammunition to their forward units.[116] Japanese authorities turned to increasingly desperate measures to supplement their dwindling petroleum stocks. A campaign to process pine roots for aviation fuel was launched but ultimately yielded only 3,000 barrels of substandard aviation fuel. Bunker fuel was supplemented with large quantities of alcohol. Unbeknown to the crews of the B-29s who began to assault Japan *en masse* in 1945, the refineries and oil storage areas they were assigned to hit had mostly run dry. Symbolizing the desperate straits of the Imperial Navy at the end of the war, the *Yamato* was dispatched on a suicidal foray to engage the American invasion fleet at Okinawa on 8 April 1945. Fuel was so short by this time that only 4,000 tons of heavy oil were spared for the mission, barely adequate for the super-battleship to execute its attack run.[117] When Japan capitulated four months later, 4,000 tons of bunker oil was all that was left in the country. Following the surrender, the US Strategic Bombing Survey concluded:

> The war against shipping was perhaps the most decisive single factor in the collapse of the Japanese economy and logistic support of Japanese military and naval power. Submarines accounted for the majority of vessel sinkings and the greater part of the reduction in tonnage.[118]

US submarines in the Pacific sank 55 per cent (4.8 million tons) of the total Japanese shipping destroyed, compared with 60 per cent (14.57 million tons) of the total Allied shipping sunk by their German counterparts in the Atlantic.[119]

While the U-boat offensive is estimated to have cost Germany 781 submarines and 39,000 men, the destruction meted out by the submarines of the United States Pacific Command was achieved at the relatively economical cost of 3,500 men and 52 submarines – lost to all causes. D.W. Waters claims that through the agency of just 5 per cent of the total Allied military power deployed in the Pacific, 'the defeat of Japan was primarily the result of sea blockade' – a feat which is 'one of the least publicized facts of history'.[120]

The inadequate protection of merchant shipping

The main reason for the Imperial Navy's abject failure to protect Japan's merchant fleet in the Second World War was that its doctrine, structure and philosophy had become almost entirely geared towards annihilating the US battle fleet in an intense conflict of limited duration. When the failure of this strategy was shown up at Midway, in June 1942, the Navy was unable to adjust to a more defensive mode of warfare that prioritized the defence of merchant shipping. Portents of Japan's vulnerability to blockade date back as far as the Russo-Japanese war and at least a theoretical understanding of the problems involved existed within the Imperial Navy prior to 1941. However, efforts to put maritime commerce protection into action were hesitant and piecemeal until hopelessly late into the war.

The 'defence of general merchant shipping routes' was mentioned in the Imperial Defence Policy of 1907, but only insofar as this did not interfere with the Navy's primary purpose; the destruction of the enemy fleet. Subsequent revisions of the Imperial Defence Policy concentrated on the need for a 'rapid war and decisive encounter' (*sokusen sokketsu*).[121] Neither the surface threat to merchantmen in the Russo-Japanese war, nor Japan's participation in ASW in the Mediterranean in 1917–18 made a lasting impression on Imperial Navy doctrine. Yet the importance of protecting far-flung SLOC was clearly understood in certain quarters. An article in the 1927 edition of *Brassey's Naval and Shipping Annual* on 'Japan's Naval Policy' by Commander Satō Ichirō, reveals an early appreciation of the vulnerability to which industrialization had exposed Japan:

> Japan is poor in natural resources and, to supply the factories, we must get raw materials from abroad. We must get many of our manufactured goods from foreign markets, too. To do this our sea-communications must be safe and secure.

It is in this context of protecting sea communications that Satō justified the existence of the Imperial Navy as 'an absolute guarantee of national existence'. Up to the Russo-Japanese war, the role of the Navy had been simpler, confined to the 'destruction of the enemy fleet and the safety of the sea-communications for the supply of expeditionary forces'.[122] With industrialization, Satō realized that trade protection had risen to become a core requirement equal to defence from invasion. Satō's analysis of Japan's vulnerability to trade disruption was remarkably prescient considering the importance he attached not just to trade flows across the Sea of Japan, Yellow and East China Seas, but to Japan's more remote sea lanes.

Satō divided overseas trade protection into three areas of priority for the Japanese Navy. Noting that a third of Japan's imports were carried across the East China Sea from the Asian mainland, he identified the security of these waters as Japan's first naval duty. Guarding the sea lanes in the China Sea, used to draw supplies of oil, rubber and metals from Southeast Asia, was its 'almost as essential' duty. The third mission of the Imperial Navy would be to keep open the more distant supply routes to Europe and America. Satō's concern with securing the sea route to Southeast Asia accurately predicted a strategic weak-point that emerged during the Pacific War:

> an item of the utmost importance coming from farther afield is fuel oil. One-half of the oil imports of Japan is drawn from the Dutch Indies,[123] and the freedom of that sea-route will be absolutely necessary for her power of resistance. The control of the routes in the China Sea is of great value to Japan, too, for the supply of rubber, clothing materials, and metals. *The protection of trade in these waters is therefore a charge against the Japanese Navy almost as essential as its first duty.*[124] [My italics]

Writing during the international naval limitations regime of the 1920s, Satō advocated the construction of auxilliary ships to extend ship protection south of the East China Sea, but such pleas fell mostly on deaf ears. In 1929, a communication was passed to the emperor written by the Naval Chief of Staff Katō Kanji on the necessity of protecting sea lanes, but failed to spell out any concrete recommendations.[125] Contemporary foreign analysts were also sensitive to Japan's 'essential sea routes, the vital arteries through which her life-blood flows',[126] while a US pre-war intelligence assessment concluded that 'Japan's lines of water and land communication provide indispensable support to her sustained war production and her deployment of armed forces and material'.[127] Imperial Army and civilian estimates before the war flagged the importance of shipping for maintaining Japanese industry and war potential, and linked success to 'the Navy's ability to secure maritime traffic'. However, concerns voiced inside and outside the Navy failed to feed through into either a review of naval policy undertaken in 1928 or the revised Imperial Defence Policy of 1936, which only mentioned shipping protection in the Tsushima Strait.[128] Once the decision was made to capture the South-East Asian oil fields, the Navy was slow to adjust existing plans despite the obvious, onerous burdens on sea transportation this would bestow. The operational plan for 1941 merely outlined the responsibility of the Navy's first-line units to protect sea communications in the waters north of Taiwan 'within the limits allowed by circumstances', something that few Combined Fleet officers had either the time or inclination to consider. When quizzed about the submarine threat to shipping and convoys in mid-1941, the Navy chief of staff Admiral Nagano brushed off the concerns of cabinet members. Even when personally questioned by the emperor about Japan's ability to 'obtain and transport oil without hindrance when faced with attacks by planes and submarines based in Australia' the naval chief of staff was unruffled.[129] Plans to protect shipping were finally extended south of Taiwan, on 5 November 1941, to include the South China, Java and Celebes Seas, through which the main Japanese invasion forces would pass. Beyond that, the commitment went no further than to 'endeavour as far as possible to defend sea lanes in the area of the Pacific Mandates, the Philippines and Sea of Okhotsk'.[130]

Critical to such sanguine attitudes was the failure of the naval command to grasp the strategic potential of the submarine, underestimating both the capability and temperament of the United States to use its submarines as a tool of economic warfare against Japan.[131] The Operations Division of the Naval General Staff regarded enemy submarines and destroyers as extensions of the battle fleet, reflecting their own doctrinal preferences. Such myopia may also have been influenced by Great Britain's attempt at the Washington Conference to ban submarine construction outright. Certain intelligence officers, Niimi in the 1920s and later Ooi Atsushi in the 1930s, had studied the German U-boat campaign in the First World War and were attuned to the sub-surface threat to merchant shipping, but were unable to influence naval policy higher up.[132]

During the Pacific War, Japanese shipping to and from the southern regions operated along two strategic sea lanes. The first, south-west route (*nansei kōro*) was strategically the most important, serving as Japan's major line of communication to the East Indies and Malay Peninsula, for imports of raw materials as well as to ferry military supplies to occupied areas in Southeast Asia. The south-east route (*nantō kōro*) stretched from Japan to the Marianas and beyond to Rabaul, in New Britain. Though of lesser economic importance, the south-east route was nonetheless vital for delivering troops, weapons and ammunition to support operations in the Solomon Islands, Bismarck Archipelago and New Guinea. At the beginning of the war, ship protection was delegated to the local Navy district commands in Japan until the establishment of the First and Second Maritime Escort Forces on 10 April 1942. The First Maritime Escort Force was assigned to protect convoys from Japan to Singapore, where it retained its headquarters under a Vice Admiral with a Shipping Control Officer (*unkōshikikan*) attached. The new unit was equipped with a force of ten aging destroyers, two torpedo boats and five converted gunboats. The Second Maritime Escort Unit, to protect merchant shipping between Japan and Truk, was smaller, initially consisting of four destroyers, two torpedo boats and one gunboat.[133] A light cruiser (*Yūbari*) was added in September.[134] Pre-war estimates had suggested a figure well in excess of 300 large escorts as the minimum needed to form a commerce protection force but the reality of finding suitable equipment for the new escort units was highly problematic.[135] At the beginning of the war, Japan had yet to develop a vessel expressly designed for merchant defence, while existing destroyers were 'considered too valuable for pure escort work'.[136] Development of the *kaibōkan*, a class of small coastal defence ships of under 1,000 tons, took several years to obtain funding in the 1930s. The first of these entered service in June 1940 and only four had been commissioned by Pearl Harbor.[137] Originally designed to protect Japan's northern fishing fleet, the *kaibōkan* were scaled down from their original design to divert extra funds into the super-battleship programme. According to Evans and Peattie, the super-battleships were a 'diversion of the navy's attention and the nation's resources from one of the most critical strategic problems that the navy faced: its utter dependence on its overseas routes and the need to acquire the ships, to form the organization, to shape the doctrine, and to develop the training that would be the most effective in protecting those sea routes'.[138]

In July 1942, merchant protection was up-graded with the establishment of the First Escort Fleet in Taiwan to extend coverage for Japan's merchant shipping in the East China Sea with a fleet of around 20 vessels.[139] Of the forces committed, many of the destroyers – like their captains – were superannuated and the sub-chasers too slow and poorly armed to venture far offshore. Lack of funding had also retarded the development of sonar and hydrophone detection technology in the 1930s which would have been invaluable to the anti-submarine effort.[140] Twenty-six improved versions of the *kaibōkan*, in two classes (*Etorofu* and *Mikura*) each of around 1,000 tons, were eventually laid down between March 1943 and May 1944, and faster vessels equipped with better ASW weapons were later added to the escort forces. But they were continually over-stretched, unable to offer more than skeletal coverage of key choke-points.[141] Japanese convoys, moreover, were tiny in comparison with Anglo-American efforts in the Atlantic.[142]

Indifference to shipping protection in the Navy's upper echelons, aggravated by bureaucratic and inter-service rivalries, manifested itself in poor organization. Unlike in Great Britain, where Atlantic shipping was overseen by a central committee from 1941, control over the Japanese merchant marine remained under separate Army, Navy and civilian administration until virtually the end of the war. Direction was left to be negotiated among the Army and Navy General Staffs and the civilian Shipping Control Board, created in April 1942. The inevitable result was duplication and inefficiency. This fragmented approach was mirrored internally within the Navy. Commerce protection was only one of several duties handled by the Defence Preparations Office of the Naval General Staff until October 1942 when a new body was created known as the Twelfth Division of the First Bureau. Yet just three staff officers were assigned to it, holding separate responsibility for convoys and routing, anti-submarine operations and the armament and communications equipment aboard merchantmen. Planners in the Navy Ministry preferred to concentrate their energies on the armament and readiness of the Combined Fleet, while in the line commands, port officers supposedly charged with shipping safety in the eight district and 'guard' units of the Imperial Navy were too habitually overburdened to give shipping protection more than cursory attention.[143] Escort operations in 1942 lacked an overarching mechanism to co-ordinate and standardize different procedures used for the control of shipping, convoying and distribution of cargo.[144] All this notwithstanding, the skill of individual convoy commanders could still frustrate American submarines when operating with good intelligence.[145]

Mounting losses in autumn 1943 demonstrated the vulnerability of cargo vessels without proper convoy protection. In March, a Second Convoy Escort

Fleet was created, ported in Saipan, with responsibility for convoys between Yokohama and Truk. But the four destroyers and two torpedo boats assigned were unequal to the task. More significantly, in November, a Grand Escort Headquarters was set up by the Chief of the General Staff, according top priority to commerce protection in all areas under its control from the Kuriles to Singapore, although its remit did not extend to the Combined and China Area Fleet sectors.[146] As a sign of its importance the new headquarters was put under the command of a former Minister of the Navy, Admiral Oikawa Koshirō.[147] However, with few officers experienced in convoying operations, the Grand Escort Headquarters continued to pay the price of the Navy's earlier indifference and frugality, having at its disposal fewer than 50 ships of 800 tons and above in addition to the 901st Air Group. The grandiose strategy developed by Admiral Oikawa's staff hardly matched the resources at their command. It relied on exploiting the partially enclosed nature of Japan's major sea lanes to Southeast Asia to shield merchant shipping from Allied submarines and air power by using Borneo, the Philippines, Taiwan and the Nansei Shotō as natural buffers against the open reaches of the Pacific. Sea-air gaps between the islands would be closed by a network of minefields and radar stations. A similar plan aimed to use the Bonin and Kazan Rettō (Volcano Islands) to screen Japan's shipping routes to the Marianas. Within these gigantic sanctuaries the forces of the Grand Escort Fleet would patrol sea lanes. A few minefields were laid towards implementing the scheme but the American juggernaut crossing the Pacific began to overrun the intended defensive perimeter in 1944, and the resulting calamities suffered by the Combined Fleet soon distracted the attention of the Naval General Staff.[148] In any case, had the scheme been made operational, it seems doubtful that the Japanese experiment with patrolled lanes would have been any more fruitful than the US and UK experience in the Atlantic (see Chapter 2).

In the first two months of 1944, US submarines sank nearly 500,000 tons of shipping causing the question of convoy escort to be brought before the emperor. Thereafter, larger and better-defended convoys were introduced, drastically improving survival rates compared to merchantmen sailing individually.[149] However, Japanese reversals in the Marianas from mid-1944 panicked the naval high command into placing Admiral Oikawa's escort assets at the disposal of the Combined Fleet. Scarce ASW vessels ill-suited to surface combat were diverted to the fleet action at Leyte Gulf and even ordered to pursue American carriers.[150] The convoy system subsequently began to disintegrate and escorts were organized on an *ad hoc* basis. In the war's terminal phase, Japanese naval tactics and armament were less and less of a match for the United States and the system of three-dimensional warfare it had perfected for waging on, under, above the waves and in the electro-magnetic spectrum. The use of radar in prosecuting night attacks removed the protective cloak of darkness for Japan's naval and cargo vessels alike.[151] Advances in signals intelligence helped steer US submarines to approximately half of their targets.[152] Fighting spirit was powerless to resist the overwhelming combination of superior technology and numbers. The last organized convoys to leave Southeast Asia in January 1945 quickly foundered in the South

China Sea. In June, US submarines penetrated the ultimate sanctuary of the Sea of Japan, regarded as a 'Japanese lake' since 1905. With the merchant marine and Imperial Navy reduced to a shadow of their former glory, a centralized command authority over shipping was finally established in May, but in the circumstances it was virtually an empty gesture.[153] By the end of the war, casualties suffered by the Japanese merchant marine exceeded one hundred thousand men of all ranks.[154]

In summary, the poor organization and neglect that characterized the Japanese maritime commerce protection effort had several underlying causes. Most important of all was the unshakeable belief of the Navy that the centre of gravity of both forces lay with the main battle fleet. Had Japan moved to implement a rearguard strategy to protect merchant shipping after Midway, then the US submarine offensive would have enjoyed something less than free rein, and might have been substantially impeded. The Navy's failure to at least accord better protection to oil imports was indeed short-sighted, for a shortage of oil became the single most important constraint on naval operations after 1943.[155] Strategy aside, rivalry among the institutions of the Japanese state took its toll on efficiency, working against centralized control at all levels of the war effort. A shortage of fiscal resources before the war also imposed practical limits on the size of any escort force, since most of the naval budget was required to keep up first-line battle fleet strength vis-à-vis the United States Navy. As Colin Gray writes, 'Strategic flexibility flows not only from sound doctrine and an open but educated mind but also from numbers; and inflexibility flows from the absence of numbers'.[156] Systemic weaknesses aside, Japan's woeful shipping protection effort was in the end a product of the Navy's indifference, which persisted even when confronted with the evidence of ship losses and the bankruptcy of the pre-war strategy. Given the disparity in resources Japan could never have hoped to win a prolonged conflict against the United States. But the Navy need not have given up the merchant fleet as cheaply as it did.

Conclusion

Modernization from the 1860s onwards locked Japan into dependence on sea transportation, underpinning the health of its economy and underwriting its war-making potential. Japan's dependence on overseas resources, especially oil, was an important contributing factor behind its decision to go to war with Great Britain and the United States in 1941. That this same dependence had transformed an undefended merchant marine into a strategic liability was not grasped by the naval high command, so intent was it on winning a quick victory over the US Pacific Fleet. The Imperial Navy developed its strategy and tactics out of limited wars fought at the turn of the century in which its major roles were to protect the short communication lines to China and Korea, and to directly challenge opposing navies for sea control. Neither the defence of merchant shipping nor the long-term security of the industrial base were essential to victory in 1895, 1905 or 1918. When the Navy tried to scale up its strategy for local war to the vast expanses of the Pacific and Indian Oceans and the total war of 1941–45, it was totally inadequate. Nevertheless, too many resources and too much pride had been invested in the Navy's 'battle faith' to be swiftly redirected into strategies for protecting maritime transportation. Once the United States had organized itself for a concerted attack on Japanese shipping, led by its submarine forces, the War of the *Maru* exposed the full extent of Japan's vulnerability to blockade. Efforts to protect merchant shipping in the form of dedicated escort forces and organized convoys arrived too little, too late. In spite of this, the little that was done to organize convoys greatly improved the survivability of Japanese merchant ships.

For most Japanese, the blockade ranks behind the atomic and incendiary bombing of its cities as the greatest hardship visited on Japan during the Second World War. After the war, the former Minister of Munitions, Toyoda Teijirō, stated in his interrogation that 'the shipping shortage and the scarcity of oil were the two main factors that assumed utmost importance in Japan's war efforts'.[157] Official testimony before the Diet was more clear-cut, acknowledging that 'the greatest cause of our defeat was the loss of shipping'.[158]

Since 1945, Japan has had no overseas territory or bases to defend and control of sea lanes on which Japan's economic security depends has been in large part the responsibility of the US Navy. However, the War of the *Maru* has continued to cast a long shadow, shaping Japan's post-war perceptions of vulnerability and bearing upon the roles and missions of the MSDF and the emphasis placed upon the security of SLOC and escort operations.

4 Japan's sea lane security in the era of defence constraints, 1945–77

Introduction

This chapter analyses the extent to which the perceived vulnerability of SLOC influenced the policies of post-war Japanese governments and other security actors in Japan from 1945–77; the era in which Japan recovered its sovereignty and established itself as an economic superpower without acquiring a concomitant military status. Japan's post-war security is normally seen in terms of the discontinuities with the pre-war status quo, as empire and militarism gave way to the peaceful expansion of trade within a security framework based on defence linkages with the United States and a system of constitutional and other constraints that strictly regulated the SDF from their formation in 1954. In the context of these changes, this chapter addresses two basic questions that are carried forward into subsequent chapters. First, to what extent did security concerns about Japan's sea lanes dispose post-war governments towards forming an alliance with the United States and acquiring independent defence capability? Second, given the domestic and international controversy surrounding rearmament, to what extent were 'sea lane defence' and the 'safety of maritime transportation' used as rationales to legitimize the creation, existence and force structure of the SDF and the MSDF in particular?

A framework is presented for analysing Japan's post-war defence and security at the levels of international systemic interaction, transnational alliance linkages and domestic politics. This is followed by an examination of the 'Yoshida Doctrine', which served as the *de facto* blueprint for Japan's security and diplomacy during the Cold War. In the section entitled Naval Renaissance, the complex and clandestine process which led to the establishment of the MSDF is profiled and contrasted with greater official resistance towards the creation of ground forces. Naval links with the United States and institutional continuity maintained from the Imperial Navy are also identified as key influences on the MSDF's structures and thinking. Planning for the protection of maritime transportation and the build-up of MSDF capabilities is then charted up to the late 1960s. Two competing visions for the MSDF are explored: Sekino Hideo's vision of a great power navy dedicated to defending SLOC, versus Kaihara Osamu's model for a limited anti-invasion force. In this context, a short-lived official attempt around

1970 to implement Sekino's 'autonomous' vision is profiled against the ascendancy of defence constraints, which were formalized with the adoption of the National Defense Program Outline (NDPO) (*taikō*) in 1976. Perceptions of a growing Soviet threat to Japan's sea lanes as far as 1977 are then evaluated, as a prelude to Chapter 5 which deals with the rise of sea lane defence to the forefront of Japan's defence and alliance policies in the 1980s.

Analytical framework for Japan's post-war security policy

Japan's post-war defence and security policy-making environment is most profitably described at three levels of analysis: systemic, transnational and domestic. Two key documents set the foundations for post-war security: the November 1946 Constitution (*kenpō*) and the 1951 Security Treaty between Japan and the United States (*nichibei anzen hoshō jōyaku*, often shortened to *ampo*), revised in 1960.

At an international systemic level, from 1945 onwards, Japan's external environment was defined initially by disarmament, occupation and the redrawing of its borders to the four main islands of Hokkaidō, Honshū, Shikoku and Kyūshū. Thereafter, it was recast in the global, bipolar schism of the Cold War and the corresponding division of Asia into Communist and Western-backed blocs. At the same time, the legacy of Japan's military expansion in the Pacific War continued to define Japan's relations with Asian countries in particular. Although the dissolution of Japan's empire (formally secured with the 1951 San Francisco Peace Treaty) removed any strategic requirement for Japan to maintain military lines of communication with overseas bases, the expansion of its industrial base after 1950 greatly increased its dependence on SLOC for imports of raw materials, energy and food (see Chapter 1), while indirect strategic dependence remained on US military SLOC for the re-supply and reinforcement of US forces in Japan and Korea.

At a transnational level, Japan's post-war political and strategic orientation was to a large extent a 'default' position determined by the role of the United States as the occupying power. Reflecting a contradiction between the initial US objective of demilitarizing Japan and Washington's subsequent drive to co-opt it as a military partner in the Cold War, Japan's post-war security linkages with the United States have acted both as a constraint and driver of Japanese rearmament. On one hand, the 1951 US–Japan Security Treaty gave Japan a *de facto* defence guarantee (made *de jure* in 1960), bringing it into the Western camp and obviating, in the perception of its post-war political leaders, any strategic requirement to deal with external security threats independently. On the other hand, transnational links pushed 'questions of military security higher up the political agenda than would have been possible in light of the organization of the Japanese government and of Japan's civil–military relations'.[1]

In an external security context dominated by linkages with the United States, Japan's post-war domestic defence 'debate' was framed between the outright opposition of left-wing parties towards rearmament and alliance with the

United States, and the conservative nationalists who favoured a more independent approach to defence and with less strategic reliance on the United States. As Katzenstein and Okawara have argued, questions of military security (in contrast to questions of economic security) were deeply contested in post-war Japan, centring on the legitimacy of the SDF and their potential to be employed in an internal as well as external security role.[2] At the level of society, pre-war popular esteem for the military was replaced by a widespread suspicion of military institutions while SDF members were held in low social esteem. After the establishment of the SDF in July 1954, their constitutionality was subject to repeated legal challenges (and upheld by the Sapporo District Court in 1973). Between these poles, post-war governments basically followed the compromise course of limited rearmament set by Prime Minister Yoshida Shigeru, who formed five administrations between 1946 and 1954. The November 1946 Constitution promulgated under Yoshida, though not preventing the establishment of the SDF in 1954, has served as the primary legal and moral reference point for successive political and normative constraints on the acquisition and use of military power by the Japanese state. Chapter II ('Renunciation of War'), Article Nine, of the Constitution states:

> Aspiring sincerely to an international peace based on justice and order, the Japanese people forever renounce war as a sovereign right of the nation and the threat or use of force as a means of settling international disputes.
>
> In order to accomplish the aim of the preceding paragraph, land, sea and air forces, as well as other war potential, will never be maintained. The right of belligerency of the state will not be recognized.[3]

Although the 1951 Security Treaty was revised in 1960 and Article Nine of the 1946 Constitution has been subject to substantial 'reinterpretation', these documents have served as the twin foundations of Japan's security policy since 1945 and symbolize the major departures from the pre-war status quo.

The Yoshida Doctrine

In the late 1940s, Prime Minister Yoshida Shigeru faced the overlapping challenges of reconstructing a shattered economy and rebuilding Japan's international reputation while still under foreign occupation. In this environment, all short-term policy imperatives pointed away from rearmament as an issue certain to be domestically divisive, internationally contentious and financially burdensome. Yoshida responded to this predicament by adopting a pragmatic national posture 'unconnected with any considerations of ideology', based on the pursuit of trade-led economic growth as the foundation of domestic stability and a minimalist politico-military footprint overseas, predicated on political and military alignment with the United States.[4] Rather than intending to set a blueprint for post-war grand strategy, Yoshida saw this approach as necessary only until such time as Japan could afford to resume full responsibility for its defence and security. However, Yoshida's expediency proved so successful that it became enshrined as the defining 'doctrine' for Japan's foreign, defence and economic policies throughout the Cold War.[5]

The Yoshida Doctrine, in essence, recognized the enormous power disparities between occupier and occupied, anticipated the emerging Cold War and charted a tactical course for Japan designed to minimize its political exposure while maximizing its economic benefits, via commercial access to the non-Communist bloc. One of the prices of this arrangement was denial of commercial access to China after 1949. As late as 1951, during the Korean War, Yoshida had still hoped to restore diplomatic and economic links with China, which had served as Japan's 'traditional' export market and supply base on the Asian Continent.[6] He also believed that maintaining economic relations with the fledgling People's Republic would induce China's Communist leaders to be independent of the Soviet Union and would later brand US containment policies based on a monolithic view of Communism 'a total failure'.[7] However, Yoshida's overriding interest lay in concluding a security treaty with the United States and the weakness of his position forced him to defer to US strategy.

Given increasing Japanese doubts about the capacity of the United Nations to function as a global institution for collective security, Yoshida appreciated that alignment with the United States brought with it a guarantee of access to an international trading system.[8] Within such a system, Japan could secure the in-flows of natural resources needed to trade its way to prosperity, based on a highly regulated home market and the creation of a world-class export sector. This prompted one of two structural shifts in the international political economy of Japan's trade. First, Southeast Asia took China's place as a substitute source of raw materials and export demand. Second, new oil finds in the Gulf region led the Middle East to become Japan's primary source of oil, replacing its pre-war dependence on North America. Thus, Japan's entry into a Western-led trading system led the sea route connecting Japan to the Gulf, via Southeast Asia, to assume central importance to its economic well-being. Sea lanes linking Japan to Australia also became essential to imports of minerals and food, while maritime access across the Pacific served both as an inward conduit for minerals and food as well as for exports bound in the opposite direction. Yoshida felt 'that Japan should and could live as a maritime nation and that cooperation with (the United States) would be the best way to acquire access to the world market and its resources and to safeguard her sea routes'.[9] By submerging Japan's political and strategic interests within *Pax Americana*, Yoshida, at the political cost of diminished sovereignty, paved the way for four decades of prosperity and the expansion of GDP between 1950 and 1990 by a factor of 152.

The Yoshida administration proposed a cooperative security arrangement with the United States as early as 1947, offering basing facilities to US forces in return for the conclusion of a peace treaty and a US defence commitment to Japan.[10] Anticipating the emergence of rival US- and Soviet-led camps in East Asia three years before the Korean War, Yoshida believed that the presence of US forces in Japan would provide an adequate deterrent against direct Soviet aggression.[11]

Yoshida believed that reciprocity in the security arrangements could be offered by conceding to the United States a liberal basing agreement that would turn Japan into a strategic, logistical and intelligence-gathering hub underpinning US military strategy in the Western Pacific. Although an exclusively non-military contribution to regional stability would avoid aggravating regional sensitivities, Japan could contribute to international security as an economic force for stability and a developmental model for decolonizing nations in Asia and beyond. This broad conception of a bilateral security arrangement was reflected in the title of the Treaty of Mutual Cooperation and Security Between Japan and the United States. References to the treaty as an 'alliance' (*dōmei*) remained taboo within Japan into the 1980s.

Although US attitudes towards Japanese rearmament were already softening with the onset of the Cold War and the Communist victory in China, it was the outbreak of the Korean War, in June 1950, that brought about a reversal in US policy towards Japan. Two weeks into the conflict, on 8 July, General MacArthur sanctioned the creation of a National Police Reserve Force (NPRF) of 75,000 men, reflecting his concerns about an internal security vacuum arising from the deployment of three US divisions from Japan to South Korea. During negotiations to conclude a security treaty, held in January 1951, Special Ambassador John Foster Dulles pressed Yoshida to transform the NPRF into an army of 350,000 capable of dealing with an external attack from the Soviet Union.[12] Yoshida, on the other hand, regarded the risk of Soviet invasion as minimal and placed at least equal weight on internal threats to national security in the form of economic sabotage or insurrection. Together with a vague offer to establish domestically recruited armed forces numbering 50,000, Yoshida reiterated the offer of bases to support the UN military effort under way in Korea, maintaining that a large-scale military build-up was both beyond the nation's means and strategically unnecessary as long as the United States maintained a military presence in Japan to ensure deterrence.

When the Security Treaty was signed on 8 September 1951 – concurrently with the San Francisco Peace Treaty – the stationing of US forces in Japan was guaranteed beyond the end of Occupation, ensuring a *de facto* security guarantee even though there was no formal commitment to defend Japan in the Treaty text.[13] However, the shift in US policy in favour of Japanese rearmament was apparent in the Preamble to the Treaty, which stated that the United States would continue to station forces in and around Japan in the expectation that Japan 'will itself increasingly assume responsibility for its own defence against direct and indirect aggression', while avoiding 'any armament which could be an offensive threat'.[14]

With the conclusion of the Security Treaty, the Japanese government thus committed itself to a policy of limited rearmament as the price of securing US military protection and a reduction in US troops in Japan, who still numbered more than 200,000. However, basic differences between the two countries over the size and function that an 'indigenous' armed force would assume remained unresolved. As far as Yoshida was concerned the primary mission of Japan's paramilitary forces was 'to preserve a satisfactory relationship with the United States'.[15]

However, in September 1952 he assented to the formation of self defence forces and agreed to include defence against external aggression as one of their basic missions.

Both governments still had to agree on manpower totals before the SDF could be inaugurated and begin drawing on US surplus equipment stocks. The NPRF and Maritime Safety Force (which MacArthur had increased by 8,000 men at the same time that the NPRF was formed) were first merged under the National Safety Agency, emerging as the 110,000-man National Safety Force in October 1952. A Security Advisory Group was formed to draw up manpower targets. Subsequently, at talks held between Foreign Minister Ikeda and Secretary of State Robertson the following October, a compromise figure of 180,000 was settled upon, clearing the way for military aid to flow via the Mutual Security Act, promulgated on 8 March 1954. After the necessary legal foundation was put into place through the Defense Agency Establishment Law and Self Defense Forces Law, the SDF were formally inaugurated on 1 July, numbering approximately 146,000 men.

The constitutionality of the SDF was based on the government's interpretation of Article Nine. The Renunciation of War clause closely bore the hallmark of US influence in its drafting. MacArthur's February 1946 draft of Article Nine was worded to reflect the immediate post-war aim of demilitarizing Japan in perpetuity, stating:

> War as a sovereign right of the nation is abolished. Japan renounces it as an intrumentality for settling its disputes and even for preserving its own security. It relies upon the higher ideals which are now stirring the world for its defence and protection.
>
> No Japanese Army, Navy or Air Force will ever be authorized and no rights of belligerency will ever be conferred upon any Japanese force.

Scope for interpreting the final version of Article Nine adopted by the Diet to allow the establishment of the SDF was facilitated by insertion of the clause, 'In order to accomplish the aim of the preceding paragraph', at the beginning of the second paragraph. This crucial re-wording was at the initiative of Foreign Minister (later prime minister) Ashida Hitoshi, during Diet deliberations prior to the Constitution's promulgation.[16] Without this addition, 'Japan would have been barred from possessing all types of armed forces'.[17] The provision in Article 66 of the Constitution that 'The Prime Minister and other Ministers of states must be civilians' – intended to distance the new Constitution from the Meiji Constitution, which had guaranteed a political role for the Imperial Army and Navy – also implied that the existence of military forces was legally recognized.

In the immediate post-Occupation period, Yoshida's administration and the ruling Liberal Party found itself under attack over its approach to defence policy from both the Socialist and Communist opposition parties, who were implacably opposed to rearmament and alliance with the United States, and from the conservative nationalist Progressive party, led by Ashida Hitoshi and Shigemitsu Mamoru, who sought to amend the Constitution to facilitate a more independent approach to defence. Reflecting the domestic controversy generated by rearmament, the institutional capacity of the defence establishment continued to lag behind efforts to boost frontline capabilities. The National Defense Council (NDC), for example, did not materialize until July 1956, two years after it was announced. Still felt to be missing, fundamentally, was a legal framework tying defence policy into the Constitution. This gap was filled with the announcement of the Basic Policy for National Defence on 20 May 1957.[18] With the Basic Policy in place, the way was finally open for a more coherent approach to defence planning through a series of four-year defence build-up plans, though at a pace gradual enough to minimize controversy and the diversion of resources from economic recovery. A further attempt was made to amend the Constitution, by the Democratic Party-led cabinet of Hatoyama Ichirō, in December 1954.[19] However, after the merger of conservative parties into the LDP the following year, inaugurating the '1955 System' under which LDP governments would rule uninterrupted until 1993, an institutional and political course was charted under which successive administrations would basically adhere to the Yoshida Doctrine. With the exception of Prime Minister Kishi Nobusuke, who briefly contemplated a policy of independent rearmament in 1957, LDP premiers throughout the Cold War adhered to Yoshida's policy of incremental expansion of the SDF, alongside the introduction of formal and informal constraints on defence capability in order to appease left-wing opposition. Bans were introduced against the overseas dispatch of the SDF (1954) and restrictions on arms exports were codified into three principles in 1967. Three other 'basic policies' adopted since 1957 have also constrained the SDF's evolution:

- An Exclusively Defense-Oriented Policy; which sanctions the use of force by the SDF only in response to an attack already initiated and limits the level of defence capability to the minimum required for self-defence.
- A policy of 'not becoming a military power that might pose a threat to other countries', which has been taken as a prohibition against acquiring 'offensive' weapons systems.
- The Three Non-Nuclear Principles, which since 1967 have proscribed the possession, production and handling of nuclear weapons on Japanese territory.

Although the JDA itself admits there is no clear definition of what constitutes 'military power' and the military relevance of a semantic division drawn between offensive and defensive weapons systems is questionable, these policies have nonetheless constrained weapons acquisitions choices, excluding ballistic missiles, bombers, large aircraft carriers, nuclear submarines and – until recently – in-flight refuelling.[20]

Without the presence of US forces in northern Japan or Korea, it is likely that a perceived 'threat from the north', based on the Soviet seizure of the four Japanese-held islands in the southern Kuriles/Northern Territories in August and September 1945, combined with Stalin's support for the North Korean invasion of South Korea in 1950, would have led Japan's civilian leadership to reconsider a defence build-up as a matter of national survival. Historically, since the nineteenth century the Korean Peninsula has been perceived emotively by Japanese strategists as a 'dagger pointed at Japan's heart'. The continuity of such strategic concerns well into the post-1945 period is apparent in the view of relatively moderate commentators such as Kōsaka Masataka, that 'if the Korean peninsula were to fall into the hands of hostile powers there would be a serious and immediate threat to Japan, and control of nearby air space and sea lanes'.[21] However, as long as the United States was committed to the forward defence of Japan in Korea and deployed 'tripwire' forces in Hokkaidō, the main function of the Ground Self Defense Force (GSDF) as far as Yoshida was concerned would continue to be the political one of raising contributory forces to maintain the diplomatic framework of the US–Japan Security Arrangements rather than any strategic role beyond Japan's post-1945 borders.

Compared with the dynamics of land-based power in Northeast Asia, Japan's post-1945 maritime strategic environment was more fully changed by Japan's alliance with the United States, in effect inverting the strategic polarity of the Pacific, transforming it from Japan's maritime frontline (as had been the case from 1905 to 1945) to the equivalent of a rear area connecting it commercially with its major export and import markets in North America and Southeast Asia, and militarily linking US forward bases in Japan and elsewhere in East Asia, with Hawaii and the US West Coast.[22] Moreover, Communist states on Asia's maritime periphery possessed only limited maritime capabilities during the 1950s, neither able nor willing to challenge US naval and air superiority over water, with the partial exception of the Taiwan Strait. In this benign maritime environment, as noted in Chapter 2, given the overwhelming dominance of the US Navy, the importance of military SLOC to US strategy tended to be obscured. However, an awareness of the naval dimension to the US security guarantee was keenly perceived both by Japan's post-war leaders and former Imperial Navy officers. Many of the latter went on to staff the MSDF itself, moved into the Diet opening up 'pipelines' connecting the fledgling military with political circles, or became businessmen 'worried about the security of Japan's trade routes'.[23] Compared with ASDF or GSDF generals, former MSDF officers would continue to have a much higher representation within industry into the 1970s.[24]

From this perspective, the underlying purpose of the Security Treaty was 'to secure Japan's lines of supply in the Pacific and Indian Oceans and to permit it access to export markets, particularly those in the United States'.[25] However, Article V of the revised 1960 US–Japan Security Treaty only obliges the United States to respond to 'an armed attack against either Party in the *territories* under the administrations of Japan'.[26] The argument that Article V of the Treaty, 'does not impose any responsibility on U.S. military forces' to respond to 'attacks against Japanese merchant shipping on the high seas' would later be used by proponents of an expanded Japanese navy and an 'autonomous' defence posture in the late 1960s.[27]

Japan's dependence on the US Seventh Fleet for security in the sea areas from Japan to the Gulf was recognized by Yoshida, who was sympathetic to a linkage between trade and the necessity for naval protection. This was reflected in the tacit support provided for the creation of post-war maritime forces by his administration, in contrast with the political resistance which met US demands to establish a large Japanese army. This difference of approach can be ascribed to several reasons. First, Japan's export-led economic growth was, in a physical sense, completely reliant on the expansion of a large, Japanese-flagged ocean-going merchant fleet – set to become the second largest in the world, at 30 million tons, by the end of the 1960s – in order to import the raw materials and fuel for industrial expansion which drove growth. The purely defensive objective of protecting Japan's commercial shipping interests thus accorded with the post-war political priority placed on economic recovery and expansion. Second, Yoshida – who maintained close links to former Imperial Navy officers during the Occupation – recognized that the political costs of maintaining naval forces, operating out of the glare of media publicity and away from foreign populations, would be much lower than for maintaining any Japanese troops on the ground in Asia.[28] Third, while the process of gradual naval rearmament was pursued with a degree of official encouragement in Tokyo, the inter-personal and institutional bonding between former Imperial Navy personnel and US Navy officers was a factor independently driving the reconstitution of Japanese maritime security forces at a transnational level. The spontaneity of rapprochement between naval veterans from both countries contrasted with Supreme Commander of the Allied Powers' (SCAP) purge of Imperial Army officers.[29]

Naval renaissance

Although nearly nine years separated the inauguration of the MSDF from the disestablishment of the Imperial Navy, a virtually unbroken institutional lineage was maintained. Compared with efforts to establish ground forces, the development of a post-war navy, although clandestine, proceeded more smoothly under the 'sympathetic guidance of the US Navy and the strong traditions of the Imperial Japanese Navy'. The strength of transnational links was reflected in the fact that the MSDF trained with and was equipped by the US Navy long before the ASDF and GSDF formed links with their corresponding US armed services. Its acquisitions were also guided towards complementing Seventh Fleet capability gaps, mainly in mine-counter measures and ASW. At the same time, the MSDF was a direct descendant of the Imperial Navy, retaining many of its personnel, as well as its customs, traditions and institutional forms. As part of this, the MSDF also inherited the ambitions of those whose 'beautiful dream' was to restore Japan's post-war navy to a fully fledged, stand-alone force whose mission would be to defend Japan's SLOC. Although partly due to a mixture of nostalgia for past grandeur and the empire-building tendencies common to all large bureaucracies, the dream of an 'autonomous' navy also reflected fears that a future *guerre de course* might be directed at Japan's commerce as well as doubts about the reliability of the US security commitment extending to Japan's merchant marine. The presence of Imperial Navy veterans at all key levels of the fledgling MSDF also ensured that the institutional memory of the wartime blockade was passed on.[30]

Although the Imperial Navy was officially abolished in November 1945, its command structures were held intact within the Second Bureau of the Demobilization Ministry Department.[31] In part, this reflected the Allies' urgent need to clear Japanese waters of approximately 100,000 sea mines, many of them air-dropped in the final months of the war. A sizeable Imperial Navy minesweeping capability had escaped destruction in the war and minesweeping operations conducted by its former officers and vessels, organized in a 'route clearance unit' (*kōro keibitai*), began shortly after the surrender on 2 September.

In August 1947, the government responded to arguments that Japan required a coast guard to protect Japanese fishing vessels from seizure and to coordinate the minesweeping effort. The Maritime Safety Board – later renamed the Maritime Safety Agency (MSA) – was created with the transfer of 28 former Imperial Navy auxiliary sub-chasers from the Demobilization Ministry. Although under the control of the Ministry of Transport (MoT), the coast guard was deliberately constituted to serve as the nucleus of a future navy.[32]

The difference between official attitudes towards naval and ground rearmament is demonstrated by the fact that even as Yoshida negotiated with the Occupation authorities over the size of a reconstituted army, in October 1950, 46 minesweepers from the *kōro keibitai*, now under MSA command, were hastily assembled and ordered to assist in mine clearance operations in support of US amphibious operations in Wonsan Bay, Korea. During operations, one Japanese vessel sank, eight personnel were wounded and one killed.[33] Subsequently, Admiral Arleigh Burke together with a circle of ex-Imperial Navy officers led by Admiral Nomura Kichisaburō (who would later embark on a political career in the Diet) jointly developed plans for Japan's maritime forces that, in addition to performing peacetime constabulary and coast guard functions, would include a role 'in the defense of her own country and in defense of the high seas surrounding the Japanese archipelago'. In April 1951, Burke wrote:

> I personally believe that the solution to this quandary lies in the formation of a small group of United States Naval Officers to study, plan, and direct the initiation of a small Japanese Navy. This Japanese Navy need not be called a Navy. It can be called a Coast Guard or anything else. ... I should think it might be desirable to augment this group ... with about ten Japanese ex-naval officers. This contingent would become the nucleus of the Japanese Navy Department'.[34]

The United States planned initially to create 'a small seagoing force' of sonar-equipped anti-submarine patrol ships in the event of a conflict with the Soviet Union. Admiral Nomura and other senior ex-Imperial Navy officers, such as Hoshina Zenshirō,[35] won the backing of Yoshida as well as future prime minister Hatoyama Ichirō for the necessity of rebuilding a Japanese Navy.[36] Although the Nomura group received a cold reception from Yoshida and Dulles for its plan to reconstitute a navy composed of 337 vessels, totalling 300,000 tons and 750 aircraft, their lobbying efforts within the US Navy and Japan's civil authorities won backing for the creation of the Maritime Guard Force (*kaijō keibitai*) as an autonomous unit within the MSA.[37] In April 1952, the Maritime Guard Force was established before the Coastal Safety Force succeeded it in August. Neither unit possessed operational capabilities beyond minesweeping, but in organizational terms they were naval in all but name and mostly staffed by former Imperial Navy officers and sailors. The NPRF and Coastal Safety Force were merged under the National Safety Agency, emerging as the 110,000-man National Safety Force and the Maritime Safety Force in August 1952. The National Safety Agency was placed under the direction of the Prime Minister's Office (*kantei*).

To equip the *de facto* navy, agreement was reached with the United States to charter surplus US vessels in November 1952, resulting in the transfer of six frigates and three landing ships in January 1953. A further Naval Vessel Loan Agreement was concluded in May 1954, paving the way for the loan of 159 ships, worth $80 million, including destroyers, support vessels and a single submarine.[38] The United States continued to supply one-third of MSDF tonnage and aircraft until 1967, when the military aid programme to Japan was terminated.

Protection of maritime transport up to the Fourth Defense Build-up Plan

Post-war Japanese proposals for a naval role in protecting shipping, in the form of convoys over the high seas, date back to 1952. In August, the *seido chōsa iinkai* (Systems Investigative Committee), was established as a supra-ministerial body designed to aid in the drafting of government policy. It incorporated a defence sub-committee responsible for drafting armed forces requirements for Japan, based on its analysis of global conditions and the Security Treaty. The newly formed Maritime Safety Force contributed its assessment, based on a long-range maritime force estimate drawn up by uniformed officials within the MSA. The sub-committee recommended that Japan would require naval forces totalling 475,000 tons. It was envisaged that this very substantial force would be constructed with the help of US military aid over a 13-year period, involving government expenditures of 8 trillion yen. The subcommittee concluded that maintaining 'supply lanes on the seas' was one of the core objectives of national defence. To this end, the acquisition of 'maritime defence potential' would serve the 'primary objective of maritime convoying and anti-submarine warfare'. Specifically, the plan recommended that: 'Convoys along coastal and territorial waters will be conducted in full, while one-third convoys on the high-sea are conducted'.[39]

This was the first official attempt to factor the security dimensions of Japan's rising economic dependence on imports into post-war military planning. The *seido chōsa iinkai* sub-committee estimated that funding for the plan would require up to 8 per cent of the government's annual expenditure to complete. The plan met with active opposition from the Ministry of Finance (MoF) in the austere conditions of the immediate post-Occupation period.[40] Such was the stringent supervision of the MoF over the JDA's budgetary claims (including via its personnel seconded to the Agency) that 'civilian control' has been seen as synonymous with MoF control.[41] After 1955, more modest acquisition targets for the MSDF were proposed, with force estimates ranging from 81,000 to 143,000 tons. However, the government was not able to embark on any long-range defence plan until the Basic Policy for National Defense was passed in May 1957. On 14 June, Prime Minister Kishi Nobusuke's cabinet embarked on the first of four 4-year defence build-up plans (*bōei seibi keikaku*).

Intended to span five years but shortened to three, the First Defense Build-up Plan (1958–60) was concerned with building up the core capability of the SDF. The tonnage of the MSDF was set at 124,000 tons. The Second Defense Build-up Plan (1962–66) ventured further, committing Japan to build up defence forces 'able to cope effectively with an aggression at or lower than [the level of] a local war, using conventional weapons'. The MSDF fleet was expanded to 140,000 tons to increase its ASW capabilities, although its logistical base remained under-developed. The Third Defense Build-up Plan outlined as a further objective for the MSDF, 'increasing the ability to defend coastal areas, straits and surrounding waters'. The NDC approved the following additions to the MSDF inventory: 56 vessels of all types amounting to 48,000 tons; 14 destroyers, including Japan's first surface-to-air missile (SAM) and helicopter-equipped models, 5 submarines as well as 60 fixed-wing ASW patrol aircraft and 33 ASW helicopters.[42]

For the first time, under the Third Defense Build-up Plan the 'protection of maritime transportation' (*kaijō kōtsū no hogo*) was officially added to Japan's defence responsibilities.[43] Specifically, the Third Defense Build-up Plan detailed emergency plans to establish two sea 'route zones' (*kōrotai*) to the southwest and southeast of Japan's major Pacific ports. The southwestern route (*nansei kōrotai*) was defined as 150 nm wide and 840 nm long, extending from Osaka along the axis of the Ryūkyū Islands/Nansei Shotō to the Bashi Channel, between Taiwan and the Philippines. A second, southeastern route zone (*nantō kōrotai*), 240 nm wide, extended 1,000 nm from Tokyo along the axis of the Ogasawara/Bonin Islands to a point north of Guam. Both 'route zones' extended approximately to the Twentieth Parallel. At this time, these island chains were still under US administration: the Ogasawara Islands were transferred to Japanese sovereignty in 1968; the Bonin Islands/Kazan Rettō in 1971; and the Ryūkyū Islands in 1972.

In testimony to the Special Committee for Okinawa and the Northern Territories, on 30 November 1970, the chief bureaucrat at the JDA, Kubo Takuya, who was to play an important role in the development of defence policy during the 1970s, became the first official to stipulate the geographical scope of the MSDF's sea lane defence concept in the Diet, stating that

> the Southeast route extends in a corridor about 100 miles wide from Tokyo Bay in the direction of Saipan for 1,000 miles. The southwest route goes through Osaka and Kyūshū to the end of the Ryūkyū island chain in a corridor also about 100 miles wide whose exact length slips my mind at the moment, but is also nearly 1,000 miles.[44]

During the 1960s, MSDF staff officers conducted a war game to determine escort requirements for convoy operations between Japan and the Philippines and Guam. It estimated that to maintain daily import requirements of 150,000 tons, a convoy of 60 ships would have to arrive every three days, requiring a total of 54 destroyer escorts (DE). However, even assuming the entire surface fleet could be tasked to convoy duties in wartime, the MSDF possessed only 38 destroyers by the end of the Third Defense Build-up Plan, in 1971. Auer's contemporary judgement was that 'if Japan's naval forces have been built up to protect its ocean-going merchant shipping, it could be considered that its relative progress has been negative'.[45]

Despite the fact that past US, British and Japanese attempts to implement a concept of patrolled sea lanes had proved disastrous in wartime compared with convoy (as noted in Chapters 2 and 3), MSDF plans for the protection of shipping embraced such a concept in response to the growing gulf between the MSDF's limited escort resources and Japan's rapidly expanding merchant fleet.[46]

Autonomous defence and MSDF capabilities

Between 1969 and 1971, during the Third Defense Build-up Plan, the question of an 'autonomous' or 'self-reliant' defence posture (*jishu bōei*) received consideration in Japan's defence and business circles. According to Nakasone Yasuhiro, who was JDA Director General from January 1970 to July 1971, the basic concept called for Japan, while maintaining exclusive dependence on the US nuclear umbrella, to 'make the Self-Defense Force the main element in the country's conventional defence and to complement this with the Japan–U.S. mutual security system'.[47] Particular emphasis was laid upon the need to develop Japan's 'maritime power', in the form of a major naval build-up, in which the JDA was backed by segments of the business community. A 'Malacca Straits defence theory' (*maraka bōeiron*) also appeared around the same time.[48]

During the drafting of a fourth plan to be budgeted from fiscal 1972–73, the JDA departed from the pattern of incremental build-up established under the first three defence build-up programmes to propose a major expansion of Japan's defense capabilities. 'Autonomous' defense arose in a strategic context shaped by the draw-down of US ground troops in Vietnam, from 1969 onwards, which for the first time challenged assumptions underlying the Yoshida Doctrine by raising questions about the reliability of US treaty commitments in Asia. This assertiveness from the Agency was closely associated with Nakasone's 18-month JDA directorship, an example of the importance of individual policy-makers in the formation of Japan's defence policy despite the 'faceless', consensual image often ascribed to decision-making in Japan.[49]

Negotiations for the reversion of Okinawa to Japanese sovereignty influenced the defence debate in several ways. In a direct sense, although US forces were to remain there, the transfer of the Ryūkyū Islands to Tokyo's control promised to extend the SDF's responsibilities for territorial defence (concerning mainly the MSDF and ASDF), virtually to Taiwan. At a jointly held JDA and MOFA press conference in May 1969, JDA officials outlined three implications of the reversion of Okinawa for defence policy:

1 While Japan's defence posture has previously been based on a gradual consolidation of defence power and maintaining the US–Japan Security Treaty in view of the internal and external situations, the growth of national power and the improvement of Japan's international status, defence efforts will be more positively pushed forward in the future, and defence power, capable of coping effectively and flexibly with the state of direct or indirect aggression, will be perfected.
2 Japan would assume primary responsibility for the defence of Okinawa after reversion. Regarding the maritime defence of Okinawa, Japan should acquire the necessary defence power for the patrolling of the sea areas around Okinawa, maintaining and controlling ports, *and the securing of the Nansei sea lane around Okinawa, in the same way as in the sea areas around the homeland.*[50]
3 For our country which is surrounded on all four sides by the sea, and which bases its existence on trade, the securing of the safety of maritime transport is an indispensable factor for the survival of our country. Further efforts will be made for the strengthening of our maritime defence power and for the improvement of defence of the straits and maritime escort.

Despite such declarations, no details were forthcoming about projected costs or equipment that the JDA intended to procure under the proposed Fourth Defense Build-up Plan until Nakasone joined the JDA. A detailed draft of the 'New Plan' or 'Nakasone Plan', so-named to advertise a departure from the gradualist pace of previous build-up plans, was released in April 1970. The plan was among several controversial moves associated with Nakasone's term as JDA Director General, including a proposal to revise the Basic Policy for National Defense to formalize a supplementary role for the alliance in Japan's defence policy.[51] The draft of the Nakasone Plan stipulated that the SDF should be able to deal independently with 'limited, direct aggression' by securing air and sea control around Japanese territory. Reflecting the importance of maritime defence, the plan called for a doubling of the MSDF fleet from 142,000 to 320,000 tons within a decade. Plans to protect maritime transportation within the *nansei* and *nantō kōrotai* were linked to the planned acquisition of two 8,000-ton helicopter carriers, each of which would be capable of carrying six helicopters to conduct ASW patrols to the Bashi channel (between Taiwan and the Philippines) and north of Guam.[52] The 'Nakasone Plan' was provisionally budgeted at between 5.7 and 6.5 trillion yen, or roughly double the expenditure of the Third Defence Build-up Plan.[53]

Support for autonomous defence was forthcoming from the Federation of Economic Organizations (*keidanren*) which was briefed by the JDA on its plans for defending Japan's commercial shipping lanes. At its general meeting in 1969, the *keidanren* passed a resolution backing autonomous defence and a doubling of the ratio of defence spending to GNP, from around 1 to 2 per cent.[54] The support expressed by business for autonomous defence in the late 1960s was driven in large part by the growth of interest in autonomous defence production, which although accounting for just 0.5 per cent of industrial output by 1970, was disproportionately important for the development of technology through research and development.[55]

In addition to the commercial interest of major corporations such as Mitsubishi Heavy Industries (which then occupied a 38 per cent market share of the defence sector) in a doubling of defence expenditure, some elements within big business were sympathetic to the argument that a long-range Japanese naval presence would reduce the vulnerability of Japanese merchant shipping and regarded a Japanese defence role in Southeast Asia as a natural extension of the development of the region as an export market and source of raw materials.[56] Other business lobby groups such as the *keizai dōyukai* subscribed to the linkage between Japan's import dependence and increasing the size of the MSDF, advocating a Japanese naval protection role overlapping its oil routes through the Straits of Malacca to the Indian Ocean.[57] Particular concern surrounded the security of the Straits of Malacca, given Japan's status as the largest user, the impending withdrawal of the Royal Navy from Singapore, an increased Soviet naval presence and rising assertiveness on the part of the littoral states.[58] (Japan's sea lane diplomacy towards Southeast Asia is explored in Chapter 6.) The President of Tokyo Electric Power, Kikawada Kazutaka, who was reportedly the inspiration behind the *maraka bōeiron*, argued that although Japan should cooperate with regional states to ensure access through the straits, an expanded MSDF should also have a role in preserving access for Japanese shipping there given the cost of diversion if the straits were closed to tankers.[59]

Since the MSDF's formation, two camps have debated its basic role: those who have argued for the necessity of an ocean-going navy to protect Japan's sea lanes, against advocates of a more limited coastal anti-invasion force. Sekino Hideo and Kaihara Osamu respectively articulated these viewpoints.[60]

Sekino's SLOC defence concept

In May 1971, Sekino Hideo, an ex-Imperial Navy officer and Commander in the MSDF (who was among those staff officers involved in the convoying exercise between Japan and the Philippines and Guam referred to above) articulated his views about Japan's strategic environment and the role of the MSDF in an essay for the *US Naval Institute's Proceedings*.[61] Sekino mapped out a maritime strategy for Japan in which the protection of sea communications would have priority.

Flanked by potentially hostile powers on the Asian mainland and dependent upon long lines of supply for imports critical to its survival, Sekino saw Japan's role as a Pacific sea power as a strategic necessity determined by geography and the distribution of natural resources rather than nostalgia for the 'mistakes' of the pre-1945 period.[62] Acknowledging Japan's inability to defend itself unaided against the Soviet Union or to protect its global trading interests independently, Sekino thought that some form of alliance with the United States would be necessary 'as far ahead as can be foreseen', while relying on diplomacy to secure commercial access to natural resources.[63] Against invasion, to compensate for the 'unchanging geographical disadvantage of insufficient strategical width', Japan would have to rely on the US Air Force and Seventh Fleet as 'the most effective power to prevent direct aggression against Japan'.[64]

Regarding the security of trade routes, Sekino acknowledged the impossibility of single-handedly defending Japan's sea lanes to the Persian Gulf and beyond. In a crisis, Japan would not be able to depend on the cooperation of oil-producing states in the Persian Gulf, nor be able to guarantee the 40 per cent of its trade, which passed across the Indian Ocean. Within the scope of practicable capabilities in the Pacific Basin, Japan could hope to maintain economic access to Southeast Asia, Oceania and the Americas through a combination of diplomacy and the 'cooperation of American and Australian sea power'. Given these strategic parameters, Sekino maintained that Japan's vulnerability was such that it simply could not afford to ignore the safety of its seaborne commerce.

Three military threat scenarios facing Japan were identified: nuclear attack, invasion and a *guerre de course*, each potentially jeopardizing the survival of the state. The probability of a nuclear attack or invasion occurring was judged to be 'virtually nil', because of the deterrent effect of Article V of the 1960 US–Japan Security Treaty. In contrast, a *guerre de course* directed at Japan's maritime commerce was judged the most likely scenario. Sekino's reasoning for this was twofold. First, with the growth of its annual imports to around 300,000 tons, Sekino believed that a blockade of seaborne imports of fuel, raw materials, foodstuffs and military supplies could choke Japan's industrial base and its war-fighting ability as it had done during the Pacific War, despite the apparent restraining influence of nuclear weapons on large-scale conflict (see Chapter 3). Second, Sekino suggested that an aggressor would actively favour the *guerre de course* as an means of applying indirect military pressure on Japan at comparatively low risk of US retaliation because, under the terms of Article V of the Security Treaty, 'Japan cannot expect the cooperation of the powerful Seventh Fleet in protecting maritime traffic'.[65] Envisaging that a Soviet naval campaign against Japanese shipping would be accompanied by domestic political unrest orchestrated by Communist sympathizers, he speculated: 'Such a two-pronged offensive would deplete both the nation's livelihood and the fighting power of the self-defense forces.' With Japan domestically divided over the legitimacy of defence and security relations with the United States, small-scale attacks on shipping might be launched in order to undermine Japanese confidence in the Security Treaty and sap the national will to resist; their 'psychological' effect achieving strategic objectives out of all proportion to the physical damage inflicted and forces committed. Sekino argued the MSDF should prioritize the protection of sea communications in Japan's defence over an anti-invasion role, to 'hold out' long enough for US forces to intervene, or to inflict sufficient attrition on enemy submarines and aircraft to force a halt to attacks on shipping.

Sekino argued that it would be a realistic objective for Japan to meet its basic monthly import requirements in wartime, at half the rate of peacetime consumption or about 150,000 tons, to fall back on Southeast Asia, Australasia and the Americas as a supply base, and establish a 'maritime safety zone' in the waters north of Indonesia for the passage of merchant vessels and military supplies. By utilizing geographic factors in its favour, Sekino thought that a viable sea lane defence concept could be developed in concert with the United States and regional states, in which the MSDF would have primary responsibility.

In case of a war with the Soviet Union, Sekino anticipated that 'attacks on Japanese sea communications by submarines and airplanes must be the main tasks of the Soviet Pacific Fleet, if it should operate against Japan'.[66] Soviet long-range, land-based aviation, principally Tu-95 *Bears* and Tu-16 *Badgers*, would be 'well suited for finding and attacking convoys'. However, since they would have to operate without fighter escort in order to attack shipping passing south of Japan, Sekino judged that 'large-scale attacks by these planes would not be expected'.[67] The major threat foreseen was from the Soviet Pacific submarine fleet, which he estimated at 100 boats of all types. Against Soviet Pacific Fleet units concentrated at Vladivostok, Japan would be able to block access from the Sea of Japan through the key straits controlling access to the Pacific and Sea of Okhotsk, by monitoring the straits in peacetime and preparing to mine them in war. Controlling the Tsugaru and Shimonoseki straits, Japan would also be able to inhibit Soviet naval passage through the Tsushima (Korea) Strait and Sōya (La Perouse) Strait, leaving only the shallow and often ice-bound Tartar Strait, separating Sakhalin and Russia's Maritime Province, wholly beyond Japan's reach.[68]

Since the blockade of straits alone could not be expected to prevent all enemy submarines and aircraft from infiltrating into the Pacific and East China Sea, Sekino proposed to exploit other features of Japan's archipelagic geography, by building chains of acoustic listening stations and air bases located on islands along its southwest and southeasterly approaches. To the southwest, the Amami and Ryūkyū Islands stretched almost to Taiwan. Beyond Taiwan, the Philippine archipelago would complete a partial barrier against the East China and South China Seas, as far south as Borneo. To the south-east, the Izu/Ogasawara Bonin/Kazan Rettō chains (Nampō Shotō), combined with the Marianas and Micronesia to form a second island screen facing the open waters of the Pacific.

In terms remarkably similar to those drawn up by Admiral Oikawa's Imperial Navy staff in 1943, Sekino envisioned the creation of a vast 'protected lake' within an arc of open water between these two elongated island chains stretching from Japan to Indonesia, through which Japanese merchant ships and supply vessels could sail in relative security, transporting enough strategic commodities and materiel to ensure national survival. Within the 'maritime safety zone' itself, patrol aircraft, attack submarines, destroyers and escorts assigned to high-value convoys would operate in coordinated fashion to minimize reaction times. Sekino was confident that 'hunter-killer teams' would be able to detect and destroy most Soviet submarines. Very-low-frequency active sonar and passive hydrophone arrays dispersed at intervals along the eastern island chain would ensure a 'high chance that targets would be detected during their passage from 100, or even 200, miles away', enabling 'patrol planes and helicopters based on some of these

Table 4.1 Sekino's optimal MSDF force structure

ASW forces (415,500 tons)
6 nuclear-powered attack submarines (SSN) of 3,000 tons each
9 conventionally-powered attack submarines (SSK) of 1,500 tons each
3 small helicopter carriers of 20,000 tons each
66 DD of 4,000 tons each
30 DE of 2,000 tons each
Counter-invasion/coastal defence (118,000 tons)
16 DD of 4,000 tons each
16 DE of 2,000 tons each
Mine warfare (32,000 tons)
60 coastal minesweeping craft of 400 tons each
4 mine-layer craft of 2,000 tons each
Air wing (570 aircraft)
198 land-based aircraft
24 flying boats
348 helicopters

Source: Adapted from Sekino, 'Japan and Her Maritime Defense', *US Naval Institute Proceedings*, May 1971, vol. 97, no. 819, pp. 98–121.

islands . . . to reach the points of detection within one hour'.[69] While Soviet nuclear submarines operating south of Japan would be unaffected by fuel limitations, Sekino claimed that their effective range would be constrained by Japan's cumulative surveillance, patrol and ASW activities.

To carry out the maritime safety zone concept, Sekino estimated that a fleet of around 500,000 tons and 570 aircraft would be needed (Table 4.1).

It was estimated that partial implementation could be achieved with 300,000 tons and 400 aircraft. With its actual strength of about 130,000 tons and around 40 ASW ships, in 1971, Sekino judged that the MSDF 'is able only to protect in convoys 20–30 per cent of the nation's maritime transportation, for a distance of several hundred miles from Japan; that is in the waters bounded by the mainland, the Nampō Islands and Nansei Islands'.[70] However, at a minimum, Sekino thought tankers could be escorted from Palau, between Saipan and Indonesia, which he proposed could be developed as a staging and storage points for Japan's oil supplies in wartime.

While the concept of a Maritime Safety Zone and the build-up of Japan's ASW forces was predicated upon a potential threat to Japanese merchant shipping, Sekino thought that Japan's military task would be:

> to relieve the U.S. Polaris submarines and the Seventh Fleet of the dangers of enemy submarines by means of the safety zone, because these forces would then be more secure in carrying out their missions. In this manner, Japan could enhance the security of sea communications which bind together, and permit the survival of, the nations of the free world in the Pacific. Furthermore, this may be the maximum measure permitted Japan at sea under our current Constitution.[71]

That Sekino's views represented more than a marginal view within the MSDF is suggested by the publication of an internal JDA instruction pamphlet dating from February 1970. The pamphlet, disclosed in a 1980 article by Nishijima Ryōichi, outlined the importance of a blue-water sea lane defence role for the MSDF, stating:

> The removal of threats against our sea lanes of communication is vital in securing survival of the nation. All threats, including the direct invasion of our homeland, could be more easily prevented in advance if the attack from the sea is stemmed or thwarted. . . . So we must try to oppose and destroy the enemy fleet to secure our sea lanes of communication. A defensive 'fortress strategy' is not a realistic one. Those large-scale offensive operations we are not allowed to carry out under the restrictions of the present constitution despite their necessity will have to be conducted by the US forces but the MSDF should work in the direction of mitigating the limitations as much as it can in order to eliminate the danger of becoming a besieged fleet.[72]

Kaihara's counter-view

Kaihara Osamu was a senior official within the NDC whose more restrictive view of defence posture was both representative of non-uniform JDA officials and a natural counterweight to the navalist views of Sekino. Kaihara held in common with Sekino that the SDF were chronically under-prepared to achieve their stated mission of rebuffing a conventional attack on Japan. However, Kaihara was determined to resist the ambitions of MSDF officers to expand the scale and scope of maritime operations to protect Japan's sea lanes, which he regarded as an echo of the strategic debates of the 1930s, when Imperial Navy officers had helped to lead Japan into an 'unwinnable' war with the United States. Kaihara would remain a forceful, public critic of the sea lanes defence concept when it resurfaced as the focus of alliance cooperation in the 1980s.

Kaihara's reading of Japan's strategic liabilities, as an island nation located near Asia's military power centres, lacking in strategic depth, devoid of natural resources and with a concentrated urban infrastructure and population, led him to the opposite of Sekino's 'unrealistic' conclusions.[73] He argued that Japan's strategic vulnerabilities would put the SDF at such an obvious disadvantage in any conflict with the Soviet Union – its main potential adversary – that its only rational mission should be conventional deterrence against an invasion. In his eyes, charging the MSDF with protecting Japan's commercial sea lanes was a nostalgically driven 'beautiful dream', reflecting a 'guilty conscience' over the Imperial Navy's negligence in failing to protect Japan's merchant arm during the Pacific War.

Kaihara criticized the use of abstract terms such as 'sea route zones' (*kōrotai*), 'protection of maritime transportation' and 'sea lanes defence' (*shiirēn bōei*) as lacking in concrete meaning or operational utility. He argued that sea lanes were not static areas of sea space capable of being defended like territory, but potentially limitless. Even if such a task were possible, Kaihara argued that Japan lacked the resources to commit to such an undertaking. Moreover, the technical difficulties involved in each of the four stages of ASW – detection, classification, localization and destruction – suggested that the MSDF would be unable to prevent a determined Soviet Pacific submarine force from attacking Japanese commerce, a force which by the beginning of the 1970s outnumbered the total US submarine fleet at the outbreak of war in 1941 by a factor of three. Furthermore, a strategic requirement to blockade Soviet submarines within the Sea of Japan would be highly provocative, probably unconstitutional and risk a pre-emptive air strike that would decimate the largely unprotected frontline equipment and infrastructure of the SDF.

Kaihara criticized Nakasone's plan to defend the *nansei* and *nantō kōrotai* from 'rampaging' Soviet submarines with two ASW helicopter carriers, as operationally non-viable. The southeastern sea route alone, 1,000 nm long and 240 nm wide, contained a surface area of 777,600 km^2, or double that of Japan itself.[74] He disputed the notion that a single-helicopter carrier deployed on patrol could establish sub-surface sea control over such a vast area of open ocean, interpreting the JDA's focus on the submarine threat as a justification for the acquisition of expensive, ocean-going ASW escorts and long-range patrol aircraft.

Kaihara argued that the defence of sea lanes, as an abstract, was an illusory concept beyond the reach of even the US Navy. He cited a 1970 assessment by a senior ASW officer in the US Navy, Vice-Admiral T. F. Caldwell, that the US Navy would be unable to mount continuous trans-atlantic convoys in wartime, and a similar statement by the Chief of Naval Operations, Admiral James Holloway, in 1975, that the United States would be unable to guarantee convoys of oil tankers from the Gulf to Europe and North America.[75] Although smaller navies such as the Royal Navy possessed the capability to secure sea transport in chokepoints such as the Dover Strait, doing so within areas of open sea was 'impossible'. If the US Navy and its western allies struggled with the task of sea-lane protection in the Atlantic and Indian Oceans, Kaihara asked, what hope could Japan have of achieving this on its own in the Pacific? Although he was not opposed to MSDF participation in patrol or convoy operations in the Northwest Pacific, if the United States requested Japan's assistance, this mission did not in his opinion equate with the security of Japan's commercial sea lanes. In contrast to Sekino's advocacy of a blue-water role for Japan extending throughout the Western Pacific, Kaihara concluded that the more operationally realistic and constitutionally legitimate goal for the MSDF should be to improve its capability to counter an invasion – a mission that would confine its duties to Japan's coastal periphery.

The primacy of constraints

From 1972, Japanese defence policy reverted to the incremental approach of previous LDP-led governments, based on the consolidation of existing capabilities. The 'dream' of autonomous defence foundered together with Nakasone's draft version of the Fourth Defense Build-up Programme, while discussion of the *maraka bōeiron* also ebbed. In the debate over what kind of defence policy Japan should develop for the 1970s, it was essentially Kaihara's viewpoint, stressing territorial defence over maritime force projection, that prevailed, although not to the extent that the MSDF was retrenched to a coastal defence force. Domestic and external constraints were instrumental in this process, while bureaucratic politics and personalities were also important.

After Nakasone left the JDA in mid-1971, the Agency suffered a succession of scandals and accidents, including the collision of an ASDF fighter and a passenger jet in July, which further disadvantaged its position as a sub-ministerial organ within the government. Nakasone's immediate successors at the JDA were short-lived in the post, less charismatic and either unable or unwilling to support the draft so closely associated with their predecessor, which was duly rejected by the NDC. A less ambitious version put forward by the Agency was returned and a third version, heavily trimmed by the MoF, was finally approved by the cabinet in October 1972.

Neither Prime Minister Satō Eisaku's administration, nor the successor government of Tanaka Kakuei had any wish to revisit the controversy generated at home and abroad by Nakasone's draft plan, and defence was subordinated to higher policy priorities in the period 1972–75, including finalizing the Okinawa reversion, normalizing relations with the People's Republic of China and implementing austerity measures to cope with the 1973–74 Oil Crisis. Although Nakasone had been intensely conscious of the need to forge greater public support for the SDF, an agenda that he would also pursue as prime minister in the 1980s, his attempts whilst at the JDA to propel policy ahead of popular and bureaucratic consensus heightened domestic divisions and aroused suspicions abroad. This experience demonstrated to the LDP leadership and civilian planners at the JDA that further increases in defence spending were politically unsupportable.

Autonomous defence also failed to gain political backing because Satō was preoccupied with the Okinawa reversion, finalized in May 1972. In addition to the practical challenges of expanded territorial defence responsibilities, symbolically, the recovery of Okinawa boosted the confidence of Japanese leaders, for whom the return of the islands and rule from Tokyo had long been a goal and as such marked a watershed in the country's relationship with the United States. The security implications of the handover were addressed in the Joint Communiqué released by President Richard Nixon and Prime Minister Satō in January 1972. By explicitly linking Japan's security with Korea and Taiwan, and the role of US bases in Okinawa to maintaining the security of the region, the Communiqué alleviated the uncertainity of Japanese decision-makers about the future of the US security guarantee which, at the strategic level, had fanned official consideration of autonomous defence. Conversely, by removing ambiguities about the freedom of US forces to operate out of bases in Okinawa, the Nixon–Satō Communiqué also settled US security concerns related to reversion, but did little to alleviate local frictions caused by the heavy US presence on the island, which would continue to dog bilateral security relations.[76] However, the political triumph of Okinawa's return was short-lived for the Satō government, which quickly foundered under the weight of political scandals and fell from power only three months later.

The incoming administration of Tanaka Kakuei, despite his own assertive brand of conservatism, was receptive to quantitative restrictions on Japan's defence capability, partly to stem opposition attacks over defence spending, which had continued to increase in the absence of a finally approved version of the Fourth Defence Build-up Plan. Moreover, China had emerged as a new foreign policy variable following President Nixon's 'shock' re-establishment of US–China relations in February 1972. China had been a vociferous critic of the Nakasone Plan and in October 1971, the official *Peking Review* signalled growing concern about Japan's ambitions to develop a naval presence in the Malacca Straits, alleging that the LDP had circulated an internal report on maritime defence including a reference to securing its 'maritime lifeline' in the straits and to building up 'the military strength to meet requirements'. In response, Nakasone's successor as JDA Director General reassured opposition parties in the Diet that it would be 'inconceivable that MSDF craft could ever operate in the Straits of Malacca, let alone the Indian Ocean'.[77]

In October 1972, while visiting Beijing to discuss normalization with the People's Republic, Tanaka offered to impose an official limit on Japanese defence spending of 1 per cent of GNP to Zhou Enlai, Mao Zedong's foreign minister. On 6 October, one week after returning from Beijing, Tanaka directed the JDA to draw up limits for 'Defense Strength in Peacetime' (*heiwaji no bōeiryoku*), partly to allay Chinese concerns about Japan's defence build-up, as well as to draw the teeth of Diet opposition shortly before the cabinet was set to approve procurement plans for the Fourth Defense Build-up Plan. Neither Satō (Kishi Nobusuke's younger brother) nor Tanaka were considered natural 'doves', but both were led by domestic and external constraints to adopt moderate stances in defence policy. When Tanaka was forced to step down over the Lockheed corruption scandal in late 1974, he was succeeded by Prime Minister Miki Takeo, a moderate on defence by conviction, rather than convenience. His leadership and that of his successors, Fukuda Takeo and Ohira Masayoshi ensured that a favourable political climate was established in which a systematic review of defence policy to formalize the *ad hoc* moderate approach of the Satō and Tanaka administrations could be achieved.

Jishu bōei also ran into opposition from the influential ministries concerning security policy. MOFA had cooperated with the JDA in 1969 in return for its assistance in brokering the technical aspects of the defence implications of the Okinawa handover with the US military, as a means of improving its bargaining position with the United States during negotiations over Okinawa.[78] This cooperation ended once the Okinawa question was superseded by normalization with China as the main diplomatic priority. However, the most trenchant opposition to an expansion of defence spending came from the MoF.[79]

From its initial 1969 announcement of a planned Fourth Defense Build-up Plan until the release of Nakasone's draft plan in April 1970, the JDA had been careful to avoid releasing detailed cost estimates. However, as the plan was understood to require a doubling of defence expenditure, the MoF regarded *jishu bōei* as a threat to its fiscal goal of maintaining defence spending within 1 per cent of GNP. In an indication of the influence which the Ministry exerted over the JDA, the MoF went as far as to issue a rebuttal to the strategic premise of the JDA's proposals for expanding Japan's maritime defence, in 1969. The MoF advanced three specific counter-arguments:

> Firstly, the reversion of Okinawa did not justify the expansion of Japan's defence capabilities, because 'it is not conceivable at all that (a foreign power) will invade Japan through Okinawa' as long as U.S. forces remained there.
>
> Secondly, convoying was no longer effective, given the increase in Japan's fuel consumption and the impossibility of directly protecting the number of tankers required to import an estimated 100 million tons of crude oil per year.
>
> Thirdly, the JDA's plans to defend maritime transportation meant exceeding the threshold of localized conflict outlined in the Third Defense Build-up Plan because attacks on Japan's shipping lanes could be conducted remotely and were likely to involve foreign merchant ships, the defence of which would exceed the constitutional mandate for self-defence.[80]

When the JDA released its 5.2 billion yen cost estimate for the Fourth Plan, in April 1970, the MoF argued against any increase on the grounds that this exceeded the projected GNP growth rate. Ultimately, a diminished budget of 4.6 billion yen was agreed upon in October 1972.[81] Defence spending nonetheless grew 17 per cent in 1972–76, even as it continued to decline as a proportion of government spending, from 7.0 to 6.2 per cent. However, a government-wide austerity programme ordered in the wake of the Oil Crisis subjected the defence budget to tighter controls as Japan was plunged into its first post-war recession in 1974 and the NDC placed a freeze on defence acquisitions in December 1975.

Acquisitions slated for the MSDF as part of the final version of the Fourth Defense Build-up Plan included a total of 13 destroyers equipped with SAM, surface-to-surface missiles (SSM) and helicopters, 5 submarines, a fleet support ship and 92 combat aircraft. However, at the end of fiscal 1976, owing to the procurement freeze, the MSDF lagged behind its acquisition targets by more than 30 per cent. Only 8 of the intended 13 destroyers had been built and the MSDF's plans to acquire its first supply ship had to be sacrificed.[82] MSDF strength in August 1975 stood at 45 escort ships, 40 mine-countermeasures craft, 35 patrol boats and 15 submarines, with vessels of all types amounting to less than 200,000 tons.

The National Defense Program Outline (*taikō*)

Reflecting the above confluence of factors, civilians within the JDA were well placed to push a moderate agenda in the early 1970s. The most important of these was Kubo Takuya, head of the JDA Defense Policy Bureau from November 1970 to June 1974 and subsequently appointed Administrative Vice-Minister – the top bureaucratic post in the agency. Kubo came to the Defence Agency from a police background, concerned that the incremental build-up of SDF capabilities should not open-ended. Beginning in 1971, he began circulating memos within the Agency written under a pseudonym, canvassing support for a strategic policy framework to guide defence policy beyond the scheduled completion of the Fourth Defense Build-up Plan, in 1976.[83] Kubo's model of a Standard Defense Force Concept (*kibanteki no bōeiryoku kōsō*) evolved gradually and was broadened through the input of civilian advisory groups to eventually underpin the 1976 National Defense Program Outline, or *taikō*, which served as the foundation of defence policy until its revision in 1995.

In common with Nakasone, Kubo emphasized that an essential condition of an effective defence capability was to build domestic support for the SDF. He also perceived Japan's defence dilemma to be peculiarly acute owing to lingering suspicions about Japanese militarism in the region, believing that any attempt by Japan to compensate for perceived vulnerability through an independent military build-up was liable to spur a regional arms race. Externally, Kubo determined that in a security context defined globally by superpower détente and regionally by the maintenance of the US–Japan security relationship, Japan's strategic environment was likely to remain benign. On this basis it was decided that the posture of the SDF could be premised on the probability that no major threats were likely to emerge within a 10-year time frame. SDF capabilities could therefore be capped approximately at the levels already attained by the early 1970s without undermining security. Kaihara thought that the qualitative force levels detailed in the final, scaled-back version of the Fourth Defence Build-up Programme, subject to qualitative improvements in certain areas, were sufficient to provide a deterrent against 'small-scale aggression' and to ensure the cooperation of the United States, upon which Japan would continue to rely for extended conventional and nuclear deterrence.

Qualitatively, the Standard Defense Force Concept recommended improvements to SDF capabilities in neglected areas owing to the bias in past procurements towards frontline capabilities. Areas targeted for improvement included force readiness, survivability, logistical support and intelligence. Maintenance of a full surveillance and intelligence posture (dubbed 'a rabbit's ears'; *usagi no mimi*) was highlighted as pivotal to the credibility of a smooth 'defence structure alteration potential in case of substantial geopolitical changes'. Intelligence was one area of defence capability in which moves towards greater defence self-reliance accelerated at a time when the build-up of frontline platforms was being de-emphasized.[84]

Kubo's first opportunity to incorporate the Standard Defense Force Concept into official defence policy came when Prime Minister Tanaka issued the 'Defense Strength in Peacetime' directive to the JDA in October 1972. The concept as announced in the Diet, on 1 February 1973, embodied most of the ideas in the Standard Defense Force Concept and outlined quantitative restrictions similar to force levels already achieved by the Ground and Air SDF:

- GSDF: 5 armies, 13 divisions, 180,000 men;
- ASDF: 3 regional air forces (8 wings); 1 composite wing, 800 aircraft;
- MSDF: 5 regional commands; 4–5 escort flotillas, 280,000 tons.[85]

However, the government was compelled to withdraw the Defense Strength in Peacetime shortly after the draft was put before the Diet, as neither the Socialists not the Communists were prepared to confer *de facto* recognition on the SDF as the price of approving quantitative limits on Japan's defence capabilities.[86] It was not until the Miki administration came to power in December 1974 that a favourable political atmosphere was re-established. Promoted to JDA Vice-Minister in July 1975, Kubo received strong support from both Miki and his new Minister of State for Defense, Sakata Michita, who would remain in charge of the JDA for an unusually long period, from December 1974 to December 1976. Between them, Kubo and Sakata presided over the task of drafting a replacement to the Fourth Defense Build-up Plan, with an up-dated version of the Standard Defense Force Concept as its centre-piece.

Under the guidance of Kubo and Sakata, parallel measures designed to build consensus behind the drafting of a successor plan were implemented. A broad-based civilian advisory panel, the 'Forum on Defense Issues', was set up to widen participation in defence policy to include business leaders and academics such as Kōsaka Masataka. The panel met several times between April and June 1975, its recommendations feeding into the Standard Defense Force Concept. The following June, to signal its commitment to transparency, the JDA released its first defence white paper since 1970, resuming annual publication thereafter.

The Standard Defense Force Concept was incorporated formally into Japan's defence policy with the adoption of the *taikō* by the National Defense Council, approved by the Miki cabinet on 29 October 1976. It identified four requirements to guide future defence capability:

1 Japan should possess the assorted functions required for national defence, including logistical support, while maintaining a balanced structure of organization and deployment.
2 A full surveillance posture should be maintained in peacetime.
3 Japan should be able to effectively deal with any situation up to the level of limited and small-scale aggression.
4 Japan should have a force structure capable of being 'smoothly adapted' when required by a serious change in circumstances.[87]

Quantitative limits on frontline platforms and combat units were set out in an Attached Table (*beppyō*) (Table 4.2).

Maritime capabilities under the taikō

Flowing largely from the operational requirements of its anti-submarine and mine warfare missions, the MSDF structure set out in the *taikō* comprised four major areas:

1 Four escort flotillas, defined as basic, surface anti-submarine units for mobile operations, would be maintained to ensure that one would be operational at all times.[88]

Table 4.2 The Attached Table of the 1976 National Defense Program Outline (*taikō*)

SDF	*Basic units*	*Main equipment*
GSDF	Regional units	12 divisions 2 combined brigades
	Mobile units	1 armoured division 1 artillery brigade 1 airborne brigade 1 training brigade 1 helicopter brigade
	Low altitude ground-to-air missile	8 Anti-Aircraft Artillery Groups (180,000 personnel in total)
ASDF	Aircraft control & warning	28 groups
	Interceptor	10 squadrons
	Support Fighter	3 squadrons
	Air reconnaissance	1 squadron
	Air transport	3 squadrons
	Early warning	1 squadron
	High altitude ground-to-air missile	6 groups
	Main equipment	
	Combat aircraft	Approx. 430
MSDF	ASW surface ship units (for mobile operations)	4 escort flotillas
	ASW surface ship units (regional district units)	10 divisions
	Submarine units	6 divisions
	Minesweeping units	2 flotillas
	Land-based ASW/patrol aircraft	16 squadrons
	Main equipment	
	ASW surface ships	Approx. 60 ships
	Submarines	16 submarines
	Combat aircraft	Approx. 220

Source: Adapted from *Defense of Japan 1995*, Tokyo: JDA/*Japan Times*, p. 270.

2 A total of 10 ship divisions would be deployed within Japan's 5 coastal defence districts, enabling one division per district to be on constant alert to carry out coastal surveillance, defence and anti-submarine operations.
3 Submarine, ASW helicopter and minesweeping units would also be maintained. Six submarine divisions, each composed of two or three boats, would be assigned to conduct surveillance of important harbours and straits. The MSDF's minesweeper force would be divided between coastal units under district-level command, and two flotillas assigned to cover the Sea of Japan.
4 Land-based anti-submarine and patrol aircraft would conduct surveillance missions, patrol nearby seas and protect surface ships.

To meet these operational requirements, relatively few changes in defence equipment were outlined, apart from the addition of two submarines and approximately 10 ASW/maritime surveillance aircraft. The totals set out in the Attached Table allowed for approximately 60 escort destroyers, 16 submarines and 220 combat aircraft. In addition, the MSDF were authorized to possess around 40 offshore and coastal mine warfare ships as well as small numbers of amphibious landing ships and to acquire a fleet replenishment vessel.

The *taikō* spelled an apparent victory for those who had sought quantitative limits against the incremental expansion of defence capability under the numbered defence plans without any accompanying strategic rationale. In other respects, the *taikō* was vague enough to allow for the open-ended qualitative enhancement of defence capability through the operation of smaller numbers of advanced platforms acquired with 'due consideration to qualitative improvements aimed at parity with the technical standards of other nations'. Nor was a completion date specified, or spending guidelines laid down. As an added constraint to mollify the opposition parties, and in accordance with of one the main recommendations of the report issued by the Forum on Defense Issues in September 1975, on 5 November, the Miki administration added the weight of a cabinet resolution to a limit of 1 per cent of GNP ratio on defence spending, which had been observed unofficially since 1967.

While the annual ratio of defence spending to GNP stayed at or below 0.90 per cent from 1976–79, annual defence budgets continued to increase by an average of 12.5 per cent during this period as the economy rebounded from the Oil Crisis. However, the one per cent ceiling helped to neutralize political opposition, enabling the government to treat defence policy increasingly as a budgetary issue to be delegated for technical management within the JDA without engendering the kind of parliamentary controversy that had attended the Fourth Defence Build-up Programme.

*Post-*taikō *maritime capabilities*

During the formulation of the *taikō*, the most keenly debated question related to SDF force structure was whether the MSDF should have four or five escort flotillas. The MSDF maintained that a fifth escort flotilla was necessary, to enable it permanently to assign one flotilla to the Sea of Japan. Given overhaul and crew-rotation requirements, it was argued that a fifth flotilla would provide a reserve capability guaranteeing the MSDF's ability to maintain two flotillas at high readiness and allow it simultaneously to cover the Sea of Japan and Japan's Pacific approaches.[89] The view of the JDA civilian internal bureaux was that four escort flotillas provided sufficient coverage. The failure of MSDF officers and civilian JDA officials to agree upon force structure had resulted in the compromise formula of 4–5 escort groups when the Defense Capability in Peacetime was announced in February 1973. However, during the drafting of the *taikō*, the MSDF's preference for a fifth flotilla was included in the draft version of the Attached Table. Although Prime Minister Tanaka indicated support for a fifth flotilla, according to a senior JDA official at the time, this was resisted by both the JDA and MoF.[90] The strongest resistance came from the MoF, which led to the number of escort flotillas in the final version of the Attached Table being revised down to four. Since 1976, this has remained the basic force structure of the Self-Defense Fleet.[91]

In contrast to the Third and Fourth Defense Build-up Plans, the *taikō* contained no reference to the protection of maritime transportation, although reference to the defence of sea routes out to 1,000 nm was included in materials used by the drafters of the *taikō*.[92] In the final version of the *taikō*, the responsibilities outlined for the MSDF emphasized operations in coastal areas and nearby seas, including surveillance and patrol, defence of harbours, straits and surface ship protection. Within the quantitative limits outlined in the Attached Table, now measured by numbers of vessel types rather than aggregate tonnage, the MSDF would still be able to operate a sizeable ocean-going surface fleet, but short of the scale and vessel types required to project power along the lines Sekino had advocated five years previously.

The *taikō* encouraged the MSDF and its fellow service arms to shift the emphasis of their defence planning away from quantitative expansion as well as promoting a better balance between frontline equipment and previously neglected areas such as logistics, readiness and intelligence. Qualitative modernization left the route open for a succession of new weapons systems approved in the late 1970s including most importantly, the P-3C, which represented a quantum leap over the P-2J anti-submarine patrol aircraft.[93] In 1979, the first of four new 8,500-ton *Towada*-class fleet-underway-replenishment-vessels was commissioned into service, extending the Self Defense Fleet's capability to undertake sustained blue-water operations.[94] Similar capability leaps were achieved by the ASDF through acquisition of the E-2C Airborne Early Warning (AEW) aircraft and the F-15 fighter.[95] Over the 20-year lifetime of the *taikō*, Japan's maritime air and defence capabilities improved far beyond the scope envisioned in 1976.

Despite the defeat of its ambitions to add a fifth flotilla to the Self Defense Fleet and the apparent primacy attached to an anti-invasion role within the *taikō*, the MSDF in other ways carried on with little overall change. The disposition of its major fleet units at Yokosuka and Kure underscored a continued southward-oriented focus on Pacific operations at odds with the growth of Soviet naval strength in the Sea of Japan.[96] Despite not being able to offer credible resistance against 'even a moderate air threat', the MSDF surface fleet continued to organize itself around 'escort ships' (*gōeikan*) grouped into escort flotillas (*gōeikantai*) that were configured for a blue-water role, rather than coastal operations in which MSDF planners had little interest.[97] While the *taikō* aligned official defence policy closer to Kaihara's coastal defence blueprint, the MSDF exploited the ambiguity of the *taikō* as a document to continue equipping and training towards maintaining its blue-water capabilities and skills, and preserving the core of a potentially expanded future navy. The roles and blue-water capabilities of the MSDF were substantially expanded in the 1980s to encompass a sea lane defence role. However, as is explored in the Chapter 5, the focus would be alliance cooperation rather than the pursuit of an autonomous capability.

Rising sea lane threat perceptions

Even as the *taikō* was being implemented, doubts about the strategic premises on which it was based began to surface. In particular, the build-up of maritime capabilities in the Soviet Far East prompted concern over the security of Japan's sea lanes at both official and private levels. The 1977 defence white paper featured several references to the importance of sea lanes to Japan's security, mainly in the context of US global strategy. In its international section, the white paper noted that 'one of the fundamental reasons behind the build-up of the Soviet navy is believed to be the creation of a challenge to the Western powers' control of the sea, particularly through the capability to prevent supply and reinforcement from the US mainland by blockading the maritime traffic lanes'. As a result of improvements in Soviet capabilities, the JDA concluded that 'the safety of the sea and air lanes from the US mainland is being jeopardized' and that in this context 'there is a renewed recognition among Western nations that their closer cooperation with the United States is of critical importance for maintenance and strengthening of their defence capabilities'.[98] The white paper described the 'sea traffic blockade capability' of the Soviet Pacific submarine fleet as a 'matter of concern to the national security of Japan'.[99]

Outlining MSDF roles as part of the Standard Defense Force Concept, the white paper included an inset diagram depicting 'ocean lane protection' along two southwesterly and southeasterly axes (see Map 4.1). While the radius for Pacific maritime patrol aircraft was set by the JDA at 300 nautical miles from the Pacific coast and 100–200 nautical miles in the Sea of Japan, in addition, one squadron would be deployed 'to each of the ocean and coastal sea lanes when the necessity for ship protection arises'.[100] Further proof that the protection of the *nantō* and *nansei kōrotai* was still extant as an MSDF mission, despite being absent from the *taikō*, came in November 1977, when Defense Agency Director General Mihara Asao said in testimony before the House of Councillors that 'Japan was ready to exercise the right of self-defense generally within 500 miles from its coasts and in important sea lanes within 1,000 miles – around Saipan to the southeast and Taiwan to the southwest'.[101]

The 1977 white paper also included a section dedicated to 'Japan and Sea Communication', emphasizing potential threats to sea lanes and the necessity of protecting marine transportation – 'the lifeline of Japan' – in a general context of trade and import dependence as well as the 1973 Oil Crisis 'which shook Japan's economic and social systems to their very foundations'.[102] Although aircraft, ship-to-ship missiles and mines were all identified as threats to marine traffic, the white paper highlighted submarines as 'the greatest menace'.

Noting that 'it is impossible for Japan alone to guarantee the safety of maritime shipping throughout the vast oceans', the JDA identified a particular need to upgrade ASW capability, in order to 'promote confidence in the Japan–US security system, the basis of Japanese defense'. The JDA's analysis of potential sea lane threats, although couched in terms of heightened economic vulnerability to supply disruptions as a result of the Oil Crisis, was, from the viewpoint of

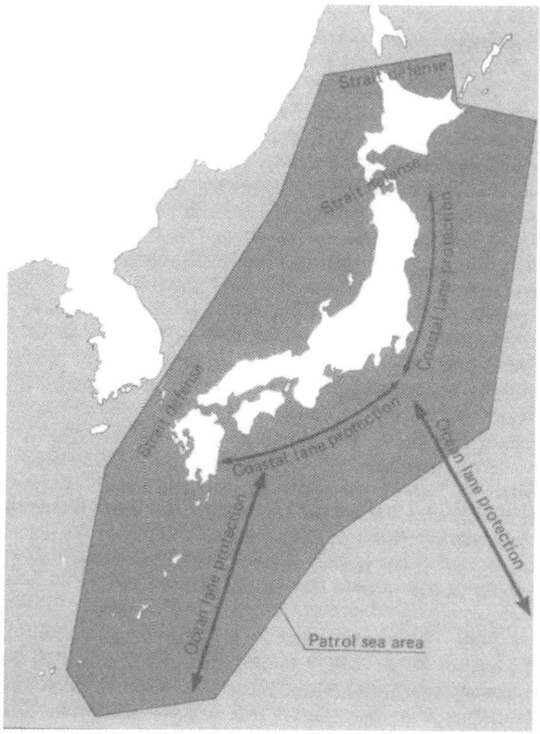

Map 4.1 JDA schematic for Marine Surface Defense, 1977.

alliance politics, partly a reaction to growing US pressure on Japan to boost the level of its ASW capability. The stress placed by the JDA on submarine threats to Japan's sea communications appeared also in the context of subsequent sections of the white paper given over to explaining the 'need for deployment of (a) follow-on ASW aircraft' and was thus partially aimed at preparing the ground for the pending replacement to the ageing P-2J, with the more expensive and far more capable P-3C.

Perceptions of Japan's potential vulnerability to commerce disruption were in evidence elsewhere. The Oil Crisis and instability in Iran in the late 1970s 'brought heated debates on the vulnerability of the sea-lanes and communication between the Middle East and Japan'.[103] In June 1977, an advisory defence report, Alternative Force Structure of Japan's Defence Force, drawn up by the defence commentator, Sakanaka Tomohisa, concluded 'In the light of its reliance on imports of food, energy and raw materials, the threat posed by interrupting the flow of raw materials to Japan would be more serious than a military threat.' The report concluded that while a general anti-shipping offensive against Japan was improbable:

> [T]he fact remains that Japan's weakness against this form of attack is conceded by nearly all analysts, whether they support or oppose an escort role for the MSDF. Initial losses would be heavy since the submarine fleets would probably be deployed prior to hostilities, and convoy systems could not be organized immediately. These sinkings, particularly if they included a few supertankers, would have great psychological impact.[104]

The report noted that Japan's vulnerability to blockade depended partly on non-military measures such as stockpiling, austerity controls and resource substitution. Moreover, the military task of protecting Japan's maritime commerce unaided in a sustained anti-shipping campaign was something Sakanaka regarded as beyond the capabilities of the MSDF. However, against the apparent impossibility of the military task, so long as the United States was committed to Japan's defence, preparing to secure at least a portion of the country's ocean-going imports would be 'worthwhile' given that the objective would be merely to ensure Japan's survival until the conflict could be terminated. Sakanaka stressed that Japan was at a strategic advantage, because Soviet naval forces based at Vladivostok were geographically hemmed in; and by the belief that Japan's cumulative ASW efforts would incrementally degrade the submarine threat.[105]

Like Sekino, Sakanaka also emphasized Japan's peculiar vulnerability to anti-shipping attacks in view of national psychology, perceived economic vulnerability and the memory of the wartime blockade as the 'the most single decisive factor in the collapse of the Japanese economy'. In the light of international awareness of these factors, a potential enemy might view low-level sporadic attacks on Japanese ships or ships bound for Japan as a low-cost, low-risk means to undermine morale and create uncertainty over the US alliance commitment, aimed ultimately at neutralizing Japan during a period of heightened tension, or non-nuclear conflict, between the superpowers.[106]

Conclusion

Between systemic pressures on Japan as an independent actor within the international system and constraints developed at the level of domestic politics, the single most important influence on the formation of Japan's defence and security policies after 1945 was the bilateral security link with the United States. After 1950, US pressure on Japan to engage in limited rearmament was the key factor in the re-constitution of armed forces. The US security guarantee also afforded Japan's post-war leaders the strategic space (or 'greenhouse', to use Hellmann's metaphor[107]) in which to concentrate on economic growth and develop a minimal approach to defence policy through formal and normative constraints that limited the size, power and legal utility of the SDF.

Although the redrawing of its borders and reliance on the United States for external security simplified the dynamics of Japan's maritime defence, the post-war expansion of Japan's international trade increased its potential vulnerability to blockade. Notwithstanding their relatively sanguine views about the military threats posed by the Soviet Union, post-war leaders such as Yoshida appreciated the particular importance of US naval protection to Japan's security and were more sympathetic to the creation of Japanese maritime forces than ground forces. Senior MSDF officers, business leaders and politicians – some of them Imperial Navy veterans – regarded the defence of SLOC as a core mission for the MSDF, given Japan's status as a major trading power and the world's largest importer of energy resources. As Sekino indicated, the desire to acquire independent naval capability also reflected doubts among MSDF officers about US willingness to extend extra-territorial security guarantees to Japanese shipping.

Among those who favoured expanding the MSDF into a fully fledged great power navy, as well as those who sought merely to build public support for the government's defence policy, there was a common recognition that the rationale of protecting Japan's commercial shipping lanes, with its appeal to 'defensive defence' and compatibility with economically defined norms of security and perceptions of vulnerability, was an elegant and useful device towards overcoming the controversy surrounding all aspects of Japan's post-war maritime rearmament. The defence of the nation's sea lanes, while having a popular resonance matched by few other potential justifications for the SDF, was also sufficiently vague and malleable to lend itself to a justification for most aspects of the MSDF's force structure and operations. For similar reasons more fully explored in Chapter 5 sea lane defence was also useful to the United States as a rationale for deepening naval cooperation with Japan in order to utilize the MSDF's complementary capabilities in ASW and mine warfare, and overcome the legal barriers to interoperability imposed by the Constitution and the Cabinet Legislative Office's 'ban' on collective self defence.

Despite Nakasone's plans to pursue autonomous defence, Japan's defence build-up was led back onto a minimalist path in the 1970s by enduring constraints reinforced at systemic, alliance and domestic levels. The JDA's flirtation with 'self-reliance' provoked political dissent from constitutional pacifists, challenged the growth-oriented priorities of the MoF, and was ultimately subordinated to such foreign policy goals as the normalization of relations with China. The adoption of the *taikō* reflected the ascendance of the minimalist vision supported by Kaihara, Kubo and Sakata over the ambitions of Nakasone and Sekino to pursue a policy of naval expansion that would have voided the constraints of the Yoshida Doctrine. However, the *taikō* also reflected the basic ambiguity of defence policy in the 1945–77 period, which was designed to appease pro- as well as anti-defence critics. Once strategic conditions worsened in the late 1970s and 1980s, this ambiguity rendered the constraining function of the *taikō* amenable to reinterpretation.

5 Sea lane defence and alliance cooperation, 1977–90

Introduction

This chapter analyses the decision-making process that propelled sea lane defence to the forefront of Japan's defence policy and alliance relations during the 1980s. Following on from the model of post-war drivers and constraints presented in Chapter 4, the major policy-making variables are considered at the levels of Japan's interaction within the international system, the US–Japan Alliance, and Japanese domestic politics. The same questions that framed Chapter 4 pertain equally to this chapter. First, how did perceptions of Japan's strategic vulnerability to the disruption of sea lanes drive decision-makers' responses in defence and alliance policy? Second, to what extent were such concerns employed 'politically' as a rationale to legitimize the existence, force structure and operations of the SDF?

In addition, this chapter seeks specifically to explore the decision-making process that led to Prime Minister Suzuki Zenkō's 'pledge' to the United States, in May 1981, that Japan would defend its sea lanes to a distance of 1,000 nm and how this shaped policy under his administration and that of his successor, Nakasone Yasuhiro. Particular emphasis is placed on developments at the level of late-Cold War US military strategy and alliance politics as factors determining the modernization of SDF capabilities and Japan's deepening military integration within the Alliance. In terms of domestic politics, the importance of Nakasone's role as an active supporter of alliance cooperation and increased defence spending is stressed. At a transnational level of decision-making, attention is drawn to the role played by MSDF officers. Served by their links to the US military, they helped to advanced sea lane defence as an issue commanding the attention of more reluctant civilian leaders, such as Suzuki, in a way that was instrumental to overcoming domestic constraints on the SDF.

The chapter briefly sets out Suzuki's 1981 statement on sea lane defence, before charting shifts in the global strategic balance and in US strategy from the late 1960s, demonstrating how these enhanced Japan's strategic importance to the United States. The process that led to Suzuki's comments is then analysed in detail, with reference to shifts in Japan's own threat perceptions during the 1970s. The Nakasone government's embrace of sea lane defence as a rationale for alliance cooperation and force modernization is then explored, together with an analysis of Japan's involvement in the 'Tanker War' during the 1980–88 Iran–Iraq conflict.

Suzuki's sea lane defence 'pledge'

On 8 May 1981, following his summit with President Ronald Reagan in Washington, Prime Minister Suzuki gave a press conference at the National Press Club. Asked about the extent of Japan's defence commitments, Suzuki stated:

> It is natural for Japan to defend its surrounding waters, which is [*sic*] our country's back-yard. We will strengthen our defence capability in order to defend several hundred miles of surrounding waters and the sea lanes to a distance of 1,000 nautical miles.[1]

The reference to defending sea lanes out to 1,000 nm attracted immediate attention from US officials. The Joint Communiqué released earlier, while affirming a Japanese commitment to boost defence efforts in surrounding sea and airspace, had not defined Japan's defence responsibilities beyond the extent of its territory. While Suzuki subsequently denied having given anything more than a non-binding statement of intent at the press conference, the 'Suzuki pledge' propelled sea lane defence to the political forefront of alliance cooperation and Japan's defence policy over the following decade. In this process, changes in US strategy brewing since the late 1960s catalysed a corresponding shift in Japanese perceptions.

Shifts in US strategy

Shifts in US strategy and the relative decline of US power from the late 1960s onwards led to an increase in burden-sharing pressure upon Japan in which naval cooperation and sea lane defence emerged as key priorities. During the late 1960s, assumptions about the economic and military superiority of the United States that had underpinned *Pax Americana* were progressively challenged. A perceived decline in US power, demonstrated by the failure to achieve a military victory in Vietnam, was judged in strategic terms against the Soviet Union and also economically vis-à-vis US allies in Europe and Asia. Popular and Congressional opposition to the war in Vietnam feeding into the 1973 War Powers Act also raised questions, political willingness aside, about the legal freedom of US policy-makers to conduct future armed interventions overseas.

The Nixon Doctrine, announced in Guam in July 1969, was designed to lessen the burden of US troop commitments across Asia by encouraging Washington's allies to assume the 'primary responsibility' of providing the manpower for their own defence. Apart from a sizeable Army commitment to be maintained in South Korea, the US post-Vietnam military presence in East Asia was henceforth to be re-configured to an 'offshore' strategy, reliant on forward-deployed air and sea power, for which the predominantly Japan-based US Seventh Fleet would be the crux. The shift from a 'two-and-a-half war' to a 'one-and-a-half war' force-sizing concept was accompanied by a substantial drawdown of US conventional forces in Asia.[2] While US allies in Asia would have to contribute more towards their conventional defence under the Nixon Doctrine, Washington would continue exclusively to provide strategic nuclear deterrence to its allies in the region. Outlining his Strategy of Realistic Deterrence, Secretary of Defense Melvin Laird wrote in 1971 that 'we do not intend to be the policeman of the world... it is realistic and more effective that the burden of protecting peace and freedom should be shared more fully by our allies and friends' [My ellipsis]. Noting that 'in escort ships, our friends and allies around the world possess a greater number than we do', Laird stated:

> Therefore it is one of our goals for the 1970s that our Atlantic and Pacific allies should provide a major contribution to protecting the convoys that in war would be carrying material for their sustenance.[3]

Also underlying the Nixon administration's willingness to reduce US military commitments on the Asian continent was its recognition of the Sino-Soviet split. Exposure of the split paved the way for the administration's diplomatic opening to China in 1971 and exploded the founding premise of pre-Vietnam strategy for the Far East, which was the containment of a monolithic Communist threat. For the remainder of the Cold War, US–China relations would increasingly take on the character of a quasi-alliance against the Soviet Union, while the diversion of Soviet conventional and nuclear strength to counter China helped to transform the US strategic position positively in Asia and globally. Even as the perceived threat of monolithic communism receded and relations with the Soviet Union warmed during the Détente period, US military planners became progressively concerned that the nuclear and conventional balance was tilting in Moscow's favour. A rise in Soviet political influence in the Middle East, East Africa and Southeast Asia was seen to be backed by a growing ability to project conventional forces and to conclude basing agreements. As a result, regions previously thought of as host to discrete proxy conflicts came to be regarded as inter-related military 'theatres' in global, strategic competition between the superpowers.

Within the US Pacific Command, concern at the modernization of Soviet strategic and conventional forces in the Far East was accentuated by the post-Vietnam retrenchment of US conventional forces in Asia and declining defence budgets.[4] Soviet naval power projection was noted with particular alarm in the predominantly maritime environment. Beginning in the early 1970s, *Delta*-class SSBNs capable of launching long-range submarine-launched ballistic missiles (SLBMs) on the Continental United States from Soviet waters were introduced into the Northern and Pacific fleets. In the 'bastion' concept, Soviet long-range ballistic missile submarines were deployed to adjoining semi-enclosed seas in order to take advantage of natural geography that lent itself to the creation of layered air and sea defences designed to protect a Soviet second-strike capability against US counter-measures.[5] The Soviet Pacific Fleet, charged with establishing an eastern bastion (to complement the primary Barents Sea bastion of the Northern Fleet) in the remote Sea of Okhotsk (see Map 5.1), expanded at a faster rate than the other Soviet fleets. Its aggregate tonnage rose from around 700,000 tons to 1.2 million tons between 1967 and 1976, including some 40 nuclear-powered submarines.[6] Defences layered concentrically around the Sea of Okhotsk bastion included radar and acoustic surveillance sites installed on Sakhalin and the Kuriles and the forward basing of a MiG-23 interceptor squadron and an anti-ship missile battery on three of the four islands disputed with Japan.

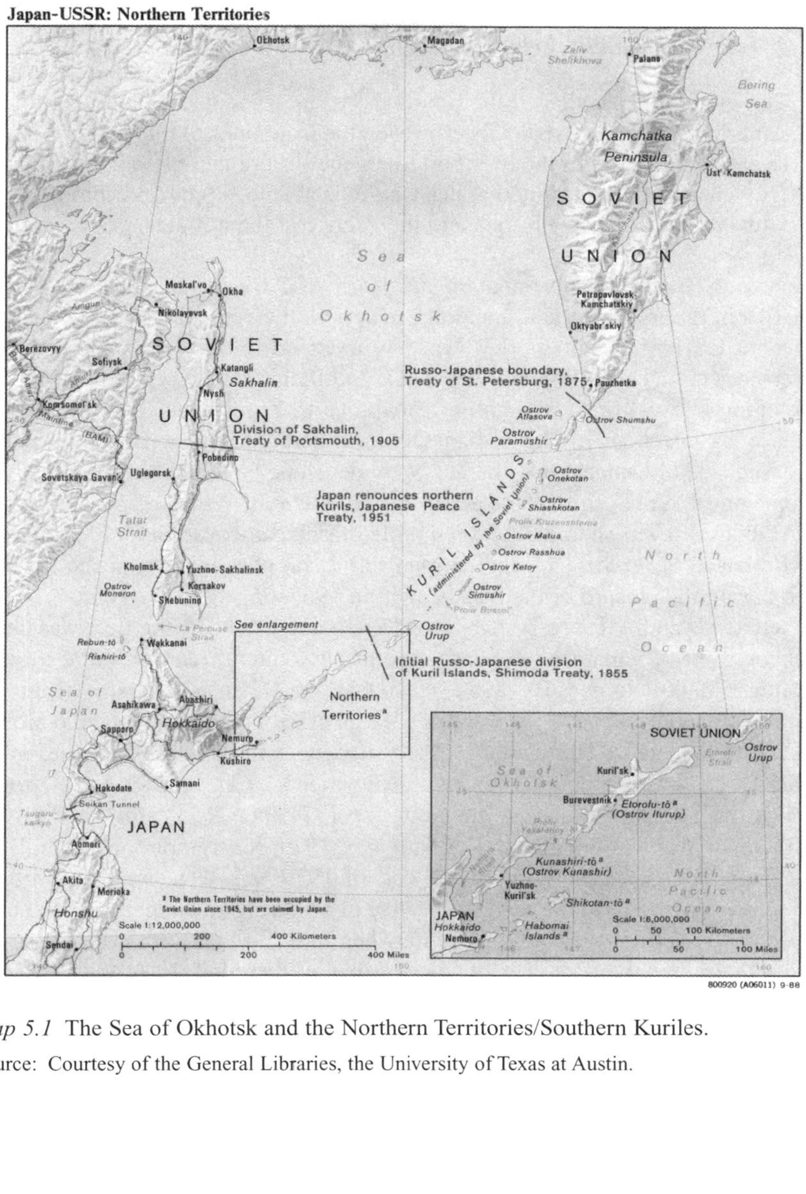

Map 5.1 The Sea of Okhotsk and the Northern Territories/Southern Kuriles.

Source: Courtesy of the General Libraries, the University of Texas at Austin.

In addition to the build-up of Soviet attack submarines, the potential threat from long-range strike aviation operating from the Soviet Far East came to dominate US naval threat perceptions in the Pacific from the mid-1970s onwards.[7] The aerial threat to US aircraft carriers was rendered more acute once the Tu-22M *Backfire*, with a supersonic combat radius of 1,000 nm and armed with the Kh-22 *Kitchen* long-range anti-ship cruise missile, began overflying the Sea of Japan and conducting simulated runs on US carrier battle groups, 'adding a new dimension to the threat to the sea lanes in this area'.[8] By the mid-1970s, US Chief of Naval Operations Admiral James L. Holloway was warning Congress that the Soviet maritime build-up in the Far East meant that US SLOC west of Hawaii could no longer be guaranteed.[9] Similar concerns were expressed by Commander-in-Chief, Pacific Admiral Maurice Weisner:

> The gradual expansion of the Soviet navy has coincided with an ebb in the American ability to expand its efforts on the front lines of the western Pacific to an all-time low. In the event of emergency, there is probably only a fifty-fifty chance that the United States would be able to supply and communicate with American troops in Asia and the Pacific in the initial stages of war.[10]

The Soviet Union's involvement in the Horn of Africa and augmented naval presence in the Indian Ocean, including access to the Yemeni port of Aden, suggested to US naval planners that Moscow intended to develop 'unprecedented power-projection capability into the Pacific and Indian Ocean regions . . . aimed at developing a two-front war-fighting capability in Europe and East Asia'.[11] To increase its coverage of the Indian Ocean, where Soviet naval activities had increased steadily since 1968, the US Navy developed a variant of its strategy to 'swing' naval forces from the Pacific to the Atlantic. While responsibility for the Arabian Sea was shared between the Mediterranean-based Sixth Fleet and the Pacific-based Seventh Fleet, this burden fell disproportionately on the Seventh Fleet during the closure of the Suez Canal, in 1967–75.

Even as Seventh Fleet responsibilities were being extended, the fleet was being cut back to pre-Vietnam levels, based around two aircraft carrier battle groups, totalling 550,000 tons.[12] By 1982, Secretary of Defense Caspar Weinberger reported to Congress that US naval force levels in the Pacific had fallen to around half their 1965 level.[13] During the 1970s, a succession of international crises in the Indian Ocean basin prompted reactive deployments of US carrier battle groups through the Straits of Malacca, including the 1971 Indo-Pakistan War, the 1973 Yom Kippur War and the Iranian Revolution of 1979. Most importantly of all, the Soviet invasion of Afghanistan at the end of 1979 was seen by some Western strategists as a revival of the czarist objective of acquiring an outlet for Russia onto the Indian Ocean. By the spring of 1980, when Iran and Iraq were also at war, the United States had two carrier battle groups deployed around the Arabian Sea and was upgrading logistic support facilities on the mid-Indian Ocean island of Diego Garcia to support a semi-permanent naval presence in the region.

With the withdrawal of most UK forces west of Suez, Washington believed that only Australia and Japan were capable of counting in the naval balance among its allies in the Pacific. Fearing that the stretching of Seventh Fleet coverage to the Arabian Sea had left gaps in the Western Pacific, the Pentagon looked particularly to Japan, highly dependent on Middle Eastern oil and owner of the largest merchant fleet in the world, to contribute naval forces to Indian Ocean patrols or to compensate locally for the reduced Seventh Fleet presence around Japanese waters. US references to Japan's security stake in the Indian Ocean are evident as far back as Defense Secretary Laird's comments in March 1971:

> The Russians have a greater (Indian Ocean) presence there than we do. It is of concern to the US of course. It should also be of interest to Japan, and I have told the Japanese that it should be so.[14]

By 1975, US officials had narrowed their preference for Japanese defence cooperation to three functions in the Northwest Pacific, namely:

- securing maritime transportation;
- strengthening ASW capability;
- improving air defence.[15]

In addition to invoking Japan's dependence on the security of its oil routes through the Indian Ocean as a means to pressure Tokyo to boost its level of maritime defence capability, US officials expressed concern at the failure of the MSDF to meet its procurement targets under the Fourth Defense Build-up Plan. These remained frozen under fiscal austerity controls imposed by the MoF at 45 escort ships, 15 submarines and 40 mine-sweepers. Based on a JDA 1974 estimate of Soviet Pacific Fleet strength (at 8 cruisers, 54 destroyers, 31 nuclear and 63 diesel submarines), the Maritime Staff Office believed that the MSDF had less than half the level of ASW capability required to secure sea areas around Japan. The director of the JDA's Defense Policy Bureau, Maruyama Subaru, stated in April 1975 that 'even if the MSDF's four escort fleets are modernised, and . . . reach 250,000 tons, it is difficult to expect them to ensure perfection in the protection of maritime transport in the sea areas around our country'.[16] Exercises conducted off Oshima in that year also reportedly exposed shortcomings in the MSDF's ASW operations.[17]

Despite the close personnel linkages and regular bilateral exercises between the MSDF and the US Navy, no formal framework existed for bilateral defence cooperation. In its absence, consultations described as study meetings were held between senior US and Japanese staff officers in late 1974 and January 1975 to discuss an operational framework for defence cooperation in the event of an 'emergency'. Participants included the Chairman of the SDF Joint Staff Council and the Commander of US Forces, Japan.[18] US military officials proposed that the MSDF should 'share, together with the US Navy, the defense of the maritime transportation line, which is the life-line for the Japanese economy'.[19] In May 1975, as Chairman of the Joint Chiefs of Staff General George Brown testified to Congress highlighting US expectations that Japan should raise the level of its ASW capability, Secretary of Defense James Schlesinger suggested that Japan should make the protection of sea lanes a priority in addition to territorial defence.[20] With the memory of the 1973 Oil Crisis still fresh, US statements began to achieve the desired effect on key figures within Japan's ruling party, with LDP Vice-Secretary Shiina declaring:

> Most of Japan's resources, in the case of oil 99 per cent [*sic*] pass from the Persian Gulf through the Indian Ocean through the Malacca and then Taiwan Strait on their way to Japan. Any minor disruption, even an isolated terrorist incident, would have a major impact on Japan's energy picture. Defence is not limited to territorial integrity alone. We must also consider how to defend Japan's interests as they exist in tankers at sea.[21]

Opposition parties expressed concerns that as a result of increasing foreign pressure (*gaiatsu*), MSDF and ASDF capabilities would not only be increased, but that escort operations could be extended geographically far beyond territorial waters, raising constitutional questions over overseas dispatch. Following reports that high-level military-to-military consultations had taken place, in March 1975, Ueda Tetsuo, a Socialist member of the House of Representatives, alleged in the Diet that a 'secret agreement' had been concluded. Under the alleged pact between military officers from both countries, Japan would take responsibility for sea lanes connecting the joint naval base at Yokosuka with Hawaii, Guam and the Philippines.[22] JDA Director General Sakata Michita denied the existence of a secret agreement, admitting only that the JDA had promoted studies on Japan–US cooperation concerning the defence of the sea areas around Japan.[23] Ueda's question nonetheless nudged Sakata into considering an official framework for bilateral defence cooperation with the United States, based on 'the premise of the general command of the seas by the US Navy Seventh Fleet, upon establishing a concept for defense in the sea areas around our country'. Sakata's interest in deepening the consultative institutional framework of the Alliance also reflected his concern to prevent SDF personnel from 'going it alone' with their US counterparts and circumventing Japan's system of civilian control.

As part of Sakata's initiative, James Schlesinger was invited to Tokyo for a bilateral defence summit in Tokyo on 29 August, setting in motion a process that would culminate in the drafting of the US–Japan Defense Cooperation Guidelines, released in November 1978. The importance of sea lanes was reflected in the text of the 1978 Guidelines, which stated that the MSDF and US Navy would 'jointly conduct maritime operations for the defence of surrounding waters and sea lines of communication'. Although the Guidelines were not subject to Diet approval and no geographical limitation was placed upon sea lane defence, mention of the MSDF's co-responsibility for defending sea lanes was especially significant in light of the fact that reference to defending sea lanes had been left out of the 1976 *taikō*, the government's defence policy outline.

Meanwhile, US political pressure on Tokyo to increase its levels of defence spending began to intensify. In the month that the Guidelines were released, a senior Democrat on the House Armed Services Committee visiting Tokyo,

Congressman Richard Wright, said that Japan's dependence on sea lanes was 'above all other nations in the Far East', and that accordingly Japan should do more to 'defend its sea lanes for shipping'.[24] During his visit to Japan in late 1978, Defense Secretary Harold Brown reaffirmed Washington's desire to see improvements to Japan's level of air defence and ASW capability.[25] During JDA Director Kanemaru Shin's visit to Washington in August 1978, Brown had warned that a *Minsk*-class vertical take-off and landing (VTOL) carrier was likely to be deployed by the Soviet Pacific Fleet in 1979 and told Kanemaru that America's naval power alone 'will not be sufficient to cope with the Soviet Navy in the Far East'. Regarding the third area of cooperation identified in 1975, the protection of shipping, Brown urged Japan to take responsibility for guarding 'branch' sea lanes extending from its Pacific ports to the seas north of the Philippines and said that the United States expected the MSDF to acquire the capability to protect shipping along a southwesterly axis – in the direction of Taiwan – and southeast, towards the Bonin islands.[26] In return, it was affirmed that in a crisis the US Navy would secure routes across the central Pacific used to transport Middle Eastern oil and other materials (if necessary deploying its entire Pacific-based carrier force of six carrier battle groups).[27]

The protection of shipping along the *nantō* and *nansei kōrotai* thus emerged at the centre of a debate within the Alliance about whether to define and apportion military roles on a geographical or functional basis. Although Kanemaru was personally supportive of an enhanced role for the MSDF in alliance cooperation, for example backing its participation in the biannual Rim of the Pacific Exercises (RIMPAC), the Japanese government was reluctant to commit the SDF to new territorial responsibilities. However, at the military level, MSDF officers' awareness of and interest in Japan's potential involvement in defending branch sea lanes in the Pacific had been expressed in a MSDF training manual as far back as 1970, which had stated:

> It will be difficult to determine whether the enemy will choose coastal routes or ocean ones to attack. The latter are generally considered more important since they provide logistic support to the US military bases in Japan and supply necessary materials to the Japanese people as well because larger vessels traverse these routes. In any case, the routes Japan wants to secure must be effectively connected with the US Central Pacific sea lanes of communication (LOC). This sea lane is to be set up in wartime as a logistic support route from the US to the far East and Australia. Effective linkage with the LOC will be the main objective of our sea lane concept.[28]

Japan's rising profile in US strategy

Military-strategic pressures

Even as the United States showed interest at the political level in broadening the geographical extent of Japan's defence responsibilities under the rubric of sea lane defence, its naval strategy against the Soviet Union was evolving towards a more offensive posture in the Pacific, in which Japan's active cooperation was deemed crucial.

In June 1979, Chief of Naval Operations Admiral Thomas Hayward said:

> An extremely large number of warships would be required to protect convoys operating over the long maritime transport routes. The United States Navy has instead adopted an offensive approach to push the enemy into a defensive position. The United States Navy and the Maritime Self Defense Force coordinate so that they do not duplicate each other's efforts. This enables American warships to operate independently. The Maritime SDF's antisubmarine P-3Cs are deployed so as to fulfil this duty'.[29]

Of the Soviet Union's Far Eastern naval bases, only the submarine base at Petropavlosk – on the Kamchatka peninsula – enjoyed unrestricted access to the Pacific. But lacking overland transport links, Petropavlosk depended on re-supply by sea and air, particularly from the main Soviet naval base at Vladivostok, facing the Sea of Japan. Japan's geostrategic position forming a natural sea-air cordon around the major Soviet bases in the Sea of Japan was described by Admiral Holloway in Congressional testimony as providing 'the most definitive military justification for a strong security relationship with Japan'.

According to Holloway, the strategic priorities of the US Navy throughout the Pacific Command could be reduced to protecting its base facilities and essential lines of communication in the Pacific and Indian Ocean:

> The success of this strategic concept depends to a large degree on the ability of the United States and its allies to block the exits to the Sea of Japan and bottle up the Vladivostok-based Russian fleet units; and the utilization of Japanese air bases as a barrier against the movement of Soviet long-range aircraft from their bases in the Vladivostok complex to the shipping lanes of the Pacific Ocean.

Holloway noted further that 'it is only with the assistance of the Japanese, operating as a military ally, that the Japanese straits can be effectively denied to the Soviets, and Russian long-range aviation prevented from overflying the Japanese archipelago'.[30] Similarly, Under-Secretary of Defense for Policy and Plans Robert Komer concluded that closing the straits would be difficult to achieve 'without active Japanese cooperation'.[31]

Accompanying the abandonment of the 'swing' concept from 1979, the concept of 'horizontal escalation' emerged as part of the US Navy's development of a new maritime strategy to underpin its global force posture vis-à-vis the Soviet Union (see Chapter 2). Contested by critics within DoD who viewed its emphasis on pre-emption as destabilizing, the concept called for US Pacific-based forces to open up a new theatre of operations by mounting reprisal strikes against Soviet Far Eastern bases in the event of a Soviet offensive in the Middle

East or Western Europe. This was based on a calculation that the isolated disposition of Soviet military infrastructure in the Far East together with US strengths in mobility, strike power and geostrategic position in the Western Pacific, would enable US forces to wage a (sub-nuclear strategic) conflict on favourable terms.[32] Operationally, the concept depended on the forward-positioned strike units of the Seventh Fleet, including carrier-based aviation as well as the then recently introduced *Tomahawk* cruise missile, which greatly complicated the Soviet defence planning environment by extending a strategic strike potential to all US principal surface combatants and submarines.[33] According to John F. Lehman, President Reagan's first Secretary of the Navy, by building up US naval forces in the north Pacific the United States 'signalled to the Soviets that if they attacked NATO Europe they could expect to see us coming at them in the Pacific'.[34] However, to be fully credible, horizontal escalation required not only Japan's passive acquiescence as a basing platform, but its active military cooperation by providing air defence over the Japanese archipelago and in closing the main egress points from the Sea of Japan.

Political-economic pressures

In addition to strategic reasons for pursuing defence cooperation, other factors in the political economy of US–Japan relations inclined Washington to apply increasing pressure on Tokyo to boost its defence spending from the late 1970s. The first stirrings of trade tension over soya beans in the early 1970s had, by 1980, sprouted into fully fledged disputes over automobile exports. This fanned Congressional charges that Japan was 'free-riding' on the US security guarantee in the same year that its bilateral trade surplus surpassed the symbolic watershed of $10 billion. Among major US allies, Japan stood out conspicuously as posting the largest bilateral trade surplus yet devoting the smallest proportion of national wealth to defence. The dominance of trade and security issues in US–Japan relations made policy linkages unavoidable, at least in Congress, in spite of the efforts of officials on both sides to separate economic ties from defence relations.[35]

Statements by senior US officials on Japan began to take on an increasingly combative tenor towards the end of the Carter presidency. Secretary of Defense Harold Brown complained of Japanese 'complacency' over defence, describing the Japanese government's plan to boost the defence budget by 7.6 per cent for fiscal 1981 as insufficient.[36] US irritation with Tokyo intensified after the Iranian revolution, following the disclosure that all six major Japanese trading houses were continuing to purchase Iranian oil, heedless of an American request for its allies to join an economic embargo in retaliation for the seizure of the US embassy and its staff in Tehran.[37] Under-Secretary of Defense for Strategy and Plans Robert Komer, visiting Japan in September 1980, impressed upon JDA Director General Omura Jōji the connection between Japan's dependence on US naval protection in the Middle East and US interest in boosting SDF efforts in the Pacific:

> The defense of the sea lanes is a problem of life and death importance for the western nations. Japan benefits most from the maintenance of the sea lanes . . . only the US can defend. It will deploy its Seventh fleet in the Indian Ocean to fulfil this responsibility. Naturally, the defense of the area around Japan will be weakened. Japan too, should recognise these circumstances and strengthen its defense power.[38]

Roles and missions

The failure of the Carter administration, despite combative rhetoric, to persuade the Japanese government significantly to raise defence budgets prompted a rethink among incoming officials of the Reagan administration in January 1981. The Republican administration came to power with two basic objectives for Japan policy: first, to maintain Japan's Western orientation; and second, to obtain 'a more equitable burden-sharing arrangement'.[39] Although these were similar to the policy objectives of the Carter administration, Reagan officials including Secretary of State Alexander Haig, Deputy Assistant Secretary for East Asia Richard Armitage and Secretary of Defense Caspar Weinberger shared the view that it was counter-productive to criticise an ally publicly. Moreover, they agreed that maintaining a focus on achieving abstract budgetary targets in the absence of an accompanying strategic rationale was unlikely to persuade a reluctant ally facing significant domestic opposition to make further defence commitments.[40] With the Defense Cooperation Guidelines already in place, an alternative strategy was suggested of assigning 'roles and missions' within the Alliance which, when linked to corresponding target capabilities, would supply their own strategic rationale for increased funding.

Although Haig is credited with coining the phrase 'roles and missions', the original architect of the approach was the Special Assistant for Japan of the Office of the Secretary of Defense, Commander James Auer, who had studied at the National Defense Academy in Yokosuka in 1970. In addition to his extensive knowledge of the MSDF, Auer had actively maintained military and political contacts in Japan. Personal links, especially those between officers from the two navies, were to play a key role in the decision-making process surrounding sea-lane defence in the 1980s. As a result of the personal network Auer had built up while an officer studying at Yokosuka, particularly his friendship with the former MSDF Chief of Staff, Kimura Hideo, he was able to consult informally with other former MSDF chiefs, Uchida Kazutomi and Nakamura Teijirō, and via these channels contact Oga Ryōhei the incumbent Chief of Staff. In Washington, close navy-to-navy links extended to Japan's Defence Attaché, Kawamura Sumihiko, a former P-3C pilot and intelligence officer, and another long-time associate of Auer. As a result, Kawamura was able to make regular, unscheduled calls to the Japan office in the Pentagon – in contrast with the more formally observed relations between counterpart personnel from other armed services.[41]

In February 1981, Armitage went to Tokyo with Auer unofficially as part of the Reagan administration's preliminary review of security policy towards Japan. Armitage met and exchanged opinions with Tanba Minoru, who was in charge of alliance relations at the MOFA, JDA Councillor for Foreign Relations Okazaki Hisahiko, then seconded from the MOFA, Shiina Motoo, the deputy head of the LDP's Policy Research Committee, and Kimura. The concept of a division of labour based on sharing roles and missions was broached tentatively, whereby the MSDF would adopt as its operational focus ASW, minesweeping and pursue the capability to block Soviet naval access to the Sōya (La Perouse), Tsugaru and Tsushima (Korea) straits, enabling the US Navy to concentrate on offensive operations.

After returning to the United States, Armitage and Auer submitted a memorandum to Weinberger outlining roles and missions for the SDF and US military, areas of responsibility in sea and air defence, and the estimated forces needed to achieve these missions. At this time, US Ambassador Mike Mansfield sent a cable to Washington requesting clarification as soon as possible of the new administration's policy on the US–Japan Security Treaty and bilateral trade issues. With Haig in favour of a less confrontational approach to alliance relations, the memorandum on roles and missions was accepted as a foundation for the Reagan administration's Japan policy.

The new administration officially pressed its case in March 1981, when Foreign Minister Itō Masayoshi visited Washington in preparation for the leaders' summit in May. Weinberger indicated interest in obtaining Japanese cooperation to defend sea areas 'west of Guam and north of the Philippines'.[42] However, Itō responded that this might contravene the cabinet-level ban on the exercise of collective self-defence and gave a commitment only to reply later, subject to further discussions.[43] In the build-up to Suzuki's visit in May, Washington's roles and missions agenda for the SDF crystallized into three key objectives:

1 To establish sea control within a fan-shaped area of the Northwest Pacific extending south of the main Japanese islands, east of the Philippines and west of Guam. Within this area the focus would be on countering Soviet submarines and *Backfire* bombers.
2 To build the capability, including mine warfare, to blockade the Soya, Tsugaru and Tsushima straits.
3 To establish an air defence screen over Japanese territory and part of the Sea of Japan to defend against Soviet fighters and bombers.

Owing to its proximity to the Soviet Far East and the decision (approved in late 1977) to acquire the F-15, Japan, so Washington believed, would be able to accomplish the second and third missions without projecting military forces beyond its air defence zone. However, the first objective entailed an unambiguous geographical expansion of Japan's defence zone, with major implications both for the SDF's force structure and conformity with the ban on collective self-defence. According to the Congressional Researcher Larry Niksch, in the zone within which Washington wanted Japan to take primary responsibility for sea control, specific MSDF tasks were to include the convoying of merchant shipping to Japan, as well as 'effective offensive and defensive capabilities against Soviet submarines, surface ships and aircraft over a wide ocean area'.[44]

In 1980, the policy-making environment in Japan was particularly sensitive to US pressure. Okazaki Hisahiko, who was at that time involved in drafting speeches in the Diet in his capacity as JDA Councillor for Foreign Relations, recalls that US frustration concerning Japan's defence spending levels, increased security concerns prompted by the Soviet invasion of Afghanistan and annoyance over continuing Japanese oil purchases from Iran, combined to make the Foreign Ministry especially anxious to placate Washington through concessions on security issues.[45]

RIMPAC participation

As a major practical step towards deepening defence cooperation with the United States, in February 1980, the MSDF sent its first contingent to the month-long RIMPAC exercises, conducted off Hawaii. MSDF officers had sought Japanese participation at RIMPAC since the exercises started in 1971, but were unable to overcome opposition from the JDA's internal bureaux. However, the Schlesinger–Sakata meeting in August 1975 swung the environment in favour of bilateral defence cooperation. Yet it was not until 1979 that backing for RIMPAC from the JDA's civilian management was forthcoming, under Director General Kanemaru Shin and his successor Yamashita Ganri.[46] Although bilateral naval exercises dated back to the 1950s, RIMPAC presented the JDA with substantial legal obstacles as a multilateral exercise focussed on a potential threat from the Soviet Union, which potentially placed MSDF units under US operational command. Negotiations to overcome these and more practical problems in the way of Japan's participation were conducted at the military level on the Japanese side by Captain Yoshida Manabu.[47] Eventually, a formula was arrived at that would allow the MSDF technically only to exercise on a bilateral level with US Navy units, as an extension of a joint US–Japan training programme dating from 1976. MSDF forces dispatched to RIMPAC in February 1980, under the command of Captain Yoshioka Tsutomu, were modest – limited to the helicopter destroyer *Hiei*, the guided-missile destroyer *Amatsukaze* and a P-2J aircraft.

Nonetheless, RIMPAC signified to contemporary observers 'momentum for... Japan's role in the joint defence of the Pacific sea lanes in the 1980s' [My ellipsis]. The exercises enabled the MSDF and the US Navy to prepare the groundwork for closer naval cooperation more than a year before the Reagan administration adopted 'roles and missions'. According to Nishijima Ryōichi, during preparations for the exercise, MSDF operational planners were already focussing on a wedge-shaped area, 'with the 20th parallel as its base and the Tōkaidō megalopolis (Tokyo–Nagoya–Osaka) as its vertex', within which the MSDF would assume primary responsibility for ASW, deploying its P-3Cs to prevent Soviet submarines from encroaching 'eastward across the Nansei Islands and westward across the Izu-Ogasawara Islands line'.[48] While this move towards adopting the defence of an area of sea space marked a departure from defending shipping directly, escorted convoys of merchant ships and tankers remained part of the MSDF's operational plans. Based on estimates of the minimum level of economic imports needed during wartime, the concept called for the MSDF to assign its four flotillas (each composed of eight vessels) to escort convoys of around 50 merchant ships dispatched at the rate of eight per month, which would receive US naval protection as far as the twentieth parallel. This roughly bisects the Bashi Channel between Taiwan and the Philippines, and runs close to Okino Tori Shima (Parece Vela), which marks the southernmost extent of Japanese territory, on the eastern fringe of the Philippine Sea.

The Suzuki pledge and its aftermath

According to Okazaki, in 1979–80 an unprecedented latitude was extended to parliamentary debate on security and defence issues, facilitating the use of previously taboo terms in the Diet, such as 'potential threat', vis-à-vis the Soviet Union.[49] In October 1980, on the heels of Komer's highlighting of Japan's dependence on US naval protection in the Middle East, Foreign Minister Itō stated before the House of Councillors Special Committee on Security:

> Japan could not help but strive to build up its defence capabilities to a certain level now that the increased US naval presence in the Indian Ocean, designed to ensure peace and stability in the Middle East region and the West's vital sea lanes there, has considerably reduced US military strength in Asia and the West Pacific.[50]

Itō's statement, the most supportive of its kind to date, was followed by Prime Minister Suzuki's appearance before the Committee on 10 November, when he said that the SDF had the legal right 'to defend Japanese shipping on the high seas if it is exposed to attack and other dangers'. Suzuki also stated that the MSDF's target of assuring the security of waters for several hundred nm from Japan's coastline and the sea routes out to 1,000 nm remained unchanged, but the SDF were not capable of protecting Japanese vessels in the Gulf and Indian Ocean. This was the first time that a post-war prime minister had asserted the constitutionality of protecting Japan's sea lanes beyond the extent of its territorial waters.[51] According to Okazaki, the brief for Suzuki's inaugural visit to Washington was prepared with the objective of presenting Japan in the most positive light possible, by re-packaging existing policy statements that were a matter of Diet record.

The Joint Communiqué issued at the conclusion of Suzuki's meeting with President Reagan in May 1981 included a recognition by both leaders of an 'appropriate division of roles' in defence. Japan would undertake to:

- defend its territory and surrounding sea and air space;
- alleviate the financial burden of stationing US forces in Japan;
- extend aid to strategically important regions.

In return, the United States affirmed that it would:

- extend nuclear protection;
- maintain offensive forces in and around Japan;
- retain forces in South Korea;
- defend sea lanes in the Indian Ocean and southwest Pacific.[52]

Although no significant Japanese defence policy concessions were contained in the Joint Communiqué, the reference to 'alliance relations' (*dōmei kankei*) itself was ground-breaking and controversial in Japan, where official reference to the Security Treaty in such terms was still taboo. Controversy over the use of 'alliance' in the official text eventually forced Foreign Minister Itō's resignation. According to Okazaki, who accompanied the premier to the United States, Suzuki was unaware of the controversy generated either by the Joint Communiqué or his subsequent press conference until he read the Japanese press coverage of the summit during a refuelling stop on his return flight to Tokyo. Only at this point did Suzuki realise that his comments on sea lanes had been taken by Washington as an official policy commitment on the part of his administration.

With US officials believing they had won a public commitment from the prime minister to assume primary responsibility for the defence of sea areas out to 1,000 nm, Washington's attention shifted to the desired level of armament for Japan to discharge its expanded responsibilities. In June 1981, at the Thirteenth Security Subcommittee meeting in Hawaii, the US side floated a force modernization proposal for the SDF that put forward quantitative targets significantly exceeding those stipulated in the 1976 *taikō* in several areas (Table 5.1).

In addition to quantitative targets, the United States recommended boosting SDF readiness and sustainability levels, including a suggestion to build up a 3-month supply of ammunition. Some Japanese observers have noted that the total of 70 destroyers put forward in the US proposal matched the MSDF's own recommendation for five escort flotillas outlined at the planning stages of the Basic Defense Force Concept, implying that MSDF officers may have fed their force structure preferences to their US Navy counterparts in Hawaii.[53] Given the closeness and informality of navy-to-navy ties, it seems highly likely that the

Table 5.1 US force structure proposals at the Thirteenth Security Subcommittee meeting

Main equipment	*Taikō*	*US proposal*
Escort destroyers	60	70
Submarines	16	25
ASW patrol aircraft	100 (P-3C and P-2J)	125 (P-3C)
Air defence squadrons	10	14
Early Warning squadrons	2	1

Sources: Oga Ryōhei, *Shiirēn no Himitsu*, Shōbunsha, Tokyo, 1983, p. 201 and Matsumae Tatsurō, *The Limits of Defense: Japan as an Unsinkable Aircraft-Carrier*, Tōkai University Press, 1988, p. 138.

US interlocutors at Hawaii would at least have been aware of the MSDF's preferences. At the same time, against increasing resistance from the Suzuki cabinet, US officials and senior officers were at pains to stress that an SDF role in sea lane security would not mean assuming a collective self-defence function, as 'Japan's capability to defend her home islands, territorial sea and air space may ultimately rest on the security she can provide to the sea lines of communications and the access they provide to the raw materials needed to sustain her in both peace and war'.[54]

Meanwhile, Suzuki had been angered by what he saw as a misrepresentation of his summit meeting with Reagan, during which the premier had stressed Japan's pacifist credentials. After returning to Japan, Suzuki sought to distance himself from his comments on sea lane defence at the National Press Club, describing them as merely 'a statement of a future objective' rather than an official commitment. Foreign Minister Itō's successor, Sunoda Sunao, equally maintained that no geographical expansion of Japan's defence responsibilities had been entered into.[55] Under pressure from those within the LDP, including Miyazawa Kiichi, who were worried at the fiscal implications of further defence commitments, the prime minister declared that strict constraints would be imposed on sea lane operations, 'if such operations are to be carried out'.[56]

Nevertheless, the Reagan administration used sea lane defence to maintain pressure on Tokyo to increase its defence efforts. In February 1982, Caspar Weinberger told Congress that Japan could increase its contribution to regional stability by strengthening its air and sea defences 'and providing protection to the sea lines of communication out to 1,000 miles'.[57] The following month, Weinberger suggested that the force structure outlined in the *taikō* could be achieved by 1990, requiring an annual increase in defence spending of 10 per cent in real terms. In July 1982, the Suzuki administration went some way towards meeting US expectations by raising the authorized total of P-3Cs to be acquired by the MSDF to 100 aircraft from 45. By agreeing to more than double the numbers of *Orions* in its inventory, the MSDF's ability to prevent the infiltration of Soviet submarines into the Northwest Pacific was greatly enhanced, with obvious implications for improving the operational environment of the US Seventh Fleet. However, the issue of how to fund accelerated acquisitions of the P-3C, F-15 and E-2C remained unresolved under Suzuki.

In 1978, the JDA formulated the Mid-Term Defense Program Estimate (MTDPE), covering fiscal years 1980–84, as the first long-term procurement plan initiated under the *taikō*. Though intended to speed up completion of the *taikō* and subject to review after three years, the MTDPE was considered within government only to have the status of JDA 'internal reference material'. As such it was not binding on the MoF, which opposed increased defence spending not least because it was attempting to rein in deficit financing by the LDP and maintain a balanced budget.[58] Without full government backing for the 1980–84 MTDPE or the revised 1983–87 version, the MoF was able to enforce cuts that led ultimately to the JDA's procurement objectives being barely half fulfilled. Although the United States interpreted the MoF's intervention as a setback in its efforts to raise Japan's defence spending, the political environment was to alter in Washington's favour under Suzuki's successor, Nakasone, who came to power in November 1982.

At the Fourteenth Security Subcommittee meeting convened at Hawaii in August, JDA interlocutors proposed that a dedicated study on sea lane defence be launched under the auspices of the Defense Cooperation Guidelines. Although initially welcomed by the US side, the JDA proposal reflected ambivalence towards sea lane defence within its internal bureaux among those who sought to delay any substantive commitments arising from Suzuki's 'pledge', by drawing out the length of the study (in a tried-and-tested technique designed to demonstrate a response to US pressure without committing to substantive policy change). As a result, the study was not launched officially until March 1983, and did not report its findings to the Japanese cabinet until December 1986, before being submitted to the Security Consultative Committee in January 1987.

Japan's changing threat perceptions

The focus accorded to sea-lane defence within Japan's defence policy during the 1980s reflected more than simply an *ad hoc* response to US pressure or opportunist attempts on the part of Japan's uniformed defence establishment to boost their legitimacy and budgetary claims. While both of these factors apply, Japan's strategic concerns were being independently remoulded in the late 1970s. First, this was in response to a perceived diminished US military commitment to East Asia, apparently confirmed in 1977 by President Carter's announced intention to withdraw US ground forces from South Korea. Second, the build-up of Soviet military capabilities in the vicinity of Japan caused mounting concern among Japanese politicians and defence planners. According to the *Report on Comprehensive National Security*, commissioned by Prime Minister Ohira Masayoshi in April 1979:

> In considering the question of Japan's security, the most fundamental change in the international situation that took place in the 1970s is the termination of clear American supremacy in both military and economic spheres.[59]

In the wake of the US withdrawal from Vietnam, opposition parties began to moderate their opposition towards the Security Treaty and the SDF. Of the four main opposition parties, the Japan Socialist Party (JSP), the Japan Communist Party (JCP), Kōmeitō ('Clean Government' Party) and the Democratic Socialist Party (DSP – a splinter party from the Socialists), the JSP and JCP were committed to abrogating the Security Treaty and regarded the SDF as unconstitutional. For their part, the Kōmeitō and the DSP began to moderate their defence policy platforms in 1975. The DSP moved from an insistence on ejecting US troops from Japan to recognizing the 'necessity' of the Security Treaty, while Kōmeitō softened its demand for an immediate abrogation of the Treaty, to doing so on the basis of mutual consent. While the Socialists refused to recognize the constitutionality of the SDF and used security policy to attack the government in the Diet (as exemplified by Ueda's questioning on sea lane defence), Party Chairman Narita Tomomi signalled a shift towards acceptance of the Security Treaty in a speech in December 1976. By 1981, Kōmeitō had recognized the SDF and put forward its own recommendations on the expansion of defence capability, passing a motion in September that recognized Moscow's build-up of the Soviet Pacific Fleet, its deployments to the Northern Territories and the invasion of Afghanistan as posing a security threat to Japan.[60] The DSP dropped its opposition to the Security Treaty and supported the creation of a standing security committee in the Diet in January 1981. Though the JSP continued to espouse unarmed neutrality, from November 1978, the party softened its opposition to the Security Treaty and brought its policy on the territorial dispute with the Soviet Union into line with the LDP.[61]

MOFA officials viewed the reinforcement of Soviet defences in the Northern Territories beginning in 1978 mainly as a reprisal for the inclusion of a 'non-hegemony' clause (implicitly directed at the Soviet Union) in the Japan–China normalization treaty signed in August.[62] JDA analysts interpreted the Soviet move as driven by the military logic of turning the Sea of Okhotsk into an SSBN 'bastion', which might lead to pre-emptive Soviet attacks on Hokkaidō or northern Honshū in order to secure transit through the Sōya or Tsugaru straits.[63] The impression of hostile Soviet intentions was sealed by Moscow's conclusion of a friendship treaty and basing rights with Vietnam in November 1978, the deployment of SS-20s missiles to the Soviet Far East, and the invasion of Afghanistan.

Around this time, the notion of a 'military threat from the north' was given popular expression through a series of books and articles published in Japan.[64] GSDF Chief of Staff Kurisu Hiromi was forced to resign in 1978 after suggesting that without a framework of emergency legislation (*yūji hōsei*) 'supra-legal' measures might be needed to respond to a military attack. In March 1979, Kurisu's successor, General Nagano, became the first figure publicly to raise revision of the *taikō* in light of the changing security environment, and in 1981 Chairman of the Joint Staff Council Takeda questioned the viability of Japan's 'defensive' defence policy.[65] Increased Soviet air activity in Japan's vicinity, meanwhile, saw the number of ASDF scrambles to intercept Soviet aircraft leap from 281 in 1975 to 939 in 1981.

Japanese sea lane threat perceptions and defence planning concepts were also evolving. Oga Ryōhei was MSDF Chief of Staff during the early 1980s. In *Shiirēn no Himitsu* ('Sealane Secrets'), published in 1983, he divided the concept of sea lane security into separate economic and military components. Economically, he argued that seaborne trade underpinned Japan's prosperity, reflecting its large population, poor resource endowment and corresponding need to import raw materials and export valued-added manufactured goods. Militarily, maritime supply routes across the Atlantic and Pacific were deemed vital to US military strategy at a global level, and US ability to defend Japan from attack.[66]

Geographically, he identified three major sea lanes as crucial to Japan's economic security:

- the sea lane connecting Japan, via the Ryūkyū island chain, Bashi Channel and either the Straits of Malacca or Lombok, with Southeast Asia and the Middle East (accounting for 60 per cent of imports);
- a southeastern sea lane linking Japan with Oceania and Australasia, via the Ogasawara/Bonin islands (16 per cent of imports);
- the 'great circle' route connecting Japan, across the Pacific, with North and South America (20 per cent of imports).

The importance Oga attached to the defence of sea lanes and a concomitant requirement for a navy capable of 'blue-water' operations bore resemblance to Sekino Hideo's blue-water vision. However, Oga's strategy – drawing heavily from that articulated by the former MSDF Chief of Staff, Uchida Kazutomi, in the 1970s – differed in other key respects. The vision of an autonomous navy still held an emotional appeal to many senior MSDF officers (many of whom, Oga included, were veterans of the Imperial Navy[67]) and certain nationalist politicians. However, by the beginning of the 1980s, MSDF plans were firmly premised on a functional division of labour defined by the ASW and mine-sweeping 'shield' provided by Japan and the 'sword' wielded by US mobile strike power.[68] Oga thus stressed that the success of Japan's defensive efforts was dependent on maintaining close coordination with US forces.

Oga's proposed 'total strategy' of sea lane defence incorporated the MSDF's anti-submarine efforts, led by P-3C aircraft and helicopter-equipped destroyers, air defence conducted by the ASDF, the blockade of Soviet egress points from the Sea of Japan as well as the direct protection of high-value units including supply ships and US aircraft carriers. The importance of boosting coordination and intelligence exchange with the MSA was also stressed, echoed by other JDA analysts.[69] From a military point of view, Oga emphasized the efficiency of closing the Sea of Japan, using the MSDF's submarines and mines, as a means to limit the potential Soviet threat posed to Japan's sea lanes. However, he also recognized that constitutional problems would be posed by the operational necessity to act pre-emptively in closing the straits in order to prevent a surge of Soviet naval vessels from the Sea of Japan. Moreover, by publicly committing itself to closing the straits, Japan carried a risk of heightened tension with the Soviet Union, which might develop a pre-emptive counter-doctrine to secure transit thought the Sōya Strait.

Assuming that a partial blockade of the Sea of Japan could successfully be mounted, Oga expected that Soviet aircraft and submarines would still be able to advance south from Kamchatka and the Kurile islands and threaten Pacific shipping by approaching from east of Ogasawara. To counter this threat, it would be necessary to establish a semi-circular blocking line stretching from Northern Japan to Kamchatka. In contrast to the previous focus in JDA white papers on Soviet submarines, Oga's analysis placed roughly equal emphasis on the threat posed by Soviet maritime aviation. The increasing Soviet air threat prompted him to draw parallels between Japan's strategic requirements and Great Britain's defence against Germany during 1940, based on a robust air defence, control over proximate straits, a unified national spirit, strong political leadership and the preservation of trans-oceanic sea lanes to receive logistical support from the United States.[70]

Other Japanese security analysts and former MSDF officers continued to increasingly focus on the Soviet submarine threat to Japan's sea lanes. Admiral Uchida, who remained highly influential within the MSDF, wrote in 1980 that Soviet naval capability posed the utmost threat in the East Asian region. Accordingly he stressed:

> An anti-submarine warfare capability must be the first charge on the resources of any nation precipitately faced with the possibility of starvation and exhaustion by hostile blockade. A force structure based upon the overall striking force of the United States and the regional defence forces of various indigenous nations must be the basic military concept in East Asia.[71]

However, the JDA's position on sea lane defence as reflected in defence white papers remained ambiguous. The 1983 *Defense of Japan* carried a section, separated by a border from the official text, entitled 'On various debates concerning Protection of Sea Lines of Communication (so-called "sea lane defence")'. Without referring to Suzuki's comments, the white paper was vague on the geographical scope of sea lane defence, noting that while Japan's goal was to achieve a capability to provide SLOC protection to 'about 1,000 nm or so', the actual scope of sea and airspace to be defended 'all depends on the situation at the time'.[72]

Regarding the defence of foreign ships bound for Japan, the JDA's position was also ambiguous, noting that although the right of self-defence would not normally be extended to foreign ships on the high seas carrying goods to Japan, 'as a matter of theory, there is an undeniable possibility that, if an armed attack takes place against this nation and if Japan is in the midst of exercising the right of self-defence, the nation attacking Japan might resort to indiscriminate attacks on third nation vessels with cargoes bound for Japan, in order to stop their transportation'. Thus, according to the JDA's interpretation, if such cargoes were deemed 'vital', SDF defence operations to halt any attacks on shipping could be construed as falling within the legal definition of the individual right of self-defence. Lastly, while noting that the denial of passage through the straits around Japan was constitutional, the white paper also stated that this would only be undertaken *after* an armed attack took place against Japan.[73]

Criticism of the SDF's involvement in sea lane defence came not only from the expected quarters of pacifist party-political and media opinion. Kaihara Osamu, a previous critic of the MSDF's blue-water ambitions, resurfaced to argue that sea lane defence made sense only as a 'a gesture or expression of willingness to cooperate with the U.S.', while independent analysts such as Maeda Tetsuo and

Chūma Kiyofuku regarded the concept as a device to justify the expansion of SDF capabilities and Japan's incorporation into US global military strategy.

Kaihara put forward counter-arguments supporting the necessity for, and the viability of, a sea lane defence concept – up-dating those he had advanced a decade earlier. Improvements to Soviet capabilities in the Far East and the further expansion of Japan's trade since the 1960s only increased his conviction that it was pointless for Japan to invest resources in protecting trade against the implausible scenario of a Soviet *guerre de course*.[74] Kaihara's analysis was, to a significant degree, borne out in the JDA's own classified operational research conducted as part of the US–Japan joint study on sea lane defence, the results of which were leaked to the *Daily Yomiuri* in December 1986.[75] Based on four scenarios for Soviet attacks against Japan (ranging from escalation over a period of six months to a large-scale assault and assuming only limited support from the United States), the JDA estimated SDF losses as involving:

- the destruction of 45 per cent of the MSDF's destroyers;
- 30 per cent of civilian cargo vessels used for transportation of oil, iron ore and grain;
- up to 80 per cent damage to radar installations, and the loss of 30–40 per cent of ASDF fighters;
- the destruction of 70 per cent of GSDF tanks and 40 per cent casualties among SDF troops.[76]

Maeda, an independent defence commentator, shared the view that the advance of sea lanes to the top of Japan's defence agenda during the 1980s owed more to its political than strategic value. According to him, the elastic spatial definition of sea lanes gave supporters of an extra-territorial defence role for the MSDF and ASDF the flexibility arbitrarily to redraw the geographical boundaries of Japan's self-defence zone without directly confronting the proscriptions against overseas dispatch and collective self-defence. Furthermore, a call to defend the nation's sea lanes could publicly be presented as an 'appropriately commercial' issue to channel the public's perception of Japan's economic vulnerability into increasing popular support for defence spending.[77] Military threats to Japanese shipping interests recalled the spectre of a resource cut-off that had generated public concern during the 1973 Oil Crisis and, further back, the 'lasting and visceral memory in the Japanese people' of the US wartime blockade. Maeda thought that the MSDF would be able to perform its ASW roles and missions against the Soviet Union adequately within its existing capabilities, given the strategic advantages flowing from its control over the major straits around the Sea of Japan. However, by linking sea lane defence to a semi-redundant convoying concept, the MSDF could better justify their status and budget-driven preference for a large surface fleet. Like Katahara (1990), Maeda too believed that the overlapping interests and close communication between the MSDF and the US Navy led both organizations to cooperate in exerting pressure on the Japanese government to allocate more resources to modernizing Japan's maritime defence capabilities. Finally, he regarded claims that the Soviet Union was targeting Japan's SLOC in the Indian Ocean and South China Sea (echoed in Japan's 1979 defence white paper) as alarmist given that Soviet bases in Vietnam located astride Japan's major economic SLOC would be vulnerable to counter-attack from US forces in the region in the early stages of any superpower conflict.

Nakasone and sea lane defence

In November 1982, Nakasone replaced Suzuki as prime minister. Nakasone was to remain premier for five years, a duration in post-war Japanese politics exceeded only by Satō Eisaku and Yoshida Shigeru. As prime minister, Nakasone adopted a less radical policy agenda than his record either as JDA Director General or junior parliamentarian. With contemporary polls recording 70 per cent opposed to revising the Constitution, he backed the status quo. Nor did he seek to revive autonomous defence.[78] However, within these constraints, Nakasone demonstrated a will to advance his policy goals ahead of the prevailing consensus in a way that few post-war premiers had done since Kishi in the 1950s.

Nakasone's approach towards defence differed fundamentally from his immediate predecessors, Suzuki and Ohira, in that he regarded it as an issue on which to demonstrate leadership on both a domestic and international stage. Nakasone's objective of awakening a 'defence consciousness' (*bōei no ishiki*) among the electorate formed part of a wider aim to achieve a 'settling of Japan's post-war accounts' including the correction of a pacifist bias in the education system dating back to the Occupation.[79] In foreign policy, Nakasone viewed defence as serving the political objective of gaining 'membership of the West'. In an international context in which the United States was pressuring its NATO allies to spend more on defence, Nakasone signed the 1983 Williamsburg G7 Summit Declaration to 'maintain sufficient military strength to deter any attack, to counter any threat, and to ensure the peace'. In a bilateral context, boosting Japan's military efforts was seen by Nakasone as a means to obtain a more 'equal' alliance relationship with the United States.[80]

Sea lane defence presented Nakasone with a ready-made platform upon which to pursue the twin objectives of boosting defence spending above the symbolic threshold of 1 per cent of GNP and bolstering bilateral defence cooperation with the United States. In January 1983, two months after taking office, he gave an interview to the *Washington Post*, in which he declared, first, that 'the whole Japanese archipelago . . . should be like an unsinkable aircraft carrier . . . against infiltration of the *Backfire* bomber'. Second, he promised 'full control of four straits that go through the Japanese islands so that there should be no passage of Soviet submarines and other naval activities'. Third, he linked these objectives to a desire 'to defend the sea lanes between Guam and Tokyo and between the Strait of Taiwan and Osaka'.[81]

Nakasone subsequently reaffirmed his intention before the Diet of achieving the levels of defence capability set out in the *taikō* as soon as possible and announced an exemption for the United States from Japan's ban on arms exports.[82] In February, Nakasone declared before the Diet that if Japan were under attack, the SDF would have the legal right to assist US naval vessels on the high seas if they were on their way to defend Japan. This expansion of the individual right of self-defence was a significant move towards broadening the scope of defence activities seen as permissible within the ban on collective self-defence.[83]

During the spring of 1983, Nakasone travelled to Southeast Asia to assuage regional concerns that Japan intended to expand the geographical range of its sea lane defence activities south of the Bashi Channel.[84] The strength of Asian reaction to his proposal, as JDA Director General in 1970, to expand the SDF had made Nakasone mindful of the importance of assuaging foreign concerns about Japan's rearmament. One major advantage of the description of 1,000 nm as a 'limit' to Japan's sea lane defence responsibilities was that Japan's defence zone could be officially kept to a point north of the Philippines, thereby avoiding inflaming regional suspicions about Japan's intentions.[85] Nakasone's enthusiastic backing of sea lane defence and commitment in time of war to a 'straits blockade' (*kaikyō fūsa*) of the Sea of Japan helped to regain US support, which had waned in reaction to the Suzuki administration's back-peddling from the premier's comments in May 1981. The commencement of the study into sea lane defence, from March 1983, reinforced Nakasone's efforts to demonstrate Tokyo's credentials as a military ally.

Nakasone was determined to breach the 1 per cent of GNP defence spending 'limit', which had stood as cabinet policy since 1976. Rather than confront the limit directly, he proposed to fund the new MTDPE for 1986–90 at a level deemed necessary to complete the *taikō*, which would automatically breach the 1 per cent of GNP threshold at some point. Since the 1983–87, MTDPE had fallen approximately 50 per cent short of its targets for want of official backing, Nakasone undertook to upgrade the new MTDPE to the status of a government programme, with the authority of cabinet backing necessary to override MoF objections.[86]

Nakasone was politically strong enough in 1985 to win backing within the LDP for this course of action. The 1986–90 MTDPE, with appropriations set at 18.4 trillion yen (in 1985 prices), was adopted as a government programme on 18 September 1985, and re-designated the Mid-Term Defense Program (MTDP). However, it failed to break the 1 per cent of GNP barrier in 1985, owing to higher than expected economic growth that year. It was not until 1987 that it was finally surpassed by a margin of 0.004 per cent. The text of the MTDP identified three defence functions to be strengthened:

1 air defence of the main islands;
2 protection of SLOC in the waters surrounding Japan;
3 capability to counter an invasion.

The MTDP thus placed the mission of sea lane defence within the framework of the *taikō* for the first time, something that the US–Japan Defense Cooperation Guidelines had not.[87] The MTDP also delineated an ambitious set of procurement targets, tailored towards offshore air and sea defence capabilities, where US expectations were highest. Allocations to the MSDF and ASDF reached a combined level of nearly 50 per cent of the budget allocated to the three SDF (garnering 23.4 and 26.4 per cent, respectively), while the GSDF's allocation fell to 37 per cent.[88]

The existing MSDF fleet was to be modernized to improve its anti-submarine, air defence and mine warfare capabilities. With nine additional destroyers to be commissioned under the MTDP, the MSDF would have a total of 62, compared to the 'approximately 60' authorized by the *taikō*. The submarine fleet was raised to 16, and a commitment to acquire a total of 100 P-3Cs, reaffirmed. Provision was also made to acquire 12 MH-53 minesweeping helicopters. This expansion of maritime aviation required the creation of two new squadrons bringing the total to 16. With these adjustments, the MSDF's unit structures and operational aircraft matched the quantitative force structure blueprint contained in the *taikō*. A new ASW centre equipped with US software was also opened at the joint naval base in Yokosuka in 1987.[89] The introduction both of new missile armament and of anti-submarine helicopters aboard escort destroyers was made a subject of studies, resulting in the decision to acquire Aegis-equipped destroyers in 1987. The Aegis radar capability would greatly expand the surface fleet's air defence at sea and improve interoperability with the US Navy from the first ship delivery in 1993. While the Aegis procurement was justified in terms of fulfilling Japan's sea lane defence commitments out to 1,000 nm, towards the end of the Cold War the specific operational role of Aegis destroyers was 'to provide a sanctuary route for US carriers coming to the defence of Japan'.[90]

The ASDF and GSDF (with the incorporation of the straits closure mission) also used sea lane defence to justify their roles and procurement plans in the mid- to late-1980s. The most significant increase to the ASDF inventory implemented under the MTDP was in the total of F-15s, 63 of which were planned for acquisition, raising the authorized tally from 155 to 187.[91] A further five E-2Cs were acquired to bolster surveillance. Among several feasibility studies authorized in the MTDP, including over-the-horizon (OTH) radar and in-flight refuelling, dedicated research into 'air defence over the sea' (*yōjō bōkū*) was commissioned in December 1987 in order to weigh procurement options in the light of new SDF operational responsibilities out to 1,000 nm. The ASDF also rationalized its plans to acquire Airborne Warning and Control System (AWACS) aircraft from the United States in terms of fulfilling Japan's sea lane defence commitments.

Although the United States aimed to build up ASDF and MSDF capabilities in particular, even the GSDF was able to use sea lane defence as a rationale to defend its predominant budgetary allocation, especially once the Nakasone administration committed the SDF to blockading the 'four straits'. Based on a scenario for a Soviet landing in Hokkaidō, the GSDF adopted 'Sea Shore Strike' as a new operational concept to orient its doctrine and procurement strategy. With the fielding of SSM-1 surface-to-ship missile units under the MTDP, the GSDF also gained an integral role in the defence of the Sōya and Tsugaru straits.[92]

Despite the Reagan administration's increasing satisfaction with Japan's defence efforts under Nakasone, pressure on Tokyo to raise its defence spending to 2–3 per cent of GNP continued to mount at the Congressional level. In June 1985, during a visit to Washington by JDA Director General Katō Kōichi, the US Senate passed a motion calling on Tokyo to increase military spending.[93] This was followed up by further legislation requiring the President to report to Congress on Japan's progress in implementing the *taikō* and towards meeting its sea lane defence commitments by 1990.[94]

Nonetheless, by the end of 1986, Nakasone's administration had done enough to head off a rupture in alliance relations that might have occurred had a less defence-minded leader been in power. Nakasone achieved a 36 per cent rise in spending between 1982 and 1987 – a rate of increase above any NATO country except the United States.[95] The tempo of alliance cooperation increased in tandem; Nakasone granted permission for the United States to station F-16s at the joint base in Misawa from April 1985, significantly enhancing US maritime strike capabilities in the Northwest Pacific. The first joint ground exercises followed in 1986, in Hokkaidō, while in the same year the MSDF sent a full escort flotilla and a P-3C contingent to the RIMPAC exercises.

The MTDP force levels were still considerably below those proposed by the United States at Hawaii in June 1981. However the pattern of procurements was clearly directed towards boosting those capabilities – ASW, mine warfare and extended air defence – in which the United States had the greatest strategic interest. A joint US–Japan study on interoperability was set up in January 1987, and exercises conducted under the auspices of the Guidelines continued to deepen cooperation and exchange between the SDF and US Armed Forces. By Nakasone's last year in office, the US administration was largely satisfied with Japan's burden-sharing efforts, and in January 1987, US representatives at the Sixteenth US–Japan Security Subcommittee meeting endorsed Japan's defence budget and its efforts to conduct the build-up within the confines of the *taikō*. Congress was less able to divorce defence cooperation (and prospective Japanese purchases of expensive US weapons systems) from mounting trade friction. In 1987, as the US trade deficit with Japan reached $57 billion, Congress passed a joint resolution demanding that Japan should devote 3 per cent of GNP to defence.[96]

Nakasone's successors returned to an essentially low-profile, 'incrementalist' approach towards defence. Defence spending continued to increase at around 5–6 per cent through 1991, but peaked both as a proportion of GDP and government spending in fiscal 1988.[97] By the late-1980s, the pendulum in US policy towards Japan, which for so long had tilted in favour of increasing the level of SDF armament, began to swing back towards the objective of keeping this within 'defensive' bounds. The US Ambassador to Tokyo during the early 1990s, Michael Armacost, later recalled that the DoD decided to 'draw a line in the sand' over the MSDF's ambitions to acquire an aircraft carrier and aerial refuelling, although he noted that this desire was 'perhaps encouraged by their counterparts in the US Navy and Air force'. In Armacost's view, while this capability was relevant to its sea lane surveillance and defence mission, it 'signalled possibly larger ambitions as well'. MSDF ambitions to acquire an aircraft carrier – an aspiration common to all large navies – were still ingrained, despite the deepening of defence cooperation with the US Navy.[98] In the late 1980s, JDA officials testified before the Diet that light aircraft carriers would be permissible under the Constitution. However, studies into the suitability of acquiring a VTOL capability to solve the MSDF's weakness in air defence at sea, concluded that *Harrier*-type aircraft would be too slow to combat the Tu-22M.[99]

The Tanker War

Coinciding with the most active phase of the debate on Japan's involvement in sea-lane defence, during the Iran–Iraq War (1980–88), Japanese shipping in fact faced a direct military threat in the Strait of Hormuz, through which around 55 per cent of its oil was shipped. As far back as 1980, Republican Congressmen Paul Findley had used the prospect of an Iranian blockade of the Strait to press Japan to contribute to US-led patrols of the Gulf.[100] As a result of repeated attacks on neutral shipping by both sides, including 71 attacks in 1984 alone, the Japan Shipowners' Association (JSA) (*nihon senshū kyōkai*) and the powerful All-Japan Seamen's Union (*zennikai*) restricted their members' activities aboard tankers in the Gulf region.[101] Despite pleas for both sides to respect freedom of navigation from Japan's UN ambassador, Kuroda Mizuo, and talks between Foreign Minister Abe Shintarō and his Iranian and Iraqi counterparts in September 1984, attacks on Japanese-owned and chartered tankers persisted. On 5 July 1984, a Japanese engineer was killed after Iranian aircraft bombed the Liberian-registered tanker *Primrose*, while it loaded oil at the Ras Tanura terminal in Saudi Arabia.

The failure of Japan's diplomatic efforts to secure its shipping interests in the Middle East, including fruitless efforts to extend a UN-brokered moratorium on attacking civilian targets to include merchant shipping, served only to underscore its reliance on the US naval presence in the Gulf.[102] This strengthened US arguments that Japan, if unable to commit naval forces directly, should at least boost its own defence efforts, enabling more Seventh Fleet assets to be released from the Northwest Pacific. Japanese-owned and registered tankers (including the 180,000-ton *Nisshin Maru* and the 227,000-ton *Diamond Marine*) were among the victims of renewed air and surface attacks on shipping by Iran in August 1987. As a result, the JSA and the All-Japan Seamen's Union on 2 September temporarily suspended all Japanese-operated ships from entering the Strait of Hormuz, while the Shipowners Labour Relations Agency began organizing three-tanker convoys for shipping already in the Gulf to minimize the risk of further attacks.[103]

In this context, reluctant to follow Kuwait's example of requesting US naval protection for Japanese shipping for fear of Iranian reprisals against Japan's economic (mainly oil-related) interests in the country, MOFA counseled financial contributions to support US operations in the Gulf which had expanded to include escort operations for Kuwaiti-flagged tankers. However, Prime Minister

Nakasone proposed dispatching MSDF minesweepers directly to the Gulf. In the face of strong opposition from within his own party, including from Chief Cabinet Secretary Gotōda Masaharu, a far less controversial decision to supply navigational aids to Saudi Arabia was made instead.[104] Nakasone's failure to win support for his initiative to dispatch minesweepers in 1987 demonstrated that in both practical and political terms, Japan's ability to extend naval protection to its shipping beyond 1,000 nm remained well beyond its reach. Although MSDF minesweepers were dispatched to the region in April 1991, this occurred only after the end of the Gulf War – underscoring the government's inability to send the SDF overseas in circumstances that might imperil its position on collective self defence.

Conclusion

Sea lane defence rose to the fore of Japan's defence policy and alliance relations in the late 1970s and 1980s owing, above all, to pressure from the United States to boost defence efforts. This reflected Washington's assessment of its own deteriorating strategic position vis-à-vis the Soviet Union and determination to transfer more of the defence burden to regional allies. Japan's dependence on the US Navy for security in the Gulf region provided a persuasive rationale for US officials to pressure Tokyo to boost its defence efforts in the Northwest Pacific to compensate for the reallocation of US Seventh Fleet assets to the Indian Ocean. This dependence was magnified once the Iran–Iraq War had demonstrated the vulnerability of Japanese shipping to attack. Moreover, US officials familiar with the longstanding ambitions of former Imperial Navy officers to develop the MSDF into a blue-water navy role knew that appealing to Japan's vulnerability to blockade was likely to register in Japan as would few other scenarios for military cooperation.

As a relative 'dove' on defence issues, Prime Minister Suzuki's May 1981 comments and subsequent retractions fit the pattern of minimalist, *ad hoc* responses to US burden-sharing demands consistent with the Yoshida Doctrine and domestic constraints laid down in the 1945–77 period. At the same time, US efforts to expand Japan's share of the 'defence burden' via sea lane defence met with support from decision-makers in the JDA, MOFA and LDP, who for their own varying strategic, bureaucratic and political reasons supported an increase in Japan's defence and alliance cooperation efforts.

Suzuki appears, at best, to have been an unwitting accomplice in setting the political agenda for sea lane defence in the 1980s. The substance of his comments in May 1981 echoed his statements before the House of Councillors Special Committee on Security in October 1980 and Diet speeches of JDA officials as far back as Kubo Takuya's statement in November 1970. Suzuki's staff had assured him that his speeches to be delivered in the United States reflected existing policy. He therefore believed he was merely re-affirming JDA plans for defending convoys dating back to the 1960s in order to appease US officials eagerly pressuring Japan for an expanded territorial defence commitment. However, to Washington, the prime minister's comments constituted official acceptance of an expanded geographical division of responsibilities within the Alliance. Resisted initially as entrapment, sea lane defence was subsequently embraced and expanded by Nakasone to include a blockade of the Sea of Japan, as a political rationale for the build-up of SDF capabilities and alliance cooperation against the Soviet Union. A defence focus suited Nakasone's moderate, nationalist domestic political agenda but was also supported by the wider perception that a relative decline in US power was detrimental to Japan's security.

Even under a sympathetic administration, the SDF struggled to find a role that was acceptable to the public and accountable to the Constitution, while able to satisfy the strategic requirements expected and sometimes demanded by the United States. Sea lane defence proved to be a highly flexible concept that lent itself to these policy needs. A shift in SDF doctrine towards an extra-territorial sea and air area defence role, functionally integrated within US military strategy, could thus be argued as falling within the right of individual self-defence, based upon a Soviet threat to Japan's sea lanes. The 'protection of maritime transportation' was maintained as part of the MSDF's rationale for sea lane defence. But this masked an incremental transformation from a limited concept of escorted convoys dating back to the 1960s, progressing through an intermediary stage of patrolled sea lanes in the early 1970s, to a concept of zonal defence by the time of Japan's entry into RIMPAC in 1980. Throughout the decade, the pattern of SDF procurement and exercises pointed to its deepening integration within US global military strategy directed against the Soviet Union. The end of the Cold War in 1990–91 abruptly withdrew the strategic rationale that had underpinned sea lane defence in the 1980s. Yet sea lane security would re-assert itself as a strategic priority for Japan in the post-Cold War era against a more diffuse and more plausible array of threats and challenges, as will be shown in Chapters 7 and 8.

6 Japan's sea lane diplomacy in Southeast Asia since the 1970s

Introduction

This chapter explores the diplomatic aspects of Japan's SLOC security, concentrating on Japan's efforts to secure its navigational interests in a region of particular importance outside the 1,000 nm perimeter of sea lane defence. The choice of Southeast Asia as a case study for Japan's sea lane diplomacy reflects the economic importance to Japan of chokepoint straits and seas in the region, as profiled in Chapters 1 and 2. These include the Straits of Malacca, Sunda, Lombok–Makassar and the South China Sea, through which pass approximately 42 per cent of Japan's trade and most of its energy imports (see Map 6.1).

Japan's first navigational interest in the region is to ensure that safe navigation is physically possible through congested, constricted and shallow waterways. Second, its status since the 1960s as the primary extra-regional user of Southeast Asia's straits and coastal seas, for shipments of petroleum products, LNG, nuclear waste and other hazardous cargoes, has also made it the object of coastal states' environmental concerns, with the potential to create political friction. Third, and potentially most important, coastal states' jurisdictional claims to the region's most important SLOC have made it vital for Japan to be diplomatically engaged, particularly as these have gained recognition in the UNCLOS.

Given the emphasis that Japan has placed on excluding any strategic military content from its diplomatic relations, especially with other Asian countries sensitive to the legacy of Japanese occupation, this case study is also concerned with the extent to which Tokyo's self-declared pursuit of 'comprehensive security' has enabled Japan to secure its SLOC access through the application of purely non-military levers.

The importance of diplomacy in securing Japan's energy supply routes was identified in the 1979 official *Report on Comprehensive National Security*, which stressed:

> It is . . . important to find ways to ensure the safe passage of tankers through the long transport route passing the Indian Ocean, the Malacca Strait, and the South China Sea. Since Japan cannot resort to its own military power to protect tankers in these areas, it must give adequate consideration to alternative policies for this purpose and be willing to support the cost they entail.[1] [My ellipsis]

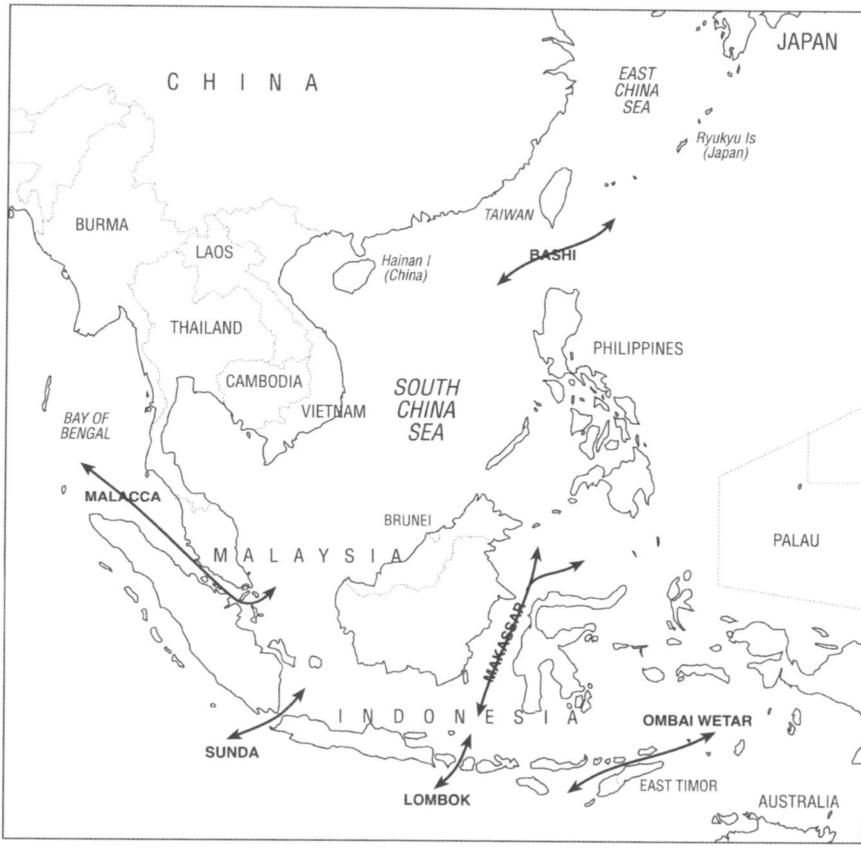

Map 6.1 Major Southeast Asian straits and channels.

These concerns are echoed in the MOFA December 2002 Energy Diplomacy statement, which declares 'maintaining and enhancing friendly relations with Middle East countries and other energy producing countries and countries along international shipping lanes' to be among Japan's foremost diplomatic objectives.[2]

This chapter charts the evolution of Japan's sea lane diplomacy from its failed bid to internationalize the Straits of Malacca in the early 1970s up to 2004. It initially locates Japan's SLOC-security interests in Southeast Asia in the general context of its regional diplomacy. This is followed by an analysis of Japan's responses to and perceptions of the UNCLOS framework. I then focus on three core sea lane security concerns for Japan in Southeast Asia. First, the Straits of Malacca demands separate consideration owing to its economic importance to Japan and the fact that jurisdiction is shared among three states. Second, Japan's diplomacy towards Indonesia is explored in the context of the latter's archipelagic doctrine and control of several other SLOC important to Japan's trade. Third, Japan's shipments of radioactive fuels and waste are examined, as the object of particular opposition from regional coastal states and beyond, and to explore the environmental aspects of SLOC security.

I demonstrate how a composite approach has developed in Japan, blending official and private diplomacy (via non-governmental and commercial organizations) as well as relying on other maritime states to pursue the more confrontational aspects of freedom of navigation in the region. Japan's diplomacy has been effective in terms of limiting its exposure to 'troublesome' conditions and tolls being placed by regional states on commercial shipping. By establishing cooperative frameworks and aid-backed good will with Southeast Asian states, Japan has reduced its own perception of vulnerability and need for compensatory defence policy responses. Potential military threats from regional states to Japan's navigational interests in Southeast Asia have been made less likely as a result of its broader diplomacy and economic linkages with the region. However, as is explored in the following two chapters, Japan's sea lane concerns in Southeast Asia extend to non-state actor threats to its shipping interests from piracy and terrorism, which require a different set of policy responses. Moreover, China's hegemonic potential and growing maritime capabilities are perceived in some quarters as posing a potential military threat to Southeast Asia's sea lanes from outside the region.

Japan's diplomacy towards Southeast Asia

Having officially forsworn military options in its dealings with the coastal states, Japan has had to rely on almost exclusively non-military means to secure access through the Southeast Asian chokepoints, making this the most critical test of its diplomatic and economic levers to deliver a liberal passage regime serving its international shipping interests. However, Japan's almost entirely commercial interest in freedom of navigation in the region has also simplified its dealings with littoral states more interested in limiting foreign military deployments for reasons of security and sovereignty than inhibiting merchant shipping.[3]

In looking after its interests in navigational access and shipping safety in Southeast Asia, Japan has generally been content to follow the lead of more assertive Western maritime states, such as the United States and Australia.[4] This reflects the pattern of Japan's post-war foreign policy approach in Asia, based on maintaining a low political profile in order to secure its resource inputs and minimize political risk to its large commercial presence in the region. Nonetheless, a policy approach relying on various non-military policy methods and a mixture of state and private sector involvement has developed gradually and proved successful in securing Japan's navigational security interests in the region from legal and environmental challenges by coastal states.

In the mid-1970s, a number of violent anti-Japanese riots in Southeast Asian capitals forced a review of Tokyo's regional policies. Since that time, the record of Japan's diplomacy with the key coastal states in Southeast Asia has been notable less for diplomatic failures or triumphs than for a stable continuum. Political and commercial relations have strengthened steadily, both at a bilateral level and through Japan's multilateral interface with the ASEAN, which was formed in 1967. Despite the implication of the non-official 'Malacca Straits defence theory' (*maraka bōeiron*) of the late 1960s that maritime Southeast Asia falls potentially within Japan's defence zone, it has been part of Japan's official defence policy to reassure Southeast Asian countries, particularly in respect of its security interest in the straits that 'Japan has only the capability of securing shipping within the range of 1,000 miles from Tokyo, Nagoya and Osaka'.[5] Visiting Japanese premiers and senior officials have tended to adhere to former Prime Minister Fukuda Takeo's formulation, outlined in Manila in August 1977, of seeking 'heart-to-heart' relations based on: (1) not becoming a 'military power'; (2) seeking closer economic, political and cultural cooperation with states in the region; and (3) promoting ties between ASEAN and Indochina.[6]

Economic relations based on the 'three pillars' of trade, aid and investment have underpinned the rhetoric of closer ties and cooperation since the 'Fukuda doctrine' was announced. Following Fukuda's visit, Japan promised $1 billion in aid. However, in large part the deepening of economic ties flowed from the revaluation of the yen under the 1985 Plaza Accords, which triggered a flood of foreign direct investment (FDI) from Japan into Southeast Asia. FDI levels increased from $855 million in 1986 to $4.7 billion by 1988, making Japan the region's largest external source of capital and Southeast Asia Japan's preferred overseas production platform in Asia. Additionally, between 1985 and 1992, trade between ASEAN and Japan rose by an annual average of 20 per cent, making ASEAN Japan's third-largest trade partner after the United States and the European Union. As the third leg of Japan's economic ties, Southeast Asia emerged as one of the primary beneficiaries of the expansion of Japan's Overseas Development Assistance (ODA) programme, the world's largest in the 1980s and 1990s until overtaken by the United States in 2001. In addition to benefiting Japanese firms relocating to Southeast Asia,[7] ODA was and is still viewed by MOFA as 'creating an international environment favourable to Japan'.[8] Some of Japan's aid to major ASEAN states, such as the Philippines and Indonesia, was labelled 'strategic' during the 1980s owing to the political importance attached to these countries' Western orientation in a Cold War context and their 'strategic location in key transit points in the world's ocean navigation'.[9]

Japan's economic decline since the collapse of the asset bubble in 1990–91 has eroded its pre-eminent economic position within Southeast Asia. Japan's economy remains five times larger than China's measured in dollars terms and Japanese FDI in the ASEAN region still amounted to $2 billion in 2000. In the wake of the regional economic crisis of 1997–98, Tokyo pledged aid worth over $30 billion via the New Miyazawa Initiative. Nonetheless, China's rising economic and political profile in the region, as exemplified by a November 2001 agreement to establish an ASEAN–China Free Trade Area (FTA) by 2010, has prompted Japan to launch competing initiatives for deeper economic ties with ASEAN states, on a bilateral and multilateral basis.[10] Such an approach is designed to maintain Southeast Asia as 'a sphere of paramount Japanese economic importance',[11] amidst growing concern that 'China wants to strengthen its influence over ASEAN members in order to challenge Japan's leadership in the region'.[12] The fact that Southeast Asia has been exempted from 10 per cent cuts to the overall aid budget implemented by Prime Minister Koizumi Junichirō's administration is testament to the importance Tokyo attaches to the value of ODA as a tool of influence in a region of high economic and strategic value – not least as a provider of mineral and energy resource exports. Koizumi has moved further than any recent Japanese premier to reinvigorate the Fukuda doctrine. During a January 2002 visit to five ASEAN capitals he announced measures to boost cooperation in education and human resources; people-to-people exchanges; an Initiative for Japan–ASEAN Comprehensive Economic Partnership; and the intensification of security cooperation, including against terrorism, piracy and human trafficking.[13] In the same month Japan concluded its first, largely symbolic FTA, with Singapore.

Japan and UNCLOS

In addition to relying on other maritime states, to avoid the impression of overt assertiveness, Tokyo has sought where possible to represent its legal and navigational safety concerns through the multilateral auspices of the IMO as the UN-level body responsible for international shipping interests. The major IMO regulations governing ship safety are: (i) SOLAS, which covers ship construction and safety equipment; (ii) the 1973/78 International Convention for the Prevention of Pollution from Ships (MARPOL); (iii) the 1972 Convention on the International Regulations for Preventing Collisions at Sea (COLREG); (iv) the 2002 ISPS code; and (v) the 1993 International Safety Management (ISM) code, which regulates operating licences among shipping companies.[14] According to Michael Leifer, Japan has 'the prospect of securing the best of both worlds in that it avoids undue tension with coastal states with whom it has close economic associations while its goal of transit passage is obtained through the diplomacy of the superpowers'.[15]

However, Japan's approach to UNCLOS has evolved unevenly. According to a personal account of Japan's 'inept' and 'dismal' negotiating performance at the second UNCLOS conference (UNCLOS II) in the early 1970s, Tokyo's view of UNCLOS was affected by a declining faith in the ability of the United States to protect Japan's sea lanes militarily. This perception led Japanese negotiators to overestimate the power of resource-supplier states while underestimating their own position. Moreover, Japanese representatives drawn from the Foreign, International Trade and Industry, Transport and Justice ministries as well as the agencies for Fisheries, Defence, Land, Natural Resources and Energy were reportedly unable even to reach a coordinated position on many issues placed before them.[16] Continued wariness about UNCLOS was behind Japan's decision to oppose the legal concept of a 200-nm EEZ, the only one of 116 nations represented at the UNCLOS III meeting in Caracas to do so.[17]

Japanese commentators have periodically expressed concerns over the implications of the UNCLOS framework throughout its 1958–94 evolution, especially in regard to 'creeping jurisdiction' and legal justifications that could be used to implement tolls and other restrictions on vessels' movements. According to Japan's senior representative to UNCLOS III, MOFA's former Deputy Director of the Sea Law Office, Iguchi Takeo, the importance of Japan's relations with Indonesia and Malaysia has increased as a result of the Law of the Sea, given its potential implications for freedom of navigation.[18] In 1980, former MSDF Chief of Staff Admiral Uchida Kazutomi commented that as long as innocent passage is respected in archipelagic waters and transit passage upheld in international straits 'few problems are likely to arise'. Equally, Uchida expressed concern about the potential for 'states with international straits within their territorial waters impos[ing] troublesome conditions beyond those related to safety and pollution' and other 'difficulties and hindrance' in archipelagic waters.[19] Vice-Admiral Yamamoto Makoto, a former Chief of the Self Defense Fleet, has identified 'unilateral declarations restricting specific waters' as among the most important potential challenges confronting freedom of navigation in the Asia-Pacific.[20] According to former JDA Administrative Vice-Minister Akiyama Masaru, until 2001 the Agency's most senior policy official, the trend among coastal and archipelagic states to claim surrounding waters, including international straits, constitutes the second-most important maritime security challenge to Japan, after China's future defence capability.[21] In part driven by such suspicions, Tokyo's diplomacy on the Straits of Malacca and towards the Law of the Sea was initially counter-productive, as is detailed in the following section.

The Straits of Malacca

As the major commercial user of the Straits of Malacca, drawing around 80 per cent of its oil and much of its LNG through the straits, the challenge for Tokyo in its dealings with the 'straits states' – Indonesia, Malaysia and Singapore – has been to segregate its interests in navigational safety as far as possible from politico-legal issues impinging on sovereignty. Generally, whenever the two issues have become entangled, as occurred in the early 1970s, Japan's relations with the coastal states have suffered.

Indonesia is by far the most important of the straits states to the navigational interests of Japan and other extra-regional maritime states given its size and geostrategic location between the Indian Ocean and Pacific. A major concern of Indonesia's post-independence leaders was to control the movement of foreign naval forces through the Straits of Malacca, which, it was feared, might otherwise continue to serve as a gateway for foreign powers seeking to intervene in the archipelago. In the early years of the Indonesian Republic, such concerns were given credence by the use of the straits by the Dutch to build up their forces in West

New Guinea and later by covert Western assistance to rebels in Sumatra and elsewhere with the aim of destabilizing President Soekarno's left-leaning government in Jakarta.

Aspirations to control the straits in their entirety periodically resurfaced during Soekarno's rule. However, Indonesia's declaration of a 12-nm territorial sea in 1957 was followed by legislation in 1960 committing Jakarta to demarcate its sea boundaries with its neighbours by means of a median line in cases where the waters dividing them were less than 24 nm wide. However, cooperation between Indonesia and Malaysia was impossible throughout the 'Confrontation' period (1957–66), when the straits were the scene of military clashes between Indonesian and Commonwealth forces. Only once the anti-Communist President Soeharto was in power and all three littoral states were linked as co-founding members of ASEAN from 1967, did cooperation on the straits again become possible.[22]

For its part, Malaysia shared the desire of many newly independent coastal states, including Indonesia, to 'wrest some control from developed nations which had by and large determined the course of customary international law particularly at the law of the sea conferences'.[23] Using powers of decree invoked to quell racial disturbances in May 1969, the Malaysian government enlarged its own territorial sea from 3 to 12 nm in August. In March 1970, the two states reached agreement to delimit a common boundary along a median line, placing a 'jurisdictional gate' across the straits. Singapore shared a common interest in improving navigational conditions in the strait. However, as it is also surrounded by Indonesian and Malaysian territory, and strategically reliant on outside powers' access through the Straits of Malacca for its survival, the joint enclosure of the straits by its neighbours signalled negative consequences for its security.

Japan's interests in the Straits of Malacca

The Straits of Malacca had served as a reliable conduit for Japan's imports and exports since recovery began in the 1950s. However, Japan's concerns about navigational safety in the straits increased in late 1960s with the introduction of the first 200,000 DWT VLCCs, which increased both the risks and stakes involved in a collision or major spill.[24] In July 1967, three months after the *Tokyo Maru* became the first Japanese supertanker to ground itself in the Straits of Malacca, Japan proposed to the Inter-governmental Maritime Consultative Organisation (IMCO), until 1982 the forerunner to the IMO, the creation of 'sea lanes' to separate east-bound and west-bound traffic within the straits. The Indonesian representative to the IMCO agreed to this suggestion in principle, with the proviso 'that such an arrangement shall in no circumstances interfere with the rights and integrity of a State in its territorial water'. It was also made clear that Indonesia would be unable to bear the costs of any associated survey and dredging work 'for the foreseeable future'.[25] Jakarta, for this reason, did not oppose a survey expedition conducted by a Royal Navy hydrographic vessel in 1967.

In July 1968, the Malacca Straits Council was formed in Japan as a private body to coordinate Japanese oil, shipping and marine insurance companies, and to represent their common interests in navigational safety and access to the straits.[26] The MoT meanwhile began to organize funding for survey expeditions to determine the suitability of the straits for large tankers.[27] In spite of Indonesia's sensitivity regarding its 'rights and privileges', and misgivings among all three littoral states over Japan's decision to appropriate the name of the straits for the Malacca Straits Council, Japan's gathering interest in improving navigational safety was not itself the object of concern for either Indonesia or Malaysia.

Changes in Southeast Asia's external security environment around this time were key to a shift in attitudes among the straits states as well as in Japan. Early in 1968, the UK government, under mounting fiscal pressure, announced that it was accelerating its military withdrawal by several years 'East of Suez' to 1971, while from July 1969, the United States began to draw down its forces in mainland Southeast Asia with the announcement of the Nixon Doctrine. The first passage of a Soviet naval flotilla through the straits in 1968 was widely interpreted as a signal of Soviet interest in filling any related power vacuum. Soviet cargo vessels carrying supplies to Moscow's Far Eastern outposts were subsequently sighted regularly in the straits.[28] To Indonesia and Malaysia, these developments represented both new uncertainties and opportunities. To the New Order regime in Jakarta, the Soviet presence prompted fears that Communist rebels would receive clandestine support and that Indonesia could potentially be drawn into a superpower clash over access to the straits. In Malaysia, questions were asked in parliament about the government's readiness to prevent unfriendly warships from using the straits even though Western forces retained a small air and naval presence on the Malaysian side.[29] By the same token, the drawdown of Anglo-American defence responsibilities in the region was an opportunity for both Indonesia and Malaysia to repair bilateral ties and to mutually assert their sovereignty claims. Obtaining Singapore's cooperation was an important objective for Indonesia, as it would enable the Malacca and Singapore straits to be presented as a single legal entity, on which a common position might be adopted.

Following the Royal Navy survey in 1967, Japan obtained permission from the coastal states to proceed with a preliminary survey of the straits from January to March 1969. The Hydrographic Department of the MSA and MoT officials also participated in the survey conducted under the auspices of the Malacca Straits Council. As a private level body with plenipotentiary powers, the Malacca Straits Council enabled the government to minimize Japan's diplomatic profile in negotiations on the straits, partly to avoid the impression of imposing its will, but also to avoid conferring *de jure* recognition of Indonesia's and Malaysia's territorial sea claims.[30] The survey identified several shoals and sunken obstacles, and plans were laid for a second expedition. In May, the MoT and MOFA held joint consultations with the US International Development Agency, with a view to presenting a plan to secure safety of navigation in the straits to other major users and to the three coastal states later that year.

However, Japanese negotiators learned subsequently that Kuala Lumpur had linked its permission for a new survey to Japan's recognition of the new 12-nm territorial sea boundary declared in August. Tokyo was reluctant to validate Malaysia's claim, since it amounted to recognition that the narrowest sections of the Straits of Malacca were entirely under the sovereign control of the coastal states. In September 1969, a Japanese naval flotilla was dispatched through the straits. The MSDF's first post-war training mission to Southeast Asia was in part a signal designed to demonstrate Japan's concern to keep the straits internationalized, as suggested by the MSDF Chief of Staff's reported comments to departing crews, framing the symbolic importance of the training mission in the context of the Royal Navy's withdrawal from Singapore.[31] When the Administrative Bureau of the Malacca Straits Council attempted to negotiate survey and dredging rights for Japanese vessels separately with Indonesia and Singapore, the approach was rejected by Indonesia.[32] The dispute was settled only in May 1970 following a direct appeal for Malaysia's consent from Japan's MOFA. A compromise was eventually reached whereby an Indonesian vessel would be used for the second survey.

Concerned at Malaysia's unexpected linkage to its territorial sea claims and at the new concert between former rivals in Kuala Lumpur and Jakarta, Japan approached the IMCO in 1970 to garner support for some form of institutional representation for itself and other shipping nations on navigational safety matters in the straits. In October, the Japanese delegate to the IMCO Subcommittee on Safety of Navigation revealed Tokyo's intention to 'set up an international co-operative system which includes three littoral countries and major shipping countries' as a prerequisite to the introduction of a TSS.[33] In early 1971, MoT representatives took the idea one stage further, by proposing to set up a Malacca–Singapore Straits Board, including representatives from major maritime states, to whom the straits states would be required to report on an annual basis. Failing to anticipate the straits states' reaction to these proposals, the issue of international regulation was pursued further by the Japanese delegation at the meeting of the IMCO Subcommittee on Safety of Navigation in London in July 1971.

Indonesia and Malaysia both registered their strong opposition to Japan's 'inappropriate' attempt to 'take away' the right to control and supervise the straits from the coastal states. On 16 November 1971, Indonesia and Malaysia bilaterally proclaimed the 'de-internationalization' of the straits in a Joint Statement, to which Singapore also partially acceded. The tripartite Joint Statement asserted:

- Safety of navigation in the Straits of Malacca and Singapore is the responsibility of the coastal states concerned.

- A body should be established to coordinate safety of navigation, composed only of coastal state representatives.
- The problem of safety of navigation and the question of internationalization of the straits should be treated as two separate issues.
- While 'fully recognizing their use for international shipping in accordance with the principle of innocent passage', Indonesia and Malaysia declared that the Straits of Malacca and Singapore were no longer considered 'international straits'. (On this point Singapore restricted itself to 'taking note' of the Malaysian–Indonesian position.)[34]
- On the basis of this understanding, the three governments approved the continuation of the hydrographic survey.

Thus, Japan's attempts to promote the internationalization of the straits had the opposite effect. Despite protesting against the Joint Statement, when questioned in the Diet about Tokyo's response to the threat of restrictions on Japanese shipping passing through the straits, the then Foreign Minister Fukuda Takeo said only that 'Japan would insist on the principle of free passage'.[35] Malaysia's and Indonesia's *fait accompli* exposed the limits of Japan's influence over the littoral states. It was also a set-back for Japan's Southeast Asian diplomacy, casting Tokyo in the role of a former occupying power attempting to impose a solution on de-colonizing states in Asia – the very perception that its post-war regional diplomacy was designed to counter.

A change in the legal status of the straits was not inherently threatening to Japan's security; the concerns of government and industry flowed more from uncertainty as to the ultimate intentions of the straits states. It was suggested at the time that Indonesia was contemplating the exclusion of large tankers from the Straits of Malacca in order to attract more shipping south through the archipelago, in support of its plans to develop the port of Tjiltjap on the south coast of Java.[36] In the follow-up to the Joint Statement, various official and non-official statements emanating from Malaysia and Indonesia gave Japan further cause for concern. In 1972, Indonesia proposed banning fully-laden VLCCs over 200,000 DWT from traversing the straits, which would have compelled Japanese supertankers either to divert through Lombok or to sail under-capacity. Both of these options were resisted for the considerable extra cost they would have incurred. On 17 April 1972, the Chief of Staff of the Indonesian Navy was reported as saying that warships and supertankers would be attacked if they entered Indonesian territorial waters.[37] VLCCs, the majority of them ferrying oil through the straits to Japan, were increasingly the object of environmental concerns in the littoral states, with Malaysian Deputy Prime Minister Tun Ismail Abdul Rahman telling an ASEAN Ministerial Meeting in Singapore that the coastal states opposed internationalization of the straits as 'such a concept would . . . endanger the livelihood of large segments of the population of our countries'.[38]

Japan was particularly concerned that the straits states would use their sovereignty claims to levy tolls similar to those charged in sea canals used for international navigation. In 1972, Tungku Razaleigh, then president of the Malay Chambers of Commerce, laid out plans – without official approval – to set up a joint Malaysian–Indonesian authority that would charge levies on ships transiting the straits, aimed in part at directing traffic to Malaysian and Indonesian ports facing the straits. The proposed annual income from levies (set at $5,000 for oil tankers, $3,000 for cargo ships and $1,000 for cargo ships calling at Malaysian and Indonesian ports) was estimated at $147 million.[39]

The early 1970s was the low-point for Japan's Straits of Malacca policy and marked the end of its attempts to gain a direct role in administering the straits through an international regime. The Joint Statement forced a re-evaluation of Japanese policy, prompting greater recognition of the coastal states' interests and the development of other non-military policy levers, mainly through increased financial and technical assistance. For their part, the coastal states subsequently moderated their stance having succeeded in extending their sovereignty over the straits. This was partly because security concerns relating to the straits lessened as the domestic and regional security environment stabilized in the 1970s. Japan's decision to part-fund Malaysia's development of Port Klang as a repair facility capable of accommodating VLCCs, thus generating local revenues from tanker traffic in the straits, may also have helped to ease Malaysian environmental concerns.[40] The change in both Indonesia's and Malaysia's positions generally reflected shortcomings in their enforcement capacity as well as their ability to finance safety measures independently. This perforce led them back to a path of cooperation with user-states. In addition, as UNCLOS III progressed, it became clear that many of the coastal states' key objectives, including recognition of the 12-nm territorial sea for coastal states as well as a new category of archipelagic state, would receive recognition under international law. The role of UNCLOS as a confidence-building legal regime through which the interests and concerns of both coastal and maritime states could be mediated was essential to restoring Japan's relations with the straits states to a cooperative track.[41]

For Indonesia, the recognition of its claim to archipelagic status – Jakarta's primary objective under UNCLOS – justified a compromise on the application of an innocent passage regime to the Straits of Malacca, especially as the eastern half of the straits fell outside its archipelagic waters claim. For the maritime states at UNCLOS, led by the United States, the *quid pro quo* demanded of the littoral states in return for recognition of many of their claims was to accept a new category of 'transit passage', a more liberal regime guaranteeing unfettered movement through straits connecting one high seas area or EEZ with another (see Appendix).[42] As UNCLOS took shape, uncertainties that had fuelled suspicions between Japan and the straits states during the Joint Statement period began to give way to the expectation of a common legal framework that would recognize the sovereignty claims of coastal states while upholding freedom of navigation through international straits. Indeed, following Jakarta's adoption of the Law of the Sea in 1985, Indonesian diplomats reverted to referring to the Straits of Malacca as an 'international strait'.[43]

The Traffic Separation Scheme and under-keel clearance limit

The next major test of Japan's relations with the straits states came when the VLCC *Shōwa Maru* ran aground in 1975, spilling more than 3,000 tonnes of crude south of Singapore. Although the spill was small in proportion to the tanker's capacity, the incident remains the worst peacetime spillage in the Straits of Malacca and sparked substantial compensation claims against the Japanese owners from all three straits states. However, the accident was successfully contained as an issue of navigational safety, with minimal political fallout on Japan's relations with the coastal states. The *Shōwa Maru* began a process that resulted in the implementation of the TSS and the establishment of the Revolving Fund, which together laid a stable foundation for Japan and the straits states to cooperate on navigational and environmental safety issues thereafter.

There are two basic approaches to improving safety for the passage of large tankers through the Straits of Malacca. The first relies on enhancing the safety parameters of the straits, by conducting surveys and dredging operations to establish optimum routes, designating separate lanes for east- and west-bound traffic and installing navigation aids. The second is to impose size and speed restrictions on vessels by setting a minimum under-keel clearance limit. While Japan's preference was for the former, the straits states pushed for an under-keel clearance limit, as this placed the onus of responsibility and cost on the vessel owners.

In the wake of the *Shōwa Maru* accident and the donation by the Japanese government of an oil-skimming vessel to Singapore, the Malacca Straits Council hosted a conference on shipping safety in Tokyo which recommended measures to improve safety in the straits, including the TSS and under-keel clearance scheme and the installation of navigational aids.[44] The JSA drafted a set of navigation rules for the MoT, including an instruction to reduce tanker speeds to 10–12 knots. A tripartite Council on Safety of Navigation and Control of Marine Pollution was then formed among the three straits states, which agreed to adopt an under-keel clearance of 3.5 m throughout the straits and to improve navigational aids further. It was also agreed that the users should bear the full cost of implementing safety measures. Following an extensive consultation process, the IMCO approved the under-keel clearance regulation and a TSS in the Singapore Strait and around One Fathom Bank (see Map 6.2). Japan accepted both initiatives, but requested a period of grace to make the necessary alterations to its tanker fleet.[45] The combined scheme was eventually introduced in May 1981, with financial and technical assistance from Japan. As a result, VLCCs over around 230,000 tons have since diverted through the Lombok Strait, for which Japan mounted joint preparatory survey expeditions with Indonesia in 1974 and 1975.[46]

The coastal states developed their own individual estimates for an under-keel clearance limit by adding values from three variables; squat (a phenomenon whereby the draught of a vessel increases as the result of a localized displacement

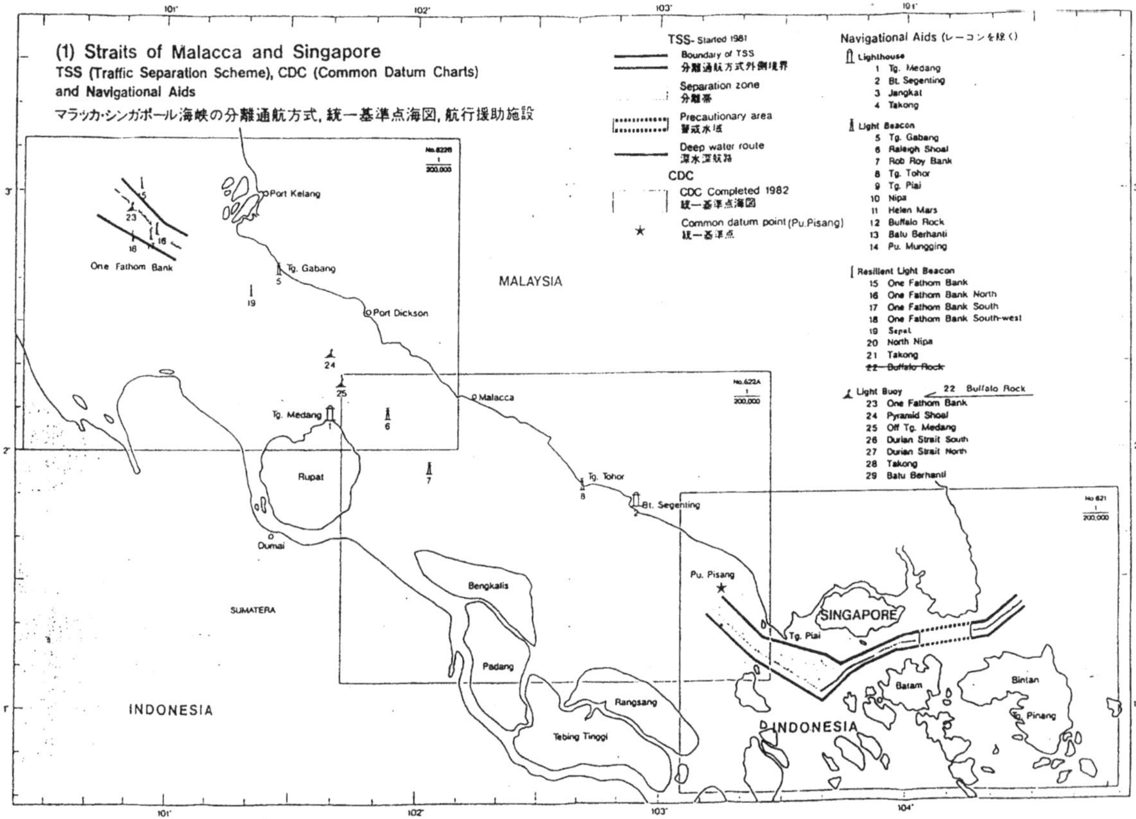

Map 6.2 The TSS in the Straits of Malacca.

Source: Malaysian Institute of Maritime Affairs/Ouchi Kazuomi.

of the water level caused by its forward motion), wave action swell, human factors and a safety margin. An under-keel clearance limit of 3.5 m was eventually adopted as a compromise figure between the Indonesian estimate of 4.5 m and the Singaporean estimate of 2.0 m.[47] A difference of even 1 m carries major commercial implications, since it means that a 250,000 DWT VLCC must reduce its load by 15,000 DWT. On a national scale, this would translate into an annual shortfall in capacity of 10 million tons according to one Japanese estimate.[48] A 1973 estimate in contemporary prices put the cost of diverting Japan's VLCCs over 200,000 DWT through Lombok–Makassar at some 10 million yen per tanker for each voyage, adding $100–270 million to Japan's annual oil import bill, which then totalled $3 billion.[49] At that time, Japan operated over 90 tankers in the 200,000–250,000 DWT range.

As of 2001, technical and financial assistance provided by Japan to the straits states through the Malacca Straits Council since 1968 amounted to over 13 billion yen. Of the 10 billion yen disbursed up to 1993, 1.4 billion was allocated to hydrographic surveys (the last conducted in 1978); 1.4 billion for the removal of four shipwrecks; 1 billion for dredging operations; 3.5 billion to install and maintain navigation aids; 502 million for a buoy tender donated to Malaysia in 1975; and 400 million to capitalize the Rolling Fund.[50] The JSA provides finance for navigational schemes in the straits via the Malacca Straits Council.[51] Since 1981, the fund has given the straits states the facility to withdraw money quickly to pay for responses in the event of serious spillages.[52] The Petroleum Association of Japan has also funded environmental clean-up exercises in the straits. In 1993, a base was established in Singapore to forward store equipment used for combating oil spills and the three littoral states have developed responses in case of oil spills through the Oil Spill Preparedness and Response (OSPAR) project, financed exclusively by Japan via the Rolling Fund.[53] In addition to the general IMO maritime safety initiatives listed earlier, particular measures to improve safety in the straits have been introduced with Japanese participation through the IMO, including a mandatory ship reporting system, STRAITREP, which has been in force in the Straits of Malacca since December 1998. STRAITREP requires all vessels transiting the straits to divulge details such as name, call-sign, position, course and speed and whether hazardous cargoes are aboard.[54]

Japanese technical and financial assistance was central to a number of other safety initiatives introduced in the straits. The hydrographic Common Datum Charts, on which the TSS was based, drew mainly from survey data collected jointly by Japan and the straits states from 1969 to 1975. From 1976 to 1979, the Malacca Straits Council compiled data on tidal ranges and currents.[55] In 1978, Japan was involved in a survey of One Fathom Bank to establish a 23 m navigable channel to service east-bound traffic. After this survey was completed in November, Japan and the three straits states agreed to the installation of additional navigational aids. In 1979, the MoT agreed to fund dredging operations required to make the new channels passable.[56] Between 1969 and 1988, the Council installed 39 navigational aids (lighthouses, beacons, buoys and surface radars) in the straits, which have since been maintained and replaced as necessary.[57]

The Malacca Straits Council and the Japan International Cooperation Agency have also discussed, as part of the ODA programme, a further round of surveys to monitor wrecks and shoals in the straits.[58] Maintenance and inspection work on navigation beacons is conducted biannually through the Malacca Straits Council, and in 2002 a replacement buoy tender was donated to Malaysia.[59] There are further official plans to help Indonesian personnel improve navigation skills.[60]

Japan also linked the legal position of the Straits of Malacca under UNCLOS to its own policy on the UN Law of the Sea. In May 1977, under the terms of the Law on the Territorial Sea, Japan extended its territorial seas to 12 nm, but opted to retain an outer limit of 3 nm in the four international straits abutting Japanese territory, Sōya, Tsugaru, Tsushima and Osumi.[61] This self-limiting ordinance was to avoid undermining its negotiating position with Indonesia and Malaysia by appearing to endorse the enclosure of international straits within territorial waters. The linkage was admitted by the government of the day:

> From the comprehensive viewpoint of the national interest of Japan, which imports the majority of its resources from overseas and depends heavily on trade and maritime shipping in particular, it is necessary to ensure free passage of merchant ships and large-sized tankers through the Straits of Malacca and elsewhere. . . . Therefore, as a provisional measure, for the time being, we shall not alter the present situation with respect to the so-called international straits of Japan.[62] [My ellipsis]

A Kra canal?

Most re-routing alternatives to the Strait of Malacca involve existing waterways passing through the Indonesian archipelago (see Chapter 1). However, Japan has intermittently expressed interest in a canal or 'land-bridge' across the Isthmus of Kra in Thailand. The original idea of a canal, which dates back to the seventeenth century, has been revived periodically in several incarnations. The land-bridge concept involves the construction of a pipeline and overland railway to connect terminals on either side of the isthmus. According to a recent estimate, the Kra land-bridge would shave 40–60 cents off the price of a barrel of oil for Northeast Asian consumers, representing an approximate saving of around 1–2 per cent.[63] However, according to Swinnerton, the 1,000 nm saved on the Straits of Malacca route (see Map 6.3), via the land-bridge, would only be worthwhile for 'Japan-bound VLCCs which would otherwise use Lombok'.[64]

In 1971, a Japanese approach was made to the military government in Thailand requesting permission to conduct a survey for possible routes across the Isthmus. The plan, similar to the land-bridge concept, envisaged 500,000-ton tankers operating shuttle runs between the Persian Gulf and a terminal at the Andaman Sea end of the pipeline. Oil would then be pumped to the Gulf of Thailand, where 200,000-DWT tankers would service the route to and from Japan. Construction was estimated to be four times cheaper than that of excavating a canal across the

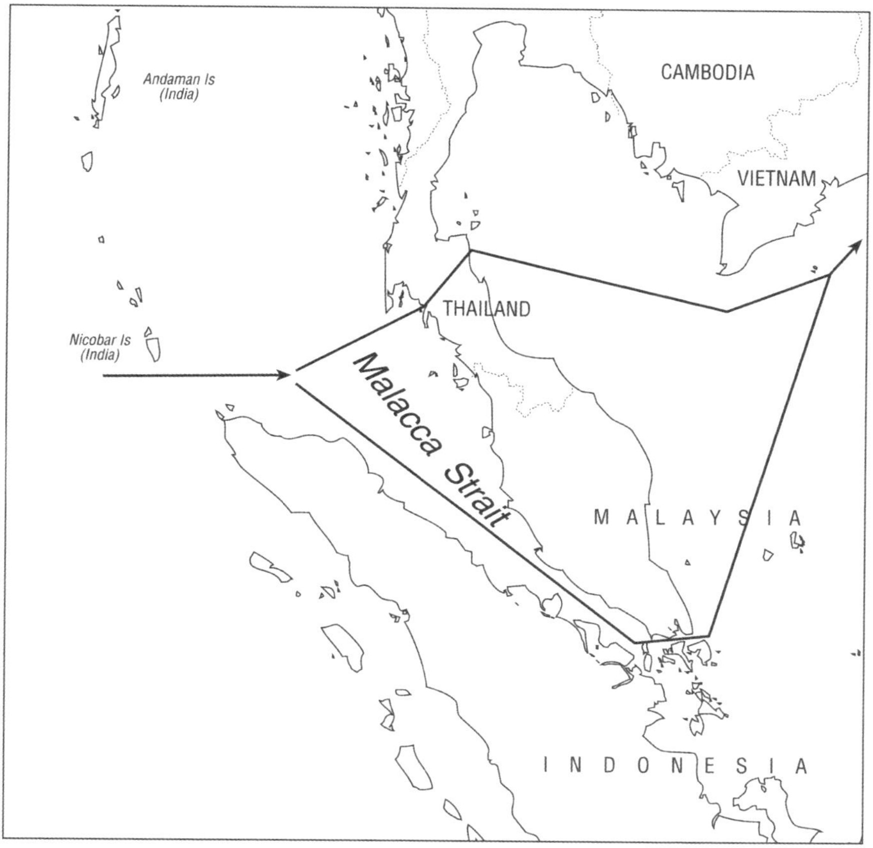

Map 6.3 Proposed Kra Landbridge route.

Kra. However, the successor to the Thanom–Praphat regime, which fell from power in 1973, did not pursue the project.[65]

The Mitsubishi Research Institute announced an interest in a Kra canal in 1986, when it included its own canal blueprint as part of a long list of infrastructure 'mega-projects' in the Global Infrastructure Fund. Some of the proposed schemes in the Fund amounted to little more than an exercise in corporate prestige. An implausible proposal to construct a canal within ten years using nuclear blast earth-clearance methods was rejected on environmental grounds. However, a Mitsubishi-funded proposal in 2000 to develop port facilities and an industrial development zone, in conjunction with a canal, received serious attention from Thai politicians eager to revive Thailand's post-1997 crisis economy with a national-scale construction project. Development costs were estimated at $25 billion to construct a two-way canal 102 km long, 25 m deep and 400 m wide.[66]

Unlike previous proposals that assumed the canal would have to be funded with external capital, it was suggested, at a seminar on the Kra Canal Project held at Hat Yai on 15 January 2000, that the proportion of foreign funding required would be as little as 20 per cent, with the remainder being sourced through a public flotation and Thai government funds.[67]

Proponents of the canal have claimed that navigational conditions would be less hazardous than in the Straits of Malacca and that it would be less prone to piracy or terrorist attack. It has also been claimed that the financial saving, relative to the cost of passage through the Malacca and Lombok Straits would range from \$37,000–120,000 per sailing. However, a 1973 survey report, based on a 12-year construction time frame, for a canal of equivalent length but only half the width predicted that the project would take more than 50 years to recoup its start-up costs.[68] Serious environmental objections have also been raised, which democratic governments in Thailand are less able to ignore than their military predecessors. Nonetheless, Prime Minister Thaksin Shinawatra's administration revived the canal proposal in late January 2003, by offering a contract to the Hong Kong-registered Phuket Pass Project (PPP) consortium to conduct a \$50 million dollar feasibility study. Japanese and Australian interests are believed to be the major financiers behind PPP, which has met local criticism due to the personal links between its chairman and the head of the government's study committee into the project. PPP's proposal, thought to be worth up to \$35 billion, envisages the construction of a trans-Isthmus canal concentrating on the ports of Chumphon and Songhkla in the Gulf of Thailand and the Andaman Sea towns of Ranong and Satun as possible sites.[69]

Doubts persist as to the commercial viability or additional security benefits of a Kra canal, particularly since the revival in 2004 of secessionist tensions and terrorism in southern Thailand. However, expressions of interest from Thai and Japanese-funded preliminary studies have, at a minimum, provided Japanese industry and officials with a form of insurance against any future attempts by Malaysia or Indonesia to place further restrictions or levies on tanker traffic passing through the Straits of Malacca, or future capacity strains on bottle-neck sections of the straits themselves.

Indonesia's archipelagic doctrine as a diplomatic challenge

Jakarta's political and military elites have tended to attach great importance to controlling surrounding waters and airspace. This aim is closely identified with the security and defence of the state, reflecting concerns over great power naval interests arising from Indonesia's geostrategic location; doubts about the fragile nature of national unity arising from the country's fragmented geography; a historically honed suspicion of outside intervention in Indonesia's internal conflicts by extra-regional powers; and a determination to maximize the country's strategic leverage and aspirations to regional leadership.[70] These concerns all informed the development of an archipelagic doctrine, first outlined in a December 1957 Declaration asserting that all waters within baselines connecting the outermost points of the Republic were 'integral parts of the territory of the Indonesian state'.[71] In 1960, this Declaration was made into law by the Act on Indonesian Waters Number Four (PRP/1960).[72] The archipelagic doctrine, or *Wawasan Nusentara*, is designed to forge a unified identity and a viable state from over 17,000 islands and dozens of ethnic and linguistic groups. It also aims to exert control over surrounding marine resources by expanding Indonesia's 'national territory' from 2 million to 5 million km^2. Thus the Indonesian government linked its claims to sovereignty over archipelagic waters to 'the country's territorial integrity, the unity and social cohesion of its people as well as national development'.[73] For these reasons, Indonesia's policy-making elites have viewed the archipelagic doctrine as 'vital to our continued survival as a nation'.[74]

As the primary alternative route for tankers unable to pass through the Straits of Malacca, and for most of the bulk ore trade between Australia and Japan, Lombok–Makassar is the second most important strait in Southeast Asia for Japan's trade.[75] These straits, together with Sunda and Ombai–Wetar, fall wholly within Indonesia's archipelagic waters claim, which received recognition from UNCLOS III in 1982, as well as a new category of ASLs passage, devised to cover routes normally used for international navigation through archipelagos (see Appendix).

The military security focus of Jakarta's position on freedom of navigation and Indonesia's expressions of 'sympathy with those who need international trade, because we are also dependent on international trade' simplified the task for Japanese negotiators at UNCLOS. This position was in contrast to Jakarta's suspicion of 'big powers' intent on pursuing 'global strategy'. According to Hasjim Djalal, Indonesia's foremost maritime legal authority and negotiator, it was the intention of Indonesian interlocutors at UNCLOS that merchant shipping would be free to transit the archipelago without restriction, with the exception of the largest categories of oil tankers and vessels carrying hazardous cargoes which demonstrate 'the need for a more regulated passage'.[76] The prospect that the coastal states in Southeast Asia would be tempted to block commercial navigation is rejected by Djalal as a 'fallacy', invoked by maritime states as 'a tactical argument during the Law of the Sea negotiations'. According to one Western observer, as long as Indonesia remains reliant on Japan as an export market for oil and gas, as well as for in-flows of aid and investment, the deliberate obstruction of Japan's sea communications by Jakarta or other Southeast Asian states would be 'akin to cutting their own throat'.[77] Hasjim Djalal echoes the logic of economic inter-dependence as a deterrent to unilateral action against Japan:

> The Japanese would like to have unimpeded passage through the straits for their own shipping, for their imported resources, and for their exports. It is in the Japanese interest to cooperate with the three coastal states, and it is in the latter's interests to co-operate with Japan as well.[78]

Sea lane closures

Indonesia has shut straits used by international shipping four times; in 1958, 1964, 1978 and 1988.[79] The first two closures were aimed at restricting the movement of British and Dutch naval vessels during periods of conflict or tension. Indonesia's motivation for the phased 48-hour closure of the Sunda and Lombok Straits in 1988, ostensibly to conduct naval gunnery drills, has been seen variously as a signal of Jakarta's displeasure over Saudi oil-pricing policies or aimed at Japan after it diversified its oil purchases away from Indonesia.[80] However, a more plausible explanation is that by temporarily closing the straits, the military, possibly in coordination with the Foreign Ministry, was testing international reaction to a legal precedent for suspending passage.[81] At the time, the assertion of Defence Minister Benny Moerdani that Indonesia was exercising its 'sovereign right' prompted a qualification from Foreign Minister Ali Alatas that the Sunda and Lombok straits were 'part of our archipelagic waters, albeit not quite full national waters'.

The Japanese authorities coordinated their diplomatic response with Australia, but did not officially protest against the closure until the next year, following protests from West Germany, the United States and Australia. As the closures resulted in little or no disruption to traffic through the straits, MOFA did not register the incident as a threat to Japan's shipping interests.[82] With a view to the risk of being denied access to various Southeast Asian straits in future, the Japanese shipping firm 'K'-line has studied alternative routes through the archipelago via the Sunda Strait, Lombok and Maluku. However, the company has not studied the much longer diversion around Australia.[83]

Archipelagic sea lanes

In August 1996, two years after UNCLOS had entered into force, Indonesia informed the IMO's Maritime Safety Committee that it had nominated three ASLs, each on a north–south axis: (i) through the Sunda and Karimata Straits to the South China Sea (aluv laut kepulauan Indonesia (ALKI)-I); (ii) through the Lombok and Makassar Straits and Sulawesi Sea (ALKI-II); and (iii) a tri-pronged ASL connecting the Maluku Sea with the Ombai and Wetar Straits and Arafura Sea (ALKI-III).[84] Despite implicitly restricting archipelagic passage along an east-west axis, Jakarta maintained in June 1998 that 'for the time being, the three north-south lanes are sufficient'[85] (see Map 6.4).

The United States and Australia were the first nations to express concern about the proposed ASLs and the implications for (principally naval) vessels wishing to sail laterally through the archipelago, from Darwin to Singapore via the Java Sea for example.[86] The absence of an east-west ASL is of less obvious economic importance to Japan than south-north ASLs, which include the heavily trafficked Sunda and Lombok–Makassar routes. Nevertheless, it is still claimed that the restriction of merchant shipping to just three ASLs would result in 'additional costs which would have to be borne in higher commodity prices'.[87]

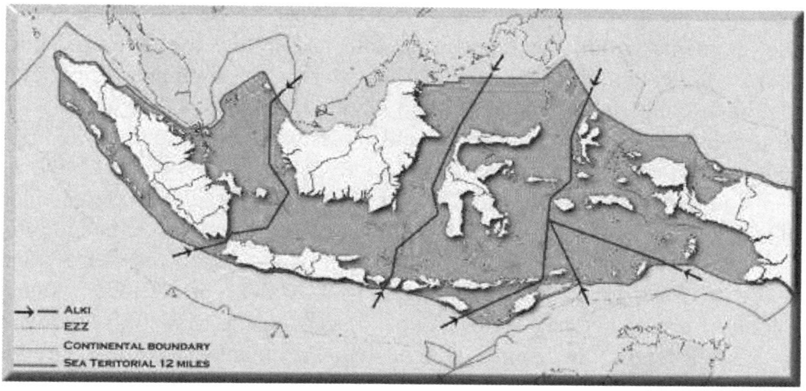

Map 6.4 Indonesia's ASLs.

Source: Reproduced with permission of Department of Marine Affairs and Fisheries, Republic of Indonesia.

Among the maritime states most obviously affected, Australia sought consultations with Indonesia through the IMO over the designation of ASLs prior to the meetings of the IMO's Maritime Safety Committee and Sub-Committee on Safety of Navigation, respectively in December 1996 and December 1997. Indonesia's response was to recognize the IMO's authority only insofar as it addresses the technical aspects of navigational safety, such as monitoring and surveillance of sea and air traffic through the ASLs.[88] In May 1998, the plenary meeting of the IMO Maritime Safety Committee endorsed Indonesia's ASLs proposal, paving the way for its entry into force from 1999. Wishing to avoid overt criticism of Indonesia and with little direct interest in lateral communications through the archipelago, Tokyo's response to the north-south ASL proposal followed a familiar pattern of reliance on other maritime states to press their freedom of navigation concerns.[89]

Prior to the fall of the Soeharto regime in May 1998, the issue of political stability in Indonesia had been considered in Japan to be 'irrelevant in the case of the Lombok or the Malacca Straits'.[90] Such confidence diminished sharply with Indonesia's economic downturn and rising social and political instability marked by the intensification of inter-communal violence and regional rebellions in provinces such as Aceh and Maluku, which are located near major sea lanes. Since 1998, an upsurge in maritime piracy (the focus of analysis in Chapter 7) has made Indonesian waters the world's most dangerous environment for international shipping. Moreover, the October 2002 Bali bombings of Western tourist targets underscored the risk that Islamist terrorist groups operating within the country could stage a repeat of the al-Qaida-linked attack off Yemen on the French tanker *Limburg* by targeting shipping in Indonesian waters. For Japan and other states with a security interest in maintaining maritime access to the archipelago, the growing and multi-faceted threat posed by lawlessness and 'rogue' elements within the Indonesian state has shifted the focus of concern away from the potential risks posed by the government's archipelagic policies to a more basic concern over its capacity to maintain political stability.

Resurgent inter-communal violence and secessionist movements, including the forced separation of East Timor from the Republic in November 1999, have revived concerns within Indonesia's body politic about foreign interference in the archipelago. This has factored into a more assertive posture to challenge foreign naval movements, particularly near politically sensitive provinces. A US warship *en route* to East Timor was challenged near Maluku in October 2000, on suspicion of providing arms to local separatists.[91] In late May 2001, Indonesian Navy vessels reportedly opened fire on two Panamanian-registered dredgers, contracted to work on reclamation projects by the Singaporean government, while in an Indonesian shipping lane near Singapore.[92]

Nuclear shipments

Japan has also faced legal challenges from Southeast Asian coastal states related to its shipment of enriched nuclear fuels. Since 1992, when Japan began importing mixed-oxide (MOX) fuel in pellet form, re-processed from Japanese nuclear waste processed in Europe, governments and private pressure groups in states along the route of shipments have sought to exclude these nuclear materials from their EEZ or territorial waters.[93] Reflecting the broadening definition of security since the end of the Cold War to include the environment, Japan's policy of importing plutonium has itself been described as a threat to Asia-Pacific SLOC, on the grounds that the shipments present an unacceptable environmental risk and an under-protected target for terrorists seeking fissile material.[94] In response to opposition from Malaysia and Indonesia, Japan was forced to route its first shipment, aboard the *Akatsuki Maru*, around Australia instead of the preferred route via the Straits of Malacca.[95] Prior to its departure, Foreign Minister Alatas stated, 'we cannot close international sea lanes, but we have called on Japan, even pressed Japan, not to use Indonesian waters'. A Japanese request to use the Lombok Strait was turned down.[96]

In May 2004, the arrival of the *Pacific Swan* at Mutsu-Ogawara, Aomori Prefecture, marked the ninth MOX shipment from Europe to dock in Japan since 1992. The nuclear shipments have followed very varied routes for security reasons, demonstrating the flexibility of shipping compared with overland modes of transport. The *Akatsuki Maru* sailed from Cherbourg, via the Cape of Good Hope, south about Australia, through the Tasman Sea and southwest Pacific to Japan. The *Pacific Pintail* sailed from Cherbourg, via the South Atlantic and Cape Horn across the Pacific. The third vessel, the *Pacific Teal*, repeated the route used by the *Akatsuki Maru*, while a further shipment left Cherbourg aboard the *Pacific Swan* and sailed to Japan via the Panama canal.[97] A return MOX shipment took place in late 2002, when a consignment of fuel originally delivered in 1999 was returned to British Nuclear Fuels Limited in the United Kingdom via the route used by the *Akatsuki Maru* and *Pacific Teal*. The use of such varied routes has enabled Japan to carry out shipments securely and largely on schedule, if at the price of alienating a larger number of coastal states.[98]

The rights of coastal states, under UNCLOS, to enforce pollution restrictions within their EEZ, or to uphold unilateral or regional nuclear-free zones, has been invoked by several coastal states along the route of the shipments. While small states such as Mauritius have had no choice but to confine their opposition to diplomatic channels, some Australasian and South American countries have dispatched naval or coast guard vessels to ensure the nuclear cargo ships remain outside their EEZ. A growing possibility that Japan's fission-based nuclear programme may be curtailed, on grounds of safety as well as local political opposition, suggests that the importance of this particular aspect of its SLOC security may already have peaked.

Conclusion

The limits of Japan's influence and shortcomings in its diplomacy were demonstrated in November 1971, when Malaysia and Indonesia jointly declared their intention to 'de-internationalize' the Straits of Malacca following Tokyo's push to secure representation for itself in an international supervisory regime governing the straits. From that low-point, Japan, acting 'privately' through the non-official Malacca Straits Council, bilaterally at the state level, and multilaterally through the IMO, has steadily built up cooperative relationships with the key straits states. These ties have generally enabled Japan to balance its interests in safety and economy with the coastal states' sovereignty concerns and desire to minimize their exposure to environmental problems, with the exception of strong opposition to Japan's nuclear cargoes. Japan's status as the only user state to have set up an institutionalized funding mechanism has won it good will among the riparian states in the Straits of Malacca, as has its provision of technical assistance.

Although some anxiety remains in Japan about 'creeping jurisdiction' in maritime Southeast Asia, no major legal restrictions on the navigation of Japanese or other vessels using the Straits of Malacca have been introduced since the under-keel clearance regulation and TSS came into effect. No Asia-Pacific state has opposed the principles of freedom of navigation or innocent passage, while UNCLOS has given Japan grounds to defend itself under international law against any future attempt by signatories to introduce tolls.[99] In this way, the Law of the Sea can be regarded as a maritime confidence-building measure, reducing uncertainties about the effects of coastal state jurisdiction on freedom of navigation and obviating the need for Japan to act unilaterally or compensate by seeking a military presence in the region. Moreover, the establishment of a universal international maritime legal framework makes it less likely that there will be a repeat crisis over the legal status of the Straits of Malacca.

Despite relying on other maritime states to press the more contentious aspects of navigational access to Southeast Asia's sea lanes, Japanese initiatives utilizing economic and diplomatic influence since the 1970s have been quietly effective in pre-empting legal moves by coastal states to restrict access to commercial shipping and at creating a cooperative framework for addressing navigational safety in the Malacca Strait. Nonetheless, such efforts have limited scope for mitigating threats to its shipping interests in Southeast Asia posed by piracy, terrorism and inter-state conflict over the South China Sea. Japan's perceptions and responses to these conventional and unconventional SLOC threats in the post-Cold War era are explored in Chapters 7 and 8.

7 Japan's post-Cold War SLOC security

Piracy and terrorism at sea

Introduction

This chapter has two purposes. The first, in the section on 'Japan's post-Cold War defence and security', is to review the major post-Cold War changes and developments within Japan's security environment, particularly regarding sea lane security, and to look at how recent Japanese governments have responded to altered strategic circumstances in terms of alliance and defence policy. In the section 'Japan: piracy and terrorism at sea', Japan's responses to maritime piracy and terrorism at sea are examined as a case study in non-state actor threats to Japan's SLOC. This follows on from the overview of piracy and terrorism at sea in Chapter 2. In Chapter 8, a second post-Cold War case study profiles Japan's state-level military SLOC security concerns, concentrating on emerging views of China as a potential strategic threat, and the existing maritime security challenges posed by North Korea. For the sake of clarity, China's alleged involvement in the 'military' category piracy is dealt with as part of Japan's piracy concerns in this chapter.

This chapter argues that Japan's post-Cold War security posture, after undergoing a period of disorientation and dislocation in the early 1990s, came under the influence of rising 'realist' perceptions about Japan's security environment in reaction to a series of regional security crises mid-decade. The resulting strategic uncertainty brought a renewed focus on the US-Japan Alliance among Japanese security policy-makers, the restructuring of the SDF to suit a more fluid security environment and the pursuit of multilateral and bilateral security dialogue and linkages. The following section profiles perceptions of potential post-Cold War maritime threats to Japan and its sea lanes as officially defined in annual defence white papers and the 1995 and 2004 reviews of the National Defense Program Outline (*taikō*). These are compared with the generalized views of individual Japanese policy-makers, naval officers and academic analysts about sea lane security. These perceptions are related to the evolving force structure of the MSDF, analysis of which is also carried over into Chapter 8.

The case study in the section 'Japan: piracy and terrorism at sea' begins by evaluating data on the scale of the piracy and maritime terrorism threats confronting Japan, before profiling Japanese policy responses at multilateral, state and private levels. Japan's responses to terrorism are further explored in the context of the MSDF's deployment of a flotilla to the Arabian Sea in the wake of the 11 September attacks in the United States and the connection this has to Japan's SLOC security. The case study demonstrates that maritime piracy and terrorism are keenly perceived as security threats in Japan. However, it also shows that Japan's attempts to gain direct involvement in anti-piracy patrols in Southeast Asia and support for anti-terrorism efforts in the Arabian Sea and Gulf region reflect their use as pretexts for developing expanded security and regional leadership roles.

Japan's post-Cold War defence and security

As shown, 'sea lane defence' served primarily as a political rationale for force modernization and deepening military cooperation with the United States during the late Cold War period. This occurred in the context of a perceived, proximate threat posed by the build-up of the Soviet Union's maritime defence capabilities. By the end of the Cold War, the SDF were approaching the force levels set out in the *taikō*, and these were fully achieved in all categories by 1995. As a result of sea lane defence, the MSDF emerged at the end of the Cold War with 62 principal surface combatants (more than the Royal Navy), 16 submarines and 30 mine warfare ships. More than half of its authorized total of 16 squadrons of ASW aircraft were equipped with P-3Cs, with the inventory eventually reaching 100 as the last P-2Js were retired.[1]

The effects of sea lane defence on major SDF acquisitions continue into the present. *Kongō*, with a loaded displacement of 9,485 tons, became the first Aegis-system equipped guided-missile destroyer (DDG) commissioned into MSDF service in 1993 and the first to be acquired outside the US Navy. Similarly, the ambitions of the ASDF to acquire AWACs aircraft, linked to 'burden-sharing issues and the SLOC defence agreement',[2] led to an order for the first two of four E-767s being placed in December 1992. Japan's air defence planners expressed their preference for an airframe 'that has a range that can fly to the Spratlys'.[3] The gradual entry into service of 98 F-2 support fighters – the costly and problematic product of the 1980s FS-X joint development programme with the United States – promises to significantly boost the anti-ship capabilities of the ASDF, although a reduction from the 130 aircraft originally planned for procurement.[4]

Upon achievement of the original *taikō* force levels, the MSDF had approximately twice as many destroyers as the US Seventh Fleet and over four times as many P-3Cs. Despite emerging from the Cold War with the largest Asian navy behind the fast-deteriorating Russian Far Eastern Fleet, a 1993 RAND study judged the MSDF to be weak in the areas of fleet air defence, power projection, amphibious operations and long-range submarine operations, due partly to its increasing integration with the US Seventh Fleet.[5] As a result of the MSDF's single-minded concentration on navy-to-navy cooperation within the US–Japan Alliance, little effort was made in the 1980s to develop a joint operational doctrine or exercise programme with the other Self Defense Forces; the first tri-service SDF drill was only conducted in November 1998, on Io Jima.[6] The lack of jointness has compounded lacunae in the MSDF's capabilities. Regarding air defence, for example, SDF doctrine stipulates that escort vessels will conduct air defence to protect vessels at sea while the ASDF will 'conduct air defence operations within its capabilities'.[7] To compensate for the MSDF's lack of organic air cover, Japanese defence analysts had realised in the early 1980s that ASDF F-15s – with an unrefuelled combat radius of 1,000 nm – could provide a significant level of protection for the Self Defense Fleet along Japan's southern approaches if forward-based on Io Jima or other outlying islands.[8] However, despite the conclusion of the official *yōjō bōkū* ('air defence over the sea') study in 1987, the ASDF continued to concentrate on the air defence of the main islands.

Yet Japan's ability to respond to the emerging challenges of the post-Cold War era was found more immediately wanting in terms of the 'software' of political constraints binding the SDF's use than the military hardware built up during the Cold War. Slow to accept US claims of an intensified Soviet threat to Japan's sea lanes in the late 1970s, the JDA proved equally reluctant to jettison the Cold War paradigm. Defence white papers as late as 1995 identified a potential threat to 'sea lanes around Japan' posed by Russia's modernizing Far Eastern maritime capabilities.[9] Citing concerns over Russia's residual capabilities, North Korea's unpredictability and uncertainty over China's long-term intentions, 'realist' Japanese scholars were sceptical about whether an end to the Cold War could even be declared in Northeast Asia.[10]

The first test of the ability of Japan's security framework to respond to post-Cold War realities came in August 1990, before the collapse of the Soviet Union. Requests from the United States to contribute militarily to the international coalition being assembled to eject Iraqi forces from Kuwait came as a shock to Japanese leaders, exposing the undeveloped state of the government's crisis decision-making machinery and a level of 'burden-sharing' expectation that the existing legal framework could not support.[11] The ability of the politically weak government led by Prime Minister Kaifu Toshiki to respond decisively to the Gulf Crisis was hindered by an alignment of opposition parties on the left, resistant to any involvement in US military interventions, and conservatives resentful of US pressure in economic matters.[12] Attempts to enact a bill to enable the SDF to participate in United Nations (UN) peace-keeping operations (PKOs) were subject to obstruction by opposition parties in the Diet. Tokyo's ultimate pledge of $13 billion towards funding the US-led campaign did little more than to confirm negative impressions of Tokyo's 'cheque-book diplomacy'. The significance of the post-*bellum* dispatch of an MSDF mine-sweeping flotilla to the Gulf in April 1991 was similarly dismissed as tokenism, even though the first overseas operational deployment of the MSDF, only four years after Nakasone had failed to do the same, represented a momentous policy departure in domestic political terms.[13]

Japan's 'failure' to respond to the Gulf Crisis provided the impetus for a review of defence policy, but political inertia and the transition, in August 1993, to the first non-LDP government since 1955, meant that an official review of the 1976 *taikō* was not ordered until February 1994. However, the Gulf War did give rise to a more immediate initiative on the part of the LDP politician Ozawa Ichirō, who launched a party Special Study Group in June 1991 to analyse *Japan's Role in the International Community* (*kokusai shakai ni okeru nihon no yakuwari*). The Special Study Group Draft Report, released in February 1992, focussed on the collective security framework of the UN Charter as a vehicle for Japan to move beyond a 'passive' posture of security reliance on the United States. Aimed at developing a political leadership role on the global stage, the centrepiece of the group's recommendations was Japan's participation in UN PKOs.[14] Ozawa's linkage of an SDF peace-keeping role to Japan's recovery of 'normal' sovereignty and pursuit of a permanent seat on the UN Security Council has been dismissed, especially within Japan, as conceived mainly to gain foreign plaudits in order to boost his domestic political standing. Japan's involvement in international peace-keeping nonetheless emerged as a major foreign policy pillar in the 1990s. The enactment of the International Peace Cooperation Law on 15 June 1993 paved the way for Japanese PKO deployments in several countries including Cambodia (1993), Zaire (1994), the Golan Heights (1996), Honduras (1998) and East Timor (2002). However, a special five-point charter heavily circumscribing the SDF's terms of participation in PKO, adopted as part of the 1993 PKO law to win opposition parties' support, excluded Japan from UN and other peace-enforcement operations.[15] Japan's hopes for the UN as a vehicle for solving regional conflicts also diminished as successive UN peace-keeping efforts faltered in Somalia, Rwanda and the former Yugoslavia from 1993 onwards.

1995 defence policy review

In February 1994, Prime Minister Hosokawa Morihiro's administration commissioned a report on *The Modality of the Security and Defense Capability of Japan* (*nihon no anzen hoshō to bōeiryoku no arikata*), from the Advisory Group on Defence Issues, under Higuchi Hirotaro, chairman of Asahi Breweries.[16] The nine-member group, including former JDA Administrative Vice-Minister Nishihiro Seiki and Aoyama Gakuin University Professor Watanabe Akio, took the Gulf Crisis as its case study in considering improvements to Japan's crisis-management capabilities and the restructuring of the SDF. Out of concern that the Advisory Group would be used to justify deep cuts to SDF force levels the JDA convened its own, parallel 'Conference to Examine the Future Modality of Defense Capability', from June–December 1993, chaired by Director General Aichi Kazuo.[17] In May 1994, JDA Director General Kanda Atsushi cited North Korea as the main reason why no dramatic cuts to the SDF's frontline strength were planned as part of the official review of defence policy.[18]

The 'Higuchi Report' premised its recommendations on a post-Cold War transition in international relations 'from the confrontational to the cooperative pattern'. During this transition, the report identified risks to global security from localized military clashes (which 'will occur more frequently and become more complex' than during the Cold War), the proliferation of WMD and the destabilizing spread of poverty and social discontent in weak states no longer supported by the major powers. Despite the report's relatively benign assessment of the global security environment, the fact that the Higuchi panel convened during the crisis over North Korea's threatened withdrawal from the Nuclear Non-Proliferation Treaty underlined to participants the importance of maintaining Japan's alliance with the United States and improving the structure of the SDF to adapt to the possibility of regional conflict, while simultaneously developing a multilateral security dialogue among Asia-Pacific countries. Multilateralism would evolve according to a three-stage agenda aimed initially at boosting confidence-building, before moving to an interim process of preventive diplomacy, with an ultimate objective of conflict resolution.[19] The attachment to multilateralism was particularly associated with Watanabe's input. From their respective inaugurations in 1994 and 1993, the ARF and the Council for Security Cooperation in the Asia Pacific (CSCAP) received financial and diplomatic backing from Japan as the respective official and 'track-two' vehicles for multilateral security dialogue. The JDA has also established over 13 bilateral defence dialogues with countries other than the United States since the end of the Cold War.[20] In accordance with a formula established under Prime Minister Miyazawa Kiichi's administration (1991–93), Japan would also seek to form *ad hoc* groupings, such as the ill-starred four-party Korean Peninsula talks involving Japan, the United States, South Korea and China (re-incarnated in a six-party format, including Russia and North Korea, under Chinese sponsorship since August 2003).

Maritime threats and capabilities

The Higuchi Report identified 'interference in the safety of maritime traffic', together with the violation of territorial air space, limited missile attack, illegal occupation of part of the country, terrorism and an influx of armed refugees among potential military dangers confronting Japan in the post-Cold War world.[21] Despite a declining probability of conventional military aggression against Japan, such as 'full-scale attacks on sea-lanes by Soviet submarines', the report's authors stressed that the safety of maritime traffic was 'a matter of life and death to Japan', due to the country's extremely high degree of overseas dependence for energy supplies and trade in manufactured goods.

Following their discussion of MSDF strategy and problems on 30 March 1994, the group met on 22 June for the fifteenth time to discuss sea lane defence, together with manning levels for the GSDF. Its members concluded that the defence of Japan's maritime interests would continue to be rooted in the Alliance with the United States with its 'overwhelming superiority at sea', supported locally by the MSDF and the MSA – since renamed the Japan Coast Guard – in its duties.[22] In terms of force structure recommendations, they concluded that the reduced threat faced by Japan justified a downsizing of the MSDF's ASW and mine counter-measures fleet. At the same time, the panel recommended establishing a 'more balanced' capability with particular emphasis on improved command, control, communications and intelligence, including the deployment of reconnaissance satellites. The SDF should also enhance inter-operability both with US forces and among its own ground, air and maritime components.

With UN PKO participation in mind, a need was also identified to expand the MSDF's ocean-going sealift and supply capabilities, the need for which had been revealed during the SDF deployment to Cambodia in 1993.[23]

The findings of the Higuchi Report and JDA study fed through to a revised version of the *taikō*, released in November 1995. As a result, the MSDF was downsized, losing one of two mine countermeasures flotillas, three regional destroyer divisions and three squadrons of fixed-wing patrol aircraft (Table 7.1). However, the core of the MSDF's force structure was preserved intact. Under the revised *taikō*, the Fleet Escort Force retained four escort flotillas, each made up of eight helicopter-carrying escorts, including a *Kongō*-class Aegis DDG to provide defence against air – and, prospectively, ballistic missile – threats.[24] The MSDF has acquired five Aegis destroyers and eventually plans to commission a total of eight, in an echo of the '8:8:8' force structure guideline (composed of twin battleship squadrons and eight heavy cruisers) adopted by the Imperial Navy in the 1920s.

Table 7.1 Force levels of the 1995 *taikō*

SDF	*Basic units*	*Main equipment*
GSDF	Regional units	8 Divisions 6 Brigades
	Mobile units	1 Armoured Division 1 Artillery Brigade 1 Airborne Brigade 1 Helicopter Brigade
	Low altitude ground-to-air missile	8 Anti-Aircraft Artillery Groups
ASDF	Aircraft control and warning	8 Groups, 20 Squadrons
	Interceptor	9 Squadrons
	Support fighter	3 Squadrons
	Air reconnaissance	1 Squadron
	Air transport	3 Squadrons
	Airborne early warning	1 Squadron
	Ground-to-air missile	6 Groups
	Main equipment	
	Combat aircraft	Approx. 400
MSDF	Destroyer units (for mobile operations)	4 Escort Flotillas
	Destroyer units (regional district units)	7 Divisions
	Submarine units	6 Divisions
	Minesweeping units	1 Flotilla
	Land-based ASW/patrol aircraft	13 Squadrons
	Main equipment	
	Destroyers	Approx. 50
	Submarines	16 (plus 2 in training)
	Combat aircraft	Approx. 170 (140 vessels and 370,400 tons)

Source: *Defense of Japan 2000*, Tokyo: JDA/*Japan Times*, pp. 89, 245.

The Fleet Submarine Force operates 16 diesel-powered, domestically manufactured boats organized into two flotillas. One new submarine is launched every year and the oldest automatically retired, creating a very modern fleet, equipped with Sub-*Harpoon* anti-ship missiles and Type-89 wire-guided torpedoes. The first of the 2,750-ton *Oyashio* class was commissioned in March 1998, built to a double-hulled design enabling longer-range, deep-water operations and equipped with hull and flank Hughes/Oki ZQQ 5B/6 sonars.[25] The operational effectiveness of the Fleet Submarine Force is suggested by reports that a Japanese submarine obtained a torpedo-firing solution against the USS *Kitty Hawk* on joint exercises east of Okinawa in November 2003.[26] Two submarines are held in reserve for training and one has been converted to trial an air-independent propulsion system, based on Kockums' *Stirling* engine design, which would enhance future submarines' capability for sustained, submerged operations.[27] MSDF submariners have bemoaned that their inability, vis-à-vis surface fleet colleagues, to eke out new roles in peace support or disaster-relief has made it more difficult to justify their post-Cold War existence. However, such worries are more than likely misplaced as Japanese strategic concerns continue to mount about the growth of China's navy and its assertive maritime activities in and around Japanese waters (see Chapter 8). As one of Japan's few, true stand-alone military capabilities, offering projectable offensive and reconnaissance potential without attendant publicity, the future of the Fleet Submarine Force in its basic form is virtually assured.

The Fleet Air Force was reduced following the 1995 *taikō* from 16 to 13 fixed-wing and helicopter squadrons. Although a domestically produced P-X jet design will probably succeed P-3C maritime patrol aircraft as they are phased out from 2010, Japan's fleet of over 80 *Orions*, together with its submarines, still constitute a potent ASW asset, capable of reaching the Straits of Malacca with a range of over 2,000 nm. In addition, five EP-3 electronic surveillance versions have been acquired since 1990 as part of a drive to upgrade Japan's intelligence-gathering capabilities, which saw the establishment in January 1997 of a new Defence Intelligence Headquarters, in Ichigaya. The fielding of four domestically produced reconnaissance satellites, the first pair of which was launched in March 2003, will further enhance Japan's ocean surveillance capabilities.[28]

In 2004, a second *taikō* review was conducted, approved by the Security Council and the Cabinet, on 10 December. The review will see the dis-establishment of one regional MSDF escort unit, which will further reduce the inventory of destroyers from 54 to 47. This cut fell some way short of the MoF's reported preference for a downsized total of 38 destroyers.[29] Cuts to the manpower levels and frontline inventory of the GSDF and ASDF were also somewhat shallower than had been expected (Table 7.2). But in recognition of a 'remarkably severe financial climate', the 22.2 trillion yen budget approved for the Fiscal 2005–09 MTDP nonetheless represents an unprecedented overall reduction in defence outlays. The fiscal squeeze on JDA procurement is likely to be augmented by the Koizumi government's December 2003 decision to proceed with ballistic missile defence (BMD). Prior to the defence outline review, the JDA had already opted

Table 7.2 Force levels of the 2004 *taikō*

SDF	*Basic units*	*Main equipment*
GSDF	Regional units	8 Divisions 6 Brigades
	Mobile units	1 Armoured Division Rapid Reaction Group
	Ground-to-air missile units	8 Anti-Aircraft Artillery Groups
	Authorized personal	155,000
	Regular	148,000
	Rapid reaction reserve	7,000
ASDF	Aircraft control and warning	8 Groups, 20 Warning Squadrons, 1–2 Early Warning Squadrons
	Fighter aircraft units (interceptor and support)	12 Squadrons
	Air reconnaissance	1 Squadron
	Air transport	3 Squadrons
	Aerial refueling/transport	1 Squadron
	Ground-to-air missile	6 Groups
	Main equipment	
	Combat aircraft	Approx. 350
	Fighters	Approx. 260
MSDF	Destroyer units (for mobile operations)	4 Flotillas (8 divisions)
	Destroyer units (regional district units)	5 Divisions
	Submarine units	4 Divisions
	Minesweeping units	1 Flotilla
	Patrol aircraft units	9 Squadrons
	Main Equipment	
	Destroyers	47
	Submarines	16
	Combat aircraft	Approx. 150

Source: JDA.

to drop a new destroyer from its requested procurement items for fiscal 2004–05 for the first time since 1954. Otherwise, the MSDF is relatively well placed vis-à-vis the other services because its principal BMD platform, the Aegis-equipped DDG, is capable of serving in a variety of naval roles.[30]

Before the 2004 review, the MSDF won budgetary approval in fiscal 2002–03 for the augmentation of a fifth vessel to its Aegis destroyer fleet, at an estimated cost of 137 billion yen. Also approved was a new 13,500 ton class of helicopter-equipped destroyer (DDH), equipped with three SH-60J and one MH-53 in forward and aft positions, provisionally budgeted at 106 billion yen in the fiscal 2003–04 budget. At a time of build-down in the MSDF surface fleet, these acquisitions represent a countervailing trend towards qualitative build up. Indeed, following on from the flat-decked *Osumi*, construction of the new 13,500-ton DDH suggests that the technological and shipbuilding capacity is being maintained so as to leave open the option of laying down a fully fledged aircraft carrier in future.[31]

Alliance factors

Despite the disappearance of the Soviet threat rationale, which had underpinned US–Japan military cooperation on sea lane defence during the 1980s, US interest in sea lane defence cooperation with Japan periodically resurfaced in the mid-1990s, focused on potential regional maritime conflict zones in East Asia. Concern in the early part of the decade that the South China Sea was a possible flashpoint led US defence analysts to conclude that 'Some nations have much more stake than the United States in free movement of ships on Southeast Asian SLOC, and these nations should be encouraged to cooperate and share the costs of SLOC protection and safe navigation'.[32]

Other regional security crises involving the United States have included a maritime dimension. During the 1993–94 North Korean nuclear crisis, the United States considered imposing a sanctions blockade against North Korea. In March 1996, Chinese missile tests in the waters north of Taiwan prompted a reactive deployment of two US carrier battle groups to the vicinity of the Taiwan Strait. Notwithstanding Japan's own concerns over Pyongyang's missile and incipient nuclear capabilities, the government's reluctance to participate in any US-led naval blockade in the Sea of Japan threatened a crisis of confidence within the Alliance recalling Japan's 'tortured response' to the Gulf Crisis.[33] Growing awareness of a potential short-term threat to Japan from North Korea and long-term uncertainty over China thus spurred Japanese efforts, at the alliance level, to revise the 1978 US–Japan Defense Cooperation Guidelines, and domestically, to draw up new legislation (*yūji hōsei*) to define rules of engagement for the SDF in emergency situations.

Following the Higuchi Report and 1995 *taikō*, moves were made to 'revitalise' the Alliance, by the April 1996 Clinton–Hashimoto Joint Declaration on Security and three major initiatives. The first two of these, the Acquisition and Cross-Servicing Agreement and the Special Action Committee on Okinawa report (dealing with local problems generated by the US bases), were respectively concluded in October and December 1996. Most significantly, a process was also begun to revise the 1978 Guidelines, the new version of which was released on 23 September 1997, and approved by the Diet in May 1999.

As the Guidelines were being reviewed, US analysts and former officials laid out proposals for a geographically expanded maritime cooperation role for Japan within the Alliance. In May 1996, one month after the Clinton–Hashimoto summit, former US Assistant Secretary for International Security Policy Richard Armitage proposed that Japan should double its geographical area of responsibility for sea lane defence to 2,000 nm in the event of a regional conflict, in effect extending the area of alliance military cooperation to include the whole of the South China Sea.[34] US concern to enlist greater Japanese cooperation in the South China Sea was also borne out in a proposed multinational security framework for 'ensuring the security of the sea lanes against piracy and other threats' laid out by Brookings Institute analyst Mike Mochizuki:

> Such a framework may eventually involve Japanese destroyers escorting merchant ships during periods of international tension in conjunction with other nations. This kind of cooperation would not be directed against China because China would be a participant. But it should restrain China, as well as other countries, from disrupting maritime traffic.

According to Mochizuki, joint US–Japan naval exercises could also 'be necessary to deter Chinese attempts to pressure Taiwan through shows of force'.[35] The text of the New Guidelines itself states only (as in the 1978 draft), that in response to an armed attack on Japan, SDF and US forces 'will bilaterally conduct operations for the defence of surrounding waters and for the protection of sea lines of communications', while the SDF 'will have primary responsibility for the protection of ships in surrounding waters, and for other operations'. However, in a departure from the original, approximately 40 new 'rear-area' joint operational tasks applying to 'situations in areas surrounding Japan' were deemed permissible under Japan's interpretation of the right of individual self defence. These included maritime surveillance, intelligence-gathering activities, logistic support, minesweeping in high seas areas around Japan, maritime traffic coordination in and around Japan, and 'inspection of ships based on United Nations Security Council Resolutions'.[36] Ship inspection operational activities include monitoring of navigation, onboard inspections, requests for route change and the approach and pursuit of non-compliant vessels.[37]

Japan's post-Cold War sea lane threat perceptions

The undiminished importance of the MSDF's role in SLOC defence in the post-Cold War era is a theme echoed by many former and serving senior MSDF officers. Admiral Akimoto Kazumine, who proposed that the MSDF redefine its post-Cold War missions by expanding its multilateral constabulary activities through an Ocean Peace-Keeping (OPK) concept,[38] also sees its core military missions as essentially unchanged from those of the Cold War, namely:

1. the defence of Japanese territory against invasion;
2. the security of maritime traffic;
3. the protection of SLOC for the reinforcement of US military forces to Japan.[39]

In Akimoto's view, what has changed since the end of the Cold War is that 'the defence of sea lanes is not so much a national interest of individual states as it is... a global interest'. In a similar vein, Admiral Kawamura Sumihiko predicts that while SLOC security 'used to be only Japan's concern, because Japan was utterly dependent on imported oil... SLOCs from the Persian Gulf will assume a much greater importance to almost all countries in the region' in light of growing energy demand across East Asia.[40] Based on a scenario of rising import demand fanning competition over limited energy resources, the importance of sea lanes 'for the survival and prosperity of countries in the Asia-Pacific region in the 21st century' is likely to intensify, according to Kawamura.[41] Senior JDA analysts and MSDF officers have repeatedly affirmed that 'the primary mission of Japan's [MSDF] is to secure the safety of maritime traffic to a distance of 1,000 nautical miles'[42] and that 'the JMSDF's basic mission of defending the homeland and protecting the sea lines of communication will not change'.[43] The Higuchi Report's description of maritime transportation as a 'matter of life and death' for Japan, is a theme echoed by former MSDF Chiefs of Staff Hayashizaki Chiaki and Yoshida Manabu.[44] Recent local press articles continue to stress that 'One of the MSDF's priority missions is to defend sea lanes in Pacific waters for commercial fleets'.[45]

Former MSDF Chief of Staff Vice-Admiral Yamamoto Makoto has argued that the value of SLOC for the deployment of military forces is a strategic constant for Japan, and that the post-Cold War expansion of trade in the Asia-Pacific has also increased the importance of SLOC to regional security. Thus, SLOC security lends itself to naval cooperation as a 'joint' undertaking among major maritime trading nations.[46] Towards a typology of post-Cold War SLOC threats to regional sea lanes, Yamamoto identified the following categories:

- disruption due to maritime accidents or disasters at sea;
- disruption to the maritime system;
- damage from piracy;
- unilateral declarations restricting specific waters;
- disruption due to regional conflict;
- intentional obstruction by a sea-denial power.

Of these six categories, Yamamoto classified the latter three as 'difficult to resolve without the employment of a military response'. In April 1998, JDA Administrative Vice-Minister Akiyama Masaru said, in the context of the debate over the geographical scope of the US–Japan Defence Cooperation Guidelines, that sea lanes were among the factors important to Japan's peace and security that may be used to define emergencies in 'areas surrounding Japan', even if far from Japanese territory.[47]

The generalized concern with sea lanes extends beyond the naval fraternity and JDA analysts to 'reluctant realists' in Japan's academic community. Soeya Yoshihide, for example, has highlighted the 'vital' importance of sea lanes among *realpolitik* considerations influencing Japan's security perceptions, in the context of its geographical location, limited resources and the increased complexity of the post-Cold War Asia-Pacific security environment.[48] In September 2002, Masuda Tatsuo, Vice President of the state-owned Japan National Oil Company and former President of the APEC-affiliated APERC cited, among the risks facing Asia's energy outlook, the risk of sea lane disruptions in the chokepoints around Southeast Asia as a result of 'military developments or terrorist attacks'. In April 2002, APERC conducted a simulation exercise on scenarios for sea lane disruptions involving participants from 20 APEC member countries at Japan's behest.[49] For its part, the MOFA 'continues to hold dialogue with energy producing countries and countries along international shipping lanes' towards meeting the country's energy security needs.[50]

According to Okazaki Hisahiko, the two most important variables defining Japan's future sea lane security are the continued forward presence of the Seventh Fleet in the Western Pacific and China's future political orientation and maritime strategy (see Chapter 8).[51] As the United States is the only country capable of guaranteeing sea control beyond 1,000 nm from Japan's shores, he suggests Tokyo should seek to develop a framework that would enable the SDF to provide non-combat support to the US Navy in operations in the South China Sea, and possibly mine-sweeping operations in the Gulf, if necessary by developing a legal framework for collective defence cooperation, ahead of any crisis.[52] Okazaki also believes that Japan's freedom-of-navigation interests in the post-Cold War era are potentially exposed to regional conflicts. Thus, in the Middle East, a single submarine could halt Japan's oil shipments through the Straits of Hormuz, while in a 'worst-case scenario' in Southeast Asia, Japan's oil routes through the Lombok and Malacca Straits could be blocked. Okazaki currently perceives no threat facing Japan in the Indian Ocean. However, in his view, if states or pirates disrupted Japan's oil tankers traversing the Indian Ocean in future, Japan's total reliance on the United States for naval protection would again expose it to charges of doing too little to protect its own shipping, as during the Iran–Iraq War of 1980–88.[53] Okazaki also believes that Japan should consider participating in mine clearance in the Straits of Malacca, for which the SDF already has the necessary level of military capability, but lacks the enabling politico-legal framework. Okazaki's prescriptions for an expanded Japanese sea lane defence role are deliberately framed as part of his long-standing advocacy of overturning the government's 'ban' on collective self-defence.

The 2000 edition of the *East Asian Strategic Review*, a quasi-official statement of JDA threat perceptions produced annually by the National Institute for Defense Studies, argued that 'Ensuring unhindered use of sea lanes and the maintenance of peace and order on the high seas have become one of the major challenges for the security of East Asia'.[54] Recent defence white papers have also continued to emphasize the military and economic importance to Japan of SLOC, 'for its survival, for sustaining its fighting capability and for securing the infrastructure for receiving support from the US armed forces'.[55] Economically, the importance of safe-guarding Japan's maritime transportation is linked to the fact that 'its prosperity is highly dependent on sea-borne traffic for importing finished goods, including machinery and equipment, natural resources, energy and foodstuffs, and for exporting manufactured goods, such as machinery and equipment and chemicals etc'. It is further stressed that 'an obstruction or a shutoff of maritime traffic to and from Japan would have serious consequences on its people's livelihood, economic activity and the sustenance of its defence capability. Indeed, Japan experienced a similar situation during World War II'.[56] Accordingly, 'Japan's maritime defense capability has an important duty to protect the safety of maritime transportation'. The 2003 white paper defines sea lanes as 'Relatively safe routes established for ships, the area and width of which vary depending upon the type of threat'. A section on Operations for Ensuring the Safety of Maritime Traffic elaborates that:

> In the case a sea lane is established, operations will be conducted to patrol the lane on a continuous basis, detect and take countermeasures against hindrance by the enemies ships and submarines at an early stage, and escort Japan's ships as necessary.[57]

Similar concerns were carried forward into the 2004 *taikō* review, which concludes that 'Japan is prone to disaster in geographical and geological terms; and that the security of sea lines of communication is indispensable to its prosperity and growth'.[58]

In summary, the collapse of the Soviet Union did little immediately to alter the linear, incremental course of Japan's post-1954 defence policy, based on a gradual military build up within budgetary, capability and operational constraints. The continuing focus on the potential military threat posed by Russia in defence white papers highlighted the rigidity of a policy outlook still frozen in the tense but predictable framework of Cold War bipolarity. The first review of this Cold War defence framework was not completed until 1995. Meanwhile, Japan's experimentation with UN peace-keeping and down-playing of the centrality of the US–Japan Alliance in the initial post-Soviet period, at a time when Japan's economic growth model was still regarded as robust (if no longer all-conquering), spoke of an attempt to re-orient the country's defence and security policies towards a new global and specifically Asian leadership role. However, by the time the 1995 *taikō* was unveiled, strategic pressures in the form of uncertainty about the regional security environment, especially concerning China and North Korea, led Japanese policy-makers to adopt a more 'realist' and independent set of perceptions and responses to their security concerns.[59] While discounting the acquisition of fully fledged independent military power, as likely only to augment regional suspicions of resurgent militarism, Japan engaged in a modified form of balancing behaviour by moving to 'revitalise' the US–Japan Alliance while at the same time exploring multilateral regional dialogue in an attempt to diplomatically pre-empt the triggers of regional conflicts. Concerns about Japan's political, economic and military vulnerability in a less stable strategic environment were borne out in perceptions of the emergence of new threats to the security of its sea lanes. The following case study will show how Japan has perceived and reacted to the emergence of piracy and terrorism at sea as non-state threats, while Chapter 8 deals with potential state-level SLOC threats posed by China and North Korea.

Japan: piracy and terrorism at sea

Following on from the general profile of piracy and terrorism at sea in Chapter 2 and the preceding overview of Japan's security and defence policy since the

Cold War, this case study analyses the particular threats posed to Japan's sea lanes by piracy and maritime terrorism as sub-state level security concerns. After gauging the scale and perception of the threat they pose to Japan, the responses of policy-makers and other actors are analysed and conclusions drawn.

The adoption, in November 2001, of the Code of Practice for the Investigation of the Crimes of Piracy and Armed Robbery Against Ships by the IMO has dispelled some of the legal confusion surrounding the definition of piracy.[60] However, uncertainty about the scale of the problem still makes it difficult to quantify the threat modern piracy poses to Japan and others. Reliable data on the number of Japanese ships and cargoes affected are obscured by opaque ownership structures associated with the widespread use of foreign charters and the reluctance of many shipping operators to report incidents to the authorities.

If flag registry is taken as the defining criterion, according to the IMB, from a total of 2,375 ships attacked in 1992–2003, only eleven were Japanese-flagged.[61] Of the 445 incidents reported globally to the IMB in 2003, a total of 24 of the ships concerned were controlled or managed in Japan, placing it fifth behind Greece (58), Singapore (55), Germany (35) and Malaysia (25).[62] According to IMO data, a total of 136 Japanese-owned or controlled ships reported piracy incidents between 1995 and 2001, peaking at 39 in 1999 and 31 in 2000 (when the global incidence of piracy also reached its high of 471 incidents).[63] Most piracy occurred in East Asian waters (28 of 39 incidents in 2000; 22 of 31 incidents in 2001 respectively), the majority in Southeast Asia.[64]

In August 1999, the Nippon Foundation (*nippon zaidan*), a non-governmental organization (NGO) and major sponsor of Japanese anti-piracy initiatives, launched an online database compiled from questionnaires distributed to Japanese shipping companies, partly to counter the suspected chronic under-reporting of piracy incidents. This survey revealed 110 cases of piracy against Japanese-managed or controlled ships between 1994 and 2000.[65] Ten per cent of these took place in and around the Straits of Malacca, the most commercially and strategically important of Japan's extra-territorial waterways.

Modern piracy has been regarded as posing a potential threat to the security of Japan's shipping lanes since incidents were first reported in the Phillip Channel in 1981.[66] Although Japanese shipping companies voiced concerns about piracy and began developing their own countermeasures in the early 1980s, official concern in Japan was first aroused in the early 1990s, when several Japanese-owned or controlled cargo and fishing vessels were either challenged or fired upon in the East China Sea. However, it took the September 1998 hijacking of the *Tenyu*, a Japanese-owned cargo vessel chartered to carry aluminium ingots from the Sumatran port of Kuala Tanjung, to focus Japanese government attention on piracy in Indonesian waters and the Straits of Malacca.[67] As the most violent and organized act of its kind, the hijack of the *Tenyu* generated media attention in Japan, but the fact that no Japanese nationals were among the 15 murdered crew limited domestic reaction.[68] Several months after its disappearance, the vessel was discovered in a south Chinese port registered under a false name, and it is believed that its $3.5 million cargo may have been sold on in Burma, via a Singaporean firm.[69]

On 22 October 1999, the Panamanian-flagged *Alondra Rainbow* was hijacked in similar circumstances in the Straits of Malacca while transporting its cargo of aluminium *en route* to Miike in Japan. Having gained control over the vessel and maintained course for several days, pirates eventually cast off the 17-strong crew, including the Japanese captain and chief engineer, in life-rafts.[70] On 14 November, following the sighting by a Kuwaiti tanker in the Arabian Sea of a vessel matching the *Alondra Rainbow*'s description, units of the Indian Navy and Coast Guard launched a pursuit. The ship, which had been renamed *Mega Rama*, flying the Belize flag, was eventually recovered 300 miles southwest of Goa, on 17 November.[71] A portion of its 7,000-ton cargo of aluminium ingots, which had already been offloaded and transferred, was later impounded in the Philippines.[72] In February 2000, a Japanese-owned freighter, the *Global Mars*, was hijacked shortly after leaving Port Klang, in Malaysia, bound for India with a cargo of palm oil, the first of several vessels to fall victim to 'a ruthless and determined gang... preying on valuable palm oil cargoes being towed off the Sumatran coast'.[73]

While such high-profile, violent hijackings have received press attention, the reported incidence of piracy in the Straits of Malacca is, by any standard, low in comparison with the volume of traffic transiting through such a narrow and congested waterway.[74] The total of eleven piracy incidents involving Japanese-owned ships in the straits reported to the Nippon Foundation throughout the seven year period (1994–2000), even allowing for gross under-reporting, pales in comparison with the annual figure of 7,146 transits made by Japanese-owned vessels through the straits in 1993. Moreover, the number of attacks against ships in transit is only around one-third of the total.[75] For example, in 2003, of the 332 actual attacks worldwide reported to the IMB, only 115 were perpetrated against ships that were steaming at the time (61 were berthed and 156 anchored), though 46 of these took place in Southeast Asian waters.[76]

When considered as a proportion of the Japanese-controlled ocean-going merchant fleet, even a relatively small number of piracy incidents can appear alarming. To take the peak year of 1999, the 39 piracy incidents involving Japanese-owned ships equate approximately to a 2 per cent probability of occurrence for each of the 1,996 vessels in the ocean-going fleet. One suspects, however, that the peak reported incidence of actual and attempted crime involving land-based corporate property in Japan would not compare unfavourably. How, then, have concerns about piracy been borne out in Japan's official and non-official perceptions? According to the MOFA's *Diplomatic Bluebook 2003*, piracy 'has become a major threat to Japan's maritime transport of its oil and other energy supplies via Southeast Asian seas on which it is largely dependent and also an adverse factor on the region's stability and economic development as a whole'.[77] For Japan's shipping companies and commodity importers, the direct costs of piracy – aside from physical harm done to the crews – include the damage (or loss) of vessels and the theft of cargoes and valuables. More commercially damaging are the indirect costs of charter delays, higher insurance premiums and increased on-board security outlays. Japanese insurers classify piracy as a war risk. Due to the high costs of war risk premiums, many Japanese ship operators limit their war-risk policies to the Middle East, although one firm has responded to the upsurge in piracy in Southeast Asia by offering a type of cover specifically for pirate attacks at one quarter of the cost of war-risk insurance.[78] Such costs directly affect Japanese industrial sectors such as shipping and non-ferrous metals importers, but not on such a scale as to pose a systemic threat to Japan's economic well-being or ability to secure sufficient resource in-flows. Indeed, in 2003–04 Japan's economy has absorbed substantial increases in shipping costs and oil prices without de-railing a return to GDP growth.

The most serious security implications of piracy rest with its potential connection to terrorist acts at sea designed to cause mass destruction, or in the 'military' category of piracy, as a clandestine means of applying strategic pressure. Piracy has also strategic value to some Japanese policy-makers and commentators in that it offers an uncontroversial pretext for exploring new security alignments with maritime states in the Indo-Pacific region that could lead to an enhanced role for Japan, or even potentially form the basis of a future coalitional containment strategy directed at China.

Although the concept of 'military' piracy is itself disputed, Japanese commentators have alleged in the past that Japanese ships were the targets of low-level, state-sanctioned harassment in the East China Sea during the early 1990s. Such harassment is perceived to have been officially encouraged by elements within China's armed forces in order to buttress Beijing's maritime sovereignty claims. These were asserted in the 1992 Territorial Waters Law which grants powers for the 'immediate eviction of foreign military vessels or vessels owned by foreign governments and used for non-commercial purposes that violate the laws and regulations of the People's Republic of China'. Japanese ships featured prominently in the wave of incidents involving harassment and shooting that swept across the East China Sea during 1991–93. Out of a reported total of 78 boarding or shooting incidents, 32 involved Japanese-flagged vessels.[79] Among the largest vessels intercepted in international waters by Chinese maritime officials and forced into port, ostensibly to clamp down on smuggling activities, was a Japanese-owned VLCC in December 1992, followed by an unsuccessful attempt to stop an 83,000 deadweight-ton Japanese-flagged LNG carrier. Crews on board these ships reported the use of firearms and uniformed personnel using small, naval-type craft. In March 1993, when the chairman of the IMO visited Beijing to raise questions about the attacks, the response of Chinese officials was to admit that 'rogue' officials were operating amongst its anti-smuggling units.

This prompted speculation in Japan that the incidents could be 'aimed purely at exercising China's *de facto* authority in these waters'.[80] Hiramatsu Shigeo, among the best-known and most 'hawkish' China scholars in Japan, claimed in a 1994 article that the attacks on Japanese vessels were part of a long-term state-sanctioned strategy aimed at turning the East China Sea into 'China's private sea'.[81] The rapid drop-off in harassment in late 1993, following protests by Japan and the IMO, and Russia's dispatch of a naval flotilla to the area with orders to protect Russian shipping, was taken as proof by proponents of this explanation that the perpetrators of the attacks were functioning within an organized chain of command.

Concern about piracy permeated the JDA's official threat assessments during the 1990s. Since 1996, the *Defense of Japan* has cited the obstruction of safe passage in the South China Sea by pirates among its concerns in Southeast Asia. Following the hijacking of the *Tenyu*, this reference to piracy was expanded to include the Straits of Malacca and Singapore in the 1999 defence white paper.[82] The 2000 edition of *East Asian Strategic Review* commented that 'piracy attacks have threatened the safety of maritime traffic in East Asia', and described piracy among the major challenges to 'ensuring unhindered use of sea lanes and the maintenance of peace and order on the high seas'.[83]

Policy responses

Japan has pursued a variety of responses at both government and private level directed at countering piracy. These can be categorized according to three general approaches:

1 coordination, cooperation and capacity building with coastal states;
2 combating piracy through international organizations;
3 non-governmental responses.

Coordination, cooperation and capacity building with coastal states

Strengthening cooperation, information-sharing links and pursuing capacity building with coastal states is the most important strand to Japan's anti-piracy strategy, in keeping with the prevailing view that the responsibility for safeguarding coastal waters should reside with the coastal state. In 1993, initiatives undertaken by MOFA and JCG with their Chinese maritime counterparts were credited with ending the spate of attacks in the East China Sea, notwithstanding concerns in Japan that China's involvement in harassment of shipping in the East China Sea had strategic overtones. Following a meeting between the Chinese and Japanese foreign ministers in February 1993, an informal bilateral summit of coast guard officials held in June led to the installation of a hot-line between both organizations. Subsequently, incidents in the East China Sea fell off precipitously to just one in 1994.[84] Since 1993, regular contacts between JCG personnel and Chinese law enforcement officials have become institutionalized, as demonstrated in a memorandum of understanding concluded between the JCG's international division and China's Public Security Agency, outlining bilateral cooperation on drugs, illegal migration and piracy.[85]

Southeast Asia has since replaced China as the focus of Japan's piracy concerns, hence the target of its cooperation efforts. Japan has initiated efforts at bilateral and multilateral (ASEAN) levels to raise regional awareness of the problem aimed ultimately at putting in place a binding framework for collaboration, while building regional anti-piracy capacity through a programme of personnel exchanges, training and technical support. At the same time JCG has pursued joint exercises with regional counterparts. In November 1999, Prime Minister Obuchi Keizō reportedly made an impromptu proposal to Indonesian President Adurrahman Wahid, on the sidelines of the ASEAN leaders summit in Manila, suggesting that JCG patrol vessels participate in multinational anti-piracy patrols of the Straits of Malacca.[86] Although ASEAN opinion was generally favourable to the prospect of increased anti-piracy cooperation and related aid projects, Malaysia and Indonesia voiced reservations over JCG vessels patrolling their territorial waters.[87] Following on from a February conference in Singapore, Obuchi invited representatives from 15 national coast guards (including China, South Korea, India, Bangladesh and the ten ASEAN states), as well as the IMO and Asian shipowners, to a Regional Conference on Combating Piracy and Armed Robbery against Ships, which was held in Tokyo in April 2000. But on the substantive issue of whether to inaugurate joint coast guard patrols in the Straits of Malacca, the Tokyo conference failed to overcome regional reservations, due principally to China's opposition.[88] The April conference adopted the Tokyo Appeal, a non-binding statement agreeing to cooperate on maintaining law and order at sea, to pursue information exchange and provide technical assistance including training and equipment to assist in capacity-building among coast guards with limited resources.[89]

Japan kept up the momentum by dispatching anti-piracy 'missions' to the Philippines, Malaysia, Singapore and Indonesia in September 2000. Tokyo brought piracy onto the agenda of the ASEAN-Plus-Three summit in Singapore in November, where Prime Minister Mori Yoshiro called for a new conference to promote anti-piracy cooperation, which was duly followed up in Japan, in December 2000.[90]

Prime Minister Koizumi Junichirō's willingness to demonstrate leadership on security issues under the rubric of counter-terrorism has extended to his enthusiastic promotion of anti-piracy cooperation with Southeast Asia. In a keynote speech delivered to ASEAN leaders in Singapore on 14 January 2002, Koizumi stated his intention 'drastically' to intensify Japan and ASEAN security cooperation on transnational issues such as terrorism and 'the plague of piracy'. He specified the need for a Regional Cooperation Agreement on Combating Piracy and Armed Robbery Against Ships in Asia (hereafter, Regional Cooperation Agreement) and to strengthen cooperation between the JCG and ASEAN counterparts.[91]

With fewer legal and political constraints on its ability to deploy vessels beyond 1,000 nm, the JCG has been at the forefront of official efforts to build anti-piracy cooperation. According to the Maritime Traffic Safety Law and Law No. 28, passed in April 1948, the JCG has exclusive responsibility in peacetime for the safety of commercial vessels. The Guard and Rescue Department of the JCG has a trans-oceanic reach, equipped with around 50 large, lightly armed patrol vessels, including 11 helicopter-equipped patrol ships with a standard displacement of 6,500 tons as well as over 70 smaller patrol vessels. Its largest vessels are essentially frigates, but armed only with four Oerlikon 35 mm anti-aircraft cannon and two JM-61 20 mm Gatling cannon.[92] JCG patrol vessels have accumulated substantial long-range operational experience, sending relief supplies to Bangladesh in 1991 and providing escort for nuclear fuel shipments from Europe to Japan since 1992. In May 1998, the Coast Guard deployed two patrol vessels to Singapore on stand-by to evacuate Japanese citizens from Indonesia.[93]

The JCG identifies 'the strengthening of cooperative relations with concerned countries to combat the issues of piracy' and 'promoting countermeasures to maritime crimes, such as the frequent occurrence of piracy in the seas surrounding Southeast Asia in particular' as part of its response to transnational crime. Cooperation activities include summits between coast guard chiefs and joint training exercises.[94] The JCG has also sought to engage in prompt information exchange; to stage mutual visits by patrol ships; to extend technical aid and to open the JCG Academy, in Kure, and Training School, in Maizuru, to regional coast guard and civilian officials.[95] Training courses on controlling maritime crime are also offered to regional officials through the Japan International Cooperation Agency.[96] Since the Tokyo Appeal Japan has dispatched JCG patrol boats to seven Southeast Asian countries including Brunei, the Philippines, Malaysia and Singapore, and Falcon 900 surveillance aircraft[97] to eight.[98]

Japanese commentators have long backed the joint patrols, initiated in the Straits of Malacca by Malaysia and Singapore in 1992, as a model to be expanded to the wider region.[99] On 20 July 2004, a new programme of three-way patrols was inaugurated in the Straits of Malacca involving Indonesia, Malaysia and Singapore. The joint patrols pool a total of 17 vessels, which are coordinated via a shared communications channel.[100] Singapore is currently especially supportive of Japan's inclusion in regional anti-piracy and maritime terror initiatives. In May, Defence Minister Tony Tan said that the convergence of piracy and terrorism threats meant Japan 'will need to get involved' to safeguard its oil supplies through the Straits of Malacca.[101]

Japan's defence white paper identifies Indonesia 'as a country located in proximity to important maritime traffic routes'.[102] In its 2001 piracy report, the IMB expressed its hope that 'the Indonesian authorities will increase their efforts, without which the area will always remain high risk'. According to Admiral Kawamura Sumihiko, as of 2001, Indonesia's current maritime patrol and surveillance capability was less than half the level required to effectively patrol the country's maritime claims.[103] In February 2002, the Indonesian Navy announced that it had 'deployed three warships on a permanent basis to guard the waters off Aceh to prevent arms smuggling and three others to contain pirate attacks on cargo vessels passing through the Malacca Straits'.[104] However, the drying up of off-budget revenues from army-owned state corporations and the run-down of the official defence budget since 1998 (supplying only around 25 per cent of military funding) have led segments of the military to supplement their incomes by engaging in extortion.[105] To address Indonesia's chronic capacity shortfall in patrol and surveillance capabilities, which as of mid-2004 were still limited to around 20 vessels,[106] MOFA has mulled the donation of patrol boats through the ODA programme, stripped of their armament to comply with restrictions on the export of military equipment.[107] The transfer to Southeast Asian countries of offshore patrol vessels or even destroyer escorts decommissioned as a result of the 2004 review of defence policy, would mark a major new threshold in Japan's anti-piracy capacity-building efforts with the region.[108]

Ties between the Japanese and Indian coast guards cemented during the *Alondra Rainbow* pursuit have led both countries to institute joint procedures for anti-piracy patrols.[109] In November 2000, JCG Director Arai Shogo flew to Chennai (Madras) to observe a joint drill designed to develop information-sharing, common communications and rescue procedures. The patrol ship *Shikishima* also sailed to Chennai, via the Straits of Malacca. According to the MOFA press release, the *Shikishima*'s visit highlighted 'the expanding cooperation between Japan and India and their resolve to check the growing menace of sea piracy and to ensure safety along Asia's busiest maritime route which is a crucial lifeline for commerce'.[110] JCG vessels currently visit the Straits of Malacca on a quarterly basis and have conducted exercises with their Malaysian counterparts since November 2000.[111] In November 2001, the JCG conducted an anti-hijacking drill with the Philippines Coast Guard off Manila, involving members of the JCG's paramilitary Special Security Team, equipped with light arms for boarding and seizure operations.[112]

While the JCG has restricted its presence in the Straits of Malacca to port visits and drills with its counterpart organizations, Japan has had an indirect interest in India's expanding naval cooperation with the United States, which yielded an agreement in February 2002 to protect commercial shipping in the Straits of Malacca. Under the agreement, India's regional naval command in the Andean and Nicobar Islands, at the western approach to the straits, coordinated patrols and the escort of high-value ships such as oil tankers and LNG carriers with US warships, which have access to bases in Singapore at the straits' eastern end.[113] India's participation in 'trial' patrols of the Straits of Malacca ran from April to September 2002.[114]

In February 2002, the ASEAN–EU Experts' Group Meeting on Maritime Security proposed the creation of a 'neutral flag patrol fleet',[115] reminiscent of a proposal put forward in the 1980s by the former MSDF Chief of Staff Sakonjo Naotoshi to set up an ASEAN 'joint sea lane defence command'.[116] However, the major impetus behind recent anti-piracy patrolling by coastal states in Southeast Asia has been a stepping up of US strategic interest in the Straits of Malacca. On 31 March 2004, the Pacific Commander, Admiral Thomas Fargo, gave testimony before the House of Representatives Armed Services Committee outlining the Regional Maritime Security Initiative (RMSI). The RMSI is aimed at working with other navies around the Straits of Malacca to build interagency and international capacity to fight transnational threats like proliferation, terrorism, trafficking in humans or drugs, and piracy 'that use the maritime space to facilitate their illicit activity'.[117] Washington has since sought to distance itself from claims that it was seeking to introduce US naval patrols or special forces in the Straits via the RMSI, following opposition voiced by Malaysia and Indonesia.[118] However, Malaysia and Indonesia's subsequent decision to join Singapore in three-way patrols appears to be at least partially reactive to the US initiative.[119]

For Japan, the recent increase in anti-piracy activity displayed by coastal states has made it less important to secure a direct role for JCG assets in regional patrols. Moreover, a JCG 'operational', as opposed to 'training', presence directed at anti-piracy in Southeast Asia remains problematic under Japanese law. Under Articles 2 and 236 of Japan's criminal code, jurisdiction covers only crimes against Japanese-flagged ships on the high seas. Japanese-owned vessels operating under flags of convenience would fall outside the law, leaving the legal basis for JCG operations to counter piracy beyond Japan's territorial waters in doubt for the majority of vessels carrying Japanese cargoes, or in cases where the perpetrators are not Japanese nationals.[120] Such jurisdictional limitations are illustrated by an April 2002 incident, when for one month Japanese authorities were unable to take into custody two Filipino crewmen who had murdered a Japanese seafarer onboard the Panamanian-registered *Tajima*, though it was docked at a Japanese port.[121] As the JCG is also proscribed from exercising with military units in other countries, joint patrols with those states that assign constabulary duties to their navy would not be permitted.[122]

Combating piracy through international organizations

Parallel to efforts to improve cooperation with coastal states, the Japanese government has sought to raise the profile of piracy via international organizations, towards ultimately locking in place a legal framework to combat the problem at a regional level. The IMO is the only forum with the necessary breadth and authority, under a UN banner, which assembles all of the major stakeholder groups affected by piracy, including coastal states, flag states and port states. In 1988, it adopted the Protocol for the Suppression of Unlawful Acts at Sea (SUA), entering into force in 1992. Also in 1992, the IMO established a working group composed of ten member states, including Japan, Indonesia and Singapore to assess, *inter alia*, the threat of piracy. In 1993, as a result of a report handed down by the working group, the IMO's Maritime Safety Committee (MSC) issued two circulars: MSC/CIRC 622, outlining recommendations for combating piracy and armed robbery against ships; and MSC/CIRC 623, detailing guidance to shipowners, operators, masters and crew on preventing and suppressing acts of piracy and armed robbery against ships, stressing preventive measures spanning watchkeeping, safe anchorage and reporting procedures.[123] Outside the IMO framework, the IMB set up the regional piracy centre in Kuala Lumpur in 1992, which has served to collate and publish an annual database of actual and attempted piracy attacks. In 2001, the IMB extended its satellite-broadcast piracy warnings to Japan, Asia, East Africa, West Africa and the west coast of South America. The warnings covered the details of recent piracy incidents and 'high risk' areas such as the northeast coast of Somalia and the Indonesian portion of the Straits of Malacca.[124]

Japan has recently enjoyed considerable success bringing piracy onto the UN agenda via the IMO and the United Nations General Assembly (UNGA). First, Agenda Item 20 submitted by Japan to the IMO's MSC on 5 March 2004 proposed the establishment of an Asian 'Information Sharing Center' charged with collecting piracy data, preparing statistics, circulating alerts and requests for cooperation and capacity building.[125] Second, the MSC's Report from its Seventy-Eighth Session, issued on 28 May 2004 extensively details Japan's efforts to introduce a Regional Cooperation Agreement, which was finalized in Tokyo in November 2003. It also reiterated the 'indispensable' need to establish an information-sharing center.[126] Third, Resolution 58/240 adopted at the Fifty-Eighth Session of UNGA calls upon states to 'cooperate in the prevention and combating of piracy and armed robbery at sea'.[127] Fourth and finally, Japan's Regional Cooperation Agreement was again raised at the Fifty-Ninth UNGA Session in June 2004, in the Report on the work of the United Nations Open-ended Informal Consultative Process on Ocean and the Law of the Sea. At a regional level, Japan's efforts also helped to bring about the adoption by the ARF of the ARF Statement on Cooperation Against Piracy and Other Threats to Maritime Security, in June 2003.[128]

Non-governmental responses

The Nippon Foundation, as the 'sponsor' of many quasi-official Japanese anti-piracy initiatives, including the conferences in Tokyo and other regional capitals, claims to have promoted counter-measures in three ways. First, it feeds information to the Japanese public and media about piracy. Second, it encourages shipping companies to pool information (including via an online database of piracy incidents involving Japanese-owned and controlled vessels). Third, it has developed *tora-nomon* (after the Foundation headquarters' location in central Tokyo), a low-cost deck-wide tripwire alarm system designed to alert crew members to boarding attempts via grappling hooks, which it began deploying in February 2000. The Nippon Foundation has also been involved in researching a radical re-routing solution to avoid high-risk piracy areas in Asian and African waters. With Norwegian and Russian support, the Foundation co-sponsored a study into the Northern Sea Route (NSR), along Russia's Arctic coast from 1993 to 1999.[129] In spite of the technical and cost challenges involved in clearing an alternative route to European ports via the ice-bound Siberian coast, the NSR has been considered as potentially commercial viable because it would halve the sailing distance between Japan and northern Europe via Suez. It would also bypass areas exposed to piratical attack and geopolitical risk, from Indonesia to Sri Lanka and the Red Sea.[130]

As with other navigational safety issues noted in Chapter 6, Japanese shipping firms and industries affected by piracy in Southeast Asia have pursued counter-measures independently and through the IMO. In 2001, Shipping industry representatives called for the creation of a regional piracy surveillance group in Southeast Asia, to be funded by all stakeholders and composed of coast guard and police patrol units. Backers of the plan thought that a new international convention might be necessary to cover the realignment of domestic law to enable suspect vessels that attempt to shelter within the territorial waters of other states to be pursued and inspected.[131] Industry concerns are ongoing and in June 2004 shipowners at the International Chamber of Commerce 35th World Congress called for coordinated naval patrols to protect shipping in maritime Southeast Asia.[132]

The JSA, in addition to sending representatives to regional anti-piracy conferences has introduced its own measures, encouraged its members to report incidents and sought to control the spread of firearms aboard ships. During the transit of JCG patrol ships to take part in drills in Southeast Asia, the JSA has conducted exercises with the Coast Guard 'that would assist it in liaising and communicating with Japanese merchant vessels which are under piratical attacks'.[133] At the level of individual ship safety, since 1983 the JSA has recommended the adoption of safety measures aboard its members' vessels aimed at reducing the risk of piracy. These include improved on-deck lighting,[134] increased watch duty, better shipboard communications and the installation of on-board alarm systems and remote ship-monitoring systems in addition to those already offered by the Nippon Foundation and the IMB's Shiploc system.[135] NYK has developed its own Fleet Remote Monitoring System to alert its central offices in case communications are disrupted with vessels belonging to its 450-strong fleet. Within the industry the greatest interest surrounds anti-boarding defences, particularly the 'Secure-Ship' system based around a deck-wide, 9,000 volt electrified fence deployed by some European shipping companies, even though fire risk has limited its use to vessels carrying non-flammable cargoes.[136] In early July 2004, Japan and South Korea announced that vessels registered under their respective flags had reached full compliance with the ISPS code, while Malaysia, the Philippines and Thailand are between 68 and 85 per cent compliant.[137] Shipowners have also been encouraged to report incidents both to coastal states and the Japanese authorities. Among the metals and shipping firms most affected by robberies and hijacking in the Straits of Malacca, Sumitomo Metal Industries, Showa Denko K. K. and Tokyo Senpaku have resorted to private arrangements with Indonesian military personnel for on-board protection during transit through Indonesian waters.[138] In some circumstances this practice simply amounts to paying for 'protection'.

Since 1992, the JSA has also sought to build links with other regional shipping firms, via the Asian Ship Owners' Forum (ASF), and to lobby governments to address piracy as a policy concern. The ASF, with members from seven states, has called on coastal states to address particular 'hot-spots' such as the Straits of Malacca and the Hong Kong–Hainan–Luzon triangle. At its 1998 meeting, the ASF praised the efforts of Malaysia and the Philippines to combat piracy in the Sulu Sea and called on 'all governments to increase patrols by police or naval vessels to eradicate acts of piracy and armed robbery against ships in their own territorial waters and the neighbouring area'. The Forum has also called on other Asian countries to join Japan, China and India in ratifying the 1988 Rome Convention for the Suppression of Unlawful Acts against the Safety of Maritime Navigation, and the Convention on Hijack Prevention under which signatories can prosecute pirates for crimes committed in another state's jurisdiction. Since 11 September 2001, the ASF's Safe Navigation and Environment Committee has also increased calls on Asian governments, especially Indonesia, to boost maritime patrols and to investigate reported incidents of piracy and armed robbery.[139]

The MSDF, piracy, maritime terrorism and operation 'Arabian Rainbow'

There have been calls within Japan to allow the MSDF to become directly involved in anti-piracy patrols 'on the high seas'.[140] Russia's naval show of force in the East China Sea in late 1993 demonstrated to Japan's naval fraternity the 'importance of the naval presence as a method of cracking down on piracy effectively'.[141] An anti-piracy role for the MSDF was also proposed in 1997 as part of an OPK concept developed by the JDA-affiliated National Institute for Defense Studies in Tokyo. The OPK concept is premised on the assumption that piracy and terrorist actions at sea are examples of post-Cold War era threats that render the 'difference between military reaction and police reaction ambiguous', justifying an expansion of constabulary duties for the MSDF on a multilateral, region-wide basis.[142] The OPK was also an attempt to develop a post-Cold War role for the MSDF to rival the GSDF's participation in UN PKOs. However, aside from constitutional challenges, a prospective MSDF role in anti-piracy patrols in Southeast Asian waters would be certain to meet strong opposition from China. The existence of separate JDA and Coast Guard anti-piracy proposals can be ascribed at one level to bureaucratic rivalry, which may be partly responsible for the failure of either to materialize as envisaged. While bureaucratic competition and duplication of effort have often marred the relationship between the JCG and MSDF – the two organizations even share some vessel names – thinking within the Maritime Staff Office in recent years has concentrated more on military than constabulary operations (notwithstanding the MSDF's ongoing role in transporting overseas humanitarian assistance to such remote destinations as Turkey[143]). At the same time, overlapping initiatives from the JCG and JDA exploring a role for Japan in anti-piracy patrols in Southeast Asia have been seen as an attempt by the Japanese government 'to reassert its waning influence in the region as a counterbalance to China'.[144] On 5 June 2004, in a speech delivered to the Third 'Shangri-La' Asia Security Conference, in Singapore, JDA Director General Ishiba Shigeru invoked the OPK concept in relation to piracy:

> The safety in this region has been at risk, as shown by the fact that 60% of the maritime piracy in the world occurred in Asia. It is important for navies and coast guards of the region to cooperate bilaterally and multilaterally to enhance surveillance efforts. Also, we should collaborate in the United Nations as well as amongst relevant states to formulate effective arrangements and resolutions. Japan, to bear appropriate responsibility in the world as well as in this region, wishes to actively speak out and take action . . . without simply becoming a financial contributor. This leads to an example of the utilization of military capability for policing purposes for the peace and stability of the region.[145]

Ishiba's reference to 'the utilization of military capability' hints at a future role for the MSDF in regional anti-piracy activities. Although both JCG and MSDF vessels currently lack a legal mandate to engage in patrols in the Straits of Malacca outside of the rubric of 'exercises', both organizations have successfully established a *de facto* presence in the straits. Furthermore, although ostensibly connected with the piracy issue, the MSDF and the Singaporean Navy have conducted bilateral search-and-rescue and other exercises since 1996. MSDF destroyers continue to send training squadrons through the Straits of Malacca on an annual basis, calling at Port Klang as they have since the late 1960s.[146] Since November 2001, the MSDF presence in the straits has been boosted with a major new operational requirement to maintain the MSDF flotilla on station in the Arabian Sea as part of Japan's response to the US-led war on terrorism.

Closer to home, Japan was exposed to mass destruction by terrorists long before the 11 September attacks, at the hands of the Aum Shinrikyō cult, which conducted the fatal March 1995 sarin gas attack on the Tokyo underground. This led the Japanese government to consider deploying the SDF in both an internal and external counter-terrorist capacity.[147] The potential threat of maritime terrorism since 11 September has led to JCG patrols around US military facilities, nuclear power stations, oil reserve storage tanks and other high-profile targets along Japan's coastline. The JCG has staged two bilateral maritime anti-terror drills with South Korea since May 2002. The second exercise conducted 1 April 2004, dealt with the scenario of an attack on a ferry from Pusan, involving the 1,200-ton patrol ship *Hakata*, three South Korean patrol vessels, 60 Japanese personnel and 180 members of South Korea's maritime police.[148]

The Japanese government has also made efforts at an inter-agency level to step up security at major Japanese ports. In February 2004 crisis management officials were appointed to Tokyo, Yokohama, Nagoya, Osaka and Kobe. An initial anti-terror exercise was staged in Nagoya, involving the JCG, Aichi prefectural police and Nagoya Regional Immigration Bureau officials, based on the scenario of a bomb threat to a cruise ship.[149] Such measures reveal the growing importance of 'homeland' aspects to Japan's contemporary SLOC security.

Tokyo's enthusiastic political backing for the US-led global 'war on terror' has also brought about a major expansion of the MSDF's roles in the Indian Ocean and Arabian Sea. After the Diet passed the Anti-Terrorism Special Measures Law in just three weeks in October 2001, MSDF warships were deployed the following month to the Middle East 'to gather information' in support of US-led operations in Afghanistan.[150] MSDF auxiliaries attached to the flotilla have since supplied around 40 per cent of the fuel requirements of US and UK vessels deployed in the Arabian Sea (as part of a force involving navies from about ten countries) to intercept suspected al-Qaida terrorists attempting to flee Afghanistan by sea via Pakistan and to prevent a recurrence of the October 2002 attack on the *Limburg*, off Yemen.[151] MSDF vessels, including the Aegis DDG *Kirishima* that sailed from Yokosuka in mid-December 2002, have since transited via the Straits of Malacca *en route* to the Indian Ocean. The deployment of three destroyers and two supply ships to the Arabian Sea was Japan's first-ever contribution of forces to an international coalition during a conflict. This was made possible without directly tackling the government's ban on collective self-defence and constitutional constraints by linking the MSDF dispatch, via the Anti-Terrorism Special Measures Law, specifically to counter-terrorist efforts against al-Qaida and Taliban forces in Afghanistan, rather than defining it as a defence contingency. The Special Measures Law, valid for two years from November 2001, was renewable for a further two years.

Operation 'Arabian Rainbow' was scheduled originally to last for six months through to 19 May 2002. However, Koizumi announced on 24 March 2002 that Japan's military support to US-led forces fighting against terrorism would continue for the foreseeable future and the MSDF's deployment in the Indian Ocean has since been extended in six month increments, most recently from 1 November 2004.[152] As of May 2004, Japan maintained two supply ships and three destroyers on station in the Arabian Sea, involving around 600 sailors. The flotilla was due to be scaled back to one *Towada*-class supply vessel and two destroyers, including the Aegis-equipped DDG, *Kongō*.[153]

The long-term deployment of MSDF units to the Gulf region under a more liberal legal remit than has governed any previous overseas dispatch in the SDF's history, carries important implications for future maritime operations beyond the ostensible purpose of aiding counter-terrorism operations in land-locked Afghanistan. Controversy arose over the potential for the terms of the MSDF's dispatch being merged into a logistic support role for the US-led invasion of Iraq in March–April 2003.

The Japanese government's original plan to commit an Aegis DDG and the 8,900 ton *Osumi* amphibious landing ship (capable of deploying MH-53 mine-sweeping helicopters from its flat deck) as part of the MSDF Indian Ocean flotilla in 2001 was postponed owing to concerns expressed by the LDP's Kōmeitō Party coalition partner and opposition parties that these capabilities exceeded the requirements necessary for operations to dislodge the Taliban.[154] However, more than one year after the overthrow of the Taliban regime, decisions were taken to reinforce the MSDF presence in the Arabian Sea by deploying the Aegis-equipped *Kirishima*, in December 2002, and *Osumi* the following February to transport a 140-man Thai engineering battalion for deployment in Afghanistan.[155]

The deployment of the *Kirishima*, with its high level of air defence capability, aroused suspicion that MSDF vessels were being eyed with a view to their possible re-assignment to support any US attack on Iraq.[156] In early 2002, as speculation arose about US intentions towards Iraq, Japanese cabinet officials said that under the October 2001 anti-terrorist legislation, it would be difficult for Japan to provide logistic support unless there was a proven connection with 11 September. Subsequently, on the first anniversary of the attacks, Moriya Takemasa, the Director General of the JDA Defense Policy Bureau, announced that Japan would be able to avail logistic support to US forces if they attacked Iraq within the framework of existing legislation, provided that military action was authorized by a UN resolution.[157]

Meanwhile, Operation 'Arabian Rainbow' was also serving to expand the range of Japan's security partners, suggesting a possible parallel aim on the part of policymakers to explore Japan's post-11 September responses in multilateral, UN-centred terms, not merely within the bilateral context of the US–Japan Alliance. In late February 2003, the Koizumi cabinet approved a move allowing MSDF vessels to refuel those from the French, German and New Zealand navies, in addition to the US and UK ships already receiving Japanese support in the Arabian Sea.[158] Under the terms of the supply agreement, ships refuelled by MSDF tenders could not participate in any hostilities against Iraq.[159] In the run-up to the war, this decision to refuel naval vessels from those countries whose governments were least favourably disposed to US military action suggested that Japan was continuing to hedge its options over whether to back the effort to oust Saddam Hussein in the absence of a second UN resolution authorizing military action. However, once hostilities had begun, the refuelling agreement was quickly extended to Spain, Italy, the Netherlands, Canada and Greece, in March.[160] Japan has itself since joined the multilateral coalition in Iraq following the passage of the Iraq Reconstruction Special Measures Law in July 2003. The dispatch of the *Osumi* from Muroran, Hokkaidō, to Kuwait in February 2004 marked the MSDF's official entry into the Iraq mission, to sustain the presence of approximately 500 GSDF soldiers in the Samawah area.[161]

Irrespective of Iraq, in the future, Operation 'Arabian Rainbow' is likely to affect the way in which SLOC security is perceived and conducted within Japan. It has established a precedent for expanding the legal framework under which the SDF may be dispatched without directly challenging the ban on collective self-defence. Thus, future MSDF operational deployments may be justified in reference to counter-terrorism, or anti-piracy by extension. The long-term operational deployment of MSDF vessels in the Indian Ocean has set another important marker in the context of Japan's SLOC security by establishing an MSDF presence along the length of its main energy supply routes to the Gulf, including in the Straits of Malacca, in the process stretching the capabilities of the Fleet Escort Force to the limit. As of February 2004, 1,000 MSDF sailors were deployed overseas, while around a 30 per cent of the Fleet Escort Force's strength of 32 destroyers and 6,500 men had participated in the Indian Ocean deployment. Around one-third of the MSDF's destroyers are normally in dock at any one time for repair and overhaul. One Aegis DDG is also usually kept on standby for any eventuality in the Sea of Japan.[162]

From the viewpoint of its legal mandate, the passage of MSDF vessels through the Straits of Malacca is unconnected to Japan's anti-piracy cooperation in Southeast Asia, and other countries' naval patrols in the area. However, the presence in the straits since November 2001 of regularly transiting MSDF vessels, in close proximity and passage communication with other naval and coast guard vessels, has inevitably created a low level of *de facto* maritime cooperation in the Straits of Malacca and their environs with important symbolic effects. In February 2003, the *Daily Yomiuri* reported that the Koizumi administration had drawn up eight 'key concerns' regarding a possible war in Iraq, including measures 'to ensure the safety of Japanese vessels in the Mideast, including oil tankers', suggesting that MSDF forces in place could in future be used in an escort role.[163] The most recent review of defence policy, completed in December 2004, affirms the importance of maintaining stability in the 'region spreading from the Middle East to East Asia' in connection with Japan's SLOC security and heavy dependence on imported resources.[164]

The decision-making process behind the choice of Japanese forces deployed to the Indian Ocean highlights one other enduring influence on Japan's maritime security. Requests from the US government in April 2002 for Japan to dispatch an Aegis DDG and P-3C aircraft were reportedly presaged by a meeting in Yokosuka of senior MSDF officers and the Commander of US Naval Forces, Japan, Rear Admiral Robert Chaplin.[165] At the meeting, MSDF officers urged Chaplin to make representations in Washington for the US government to 'strongly request' such a deployment from Japan. Later that month, US Deputy Defense Secretary Paul Wolfowitz duly requested the dispatch of an Aegis destroyer and P-3C aircraft in talks with senior politicians from Japan's ruling coalition.[166] In this way, the close navy-to-navy relationship established after 1945, which played such an important role in sea lane defence during the 1980s, still functions at the transnational level as a semi-independent and occasionally pivotal influence within Japanese defence policy decision-making. According to Japanese media reports, the United States is planning to follow up the 2000 'Armitage Report' on US–Japan security relations by urging 'Japan to defend its sea lanes for 5,000 nautical miles or as far as the Persian Gulf'.[167] This reported proposal to resurrect sea lane defence as a rationale for expanding alliance cooperation to the Middle East is attributed to Deputy Assistant Secretary of State Torkel Patterson, former country director for Japan at the Pentagon, who is fluent in Japanese and retired from the US Navy in September 1994, having served as Aide to the Commander US Naval Forces, Japan.[168]

Conclusion

Japan is the leading user of waterways between the home islands and the Middle East that overlap the major piracy 'hot-spots' identified over the last decade. This has ensured that modern piracy is viewed within government and industry as a genuine concern, reflective of the rise of non-state actor security challenges since the end of the Cold War. Yet the widespread perception of maritime piracy as a threat to the security of Japan's sea lanes sits at odds with the small number of incidents involving Japanese ships relative to the volume of Japan's seaborne trade.

Relative to the scale of trade flows through affected waters, piracy could be seen as more of an 'irritant' to the global maritime trading network than the systemic economic threat it is sometimes portrayed to be in Japan. However, widespread perceptions of piracy as a national security threat are constantly borne out both in Japanese official statements and the views of private analysts. Apart from concerns about piracy's immediate economic and commercial impact, the suspicion that Japan was the target of 'military piracy' in the East China Sea during the early 1990s, as part of a clandestine Chinese policy of asserting its sovereignty claims and testing Japan's resolve, appears genuine in realist quarters. Such a scenario echoes Cold War fears that the Soviet Union would use shipping as a low-cost means to exert political pressure on Japan.

As 'new' security challenges, the potential of anti-piracy and counter-terrorism to be used as rationales to generate post-Cold War missions and budgetary claims on the part of the JCG and MSDF can be partly attributed to bureaucratic self-preservation (especially for the JDA, post-Soviet threat) and competition for a diminishing pool of central government funds. However, the level of political commitment to anti-piracy initiatives since 1998, particularly under the Koizumi administration, reflects more than mere bureaucratic rivalry. Providing technology and know-how to help Southeast Asian law enforcement combat piracy is seen as a measure by which 'Japan can match the growing influence of China' in the context of an increasingly competitive dynamic to establish leadership credentials in the region.[169] Piracy has also handed advocates of an expanded security role for Japan a politically safe pretext to explore cooperation with Asia Pacific maritime countries, including India as well as in Southeast Asia. Japan's responses to piracy accord with a generalized post-Cold War perception that expanding multilateral security linkages with other Asia Pacific states has a positive effect, by communicating reassurance to the region about Japan's benign intentions while also serving to mitigate sources of regional conflict. A realist logic also informed the Higuchi Report's emphasis on multilateralism. For by broadening the basis of its post-1945 security posture based on Yoshida's doctrine of reliance on the United States, Japan could hedge against a future ebbing of the US security commitment to Japan, especially if it might have to face an assertive China without alternative allies. Japan's SLOC security in the context of a rising China is the subject of the next case study, in Chapter 8.

Since 11 September 2001, the rise of Islamist terrorism has presented Japan's SLOC security with fresh challenges, given the particularly high risk attached to al-Qaida-linked actions against shipping and port infrastructure in the Middle East and Southeast Asia. Notwithstanding Japan's particular receptivity to counter-terrorist cooperation, the MSDF dispatch to the Arabian Sea in 2001 was in an immediate sense a 'political' response to avoid a crisis in alliance relations with the United States akin to those of 1990–91, over Iraq, or 1993–94, over North Korea. The decision in 2003 to extend support for the US-led reconstruction effort in Iraq followed on from this logic. From a wider perspective, the MSDF deployment has established a naval presence along the length of Japan's energy supply routes to the Gulf and expanded the scope for new maritime security roles and linkages in the Indian Ocean region.

8 Japan's post-Cold War SLOC security

China, North Korea and regional conflict

Introduction

This chapter explores potential military threats to Japan's SLOC in the post-Cold War era, focussing primarily on China and secondarily on North Korea. As shown in Chapter 2, the outbreak of conflict in a number of regions adjacent to key Indo-Pacific shipping lanes, including the Gulf, South China Sea, Taiwan Strait and Korean Peninsula, could have a major impact on the security of shipping and disrupt international trade. A major conflict in the Gulf, while serious for Japan's security in terms of the potential for energy supply disruptions, would automatically be internationalized, given the region's importance to global energy supplies. Japan's main problem, as in 1991 and 2003, would be the political one of whether or how to organize a contribution to a US-led military coalition. The most serious regional flash-points, from the viewpoint of Japan's SLOC, are the more proximate concerns of the South China Sea, Taiwan Strait and Korean Peninsula. North Korea, even with its limited capability, could potentially threaten Japan's SLOC where they are most vulnerable, using sea mines and small submarines in the approaches to Japan's ports and straits. However, the disposition of forces in the Peninsula is such that the ground and air dimensions would predominate, unlike in the South China Sea or Taiwan Strait, where the maritime dimension would shape any major military conflict primarily as a naval and air war. (China's missile build-up opposite Taiwan means that a cross-strait conflict could conceivably be limited to a missile exchange.) China is seen in Japan as by far the most important state-level variable bearing on Japan's SLOC, as a party to sovereignty disputes in the South China Sea and Taiwan Strait. Japanese concerns reflect China's geographically dominant position along East Asia's coastal periphery, its growing economic and political influence within the region, and its military and especially naval modernization.

This chapter focuses on aspects of Sino-Japanese relations that have a particular bearing on Japan's sea lane security and China's potential to emerge as a strategic threat. It does not attempt to describe the broader dynamics of bilateral ties between Japan and China, which unlike Japan's monolithically adversarial Cold War relations with the Soviet Union, have evolved complex economic and political inter-linkages, with two-way trade expanding by 30 per cent year-on-year in 2003 to $132 billion.[1] In spite of this growing economic inter-dependence, a shift towards a more 'realist' view of China among Japan's policy-makers, is widely acknowledged to have occurred since the end of the Cold War.[2] Although many agree that China will be the most important long-term determinant of Japan's future security policy, opinion diverges on whether the dynamic most likely to develop will be cooperative, accommodative, benignly competitive or confrontational. Some regard it as likely that Japanese realism toward China will assert itself in the form of an accommodation with Beijing in recognition of China's 'historic' role as Asia's dominant power.[3] Alternatively, Tokyo's increased support for the US–Japan Alliance since the mid-1990s, and diplomatic overtures to Southeast Asia, could be seen as evidence of Japanese policy-makers engaging in balancing behaviour against China's hegemonic potential. Equally, Japan's pursuit of multilateral security linkages with states around Asia's coastal periphery could attest to a deeper interest in exploring options for a future maritime axis to check China's power should the United States itself seek an accommodation with China.

The major objective of this chapter is to analyse perceptions among security policy-makers (in China as well as Japan) in as far as these relate specifically to sea lanes, and to draw conclusions about how these perceptions inform the strategic dynamic of Sino-Japanese ties. Initially, I assess the influence that SLOC have had in the development of China's emerging maritime strategy, its operational concepts and naval doctrine. China's maritime capabilities and force development are then profiled, leading into an assessment of how China perceives the issue of Japan's SLOC security. This is followed by an analysis of perceptions held by Japanese defence decision-makers, security analysts and former and serving military personnel regarding China's potential to imperil the security of Japan's major SLOC to Southeast Asia and the Middle East. Consideration is then given to the conventional and non-conventional threats that North Korea presents to Japan's SLOC. I argue that although North Korea's maritime capabilities and threat potential (excluding its missile and incipient nuclear capabilities) are modest compared with those of China, North Korea has had an important political effect in terms of driving recent changes in Japan's defence policy.

China's naval modernization and maritime strategy

In the early 1980s, under the direction of Admiral Liu Huaqing ('China's Gorshkov'), the People's Liberation Army Navy (PLAN) moved from a doctrine of 'people's war at sea'.[4] Liu expanded the scope of limited, inshore operations in support of PLA ground forces, to a limited war doctrine extending to ambitions for a 'blue water' fleet, equipped for power-projection.[5] The PLAN's blue-water ambitions have evolved in step with China's expanding maritime interests, which can be grouped into three core concerns:

1 *Territorial claims*: China's most important maritime concern is the security and sovereignty of its 18,000 km coastline, including the protection of

coastal regions where the new prosperity is concentrated, as well as the 3.6 million km^2 of 'territorial waters' claimed. As sovereignty over two-thirds of this area is disputed, the affirmation of Chinese maritime claims is a major role, or ambition of the PLAN.

2 *Resource protection*: The exploitation of marine resources in relation to seabed minerals, especially hydrocarbons, has grown in importance since China became a net energy importer in 1993 (importing 48 per cent of its oil in 2004; in 1980 it exported 20 per cent of production[6]). In 2004, China overtook Japan as the second-largest consumer of oil.[7] China also owns the world's largest fishing fleet.

3 *Trade protection*: The conduct and protection of seaborne trade has emerged as a major and rapidly growing priority. Since China's entry into the WTO in December 2001 cemented its position as the 'factory of the world', the export of Chinese-made goods to the United States has already overtaken those of Japan.[8] China's exports are projected to continue expanding rapidly, fed by a surge in FDI which exceeded $50 billion in 2002, making China the most favoured destination for FDI globally. Shenzhen and Qingdao have now joined Shanghai among the world's top-20 container ports, while Hong Kong – the leading port – has been under Chinese sovereignty since 1997.[9] In 2004 alone, Tianjin's authorities predicted that the volume of bulk and container traffic at the port increased by 25 per cent, and plan to invest $3 billion in new capacity over 5 years.[10]

The role of SLOC in China's maritime strategy

PLAN strategists have proposed the establishment of maritime defence perimeters to varying depths. Admiral Liu's more limited 'green water' navy concept, apparently influenced by Japan's 1,000 nm sea lane defence concept, would basically extend PLAN coverage to the limit of its territorial claims in the East and South China Sea (China's South China Sea claims are shown in Map 1.2). Admiral Zhang Xusan, the former chief of the naval staff, envisaged a navy capable of operating from the Sea of Japan to the Straits of Malacca and defined China's eastern defence perimeter as including the 'first island chain', comprising the Indonesian, Philippine and Japanese archipelagos and Taiwan (Map 8.1).

Other Chinese defence analysts have identified strategic weaknesses in designating the first island chain as the limit of China's defence zone, 'with most of our lanes to the high seas being interdicted by the island chain, so that access to the high sea of the Chinese Navy is controlled to a certain extent by others, who are very likely to close it off in wartime'.[11] A more ambitious defence-in-depth concept extending to the 'second island chain', has been advanced, including the Bonin, Mariana, Guam and the Caroline Islands in Oceania.[12] This is partly on the grounds that the increasing range of modern tactical missiles requires that enemy forces be intercepted at distances beyond 1,000 nm.[13] The establishment of military facilities in, and defence links with Burma and port calls to South Pacific nations have been seen as evidence of growing Chinese interest in acquiring the

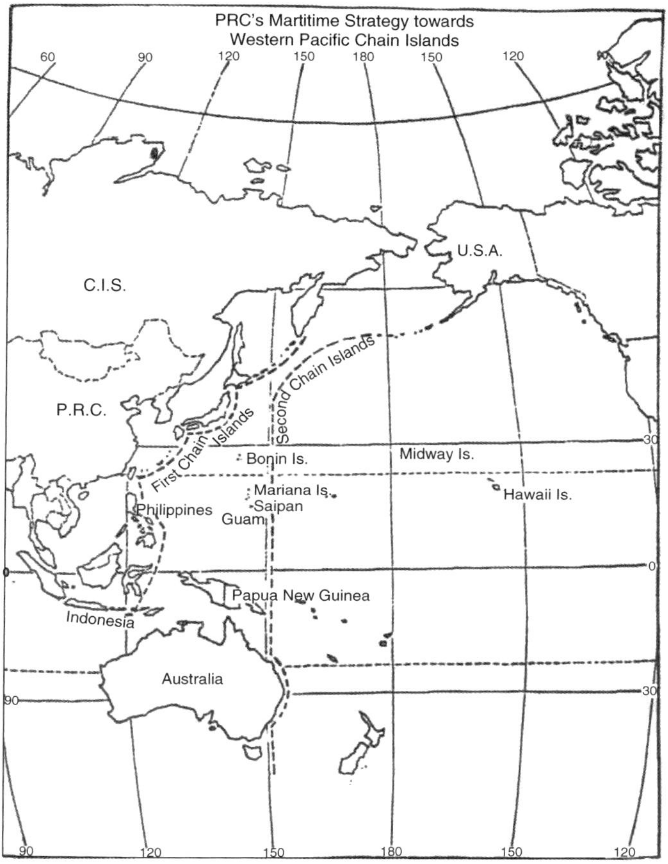

Map 8.1 The First and Second Island Chains in China's maritime strategy.

Source: S. Konapalli, *China's Naval Power*, New Delhi: Knowledge World in association with Institute for Defence Studies and Analyses, 2001, p. 4. As reprinted in Liao Wen-chung, 'China's Blue Water Strategy in the 21st Century: From the First Islands Chain Toward the Second Islands Chain', *Occasional Paper Series*, Taipei: Chinese Council of Advanced Policy Studies, 1995, Appendix 1.

experience and base infrastructure to support long-range operations in the Pacific and Indian oceans.

Some Chinese commentators have emphasized the control of key straits and chokepoints, giving rise to the belief that 'the Chinese Navy is going to have to have enough might to effectively control when necessary the key sea lanes from Chinese sea-space to the high seas [including] the Korea [Tsushima] Strait and all straits or channels in the Ryūkyū Islands'. Owing to the perception that 'the concerned countries keep a quite tight peacetime security, warning, and control of these straits' the same writer predicts that 'the wartime struggle to control these straits will be very intense'. To the south, it is seen as strategically necessary to control the Bashi, Malacca, Sunda and Lungmu [Lombok], Straits as well as 'all straits in the Philippines'.[14]

To China's naval planners, the control of Taiwan has strategic value, as a 'gateway' giving unobstructed access to the Pacific. It is also prized for its sea-denial value astride US military and Japanese economic SLOC: 'As such, it may be used to adversely affect the US's forward deployment [and] Japan's economic lifeline'.[15] Early post-war US assessments of Taiwan's strategic value, drawn up by the Joint Chiefs of Staff in November 1948, concurred that control of the island by a hostile power would confer on it the 'capability of dominating to his advantage and our disadvantage the sea routes between Japan and the Malay area'.[16] Taiwanese officials and political leaders continue to draw external powers' attention to the island's geostrategic importance as a means of eliciting interest in its defence, a strategy that has much in common with Singapore. In 2002, Taiwan's foreign minister stressed the importance of the Taiwan Strait as a 'lifeline' to Japan.[17] In August 2004 opposition Kuomintang leader Lien Chan reminded a visiting Japanese political delegation that 60 per cent of Japan's sea traffic passes through the Bashi Channel as the basis for his claim that Japan and Taiwan share 'a common basis of geopolitics and security structure'.[18] Taiwan's senior naval commanders, for their part, describe the security of SLOC 'on which the very survival of Taiwan depends' as their 'uppermost duty'.[19] One Chinese source comments:

> The island of Taiwan holds the most crucial 'central position' on the Chinese coast, as well as the 'central position' in the first island chain. It overlooks the Western Pacific shipping lane outside of the first island chain from the Bering Strait and the Aleutian Islands . . . guarding the Bashi . . . and Taiwan Strait, and controlling the throat of the shipping lane from the Malacca Strait north through the South China Sea, which gives it a very advantageous geographic location of great strategic value.[20]

The same writer describes the Paracel and Spratly Islands in the South China Sea as 'crucial footholds that can effectively control [China's] maritime space and the shipping lane from the Malacca Strait through the Philippines west to the Bashi Strait'.

Four core roles outlined by Admiral Liu have defined the PLAN's capabilities and missions:

1 the ability to conduct campaigns for defending or disrupting SLOC;
2 the ability to conduct sea battles with less than first-rate sea powers;
3 the ability to capture, occupy and defend islands;
4 deterrence.

In spite of a shortage of battle experience and limited resources, the PLAN places priority on SLOC defence as a matter of China's 'economic survival', in terms of trade protection and the protection of oil routes from the Gulf. China's reliance on imports of strategic resources, such as oil and mineral ores, that are shipped through Indian Ocean sea lanes, 'means that the Chinese Navy has to have enough might to cover the sea lanes through the Malacca Strait to the southern Indian Ocean, to ensure that our strategic resources are not interdicted'. Nonetheless, the PLAN itself has identified the following operational and tactical difficulties confronting the SLOC defence mission:

- a necessity to operate at long distances from its home bases, as far as the Gulf, stretching its surface and submarine escort capabilities to the limit;
- a loss of initiative, due to the defensive nature of the escort mission, which allows an opponent to choose the location, method and timing of his attacks;
- tactical vulnerability for surface escorts arising from the necessity to operate at slow speeds in convoy formation.

However, SLOC disruption is seen as integral to the navy's future operational plans, first, because long-distance lines of supply are regarded as a weakness of great power navies; and second, because a blockade of Taiwan is regarded as a serious military option in case of a cross-strait conflict. The following principles for SLOC interdiction have been put forward:

- priority should be given to selective attacks on enemy SLOC;
- to avoid damaging counter-attacks, PLAN units should be dispersed while carrying out supplementary 'small-scale disruptive activities' during the campaign;
- anti-SLOC campaigns should be conducted mainly within range of land-based air cover;
- SLOC disruption should also include attacks on enemy ports, while the number of targets should be limited.[21]

PLAN force modernization

The PLAN expected to complete its first stage of modernization by the end of the 1990s. During this phase, while avoiding direct confrontation with other navies as far as possible, the onus of development would fall on land-based medium-range aviation and attack submarines while the PLAN's three fleets (Northern, Eastern and Southern) would build an ocean-going task force to practice blue-water operations. In the second stage, lasting until 2020 or 2030, the PLAN would move to a blue-water configuration capable of three-dimensional naval conflict, equipped with SSBNs, aircraft carriers and other major surface combatants.

In the 1990s, the PLAN moved some way towards meeting its first stage objectives, scrapping more than half of its vintage *Romeo*-class submarines and all of its first-generation destroyers, acquiring two 8,000-ton *Sovremennyy*-class destroyers and four *Kilo*-class submarines from Russia. The *Ming* and *Song*-class submarines and the *Luhu*-class DDG were produced domestically, and existing surface combatants were retrofitted with SAM. Submarine development received priority in PLAN planning during the 1990s. Although the PLAN experienced inertial problems operating and training crews for the *Kilo* submarines, a decision to treble its Russian-bought fleet in part was aimed to compensate for the failure of the *Song* programme to develop according to schedule, following its poor performance during sea trials in 1995.[22] In June 2002, as part of an arms deal with Russia worth $4 billion, which has helped to make China the world's largest arms importer, Beijing agreed to buy a further two *Sovremennyy* destroyers (equipped with the supersonic SS-N-22 'Sunburn' anti-ship missile) and up to eight more *Kilo* submarines (all of the improved '636' design and offered at a 'below-market' unit price of $200 million) equipped with the *Club* anti-ship missile, with a range of 225 km. China has yet to develop OTH targeting capabilities to utilize these missiles to their full range, but has put a developmental premium on OTH radar and space-based surveillance and targeting systems to this end. Not surprisingly, the PLAN has experienced teething problems in the transition to a smaller, more modern and potent submarine fleet (with half as many boats as a decade ago), requiring it simultaneously to assimilate imported off-the-shelf technology while developing domestic designs.[23] Once the PLAN has mastered these problems however, it plans to reinforce its submarine fleet to secure maritime control in areas beyond the 'first island chain'[24] and will 'be able to form an ambush platform at the strategic chokepoints in the West Pacific such as around the Bashi Channel and the Taiwan Strait'.[25] Operationally, although the pattern of recent PLAN training activity has been limited, it has made progress towards developing its long-range capabilities, with the destroyer, *Qingdao*, completing China's first naval circumnavigation in September 2002 in a four-month voyage, visiting 10 countries.[26]

The PLAN currently numbers 290,000 personnel, fielding around 60 destroyers and frigates, around 50 conventional and 6 nuclear submarines, as well as an air arm with over 500 fixed-wing aircraft and 50 helicopters. Forty Su-30MKK maritime-strike variant aircraft were also included in the 2002 arms deal with Russia. Despite recent advances in force modernization, the PLAN has made greater progress in its strategies and organizational restructuring towards becoming a blue-water force than it has in hardware or operational terms. Despite a total displacement tonnage of nearly 1 million tons, most of the PLAN's vessels 'are obsolete and small, and most of the major ships are without anti-air missiles'.[27] The US DoD identifies one of China's main military weaknesses as its limited capacity for protecting SLOC against superior naval and air forces.[28] Air defence for the surface fleet remains limited to point defence. Moreover, the PLAN does not have any capability to defend itself against cruise missiles. The indefinite postponement of plans to acquire an aircraft carrier in conjunction with the expansion of its submarine force and land-based naval air arm appear to signal a more limited ambition to pursue sea control in coastal and offshore areas, and the pursuit of a sea-denial capability that 'could form the core of a force to allow China to blockade Taiwan's ports'.[29] The acquisition of such a capability would also have both political and military value, by raising the costs to the United States of sending its Navy and Air Force to operate in and around the Taiwan Strait, and possibly the South China Sea as well. During the 1982 Falklands War, the single Type-209 submarine possessed by the Argentine Navy, *San Luis*, distracted the British naval task force, forcing it to divert scarce resources to ASW throughout the three-month campaign.[30]

China's territorial claims and SLOC

At the diplomatic level, China has given assurances that it 'attaches great importance to the safety and free passage of South China Sea international sea lanes'.[31] After the February 1995 stand-off between the Philippine Navy and Chinese vessels near Mischief Reef, 'respect for free navigation' was affirmed at a vice-ministerial level meeting between Chinese and Philippines diplomats in early August 1995. At a news conference in November 2000, Deputy Foreign Minister Wang Ri, addressing proposals for a Code of Conduct in the South China Sea with rival claimants in the ten-member ASEAN, affirmed that 'There is no problem with the international sea lanes . . . at this stage and there won't be a problem in the future'.[32] China's switch to a more accommodative position over its territorial disputes in the South China Sea since the mid-1990s, for example signing the Code of Conduct with ASEAN in member states in November 2002, has been perceived as a tactical shift reflecting the preoccupation of China's strategists and political leadership with Taiwan since the crisis in cross-strait relations that erupted in 1995–96.[33]

According to the US DoD annual report on China's military capability released in July 2002, Taiwan is 'the major focus of China's military modernization'.[34] China's military strategy towards Taiwan is aimed at developing a range of 'credible' military options designed to maximize Beijing's leverage in negotiations, which 'may reflect an increasing willingness to consider the use of force to achieve unification'. Among its options are air and missile strikes launched from within the Nanjing Military Region, cyber-warfare and a blockade of the island.[35]

Taiwanese defence analysts have long perceived a merchant blockade of the island as consistent with precepts of Chinese strategy that put political and psychological factors at least on a par with military factors in the use of force. According to Michael Tsai and York Chen, a commercial blockade of the island may be favoured by China's military authorities as a means of applying Sun Tsu's strategic dictum of *fu gong* ('capturing a fortified city without attack'). A blockade would provide a means of exerting pressure on the island's leadership politically, economically and psychologically, given the perception that the 'symbolic' sinking of even 'one or two Taiwanese merchantmen . . . will drastically weaken the security of Taiwan's maritime traffic'.[36]

One of two options is foreseen in the event of a merchant blockade, involving either a 'close' blockade in the island's vicinity, or one executed at some distance. Since 93 per cent of shipping normally docks at one of three ports – Kaohsiung (51 per cent), Keelung (26 per cent) and Taichung (17 per cent) – the former option, conducted via a submarine-led blockade of the approaches to the island's major commercial ports, would simplify the problem for the PLAN of how to distinguish between trade bound for Taiwan and cargoes for other destinations, reducing the political risks of internationalizing the conflict. A close blockade would also benefit tactically from the unavoidable concentration of shipping in the approaches to terminals. Against this, a close blockade would entail higher military risks, given closer proximity to the island's armed forces and port defences, as well as the defenders' familiarity with the operating environment.[37] A remote blockade would severely constrain the ability of Taiwan's navy and air force, forcing them to disperse their forces and reducing the military risks to China's forces.[38]

Although the PLAN could release assets from all three of its fleets for use in a distant blockade against Taiwan, their effectiveness would be reduced if operating far from their own bases. According to Tsai and Chen's scenario, if a blockade were undertaken, China would commit the four submarine squadrons at the disposal of its Southern and Eastern fleets. In conjunction with surface and signals intelligence operations, these forces could be deployed in inner and outer blockade lines; the former blocking traffic and raiding Taiwan's civilian and military harbours, while the outer 'ring' would target any merchant vessels attempting to break the blockade, concurrently deterring US attempts to dispatch seaborne supplies or to intervene directly (from Okinawa and other Pacific bases).[39] According to US estimates, China has enough mine warfare assets (including bottom-laid mines, moored-influence mines, mobile mines, remote-controlled mines, and propelled-warhead mines) to lay 'a good defensive and a modest offensive minefield'. These mines could be laid in areas where merchant ships are likely to be concentrated, by submarines and/or Chinese commercial and fishing vessels.[40]

Chinese perceptions of Japan's SLOC

Japan's own naval modernization programme, its alliance relationship with the United States and alleged militarist tendencies have been presented by Chinese analysts as posing a potential threat to China and its maritime security.[41] The overlap between both countries' maritime defence zones, including the disputed Senkaku Islands, in the East China Sea, presents a further potential source of tension.[42]

Chinese analysts are also aware of Japan's vulnerability to a blockade:

> From the Western Pacific to Southeast Asia, the maritime shipping lane through the Straits of Malacca to the . . . Persian Gulf is called Japan's economic 'lifeline', with the Straits of Malacca . . . being the key link of that lifeline. The obstruction or even blockade of that shipping lane would cut off Japan's economic lifeline, paralysing the Japanese economy and society. Keeping this shipping lane open is a key condition for Japan's survival and development, as well as a crucial mission in the development of the Japanese SDF.[43]

Indeed, some Chinese analysts argue that Japan could use the perceived vulnerability of SLOC as a pretext to justify involvement in a dispute over Taiwan, using 'the right to maritime freedom [to] ignite a conflict'.[44] Right wing forces in Japan are, by the same token, portrayed as using sea lane security concerns to revive a 'southward' expansionist strategy 'to seize raw material bases'.[45] At the same time, since 1994 China has judged the MSDF, to be 'the Asian naval armed force with the strongest ocean-going escort and offensive-defensive combat capability', able to operate independently in the South China Sea.[46] The *Zhongguo Tongxun She* news agency reported that in 1996 the JDA published an internal report concluding that China will 'bring about a pattern of military confrontation in its relations with Japan' and that China will 'pose threats to Japan's maritime lifeline'.[47]

Japanese perceptions of China's potential naval threat

Since the early 1990s, concern has grown among Japan's policy-makers over the direction of China's foreign and defence policies and the implications for Japan's long-term maritime security. Official concern in Japan was awakened in February 1992, with China's promulgation of the Territorial Waters Law, legally affirming sovereignty claims based on China's continental shelf claim (see Chapter 7). This included the Paracel and Spratly island groups disputed with Taiwan and several Southeast Asian states in the South China Sea, and waters in the East China Sea that fall within Japan's EEZ, demarcated by Tokyo along a median line between the two countries' coastlines. The Law 'shocked' Japan by appearing to revive the territorial dispute over the Senkaku Islands.[48] Prime Minister Miyazawa Kiichi sought clarification of the Territorial Waters Law from Chinese Communist Party Chairman Jiang Zemin, during the latter's visit to Tokyo in April 1992.[49] The JDA has also expressed concerns that the Chinese Communist Party's Fourteenth Congress in October 1992 'made clear that defending the interests of the territorial waters is part of the [PLA's] mission for the future', a theme it claims is substantiated in China's National Defence Law of March 1997.[50]

Japanese security concerns were heightened by the stepped-up activities of Chinese survey vessels within Japan's EEZ after 1994 and the growing presence of Chinese naval vessels and aircraft around the Senkaku Islands, Okinawa and as far north as the Tsugaru Strait.[51] The February 1995 Mischief Reef incident was viewed with alarm in Tokyo as an indication of China's increased assertiveness.[52] At Manila's prompting, the issue was raised by Japan's MOFA at a vice-ministerial level meeting in Beijing on 2 March and again by Prime Minister Maruyama Tomiichi during his visit to China in April. In August, at the second meeting of the ARF, Foreign Minister Kōno Yōhei raised Japan's concerns over freedom of navigation in relation to the Spratlys dispute and stated Japan's concern for a peaceful solution.[53] Before the Diet in October 1995, Kōno took the unprecedented step of citing China's territorial policies and military buildup as potential sources of instability.[54]

Growing concern at the rise of pro-independence political forces in Taiwan led the PLA to conduct an initial round of coastal military exercises and missile tests in the island's vicinity in July 1995, in an attempt to signal China's displeasure.

As the March 1996 presidential election loomed, China resorted to a second, larger round of coastal military exercises in Fujian province, opposite Taiwan, and a battery of short-range ballistic missile tests. Japanese anxieties were sharpened by the fact that some of the missiles landed in waters only 60 km from Yonaguni island, at the extreme, southern end of Okinawa prefecture.[55] A MOFA spokesman, while avoiding outright condemnation, described the missile tests as 'undesirable' and said that they 'may create problems for shipping in neutral waters off the place of their fall'. On 12 March as the second of three phases to China's exercises began, Prime Minister Hashimoto Ryūtaro expressed his concern that many commercial flights and aircraft had been forced to divert around the areas affected.[56]

Although collective self-defence considerations ruled out any official Japanese military deployments in coordination with the US deployment of two aircraft carrier battle groups in the vicinity of the Taiwan Straits, Japan nevertheless dispatched ASDF E-2Cs and an MSDF EP-3 under the pretext of its own exercises to collect intelligence on Chinese activities during the crisis.[57] The JDA Vice-Minister Murata, visiting China in August 1996, reiterated Tokyo's concerns with 'the exercises which took place in commercial shipping lanes'.[58] As the revised US–Japan Defense Cooperation Guidelines were debated in the autumn of 1997, Chief Cabinet Secretary Kajiyama Seiroku stated, controversially, that Taiwan would be included within the scope of the US–Japan Defense Cooperation Guidelines, then in the process of being redrafted.[59] Attempts to delimit the scope of the Guidelines geographically were dropped in favour of a vague formula to minimize controversy, whereby the Guidelines would apply 'in situations and areas surrounding Japan', at the same time preserving ambiguity over whether Japan would assist US efforts to repel Chinese aggression across the Strait.

Japanese concerns about China had already featured in the August 1994 report drawn up by the Advisory Group on Defense Issues. In their assessment of Japan's security environment, the report's authors highlighted China, among other Asian countries, as possessing the political motives and economic foundation to modernize its military power in addition to the risk of conflict erupting over its disputed maritime territorial claims.[60] In 1995, Chairman of the SDF Joint Staff Council General Nishimoto Tetsuya became the most senior SDF officer to visit China, appealing for greater transparency in its defence and nuclear weapons policy. Japan's 1996 defence white paper, while characterizing the pace of China's defence modernization as 'moderate', noted that 'we need to continue to watch Chinese actions, such as the modernization of its nuclear forces, naval and air forces; expanding its scope of activities in the high seas; and the growing tension in the Taiwan Strait caused by its military exercises'.[61]

Outside the white paper framework, one Japanese security analyst, a former GSDF general, expressed the more overt concerns that:

> If China conducts military drills to intimidate Taiwan, or actually launches hostile actions in the waters around Taiwan, it will seriously impact the safety of the Japanese territory and its SLOC even if the areas involved are on the high seas. Furthermore, it will arouse and inflame the latent and instinctive fear of the Japanese people creating a condition of an open crisis.[62]

The *East Asia Strategic Review 2000* stated that China's survey activities and naval presence around the Senkaku had 'aroused the fears of Japan'.[63] The review's authors claimed that China's increasingly assertive presence in areas surrounding Japan was aimed at bolstering its long-term claim to marine resources, including possible oil deposits around the Senkaku. Furthermore, the timing of Chinese naval activity was interpreted within the JDA as a political signal intended to discourage the passage of Guidelines-related legislation by the Diet. *East Asia Strategic Review 2001* noted that Chinese oceanographic vessels conducted surveys within Japan's EEZ 16 times in 1998, 30 times in 1999 and 24 times in 2000, when PLAN vessels were, in addition, spotted 3 times.[64] In 2004, a total of 19 'violations' of Japan's EEZ were reported in the 5 months to May. In April, at a working-level meeting in Beijing, Japanese officials raised the issue of China's oceanographic survey activities in its EEZ as far south as Okino Tori Shima.[65] Japan's concerns intensified in October, following reports that China had granted natural gas exploitation rights within Japan's EEZ, behaviour described as 'unfriendly' by METI Nakagawa Shoichi.[66] The December 2004 official review of defence policy concluded that 'Japan must pay close attention to China's modernization of its military and the expansion of its maritime activities'.[67]

The presence of warships in Japan's EEZ is not illegal under the UNCLOS, or Japanese law. However, approaches by Chinese combat aircraft and submarines have occurred in the vicinity of the Senkaku Islands since the mid-1990s. On 16 August 1995, ASDF F-4 fighters based at Naha, Okinawa were ordered to intercept a pair of Chinese Su-27s approaching at high speed, before turning short of the islands.[68] The following August, two Chinese submarines were reported to pass close by.[69] Although reports of Chinese submarine incursions in the Japanese press were not officially acknowledged in Tokyo, in October 1996, the Defense Agency sought cabinet backing for tougher regulations to allow MSDF vessels to force unidentified submarines in Japanese territorial waters to surface. Ostensibly this was in order to respond to the threat of North Korean submersibles following a serious incursion incident in South Korean waters.[70] However, on 24 December, the Hashimoto Cabinet approved these measures, also with China in mind. Indeed, it has been claimed that Chinese oceanographic survey vessels have been engaged in 'information-gathering for future Chinese submarine operations in passages around the Ryūkyū Islands'.[71] In May 2000, China sent a *Yanbing*-class ice-breaker reportedly sea-bed mapping through the Tsushima and Tsugaru Straits, prompting Japanese defence officials and diplomats to raise the issue with their counterparts during bilateral talks in Beijing, on 19 June 2000.[72] In November 2003, a *Ming*-class submarine was discovered by a US P-3C navigating off the coast of Kagoshima.[73] The most serious submarine incursion occurred in November 2004 when, amidst rising concern in Japan over China's commercial and strategic maritime activities and pending the release of a major review of defence policy, a submerged *Han*-class SSN briefly entered Japan's territorial waters near Sakishima, 120 km south of the Senkaku Islands. The incursion prompted the government to initiate an order to conduct maritime security operations, for only the second time in the MSDF's 50-year history, and later to lodge a formal diplomatic protest.[74] After the submarine had left Japan's territorial waters, MSDF P-3Cs, and 2 DDH continued to track it northward, then westward towards the Bohai Gulf.[75]

Kyōrin University professor Hiramatsu Shigeo's views on China's 'use' of piracy as a security threat to Japan were outlined in Chapter 7. Hiramatsu was among the first Japanese analysts publicly to warn of an 'emerging threat of Chinese military expansion', particularly the country's growing ability to project naval power into surrounding seas, and he has advocated making an official commitment to include Taiwan within the scope of the US–Japan Alliance.[76] Okazaki Hisahiko, former Ambassador to Thailand, Saudi Arabia and director of intelligence at both MOFA and JDA, while uncommonly vocal among retired Japanese officials represents a strain of realist, balance-of-power thinking widely subscribed to within conservative policy-making circles, into which he has had access via the LDP defence expert (*zoku*), Shiina Motoo.

Hiramatsu asserted that by applying indirect pressure on Japanese shipping, or by interdicting sea lanes in the South China Sea, China could 'deal a serious blow' to Japan and Taiwan without using force. Notably, *Safely by Sea*, a 1990 collection of papers given at the biannual Asia-Pacific SLOC conferences since 1982, prefigured such concerns arguing:

> Far more likely [than a Soviet direct assault] would be the use of direct, or through surrogates, indirect pressure upon Japan's SLOCs at a distance beyond the reach of the [MSDF]. The confined and relatively shallow waters of the archipelagoes [*sic*] bounding the South China Sea appear more attractive for such operations, particularly if they can be disguised behind existing regional conflicts or acts of piracy.[77]

Given this assumed vulnerability to SLOC disruption, China's perceived determination to exert control over oil resources in the South China Sea, and preparedness to use military pressure for political leverage, Hiramatsu recommended that Japan should consider a collective security arrangement with the littoral states of Southeast Asia. Okazaki, himself born in Dalian in 1930, regards China's approach to military power as one strand in a composite strategy that combines political and psychological factors, aimed at 'the deprivation of the opponent's will to fight through psychological warfare of the threat of violence'.[78] According to this logic, though China will not attain sufficient conventional military power to constitute a 'real threat' to Taiwan and other countries until 2020, it will probably have enough force to 'exert credible psychological pressure' by 2010. Writing in 1998 Okazaki stated that 'If an armed conflict developed now between Chinese naval and air forces and Japan's [MSDF] and [ASDF] in the Senkaku Islands area, Japan's victory would be only a matter of hours'.[79] However, during future periods of tension between China and Japan, China may seek to influence the Japanese government's position by applying indirect pressure on commercial SLOC in the South China Sea.[80] This 'psychological' aspect of the use of military pressure on 'fragile' sea lanes, is echoed in Japanese perceptions throughout the post-1945 era, as seen in Sekino Hideo's views profiled in Chapter 4, and it is a mindset still entrenched in the MSDF.[81]

During the Cold War, Japanese defence planners commonly regarded China as lacking the industrial base to support a submarine force capable of long-range operations. The projection of China's continental shelf far out to sea was also recognized as rendering its submarines tactically vulnerable in coastal waters by limiting their ability to submerge. Even late in the Cold War, despite having over 50 attack submarines (mostly small, *Romeo*-class boats), MSDF officers assessed China (and North Korea) to be lacking 'sufficient capabilities to attack Japanese sea lanes in the foreseeable future'.[82] By contrast, in the post-Cold War era, China's potential to use its submarines to blockade Taiwan and to threaten US and Japanese naval forces nearby is viewed by MSDF officers as potentially their most challenging operational problem.[83] The JDA concerns centre on the deep-water trenches off Taiwan and Okinawa, where the acoustic environment severely hampers detection, a natural hazard complicated by the PLAN's acquisition of the ultra-quiet *Kilo*-636 submarine. The particular difficulties of locating Soviet submarines operating in this area led the MSDF, in the late 1980s, to acquire 2 *Hibiki*-class acoustic intelligence vessels equipped with Surveillance Towed Array Sensor System (SURTASS).[84] However, the survivability of such platforms is questionable without screening forces, which might not be available in wartime.[85]

Izumi Hajime wrote in 1993 that Japan cannot 'wait and see the expanding Chinese naval activities on the Spratly Islands located on an important transportation sea lane. This standpoint of Japan would meet with sympathies even in the international community'.[86] According to Okazaki, by the late 1990s, China already had the military capability to control sea lanes in the South China Sea through air power alone, based on its acquisition of Su-27s and other fourth-generation strike aircraft, which if based in Hainan and the Paracels would extend air coverage throughout the South China Sea. However, against a military threat to commercial navigation in the South China Sea, Japan would retain the option of diverting its imports round the South China Sea and absorbing the higher shipping costs involved. While Okazaki believes that Japan's oil shipments could be maintained at additional cost by diverting round Australia, Japan's interest in the South China Sea is perceived in much broader terms than simply as a physical conduit serving its economy. For Okazaki, the potential 'Finlandization' of the littoral states in the South China Sea is the political consequence likely to flow from an assertive China, backed by its limited maritime interdiction capability in the South China Sea. For this reason, the security of the South China Sea is viewed as a security concern to Japan that would necessitate the SDF's active defence involvement in conjunction with the United States.[87]

Some of these assumptions have been challenged by the *Asahi Shimbun* veteran military analyst Taoka Shunji, who questions the suitability of islands and atolls in the Spratlys and Paracels (including the airstrip on Woody Island) for combat operations, much as the strategic importance and survivability of Soviet bases in Vietnam were questioned in the late 1970s and 1980s. Taoka also dismisses 'amateur' fears that a South China Sea conflict would severely disrupt Japan's oil supplies, arguing that the additional cost of diverting tankers through Lombok (and east of the Philippines) would add only 0.18 yen per litre to the cost of oil in Japan.[88]

Regarding perceptions within the MSDF and its sizeable coterie of conference-going retired admirals, at one extreme Hirama Yōichi has compared China's 'oceanic living space concept' with pre-war Germany's expansionist *lebensraum* philosophy, driven by an 'insatiable desire to obtain marine resources'. Admiral Liu's offshore defence concept is described as the extension of a 'continentalist' strategic culture to the maritime plane.[89] Those like Hirama who hold deep suspicions about China's long-term intentions also recognize short to medium-term constraints on its power-projection capabilities and capability gaps in electronic support measures, electronic counter measures, air defence and ASW, which unless addressed will leave it essentially a coastal navy. Hirama also cites 'many geographic, political and racial problems that will impede China's Navy from developing into a blue-water navy', suggesting that Mahanian and cultural-determinist explanations still have their place in contemporary Japan's strategic thought. What is feared most is that China's 'strategic genius' rather than brute military strength will effectively identify and exploit Japan's political and economic vulnerabilities.[90]

Mid-ranking MSDF officers have expressed concerns about China's 'extremely unsettling' defence modernization programme and assert that its military involvement in conflicts over the Spratlys and Paracels would 'pose a threat to Japan's sea lines of communication'.[91] China has also been used, within the MSDF and more broadly, to justify the MSDF's post-Cold War role and the retention and modernization of its capabilities. Commander Mitsuhisa Masahiko identifies China's 'outright expansion of the naval strength' as 'likely to become a significant threat to [the] Southwest Islands and maritime traffic of Japan'. Accordingly, it is argued that the MSDF 'will have to maintain a certain degree of defense capability so Japan can resolve this issue *by itself*', owing to doubts about whether the 'full military support' of the United States would be forthcoming in the event of a Sino-Japanese clash.[92]

The MSDF, moderately downsized as a result of the 1995 and 2004 *taikō* reviews, still has major functional gaps preventing the development of an autonomous power-projection capability. Nonetheless, the steady qualitative improvement of its existing capabilities, and an expanding programme of exercise partners, exercise activities and overseas deployments invite the question as to where its own intentions lie. Although Japan already possesses one of the largest and most modern naval fleets in Asia, the MTDP for fiscal 1996–2000, included scheduled naval construction amounting to 100,000 tons, including 8 destroyers , 5 submarines, 18 other vessels and 37 SH-60J patrol helicopters.[93] Procurements for the 2001–05 MTDP (including the new DDH and additional Aegis-equipped destroyers) are, according to *Sankei Shimbun* 'aimed at dealing with Chinese submarines operating in the shallow waters of the East China Sea', as part of a general rationale linked to the defence of surrounding maritime areas and the maintenance of maritime traffic safety.[94] The MTDP for fiscal 2005–09 includes approximately 60,000 tons of naval construction, including 3 Aegis DDG, 5 DDH, 4 submarines and 11 other vessels. Four new-generation fixed-wing maritime patrol aircraft will also be ordered in addition to 23 SH-60K patrol helicopters and three minesweeping and utility MCH-101 helicopters (Appendix 2). In spite of cutbacks to its regional divisional structure under the 2004 *taikō*, the MSDF has again preserved its core surface fleet based around four escort flotillas, comprising eight divisions. While the operational submarine inventory remains unchanged at 16, the number of divisions is being consolidated from 6 to 4. This is in accordance with the aim expressed in the MTDP to 'transform' the submarine fleet, presumably in line with a reorientation from the Cold War mission of straits defence to more wide-ranging operations in Japan's southern approaches. The number of maritime patrol squadrons has also been cut from 13 to 9, with the total of aircraft reducing from around 170 to 150 (see Figure 7.2).

The ambiguity of the MSDF's post-Cold War strategic outlook and the continued orientation of its capabilities towards 'blue-water' formations has led some Japanese analysts to conclude that it may be aiming to establish a presence in the South China Sea.[95] The desire of the ASDF to have the capability to maintain AWACs coverage as far as the South China Sea was noted in Chapter 7. The MTDP for fiscal 2005–09 rationalizes plans to procure next-generation P-3Cs and E-767s 'in order to warn and survey in the surrounding sea areas and deal properly with armed manoeuvring ships or foreign submarines transiting through [or] under Japanese sea territory'.[96] Since 1999, ASDF E-2Cs and F-15s have deployed as far south as Guam for bilateral exercises with the United States.[97] The acquisition of KC-767 tankers will provide the ASDF with the capability to project air superiority and support fighters to at least the northern half of the South China Sea.[98] The South China Sea offers a favourable operational environment for submarines (the Imperial Navy built a submarine base in the Spratly group after occupying and annexing the islands in 1939). In 1997, the former commander of the MSDF's Fleet Submarine Force, Nishimura Yoshiaki, expressed the view that 'unless the battle zone is pushed to the enemy's coastal area [at a chokepoint], our nation will suffer damages. Therefore . . . we need to travel to a certain extent, and only submarines can accomplish this'.[99] In October 2000, the MSDF sent the submarine *Asashio* to the South China Sea, as part of the quadripartite Exercise Pacific Reach 2000 involving Singapore, South Korea and the United States, each of which supplied a submarine to 'practice rescuing submarines in distress and their crews'.[100] In June 2001, MSDF vessels took part in a multilateral exercise off Singapore, involving units from 16 states represented within the Western Pacific Naval Symposium.[101] In December 2004, the Singaporean Navy announced that it was planning to request naval forces from Japan, the United States and others to participate in minesweeping exercises in the Straits of Malacca, following joint drills staged with Indonesia in May.[102] Asked if Japan's participation in actual minesweeping in the strait might breech the ban on collective self defence, a JDA official reportedly responded that minesweeping activities could be conducted 'under a collective security framework involving the United Nations in the event of any attacks'.[103]

Concern about China is echoed among more senior and still-influential former and serving MSDF officers and defence officials. Former MSDF Chief of Staff Sakuma Makoto has highlighted China as the most important challenge facing Japan's security in the post-Cold War age. China's maritime strategy is seen as driven by a desire to 'retain control of ocean resources while expanding its sphere of influence' towards the creation of a 'new oceanic order' in Asia.[104] Similarly, Admiral Kawamura Sumihiko attributes China's 'advance' into the South China Sea to Beijing's determination to secure control over energy, mineral and food resources.[105] However, China's growing dependence on oil imports, which is forecast to rise to 77 per cent of its needs by 2020,[106] is also recognized by Kawamura as potentially increasing the constraints on its scope for adventurism as it gains a stake in maintaining the security of oil shipments through the South China Sea.[107] Nonetheless, there are fears that if the PLAN maintains its current pace of naval modernization, China will 'become fully capable of challenging its rival navies in the Pacific and the Indian Ocean in the future'.

A former MSDF Chief of Staff, Hayashizaki Chiaki, outlining a post-Cold War strategy for the MSDF has compared China's offshore defence plans, encompassing parts of the Sea of Japan, East China Sea, and South China Sea, with the expansion of the Soviet Far Eastern Fleet during the 1970s and 1980s. Another former Chief of Staff, Admiral Sakonjo Naotoshi, while not dismissing China's long-term threat potential, more cautiously assesses that China's naval capabilities lag behind those of Japan by about 20 years. Even assuming a steady increase in China's defence budget, the SDF is likely to retain a technological edge over the PLAN until approximately 2020. China's acquisition of an aircraft carrier would not necessarily change this, as it would both absorb significant defensive assets and constitute a 'big target' for any opposing force.

Among serving staff officers, the view is shared that China still lacks a power-projection capability, but there is particular concern over its missile capabilities and willingness to use these in connection with political goals, as demonstrated from a much lower capability base vis-à-vis Taiwan in 1995 and 1996. Any use of force in the Strait would be seen as automatically threatening Japan's SLOC. Viewed simply as a narrow security concern over the safety of shipping, most tankers and container vessels in transit through the East China Sea would have the option to divert to safety unless China adopted a remote blockade. However, the more worldly MSDF officers appreciate that the overriding, political determinant of Japan's reaction to a cross-strait crisis is whether the United States decides to intervene. Were it to do so, it is felt that this would trigger irresistible pressures within the Alliance for Japan to provide defence support under the terms of the new Guidelines.[108]

Long-term concern about China extends to the top of the civilian hierarchy within the JDA. Former Administrative Vice-Minister Akiyama Masahiro has identified China's future defence capability as Japan's single most important maritime security challenge. In his view, Japan should match any decision by the PLAN to acquire an aircraft carrier. Under Akiyama's tenure at the JDA, the annual defence white paper assessments of China's military power expanded from three pages in 1995 to nine pages in the 2001 edition. He believes that Japan may have to expand its sea lane defence commitment beyond 1,000 nm in future.[109]

In 2004, Kyodo reported that it had obtained confidential JDA documents revealing plans to deploy over 7,000 GSDF troops to defend outlying islands in Okinawa Prefecture against the possibility of Chinese landings to block US– Japan intervention in a conflict over Taiwan.[110] Such leaks may have served the political purpose of safeguarding GSDF force levels from deep manpower cuts, anticipated as a likely recommendation of the 2004 review of defence capability. However, the proximity to Taiwan of remote Japanese islands such as Yonagunijima and Miyakojima is now genuinely perceived in Japan as a strategic vulnerability, while the territorial dispute with China over the Senkaku is an ongoing concern.[111] Indeed, official recognition of a requirement to maintain 'necessary defence structure to respond effectively to invasion against islands' was included in the new *taikō*.

At a wider level in policy-making circles and in society, Japanese attitudes towards China since the end of Cold War have been marked by ambivalence. An alleged sympathetic bias towards Beijing has often been attributed to the 'China School' of MOFA's Asian Affairs Bureau, big business, and segments of the mass media (especially *Asahi Shimbun*) and LDP.[112] The rise of a new political generation and the demise of ideology as a significant factor in Japan–China relations have combined to open up political debate on China and to weaken political taboos against criticizing the country, while support for China among the general public has been in decline for several years. The retrenchment of LDP politicians regarded as broadly sympathetic to China, in particular former party Secretary General Katō Kōichi, has helped to shift the balance of political opinion towards nationalist platforms within the controlling party. In 1995–96, LDP deputies called (unsuccessfully) for a freeze in yen loans to China in protest at Beijing's nuclear testing programme.[113] More recently, Japan's overseas development aid to China has come under pressure for cuts in response to China's continued high military spending. A perceived increase in the tendency of Chinese officials to use 'history problems' (*rekishi mondai*) from the pre-1945 period as moral leverage to block undesirable aspects of Japan's foreign and defence policies is also resented.[114] Outside the LDP, the same trend is exemplified by the political resurgence of the mayor of Tokyo (and advocate of naval expansion), Ishihara Shintarō, whose strident criticism of Beijing and criminal activities attributed to ethnic Chinese in Japan contrasts starkly with his appeals to Pan-Asianism in the 1980s. Within the LDP, politicians concerned at the escalating trend in relocation of Japanese firms to Asia have branded China as an economic threat to Japan as well as a latent strategic challenger. A growing 'realist' perception that China poses a potential security threat to Japan has also been borne out among centrist opposition parties. For example, the opposition *shinshintō* party, in 1995, included the Spratlys among sources of regional insecurity in its party policy outline and in 1996 issued a communiqué calling on China to halt its missile tests near Taiwan.[115]

Although Soeya Yoshihide has described the 'China threat' thesis as 'alien' to the Japanese government and people, and also to the country's post-1989 policy of supporting China's economic modernization, an 'unmistakable' shift in Japanese official and popular attitudes has occurred since the mid-1990s.[116] Mainstream Japanese international scholars, including Etō Shinkichi, Iriye Akira and Inoguchi Takashi followed a liberal-institutionalist approach towards relations with China up to the early 1990s. This was based on the assumption that 'Under present circumstances . . . there is no possibility of China's emerging as an expansionist, hegemonic power wielding military force against its neighbours to augment its own territory'.[117] However, the perceptions of China held by a younger generation of Japanese academics, of whom Soeya is representative, have undergone a transformation in the post-Cold War period. In 1993, Soeya wrote that 'With its status as an economic superpower and its strictly defence-oriented security policy Japan is in a good position to demand that China act with restraint in the South China Sea'.[118] At the time, such views were echoed by other Japanese observers who thought that the threat of Japanese economic sanctions 'acts as an important check on Chinese ambitions' and believed that Japan's status as a non-claimant in the South China Sea qualified it to broker a solution to the territorial disputes over the Spratlys and Paracels.[119] However, after the Mischief Reef episode, the Taiwan missile crisis and China's nuclear tests in August 1995 and July 1996, Soeya urged the need to be 'vigilant' against Chinese moves in the South China Sea as 'one of the few cases where Japan's national and security interests are evidently at stake in the post-Cold War era'.[120] Since Japan 'is in no position to deal with China by itself', he concluded that it faced a 'highly strategic' need to adopt closer defence relations with the United States as the only 'viable counterpart to the Chinese military'.

One Japanese security analyst has recently proposed the 'construction of a multilateral cooperative system in which all regional players participate' as 'vital to the security of sea lanes in the Asian region'. This concern has particular significance in a cross-strait context:

> [S]uch an international cooperative system cannot be considered complete without the participation of an important regional naval power like Taiwan . . . [which] will have a very hard time achieving this objective by itself. . . . Japan's role and responsibility is great, as a country that shares most sea lanes with Taiwan. For Japan to agree to exclude Taiwan . . . is for Japan to agree to the creation of a gaping hole in the security of sea lanes connecting Japan with the Middle East. Whenever there are international discussions about maritime security, Japan must keep its national interests firmly in sight and make its position abundantly clear. The Japanese government should be aware that [this] is as much in the interest of Japan's national dignity as its national interest.[121]

North Korea's SLOC security challenges

While Japan's maritime military threat perceptions are focused on China in the medium to long term, North Korea presents a broader, less predictable set of challenges and potential threats to Japan's SLOC security. These can be divided into three categories:

1 conventional military threats, posed by North Korea's navy and special forces;
2 transnational criminal challenges, posed by North Korea's maritime incursions and illicit activities in Japan;
3 proliferation of missiles and WMD by sea.

Conventional threats

In terms of a conventional threat to Japan's SLOC from North Korea, the maritime component is not usually viewed as central to scenarios for resumed conflict on the Peninsula. Nonetheless, infiltration from *Sango*-class submarines into South Korea has resulted in armed clashes in the last decade, the most serious in September 1996 when North Korean commandos came ashore. A second submersible was destroyed off South Korea's southern coast in December 1998. South Korean ASW operations against two suspected submarines off South Korea's east coast were reported by the local media in October 2004, although any incursion was subsequently denied in Seoul.[122] North Korea's possession of 22 *Romeo*-class submarines has been evaluated by the former head of the MSDF's Fleet Submarine Force as 'quite ominous'.[123] Also of concern to Japan's defence planners is North Korea's capacity to deploy sea mines, as occurred during the Korean War, and its possession of an estimated 135 air-cushioned landing craft, which could be used to infiltrate a small number of the country's 100,000-strong Special Forces by sea.[124] Irregular attacks against US military installations in Japan and nuclear power stations along the Sea of Japan coast are particularly feared.

Transnational criminal challenges

Between 1963 and the end of 2002, the JCG identified a total of 21 'suspicious vessels' (*fushinsen*) believed to have originated from North Korea, 18 of which were detected in the Sea of Japan and 12 inside Japan's territorial waters. North Korean 'spy ships' have gained notoriety in Japan in recent years. In March 1999, the unsuccessful pursuit by MSDF ships of two high-speed *fushinsen* in the Sea of Japan, off the Nōto Peninsula, demonstrated the vulnerability of Japan's EEZ and territorial seas to covert intrusion. North Korean incursions along Japan's western coast, allegedly organized by the 727 Liaison Office, are widely thought to have involved intelligence collection, the smuggling of drugs and counterfeit goods, and the infiltration and exfiltration of covert operatives.[125] According to the National Police Authority, North Korea was the source of over one-third of the illegal stimulants impounded in Japan from 1998 to 2002, including a single seizure of more than 2 tons in 1999.[126] North Korean state involvement is also alleged in the export from Japan of stolen electronic goods, cars and semi-legal cash remittances that are shipped in collaboration with local criminal gangs.[127]

However, since Prime Minister Koizumi Junichirō's visit to Pyongyang in September 2002 Japanese public threat perceptions have overwhelmingly focused on Kim Jong Il's admission that North Korean operatives abducted several Japanese citizens from the Sea of Japan coastline during the 1970s and 1980s.[128]

In December 2001, the pursuit of a 'spy ship' by the JCG culminated in a firefight southwest of Kagoshima and the vessel's sinking inside China's EEZ. This unprecedented use of lethal force by the Japanese state in the post-war era was endorsed at the time as a 'resolute action' by US Deputy Secretary of State Richard Armitage.[129] The same *fushinsen* is alleged to have been involved in an aborted operation, in August 1998, to infiltrate 300 kg of stimulants off the coast of Kōchi.[130] Upon its recovery from the seabed in 2002, the vessel was revealed to be armed with rocket launchers, SAMs and anti-aircraft machine guns, as well as containing Japanese-manufactured mobile phones, satellite navigational devices and a detachable water scooter.[131]

The military and transnational crime threats posed by North Korea to Japan's maritime security have provided impetus for legislative moves to relax restrictions on the use of force by the JCG and MSDF, and efforts to boost inter-agency cooperation and information-sharing.[132] Several significant legal and operational precedents were set as a result of the North Korean 'spy ship' incidents in 1999 and 2001. During the March 1999 incident, for the first time in the history of the MSDF, Prime Minister Obuchi Keizō ordered maritime security operations, under Article 82 of the Self Defense Law, culminating in warning shots fired from MSDF vessels.

Both the JCG and MSDF have successfully argued the case for new capabilities to cope with North Korea's maritime intrusions. The MSDF ordered guided-missile patrol boats after the 1999 sea chase, capable of making 44 knots, armed with anti-ship missiles and 12.7 mm machine guns.[133] The JCG, which considered acquiring its own high-speed vessels equipped with heavy machine guns, has also stepped up inspections of North Korean vessels visiting Japanese ports, in particular the *Manyongbong*-92 ferry, which calls at Niigata.[134] In the wake of the 1999 incident, the MSDF and JCG conducted their first joint exercise and agreed to draft a joint manual to coordinate responses to similar incidents in future.[135]

The JCG's use of lethal force in December 2001 was justified with reference to the Fisheries Law, as the only domestic statute outlawing activities within Japan's EEZ.[136] The incident spurred a formal declaration by the government backing the use of SDF assets against suspected 'suspicious ship' intrusions into Japan's EEZ.[137] It also gave longer-term political momentum to the introduction of emergency laws that would enable the MSDF to launch ships at its own discretion to cope with suspected maritime intrusions.[138] The government initially considered drafting special legislation that would enable discriminatory measures to be taken against North Korean vessels within Japan's EEZ.[139] However, the basis for doing so under UNCLOS, which allows only for the interception of vessels related to fisheries stocks and dangerous cargoes, is doubtful. Instead, legislation was enacted in 2004 giving the cabinet powers to declare a discriminatory ban on ships that are either flagged or arriving from a particular country, preventing them from calling at Japanese ports. While North Korea is not named, North Korean vessels and the *Manyongbong*-92 ferry in particular are the suspected targets of the law, which imposes up to three years imprisonment and/or a fine of up to 1 million yen on offending captains.[140]

One of seven bills introduced to the Diet in 2004, as part of the *yūji hōsei* framework of emergency legislation, empowers MSDF units to conduct maritime intercept operations during an actual or impending attack on Japan. Specifically, this would allow the MSDF to inspect ships suspected of carrying weapons and to confiscate their cargoes. The MSDF would be authorized to fire on ships refusing to submit to inspections, at first in warning but ultimately including shots at their hull.[141] The government was also reported to be considering introducing legislation which, in the event of a military crisis, would enable the head of the JCG to restrict the passage of ships in officially designated areas, where under existing laws the JCG has the power to control shipping in only a few waterways, such as Tokyo Bay.[142]

The new ports legislation gives the Japanese government authority virtually to cut off direct flows of people and goods between Japan and North Korea. As such it is regarded by the Koizumi administration as an important 'stick', to reinforce dialogue with Pyongyang in respect of Japan's nuclear and missile security concerns, and towards obtaining a fuller accounting of Japanese abductees. In conjunction with revisions to the Foreign Exchange and Foreign Trade Law, to restrict the direct flow remittances from Japan to North Korea, the port ban lays the framework for bilateral sanctions, should Tokyo opt for coercive diplomacy.

Despite these moves to put in place a legal framework for sanctions, and widespread public antipathy towards Kim Jong Il's regime, Tokyo's North Korea policy has overall been poised between 'dialogue and pressure', as evidenced by the terms of the September 2002 Pyongyang Declaration. The declaration opens the way for diplomatic normalization, which would include aid-as-compensation potentially worth several billion dollars, once bilateral concerns are resolved to Japan's satisfaction. Koizumi himself has cautioned against 'emotional' responses to the abductions issue. However, even if a decision to enforce the ship ban is not taken, the increased stringency of Japanese inspections of North Korean vessels and enforcement of port state controls has already had an effect, causing the number of North Korean ship visits to Japanese ports to fall from 1,415 in 2002, to 1,007 in 2003. This drop was reflected in an estimated 30 per cent decline in North Korea's official imports over the same period, from 29 billion to 20 billion yen, reinforced by an increasingly hostile political climate towards commercial activities with North Korea.[143]

Proliferation of missiles and WMD by sea

The third maritime security challenge that North Korea poses to Japan relates to its export trade, by sea and by air, of missiles and missile technology, and its assumed potential to transfer WMD via the same network. North Korea has reportedly sold *Nodong* missiles to Iran, Iraq, Syria and Pakistan since the early 1990s, including shipments to the Middle East estimated at $580 million in 2001.[144] According to a defector's testimony in May 2003, over 90 per cent of the components inbound for North Korea's missile programme was smuggled on board ships from Japan. Japanese judicial authorities have also prosecuted a Japan-based trading company for trans-shipping to North Korea, via Thailand, electronic components with suspected dual-use applications.[145]

Japan's primary response to the maritime proliferation threat was to join the 'core group' of participants in the PSI, at its inception announced by President George W. Bush in Warsaw in May 2003. PSI's other ten original members are Canada, France, Germany, Italy, the Netherlands, Poland, Portugal, Spain, the United States and United Kingdom. Norway, Russia and Singapore have joined since. Based on the Statement of Interdiction Principles agreed at Paris in September 2003, PSI is aimed at countering the global threat posed by WMD, by promoting intelligence exchange and maritime law enforcement cooperation. Although not directed at any state, commentators have most often linked PSI to North Korea.[146] North Korea's official media have singled out Japan's participation in PSI for particular invective, accusing it of 'targeting our republic by servilely following the United States' policy to isolate and blockade the DPRK'.[147]

Although an enthusiastic supporter of the Initiative present from the outset, Japan's operational commitment to PSI was initially limited to the civilian JCG. The authorities also waited until October 2004 to host the first PSI drill in Japanese waters. However, Japan held a seminar, 16–30 May, to which ASEAN, South Korean and Chinese representatives were invited, including broad discussion of nuclear proliferation threats and export controls, and a demonstration ship inspection conducted by JCG officials in Kobe harbour.[148] On one level, Japanese officials' caution regarding the timing of Japan's (and Asia's) first PSI exercise probably reflected a concern not to derail Prime Minister Koizumi's impending second visit to Pyongyang, also in May, or the June convening of the third round of the Six Party nuclear talks in Beijing.[149] However, Tokyo's decision to stage a regional seminar ahead of the PSI October drill was – on the model of Japan's anti-piracy initiatives – principally aimed at persuading ASEAN's more reticent members, of the counter-proliferation value of PSI, and overcoming the particular reservations of South Korea and China, whose cooperation would be a pre-requisite to any comprehensive counter-proliferation strategy towards North Korea.

PSI is consistent with UN Security Council Resolution 1540, adopted on 28 April 2004 and UNCLOS. Its applicability beyond high seas areas depends also on meshing with existing national legal frameworks among littoral states, flag states and port states. As North Korea is not a signatory to the Missile Technology Control Regime (MTCR), the closest that exists to an international anti-missile proliferation treaty, the basis for challenging its missile exports to other MTCR non-signatories has proved problematic in the past. This was demonstrated before PSI was inaugurated, in December 2002, when a concealed consignment of *Scud* missiles on board the Singapore-registered *So San* was intercepted on the high seas by Spanish marines in the Arabian Sea. After establishing that the Yemeni government had legitimately ordered the missile consignment, Western authorities had little alternative but to allow *So San* and its cargo to proceed to its destination.[150] PSI, though highly effective as a demonstration of international will and cooperation to curb proliferation, also faces practical limits in terms of participants' ability to detect small objects concealed in ships. Compared with ship inspections, the options for interdicting suspect cargo flights are starker and carry a greater risk of military escalation.

As of 2004, Japan remained the only Asian PSI participant with the exception of Singapore. Nonetheless, in the prevailing post-11 September international context, PSI offers distinct advantages for Japan as a vehicle for exploring maritime cooperation among 'willing' states in the Asia Pacific and Europe: it is global in scope, groups together several major and medium maritime powers and enjoys the added legitimacy of a United Nations Security Council (UNSC) Resolution on counter-proliferation. Japan's membership of PSI has also latterly served to advance the MSDF's institutional agenda of seeking a wider operational role. Because the SDF currently lacks a legal basis to conduct maritime interception operations outside of wartime, Japan's operational involvement in previous PSI exercises had been limited to JCG units. However, MSDF assets, including destroyers and P-3Cs, took part for the first time in the exercise hosted by Japan near Tokyo Bay in October 2004.[151]

Outside of a narrow maritime security context, the potential missile and nuclear threats North Korea poses have already nudged Japan over some important security policy thresholds and towards others. Should diplomatic efforts to resolve the ongoing nuclear dispute stall, Japanese officials have for some time regarded the test-launch of a *Nodong* or other missile as the most likely act of brinkmanship on the part of Pyongyang.[152] In early 2003, the Koizumi government prepared a response plan to deal with a missile launch. In the event of a test flight over Japanese territory or waters, the JDA Director General would reportedly be given authority to order the MSDF to 'engage in coast guard duties' and 'guard against violations of Japanese airspace'.[153] While the MSDF's Aegis destroyers can track missiles, such as the *Taepodong*-1 that overflew Honshū in August 1998, they do not yet have an interception capability. Concerns about a missile test resurfaced in October 2004, based on unusual military activity levels observed in North Korea.[154]

In the Pyongyang Declaration 'The DPRK side expressed its will to extend its moratorium on missile tests beyond 2003'. However, continuing concern in Japan about North Korea's missile capabilities contributed to the Koizumi government's decision, in December 2003, to upgrade US–Japan joint research cooperation on BMD to full deployment. As BMD remains technically unproven and some years away from full operational status, the North Korea missile threat has fanned discussion in Japan about the acquisition of a conventional strike capability, to provide a level of conventional deterrence in parallel with BMD.

In September 1998, following the *Taepodong* launch, JDA Director General Nukaga Fukushirō stated that Japan had the right to retaliate against missile bases overseas.[155] This was based on the position of the Hatoyama administration in 1956, that 'In the case of an attack by missiles . . . Japan can take the minimum necessary measures to prevent such an attack, and if it is deemed to be the only method to prevent the attack, the country should be able to attack the missile base, etc. as a legal invocation of its self-defense rights.' The JDA's view is that pre-emptive attack is not constitutional. The 2003 defence white paper comments nonetheless that the actual starting point of an attack should be defined 'case-by-case' according to such criteria as 'the prevailing international situation, the explicit *intention* of that country, measures and types of attack'.[156] Such criteria would appear to offer considerable scope for interpretation.

Regarding the possibility of Japan acquiring a strike capability, the commentator Sakurada Jun and the Minshutō opposition Diet member Maehara Seiji have publicly raised the possibility of Japan acquiring cruise missiles in the future. According to local media, around $10 million was set aside in FY (financial year) 2004 to equip the ASDF with the US-made Joint Direct Attack Munition (JDAM), which would inexpensively convert Japan's existing stock of free-fall bombs into precision-guided munitions.[157] The ASDF's acquisition of Boeing-767 aerial tankers, an impressive suite of AEW and Control aircraft, F-15 interceptors and JDAM-equipped F-2 support fighters would give Japan, in pure capability terms, sufficient range to operate over the Northeast Asian littoral and the potential to conduct all-weather precision strike operations. There is no indication that the ASDF are developing the doctrine and training required to carry out long-range strike missions against foreign installations, or that cruise missiles are under active consideration. However, it is notable that in March 2003 JDA Director General Ishiba told the Diet that the acquisition of strike capabilities was 'worth considering', while an advisory panel reviewing the level of Japan's defence capability in late 2004 also reportedly examined the issue.[158]

Conclusion

In the context of an emerging strategic dynamic in Japan–China relations, sea lanes have acquired renewed relevance as a military security concern for Japan since the end of the Cold War. China is widely perceived as possibly threatening Japan's sea lanes over the long term. This is based on the underlying assumption that China eventually intends to establish itself as the pre-eminent power in East Asia; extending sovereignty over the South China Sea and Taiwan, while exerting a level of influence over Southeast Asia. Equally, the PLAN's perceived determination to maintain its current pace of military modernization in pursuit of a blue-water capability is seen as underpinning hegemonic ambitions with real military potential by 2020–30.

Japanese strategists fear that if China acquires the military capability to interdict Japan's sea lanes, this could be used as strategic leverage to discourage Japan from providing military and diplomatic support for the United States, particularly in the context of Taiwan. Fears that China could at some point in the future apply direct pressure to Japan's SLOC, for example by restricting navigational access in the South China Sea, reflect an ingrained self-perception that Japan remains vulnerable not only economically but as a politically 'handicapped' state.

North Korea's short-term challenge to Japan's maritime security is, of itself, less strategically significant than the long-range challenge posed by an assertive China. However, North Korea's resort to a broad spectrum of behaviour threatening to Japan and regional security, from an involvement in transnational crime to its nuclear weapons ambitions, has done much since the end of the Cold War to convince both elite and mass opinion in Japan of the necessity to readjust the country's minimalist security posture as laid down by Prime Minister Yoshida in the early 1950s. While military security remains a keenly contested area of Japanese policy-making, North Korea's influence in creating the political space within Japan to move beyond the confines of constitutional pacifism is likely to outlast the North Korean state itself.

The continuing attention focused within Japan on SLOC security issues, despite the disappearance of the singular military threat posed by the Soviet Union, demonstrates that its value as a security concern is deeply enduring and transcendent of change within the international system. It is ironic, yet instructive, that the southward strategic orientation of the Imperial Navy in the 1920s and 1930s, against an Anglo-American threat to Japan's resource supplies, should be mirrored in the contemporary orientation of the MSDF towards the possible emergence of a Chinese maritime threat in the same expanses of the Western Pacific fought over during the Second World War. Rather than being indicative of a recidivist militarism, the recurrent nature of these threat perceptions and the MSDF's interest in establishing a South China Sea presence point instead to the enduring nature of Japan's strategic geography.

With regard to the other recurrent theme of this book, sea lane concerns have also offered Japan's post-Cold War defence decision-makers important arguments to justify and expand the scope of their policy options. While Japan's Cold War security concerns have fragmented to include non-state and state-level threats in geographically disparate areas that are no longer bound by the unifying security framework of global bipolar rivalry, the security of sea lanes still constitutes a readily identifiable core security concern. Theoretically, Japan's involvement in any maritime contingency from Yokohama to the oil terminals of the Gulf could legitimately be argued as falling within the ambit of Japan's SLOC security, in which national security is at stake by extension. As in the 1980s, when the image of Japan's vulnerability was invoked to convince a sceptical public of the need for an expanded maritime defence role with the United States, sea lane security has continuing utility for Japanese policy-makers keen to elicit domestic support for a 'normal' security posture, to retain a large, conventionally structured navy, and to establish a common agenda for security cooperation with other maritime states in Asia.

Conclusion

Returning to the two guiding questions raised in the Introduction, first, I asked how Japan's vulnerability to the disruption of its sea lanes has defined its strategic security imperatives and policy choices from the pre-war period to 2004. Second, I asked to what extent have strategic concerns about securing SLOC in the post-1945 era been used instrumentally to legitimize constitutionally and politically problematic security activities. Two underlying themes emerged. First, Japan's strategic geography has exerted a secular influence over its security policy decision-makers, transcending major changes to the domestic and international order. Second, security and defence decision-making in Japan since 1945 has been driven at domestic, systemic and transnational levels, the discrete nature of which is sometimes compounded by Japan's heavily compartmentalized governmental structure. The primacy of domestic constraints has yielded latterly to increased 'realism' about systemic pressures, while the transnational Alliance has, throughout, occupied a pivotal position in between.

The strategic imperative of SLOC protection has remained a constant for Japan throughout the period of study, notwithstanding the pronounced divide between post-1945 and pre-1945 approaches to military security. The unchanging fundamentals of Japan's maritime geography and poor resource allocation have ensured that its policy-makers consistently view the security of sea lanes as 'a matter of life and death'. This imperative has driven official responses in such diverse fields as economic policy, diplomacy, alliance relations, military strategy and law enforcement. This challenges the widely held view of Japan's security in terms of historical discontinuity; reflecting the transformation, since 1940, of its political and military institutions, economic structure and policy-makers' external threat perceptions and normative approaches to security.

However, the emphasis placed on the vulnerability of Japan's SLOC in post-war defence planning and in the outlook of the MSDF can be fully understood only in relation to its use in justifying controversial aspects of defence and alliance policy to a domestic and international audience. The notion of protecting maritime trade, with its appeal to widely accepted economic norms of security and the avoidance of military entanglements on land, has retained an enduring value for Japan's policy-makers in the highly politicized context of defence policy since 1945, assisted by transnational navy-to-navy links with the United States.

SLOC as a strategic imperative

Chapter 1 charted Japan's long-term import dependence as the essential 'pre-condition' for its SLOC security concerns. Prolonged disruption to the import of fuels, food and raw materials would undermine the ability of the Japanese government and industry to sustain all but the most basic economic activity, eventually threatening national and even human survival. Japan's potential vulnerability to supply disruptions has fed through into a particular defence policy concern with the security of SLOC.

Chapter 2 showed the evolution of SLOC security as a strategic concept over the last century. I concluded that while the nature of maritime threats is far more complex and varied than was the case when Mahan and Corbett developed their theories of sea power, the military and economic importance of securing lines of communication over the sea remains a strategic constant for maritime states. I broke down SLOC security into its constituent parts of sea power and lines of communications to arrive at a definition. I traced the control of communications as a concept integral to theories of sea power developed in an era when naval strategy was concerned with the mono-dimensional objective of attaining command of the sea over rival surface battle fleets. The advent of total warfare on a global scale in the first half of the twentieth century blurred the distinction between 'military' and 'economic' SLOC. Submarine-led anti-shipping campaigns threatened the survival of maritime powers, establishing that a strategy of 'sea denial' could be prosecuted independently of surface sea control, for a relatively modest commitment of resources. This observation remains relevant in a global security environment where a single superpower exerts naval hegemony. While Japan's defeat in 1945 proved the strategic vulnerability of maritime powers to blockade, the US–UK experience in both battles of the Atlantic demonstrated that sea communications could be maintained under sustained military pressure, once measures for the defence of shipping (convoy in particular) were organized. Of enduring importance, the world wars gave a real-world corrective to the conceptual allure of SLOCs as strategic entities that can be protected independently of ships. The belligerents uniformly abandoned patrolled sea lane concepts as costly failures. Regarding regional conflicts, the flexibility of commercial shipping to follow diversionary routes usually offers a simple solution to localized threats to particular waterways, with the exception of ports and terminal approaches.

Despite the diminishing incidence of high-intensity naval conflict in the nuclear era, Western military planners in the 1970s and 1980s took the potential threat of the Soviet Union to interdict Western military SLOC extremely seriously, as shown in Chapters 2 and 5. With the end of the Cold War and the run-down of the former Soviet fleet, the risk of a naval conflagration in the open seas diminished sharply and, with it, the prospect of any short- to medium-term military threat to Western military SLOC in the Atlantic or Pacific, beyond the littoral seas. A diffuse set of threats and challenges has emerged in place of the perceived, global Soviet maritime threat. The definition of SLOC security has expanded to encompass environmental concerns, attempts at legal enclosure, piracy and terrorism, as well as residual military threats to navigation from regional conflicts, the most potentially serious of which are located astride Japan's strategically vital seaborne trade routes in the Indo-Pacific region.

As Japan's industrial development proceeded from 1868 and its population grew rapidly, it became locked into a cycle of dependence on imports in order to meet its basic nutritional, energy and raw materials requirements. The drive to establish a captive resource base was a crucial determinant of Japan's imperial expansion in Asia from the 1890s onwards and led ultimately to the reckless gamble of going to war with the United States and Great Britain in 1941. Chapter 3 showed that the US submarine anti-shipping campaign against Japan wrought strategic effects at comparatively little cost and could even have caused Japan's defeat unaided. In Japan, the trauma and shame of the wartime blockade, though less visible in the public eye than the atomic and incendiary bombing of the homeland, left an indelible imprint on the 'culture' of the MSDF, extending to wider elite and societal perceptions of Japan's vulnerability in a hostile international system.

After 1945, the enforced transition was made from imperial autarky to a liberal trade model, within the wider security framework of *Pax Americana*, as the means for Japan to secure access to resources it lacks naturally. This structural shift brought about a major geographical reorientation of its supply base and export markets, enhancing the importance of the Middle East, Southeast Asia and Australasia as providers of the energy and industrial commodities that fuelled rapid industrial growth from the late 1950s to the 1970s. This involved a massive expansion both in the volume of goods imported and the distances over which they were transported via three key southwestern, southern and eastern commercial shipping streams respectively connecting Japan with the Middle East and Southeast Asia; with Australia, and with the Americas. The strategic importance of chokepoints where shipping was concentrated along these routes increased concomitantly, especially the Straits of Malacca, Japan's maritime 'life-line'.

In Chapter 1, I examined ways in which Japan has the capacity, through economic policy measures, to reduce its vulnerability to supply disruptions. Government and industry efforts to diversify Japan's supply base trans-regionally and to build up stockpiles of oil and raw materials to soften the impact of any short-term supply disruption were profiled and assessed. I concluded that a combination of stockpiling, resource substitution and supplier diversification, and the adoption of progressive energy policies since the 1973 oil crisis have given the Japanese economy a limited cushion against the interruption of imports along its SLOC. If the government's objective in a security crisis was merely to survive the duration, austerity controls would provide it with the economic leeway to reduce its import requirements to one-third of normal levels, or even less if it chose to switch productive capacity from the export sector to meeting domestic demand. Against this more qualified picture of economic vulnerability and the ability of commercial shipping to detour around most localized trouble-spots and obstructed chokepoints between terminals, the consistently high level of attention paid to SLOC disruption in Japan's post-war defence and diplomacy appears extremely risk sensitive, considering that the only major commodity supply shock to Japan's economy was delivered at source, as a result of the 1973 Arab oil embargo, rather than in transit.

Yet in spite of the hugely expensive efforts since 1973 to create a cushion against import disruption, Japan still has only limited capacity to insulate itself from a prolonged interruption to seaborne transportation. The very fact that since the oil crises Japan's industry has developed one of the leanest energy consumption profiles of any advanced economy means that little 'slack' remains within the system, limiting capacity to further cut energy use without curbing production or transportation. Japan's paucity of natural resources is so extreme relative to its basic needs that, barring a technological breakthrough in energy production releasing it from dependence on imported hydrocarbons, any serious and sustained disruption to in-bound shipping flows would inevitably be perceived by the Japanese authorities as a threat to national survival, regardless of the temporary respite afforded by stockpiles. This remained the case in 2004 as it was in 1944 when Japan's latent vulnerability to blockade was exposed.

In the 1945–77 period, although strategic pressures and alliance politics weighed in favour of Japan's rearmament, domestic constraints were paramount, as seen in the rejection of autonomous defence proposals in the late 1960s and the adoption of limits on defence capability within the *taikō*. Japan's pre-1945 military-dominated government was replaced after the war by a civilian leadership and the constitutionally enshrined goals of state non-belligerency and civilian control. Since the Pacific War, without overseas territories or military bases, Japan has had no independent need for SLOC to project military power. Aside from an indirect dependence on US trans-Pacific SLOC to provide military reinforcement in case of external aggression, its interests in sea transportation have remained those of a commercial maritime power. However, despite the clear political and strategic departures from the pre-war situation, Japan's vulnerability to the disruption of its SLOC is striking as a strategic constant that straddles the pre- and post-1945 divide.

Some 'traditional' concerns of strategic geography have certainly carried over from the pre-war period, for instance in a basic continuity in Japan's perceptions of the Korean peninsula as physically integral to its security. However, Japan's interest in SLOC is peculiar among its post-war security concerns, more notable for their diminished strategic content, in that its potential exposure to a major disruption of seaborne imports steadily increased, in line with the exponential growth of its overseas trade and resource demands. By deepening its dependence on foreign sources of supply, and on a new and more geographically remote set of nations, many of which are located in areas of high geopolitical risk, Japan's integration within the Western liberal economic trading system brought about a concomitant *strategic* requirement to ensure that an adequate level of naval protection (direct or indirect) is maintained in the Indian and Pacific Oceans. The expansion of Japan's overseas trade thus formed its own powerful rationale to maintain a military alliance with the only maritime power capable of extending such protection – the United States. The importance of the maritime influence on

Japan's strategy is reflected in its predominant pattern of alliances with naval hegemons (Great Britain from 1902–22 and the United States from 1951 to the present). Apart from the brief and largely passive wartime 'axis' with Germany and Italy, Japan has elected to aggregate its capabilities with the globally dominant maritime power as a more enduring response to the strategic problem of how to secure overseas access to markets and natural resources.

In Chapter 4, I showed how Japan's post-1945 security policy was redefined, against the backdrop of sweeping change at the systemic, transnational and domestic levels, in the Yoshida Doctrine. The doctrine reflected reduced threat perceptions compared with the pre-war period and Yoshida's perception that Japan's resource needs could optimally be met via entry into a US-led trading order, within which Japan's external security would be guaranteed. This left the government and private industry free to concentrate their energies on reconstruction and recovery.

Arguments in favour of the development of a large navy configured for an independent 'sea lane defence' role resurfaced surprisingly quickly in Japan after the Second World War and received a level of political support that contrasted sharply with official reluctance to accede to US pressure to create a large army. Yoshida and subsequent administrations acknowledged that contributory forces were a *political* necessity. However, in the case of naval forces, official support was also forthcoming owing to the *strategic* premium attached to protecting Japan's seaborne trade beyond its territorial waters.

As demonstrated in Chapters 3 and 4, those former Imperial Navy officers who filled the ranks of the post-war maritime security forces, or who entered business and politics, carried their wartime experiences with them and the conviction that the Imperial Navy had erred in not doing more to protect Japan's merchant fleet. The task of trade protection was thus quickly established as a core priority for Japan's reconstituted naval forces; a 'lesson learned' from the Pacific War.

Japan's security links with the United States, especially close navy-to-navy relations, were crucial to the formation, structure and operational orientation of the MSDF. However, concerns about the security of sea lanes also drove Japanese decision-makers' perceptions and responses independently, exposing a perceived weakness in the territorial security guarantee extended to Japan by the United States, under the terms of the Security Treaty. As seen in Chapter 4, Sekino Hideo's notion of a stand-alone Japanese navy oriented to a SLOC protection role in the Western Pacific stemmed partly from a lack of confidence that the US defence guarantee would apply to Japanese shipping on the high seas. This fed concern that a hostile power might look to target Japan's SLOC, in addition to their constituting an independent strategic weak-point, as the Achilles heel of alliance cohesion.

The vulnerability of SLOC has thus been perceived in Japan in political as well as military and economic terms. In Chapters 4–8 Japanese analysts' and defence planners' concerns about the 'psychological' impact of attacks on shipping surfaced repeatedly. This partly reflects concern that attacks on shipping could be used to test the strength of the US security guarantee at its peripheries. At a domestic level, politicians and defence officials also feared that hostile states could conduct small-scale or clandestine attacks on Japanese shipping to exacerbate political divisions over questions of military security and the constitutional legitimacy of the SDF, or to put pressure on the government to adopt an accommodative posture in relation to maritime territorial disputes.

Chapter 5 demonstrated that in the period 1977–90, alliance politics were the main imperative of Japan's SLOC security policy responses and the main driver of change in Japan's approach to defence. Although defence constraints remained in place, Tokyo's acquiescence in closer defence cooperation reflected not only a 'political' response to the US burden-sharing pressure, but the emergence of independent concerns within Japan about the relative decline of US power and the Soviet military build-up in the Far East. The rise of the Soviet sea lane threat to the top of the Alliance agenda in the late Cold War reflected a wider strategic context shaped by the relative decline in US military power vis-à-vis the Soviet Union and Washington's determination to boost defence cooperation and the SDF's maritime capabilities. MSDF plans for the protection of shipping in Second World War-style convoys, in place since the 1960s, had by the 1980s given way to a more expansive concept of area defence. The prospective role of the MSDF in sea lane defence was no longer limited to the defensive task of convoying oil tankers and commercial shipping. In the event of a superpower conflict, Japanese forces would have operated at a functionally integrated level alongside US forces deployed to carry out the US Maritime Strategy in the northwest Pacific. Indeed, the success of US war plans depended on SDF cooperation sealing in Soviet forces in the Sea of Japan, and coordinated efforts to track and destroy Soviet submarines in the open waters of the Pacific. Suffice it to say this went beyond the scope of Japan's official defence posture, as outlined in the *taikō*, of dealing 'with any situation up to the level of limited and small-scale aggression'.

In the context of various state and non-state level potential threats faced in the post-Cold War period, Japan's independent strategic perceptions are gradually rising to the fore as a defence policy imperative for the first time in post-war era. In Chapter 7, Japan's security policy-making community was shown to be moving towards a more 'realist' understanding of regional and global security, a shift of perception that has firmed official support for the US–Japan Alliance and its reshaping from an anti-Soviet compact in the late Cold War to a 'situationally' defined framework for bilateral defence cooperation extending potentially as far as the Gulf. I also examined how Japan has adopted security initiatives independently of the United States, via its involvement in United Nations peace-keeping, its exploration of multilateral security dialogue and development of bilateral defence links with a range of third countries, focused on the Asia-Pacific region, where the most obvious candidates for potential state-level threats to Japan's security are located. It is at least of symbolic importance that Japan's naval flotilla in the Indian Ocean since November 2001 and ground contingent in Iraq since July 2004 have generated Japan's first *military* SLOC requirement since 1945, extending over 5,000 nm from Yokosuka to the Gulf.

In a more uncertain post-Cold War environment, geopolitical risk is present along the length of Japan's major energy arterial, from the Gulf, via South Asia, Southeast Asia and East Asia. Chapter 8 concluded that among potential state-level threats, China has assumed central place in Japanese defence planners' long-range view. Japan's economically crucial SLOC to the Middle East and Southeast Asia are seen as potentially exposed to a rising naval power with a long seaboard flanking Japan's southern maritime approaches. The potential for China's expanding economy and rising resource needs to develop in competition with those of Japan and other import-dependent states in Asia has resurrected the potential threat of deliberate interdiction of Japan's supply routes by a hostile maritime power.

Japanese policy-makers recognize that the PLAN lags significantly behind MSDF capabilities in most areas, quite apart from the gulf that separates it from the US Navy. However, concern about China's naval modernization is long term and relates not only to future material potential, but equally to the perceived skill of its policy-makers in blending military pressure with composite elements of national power in the pursuit of a clearly defined grand strategy. Japan's concern about the security of its sea lanes is honed in the context of fears that China is pursuing a long-term strategy aimed at establishing hegemony; on land, over the Korean Peninsula, Taiwan and continental Southeast Asia, and maritime sway over the East and South China Sea. The ambition of those within the PLAN who aim to extend China's maritime defence zone to Southeast Asia and the 'second island chain' in the Western Pacific is viewed as inherently threatening in Japan, given the overlap with its most important economic SLOC and EEZ.

Chapter 2 concluded that piracy is more of an 'irritant' to the global maritime transportation system than a systemic threat. However, Chapter 7 made equally clear that piracy, as an active threat, commands a lot of private and official attention in Japan. This is reflected in a significant commitment of Japanese resources and diplomatic energy to promoting regional anti-piracy cooperation. The threat posed by Islamist terrorism potentially exposes to attack Japan's oil supplies and shipping routes passing through the Middle East and maritime Southeast Asia. However, the *possibility* of maritime terrorist attack to cause economic dislocation must be weighed against the *probability* that piracy will, at a much lower level, continue to disrupt Japanese shipping.

Japan's sea lane diplomacy has sought to maintain the physical parameters of safe navigation in the Straits of Malacca and to limit the impact on navigational access of jurisdictional claims by regional states, especially Indonesia. In Chapter 6, I concluded that Japan's failure to secure a role in the administration of the Straits of Malacca in 1971, which led to the joint Indonesian–Malaysian declaration 'de-internationalising' the straits, marked the low-point for its SLOC diplomacy in the region. In the context of this failure and anti-Japanese riots across Southeast Asian capitals in the mid-1970s, Tokyo re-evaluated its diplomacy towards the region, prompting a major redirection of aid flows to reflect Southeast Asia's strategic importance to Japan. Technical and financial assistance disbursed to the coastal states through the Malacca Straits Council established a quasi-official framework of cooperation with Indonesia, Malaysia and Singapore leading to the adoption of the TSS and Under-keel Clearance limit. These regulations have facilitated safe access through the straits and lessened coastal states' concerns about collisions and spillages resulting from unregulated shipping traffic. Japan's financing of the Rolling Fund has contained disputes with the straits states about how to apportion the financial burden of navigational safety measures in the straits. Generally, Japan has benefited by conducting its sea-lane diplomacy indirectly through the Malacca Straits Council and Nippon Foundation, while relying on the IMO and other states to press overtly for navigational freedoms to be upheld. With the exception of the transit of nuclear cargoes through the region, on which it has faced firm opposition, Japan has avoided any serious limitation to its commercial transit rights resulting from coastal states' jurisdictional claims.

Japan's sea lane diplomacy in Southeast Asia has succeeded in balancing free and safe navigation with the sensitivities of coastal states. Tokyo has also had some success in building regional support and capacity for anti-piracy cooperation, overcoming limited enthusiasm for Japanese participation in actual patrols. Japan's diplomatic ability to influence the potential for Islamist terrorism or regional conflict in the South China Sea is more limited. Regarding the latter, China's position as an extra-regional great power less beholden to aid and other forms of 'soft' leverage, is the key strategic variable, rendering Japan's sea lane diplomacy in Southeast Asia ultimately subordinate to balance-of-power concerns.

SLOC security as an instrumental policy concern

Notwithstanding the depth of genuine concern in Japan about the vulnerability of its SLOC to disruption, the use of responses aimed at securing maritime traffic or lessening the vulnerability of sea lanes in order to justify controversial aspects of defence policy is an undercurrent present throughout this narrative. At various times, in its different guises, SLOC protection has been employed as a rationale to build up, and preserve, the level of Japan's post-war naval capabilities, to expand the functional and geographical scope of US–Japan Alliance cooperation and to explore security cooperation with other maritime states in the Asia-Pacific. Towards achieving these aims SLOC protection has offered advantages in several areas.

First, sea lane defence has presented the MSDF with a rationale that has enabled its officers and other pro-naval advocates to defend their budgetary claims and to argue the necessity of a large surface fleet configured for blue-water operations. Mahan's dictum that the necessity of a navy springs from the existence of peaceful shipping has proved useful in the context of Japan's constitutional pacifism for rebutting the arguments of critics such as Kaihara Osamu, that the MSDF should be downsized and reconfigured to serve in a minimalist counter-invasion and coastal defence role.

Second, the rationale for a Japanese naval role in trade protection accorded with the priority given to economic security and defence constraints within the Yoshida Doctrine. Widespread consensus among the various government actors with responsibility for security policy that Japan required reliable and safe access to natural resources overseas helped the cause of naval rearmament to proceed more smoothly than that of the GSDF, aided by the less visible, less controversial profile of navies compared with armies. As a 'defensive' task, sea lane protection could be accommodated more easily within the constraints of the Constitution than any other strategic rationale involving the extra-territorial dispatch of the SDF. Chapter 5 showed that in the 1970s and 1980s, both the popular memory of the wartime blockade and fears of supply disruptions re-awoken by the 1973 oil crisis were marshalled to persuade a domestic audience of the need for Japan to engage in deeper maritime defence cooperation with the United States.

Third, as a concept that is inherently vague and elastic in geographical and operational terms, sea lane defence lent itself particularly well to justifying expanded defence cooperation with the United States during the late Cold War. During the 1980s, such cooperation drew Japan steadily closer towards a *de facto* collective self-defence posture vis-à-vis the United States, as a military ally integrated into US Cold War military strategy. Without the political 'cover' afforded by sea lane defence, intensified alliance cooperation would certainly have encountered greater political resistance within Japan.

Fourth, in the post-Cold War era, appeals to sea lane security have continuing value not only in the context of legitimising defence policy to a domestic audience, but also in presenting the protection of maritime transportation as a common concern to all maritime trading states in the Asia Pacific. For advocates of an expanded security role in Japan, as seen in Chapters 7 and 8, it has thus provided a non-threatening platform on which to build security cooperation with Asian maritime states that share overlapping interests in seaborne trade and imported energy resources.

Fifth, Chapter 7 showed that piracy is a particular issue of sea lane security that has been used as a pretext to develop Japan's regional security role since the end of the Cold War, with partial success. It has been used as a vehicle both to explore security cooperation with other states in East Asia, Southeast Asia and South Asia, as well as to establish a limited Japanese maritime presence in the Straits of Malacca, through the JCG. As a constabulary concern, Japan's anti-piracy involvement offers political advantages, by offering a focus for security cooperation that does not target any particular state, thus lowering the political costs for participants – a point that applies equally to Japan's involvement in the PSI. Anti-piracy initiatives are also pitched as a confidence-building measure designed to demonstrate Japan's reliability and responsibility as a security partner, particularly to Southeast Asian states; the maritime equivalent of Japan's UN peacekeeping troop deployment to Cambodia in 1993. Moreover, it is an area in which Japan can draw on its comparative advantage in capacity-building, as a donor of technical and financial aid. In strategic terms, Japan's sponsorship of anti-piracy cooperation serves the unstated purpose of demonstrating leadership credentials.

Such frameworks for maritime security cooperation also lay a contingent infrastructure for coalition building, should the Japanese government decide in future that it needs to counter a more assertive China, or to compensate for a weakening of its Alliance with the United States. Japan's enthusiastic promotion of PSI in Asia is the clearest example yet of it adopting an activist role to maritime coalition building to face post-Cold War threats.

The MSDF has proved institutionally adept at deploying sea lane security and the safety of maritime transportation as pretexts and precedents to widen the legal and geographic scope of its operations. Although, as seen in Chapter 4, the 1976 *taikō* did not mention sea lane defence among the MSDF's roles, during the 1970s the MSDF retained its blue-water escort flotilla formations in spite of a political and fiscal climate that favoured the formalization of defence constraints. Chapter 5 showed how, in the late 1970s and early 1980s, the rationale of defending Japan's sea lanes – in tandem with US political pressure – enabled the MSDF to expand its budgetary claims and deepen its cooperation with the US Navy. In terms of force structure, acquisitions justified under the rubric of sea lane defence facilitated improvements in anti-submarine and mine warfare capabilities that had outstripped those of the US Seventh Fleet in certain areas by the end of the Cold War and transformed the MSDF into a highly potent navy. Ongoing appeals to the primacy of the SLOC protection mission have enabled the MSDF to preserve its core force structure through two reviews of post-Cold War defence capability. The MSDF also argued successfully for its participation in the RIMPAC exercises on the strength of its SLOC defence responsibilities. In turn, the ASDF and even the GSDF recognized the value of sea lane defence as a rationale to boost or to defend their budgetary shares in the 1980s.

As seen in Chapter 7, the MSDF's deployment to the Arabian Sea since November 2001 extrapolates the same trend in a contemporary context. The MSDF flotilla was dispatched under the terms of the Anti-Terrorism Special Measures Law, initially for a period of six months to 'gather information' in support of US-led operations in Afghanistan. Since then the deployment has been repeatedly extended, merging logistically with support for the GSDF contingent now in Iraq, though governed by separate legislation. The terms of the MSDF's activities in the Arabian Sea have also been expanded to include refuelling naval vessels from several other countries. The government has reportedly drawn up plans to protect oil tankers in the Gulf, for which the forces in place in the region could readily be used. The MSDF's deployment has thus established a precedent for a future Japanese naval presence in the Indian Ocean and along the length of its most important economic SLOC to the Gulf, a *fait accompli* which is also likely to be taken on board in future Alliance initiatives to re-define frameworks for bilateral defence cooperation.

Japan's SLOC security prospects

This book has established that SLOC security is a 'permanent' strategic problem for Japan's security decision-makers, as a function of the country's industrial structure, resource allocation and geopolitical location far from its sources of supply and close to potentially hostile powers. It is thus certain to register as a policy issue in future, though in what way depends on the course of several economic, political and strategic trends.

Japan's demographic transition to a smaller, older population and the hollowing out of its industrial base, although not irreversible, are both likely to continue. This will have a significant impact on medium- to long-term consumption trends, reducing Japan's absolute energy and resource requirements. Increasing use of natural gas, most promisingly in relation to Sakhalin, will continue to lessen oil's share in primary energy production and could significantly shorten Japan's supply chain. However, the nuclear sector is unlikely to fulfill the promise of energy autonomy that it once held out to policy-makers. The needs of a residual onshore industrial base, domestic transportation and residential power demand will continue to require large inputs of imported resources, and the economy will thus remain reliant on oil for at least another 30–40 years. The cultivation of Russia and other non-Gulf-based producers does hold out some prospect of reducing Japan's very high dependence on Middle Eastern oil. But the draw-down of Southeast Asian oil and gas exports to Japan, the global dominance of Gulf-region reserves, and increasing competition with China for ownership of alternative upstream energy resources, is unlikely to prompt a radical change in Japan's energy import patterns until technology supplies cheaper alternatives to fossil fuels. Ensuring the security of its southern SLOC to the Middle East will therefore remain essential during this timeframe, potentially drawing Japan into a maritime security role.

Most of the projected increase in maritime traffic through the Straits of Malacca will be created by other countries. Japan will progressively cede its position as the primary user of the straits to China, whose resource imports and manufactured exports will continue to grow, provided the country's domestic growth potential can be sustained and multinationals continue to relocate production there. The growing portfolio of non-Japanese cargoes in the Southeast Asian SLOC will in one sense simplify Tokyo's task of maintaining safe navigational access, by further internationalizing the issue. But unless Southeast Asian states respond positively to the prospect of Japan as a strategic counterweight to China, the leverage of its negotiating position in the region is likely to decline over time as its economic pre-eminence is eroded. However, short of a major regional conflict, fears that Japan would be denied navigational access to Southeast Asia, or that resource shipments bound for China would physically crowd Japan out of the Straits of Malacca appear somewhat overblown. Japan would in any case retain several options for diversionary re-routing, as long as spare capacity is available to compensate for the lengthening of its maritime supply chain. With regard to the terrorist threat to Japan's SLOC interests, now that the ISPS code has greatly improved ship security, the most pressing challenge for Tokyo will be to contribute to multilateral efforts to improve security around the hard and soft infrastructure of major Asian ports, where it is most concentrated and vulnerable.

At the time of writing, in December 2004, the nuclear and missile threats posed by North Korea commanded the most immediate attention in Japan, though a recent Chinese submarine incursion underlined growing unease about China's medium-to-long term strategic intentions. The question of how far to extend diplomatic and military support for the US-led 'war on terror' also loomed over Japan's policy-makers' short-to-medium term horizons. How they respond to these concurrent challenges is likely to have an important bearing not only on the future of Japan's SLOC security, but also on the basic orientation of its defence policy.

The North Korean nuclear crisis, the second in 10 years, has already fostered the development of a more assertive defence posture for Japan. This process is unlikely to change radically even if the stand-off between Pyongyang and Washington is resolved diplomatically. The broad array of potential threats posed by North Korea, from transnational crime to nuclear-tipped missiles and WMD proliferation, constitutes a source of external strategic pressure upon Japan. Domestically, the negative disposition of Japanese public opinion towards the North Korean regime, especially since its admission to abducting Japanese nationals, has yielded a peculiar tolerance of measures justified in relation to the 'North Korean threat', as seen with Tokyo's decision to participate fully in BMD and the law empowering a ban on ship visits. *Faits accomplis*, whether established in the particular context of North Korea, counter-terrorism cooperation in the Indian Ocean, or reconstruction efforts in Iraq, serve in the abstract to advance the range of legally and politically acceptable defence activities. This is in conformity with a pattern of incremental change in Japan's defence policy observed since 1954. The Koizumi administration has substantially upped the pace of adjustment in Japan's defence and security policy since September 2001, while adhering to the basic post-war model based on the 1946 Constitution and the US–Japan Alliance. A more radical departure could follow if the LDP in future unites behind a popular nationalist figure outside of the formal party structure, or if a major military contingency erupts in Korea or Taiwan. However, the 'dream' of autonomous defence is unlikely to be resurrected, or with it the notion that Japan could independently secure sea lanes which extend globally. The record of Nakasone Yasuhiro, a conservative nationalist who followed a less radical defence policy agenda as premier than he had advocated as a Diet politician or JDA Director General, underlines that incumbency usually imposes its own constraints, reinforced by the inertia of the Japanese political system. Though the left may be an eviscerated force in contemporary politics, many ordinary Japanese and elected officials remain genuinely reluctant to jettison post-war constitutional constraints on defence capability. Moreover, the two-thirds Diet majority and referendum required to amend the Constitution set a high procedural bar for change. The trend toward the 'normalization' of Japan's security and defence policies is such, however, that an LDP-led administration if not Koizumi's immediate successor, is likely to sanction the exercise of collective self defence within the Alliance framework, while gathering the necessary bipartisan support in the Diet to revise the Constitution within a 5–10 year timeframe.

Despite the immediate 'political' preoccupation of Japanese security planners with North Korea and the 'war on terror', Japan's longer-term strategic focus will be on ways to cope with the rise of China and concerns about a relative diminution of Japan's influence in Southeast Asia and elsewhere on the Asian continent. The abiding perception that Japan's SLOC are most vulnerable to interdiction beyond the Bashi Channel, and particularly in the South China Sea, will reinforce the MSDF's southward strategic orientation. This is likely to be borne out in a more regular MSDF and ASDF presence in the South China Sea. The Fleet Escort Force's capabilities were not seriously attenuated as part of the 2004 *taikō* review, and the MSDF is set to acquire enhanced long-range capabilities with the commissioning of its new DDH, more Aegis DDGs and the follow-on to the P-3C. The logistical difficulties of sustaining long-range operational deployments could even prompt diplomatic efforts to secure staging arrangements in Southeast Asia. While remaining in the vanguard of theatre-level missile defence, the MSDF will probably press for its inclusion in the development of a limited conventional strike capability should the government decide in future to support this major shift in the SDF's orientation. While continuing to eke out new roles and seek international partners, for example through greater involvement in PSI, a leaner MSDF will at the same time be more constrained by the need for greater jointness and inter-operability with the other SDF and the US Navy. Missile defence in particular is likely to drive the functional integration of Japanese and US weapons and surveillance systems under streamlined, partly automated command arrangements.

In the future, SLOC security will continue to serve as the nexus for several strands within Japan's defence and security policy-making. Economically, concerns over supply disruptions in transit will drive self-help policies to lessen their potential economic impact, while increased competition for Middle Eastern oil is likely to re-invigorate efforts to diversify Japan's energy mix and supply portfolio. Diplomatically, Japan will continue to prioritize free and safe navigation in its relations with coastal states adjacent to its SLOC, in Southeast Asia and beyond. Strategically, as in the 1980s, sea lane defence could be revived as a rationale to expand Tokyo's territorially defined defence interests along a vast maritime arc linking Japan, via Southeast Asia, to the Gulf. This could provide the impetus for a forward maritime defence posture, either in alliance with a naval hegemonic power or as part of an as yet undetermined maritime coalition.

Appendices

Appendix 1: Major navigational concepts introduced under the UNCLOS

The entry into force of UNCLOS in 1994 introduced the following jurisdictional concepts into international law, although their development over the three Law of the Sea Conventions (1958, 1973 and 1982), and through state practice and customary law was an incremental process:

Territorial seas. UNCLOS recognizes the right of coastal states to extend their territorial waters to 12 nm, throughout which sovereignty is fully exercised, and to exercise customs and immigration controls in a contiguous zone for a further 12 nm.[1] Prior to UNCLOS, territorial seas of widely varying dimensions had been claimed, varying from 3 to 200 nm, but the 12 nm limit had become established as an international norm long before the Convention entered into force. The extension of territorial seas has brought a number of straits used for international navigation which formerly contained high-seas corridors, within the sole or shared jurisdiction of coastal straits.

Archipelagic waters. The waters enclosed within baselines drawn from the outermost edges of the 14 designated archipelagos under UNCLOS have a legal status similar to territorial seas. However, one of the 'grey areas' identified in UNCLOS legislation concerns whether prescriptive and enforcement jurisdiction that applies in territorial seas extends to archipelagic waters.[2]

Exclusive Economic Zones. Part V of the 1982 UNCLOS draft recognized EEZ out to 200 nm. The concept of the EEZ arose as a compromise aimed at providing coastal states with legal ownership over marine resources out to 200 nm, as a *quid pro quo* for confining their territorial-sea claims to 12 miles. Within their EEZ, coastal states are empowered to apprehend vessels that pose a risk of pollution to the coastline or resources of the EEZ.[3] The authority of coastal states does not extend to naval vessels or military aircraft, however, which enjoy high-seas freedoms outside territorial seas or archipelagic waters.

A number of military maritime zones with the potential to affect shipping and aviation have also been declared outside of the framework of UNCLOS. These include warning and exclusion zones declared by China, in the north of the Yellow

Sea and north of Taiwan; Taiwan's own exclusion zone in the Taiwan Strait; North Korea's 70-nm military zones off both its coastlines and the United States has a 200-mile warning area in effect around its missile testing range, near Kwajalein in the Pacific.[4] A number of states, including Japan, and regional organizations such as the ASEAN have declared nuclear weapons free zones, banning the admission of nuclear weapons and/or nuclear-powered warships.

Passage regimes. Aside from high seas passage, which was legally unaffected by UNCLOS (although the area of high seas itself was dramatically curtailed), three transit regimes were eventually adopted as part of the new regime. First, the pre-existing concept of 'innocent passage' was incorporated, applying to navigation through territorial seas and, generally, within archipelagic waters. Second, the regime of 'transit passage' was created to deal with transit through international straits. Third, 'archipelagic sea-lanes passage' was developed to govern passage through sea lanes designated within archipelagic waters:

- *International straits containing high seas areas.* Where international straits are wide enough that a high-seas corridor remains despite the extension of territorial seas to 12 nm, or in such cases where the coastal state has chosen not to extend its territorial sea, navigation is legally unencumbered by UNCLOS. High-seas corridors remain in the Sōya, Tsugaru, Tsushima and Osumi straits around Japan, the Taiwan and Luzon Straits/Bashi Channel, the Torres Strait and the Strait of Hormuz.
- *Innocent passage.* The rules of Innocent Passage, under Article 19(2) of UNCLOS, confer passage rights through territorial waters for ships (and aircraft), provided they engage in 'continuous and expeditious passage which is not prejudicial to the peace, good order, or security of coastal states'. Although there is nothing expressly to exclude naval vessels from innocent passage in the UNCLOS text, some states request prior notification before foreign naval vessels enter their territorial or archipelagic waters.[5] Under the terms of innocent passage, warships are not supposed to engage in flying operations and submarines are required to proceed, surfaced, with their flags displayed. In archipelagic waters, innocent passage applies outside of nominated sea lanes where more a liberal transit regime obtains. Coastal states have limited rights to suspend innocent passage for security reasons or to carry out weapons exercises, provided such closures are temporary and do not discriminate between different flag-states.[6] Non-suspendable innocent passage, as formerly applied to international straits was superseded in UNCLOS by the new regime of 'transit passage'.
- *Transit passage.* Transit passage confers the right of transit through a strait connecting one high seas area or EEZ with another, provided passage (and overflight) is continuous and expeditious. Under the regime of transit passage (which, unlike innocent passage, is non-suspendable) warships and military aircraft may proceed in their normal operational mode.[7] The terms of transit passage under UNCLOS met most of the criteria of 'free passage in international straits' set by the maritime powers, representing a victory

over the coastal states' attempts to gain uniform application throughout their territorial waters, regardless of their use for international navigation.

- *ASL passage*. UNCLOS allows for archipelagic states to designate special sea lanes within archipelagic waters, conferring 'the exercise of the rights of navigation and overflight in the normal mode for the purpose of continuous and expeditious transit through an archipelago between one part of the high seas or an exclusive economic zone and another part of the high seas or an exclusive economic zone'. These sea lanes, which may be up to 50 nm in width are in effect 'virtual straits' where vessels enjoy the same rights as under-transit passage. Although the advantage of ASL passage to the maritime state is that it confers more liberal transit conditions than innocent passage, concern has been expressed at the potential for archipelagic states to compel foreign shipping to pass through ASLs, nullifying the application of innocent passage elsewhere within archipelagic waters.

Appendix 2: Planned procurements during the MTDP (Fiscal 2005–09)

SDF	*Main equipment*	*Unit numbers*
GSDF	Tanks	49 vehicles
	Artillery (excluding mortar)	38 pieces
	Armoured vehicles	104 vehicles
	Combat helicopters (AH-64D)	7 aircraft
	Transport helicopters (CH-47JA)	11 aircraft
	Medium-range surface-to-air guided missiles	8 companies
MSDF	Improve capability of AEGIS-equipped destroyers	3 ships
	Destroyers	5 ships
	Submarines	4 vessels
	Other vessels	11 ships
	Total number of ships to be built	20 vessels (Approx. 59,000 tons)
	New fixed-wing patrol aircraft	4 aircraft
	Patrol helicopters (SH-60K)	23 aircraft
	Minesweeping and transport helicopters (MCH-101)	3 aircraft
ASDF	Improve surface-to-air guided patriot missiles	2 groups
	Modernized fighters (F-15)	26 aircraft
	Fighters (F-2)	22 aircraft
	New fighters	7 aircraft
	New transport aircraft	8 aircraft
	Transport helicopters (CH-47J)	4 aircraft
	Aircraft equipped with in-flight refuelling and transport aircraft (KC-767)	1 aircraft

Source: JDA.

Notes

Preface

1 For example, R. Oga, *Shiirēn no Himitsu* ['Sea Lane Secrets'], Tokyo: Shōbunsha, 1983; and S. Murai, *Shiirēn: Umi no Bōeisen* ['Sea Lanes: Defence Lines of the Sea'], Tokyo: NHK, 1983.
2 J. E. Auer, *The Postwar Rearmament of Japanese Maritime Forces, 1945–71*, New York: Praeger, 1973; and P. J. Woolley, *Japan's Navy: Politics and Paradox, 1971–2000*, Boulder, CO: Lynne Reiner, 2000.
3 L. Wells II, *The Sea and Japan's Strategic Interests 1975–1985*, unpublished PhD thesis, Ann Arbor, MI: Johns Hopkins University, Xerox University Microfilms, 1975.
4 J. Chapman, R. Drifte and I. Gow, *Japan's Quest for Comprehensive Security: Defence, Diplomacy, Dependence*, London: Frances Pinter, 1983; and G. Friedman and M. Lebard, *The Coming War with Japan*, New York: St Martin's Press, 1991.

Introduction

1 For example, Advisory Group on Defense Issues, *The Modality of the Security and Defense Capability of Japan*, Japanese government translation GM:3338-, 12 August 1994, p. 22; and M. Yoshida, 'Resources, Maritime Transport and SLOC Security', in M. O'Connor and M. J. Kennedy (eds), *Safely By Sea*, Lanham, MD: University Press of America, 1990, p. 36; and C. Hayashizaki, *Securitarian*, November 1996, pp. 15–19.
2 *National Defense Program Guideline for FY 2005 and After*, unofficial translation, December 2004, p. 3.
3 M. Kōsaka, 'Diplomacy and Security in the Twenty-first Century', *Japan Echo*, Winter 1996, p. 6.

1 Japan's maritime trade and trade routes: an empirical analysis

1 *Asahi Shimbun*, *Japan Almanac 1999*, Tokyo: Asahi Shimbunsha, 1998, p. 60.
2 National Institute of Population and Social Security Research, 'Population Projection for Japan from 2001 to 2050: With Long-range Population Projections, 2051–2100', Online. Available www.ipss.go.jp/English/ppfj02/suikei_g_e.html (accessed 15 December 2002).
3 O. Nariai, *History of the Modern Japanese Economy*, Tokyo: Foreign Press Center, Japan, 1997, pp. 33–5.
4 R. Drifte, *Japan's Foreign Policy*, London: Royal Institute of International Affairs/Routledge, 1990, p. 65; and United States Federal Research Division, *Japan: A Country Study*, Washington, DC: Library of Congress/Department of the Army, 1992, p. 270.

5 B. Dolven, 'A Blueprint for Recovery', *Far Eastern Economic Review*, 31 October, 2002, pp. 44–8.
6 Foreign Press Center, Japan, *Facts and Figures of Japan*, 1997 edition, Tokyo: Foreign Press Center, Japan, 1997, pp. 40–3.
7 Y. Gotō, 'Rush into China Lacks Rational Basis', *The Nikkei Weekly*, 2 December 2002, p. 7.
8 Japan Iron and Steel Federation figures cited in *Asahi Shimbun*, op. cit., p. 152.
9 Foreign Press Center, Japan, op. cit., p. 42.
10 'GDP Sags under Deflation, Reform Fears', *The Nikkei Weekly*, 18 November 2002, p. 1.
11 US Department of Energy, Energy Information Administration, Country Profile, Online. Available www.eia.doe.gov/emeu/cabs/japan.html (accessed 12 February 2003).
12 Nariai, op. cit., pp. 45–9.
13 Japan's per capita energy consumption is less than that of France or Germany and almost half that of the United States: *Asahi Shimbun*, op. cit., pp. 174–5.
14 Ministry of Economy, Trade and Industry (METI), *Energy in Japan*, September 2001: Agency for Natural Resources and Energy, METI, p. 34; and *Asahi Shimbun*, op. cit., p. 171.
15 'Japan's Nuclear Fuel Recycling Policy Thrown into Doubt', *Kyodo*, 18 May 2004; and 'Nuclear Plant Accident Splits Japan Press', BBC News Online. Available www.news.bbc.co.uk/1/hi/world/asia-pacific/3551902.stm (accessed 10 August 2004).
16 METI policy document, *Energy in Japan*. Online. Available www.meti.go.jp/english/aboutmeti/data/a231201e.html (accessed 2 January 2002).
17 METI, op. cit., pp. 11–14.
18 US Department of Energy, Energy Information Administration, Japan Country Analysis Brief. Online. Available www.eia.doe.gov/emeu/cabs/japan.html (accessed 28 December 2004).
19 M. J. O'Connor and M. J. Kennedy (eds), *Safely By Sea*, Lanham, MD: University Press of America, 1990, pp. 37–8.
20 D. Shilling, 'A Reassessment of Japan's Naval Defense Needs', *Asian Survey*, 1976, 16(3): 216–29.
21 Japan Shipowners' Association (JSA), *The Current State of Japanese Shipping*, March 2004, p. 2. Online. Available www.jsanet.or.jp/e/shipping-e/pdf/currentstate_e2004.pdf (accessed 18 November 2004).
22 Ministry of Foreign Affairs (MOFA), Japan, 'Japan and the U.N. Convention Law of the Sea'. Online. Available www.mofa.go.jp/policy/economy/sea/convention.html (accessed 7 November 2003).
23 Interview with Mining and Mineral Agency materials supplied by Iimura Akiko, Deputy Director, International Division, Agency for Natural Resources and Energy, METI, Tokyo, 28 February 2002.
24 METI, op. cit., p. 17; and Foreign Press Center, Japan, op. cit., p. 58. Despite the reduction in oil dependence, Japan's reliance on oil for energy production compares only with Italy among other G8 members.
25 *Asahi Shimbun*, op. cit., p. 171.
26 'Crude Oil Imports Decline 13.4%', *The Japan Times*, 1 March 2002, p. 9.
27 The figures do not include bunker and aviation fuel stockpiled either by the Japan Defense Agency (JDA) or the US military in Japan. (Interview with Arima Jun, Director for International Energy Strategy, METI, Tokyo, 28 February 2002.)
28 METI, op. cit., pp. 17–18.
29 Ibid., p. 22.
30 Ibid., p. 28.
31 J. W. M. Chapman, R. Drifte and I. T. M. Gow, *Japan's Quest for Comprehensive Security: Defence, Diplomacy, Dependence*, London: Frances Pinter, 1983, p. 198.
32 *Asahi Shimbun*, op. cit., p. 139; and Chapman *et al.*, op. cit., p. 206.

33 Food self-sufficiency is calculated in different ways, such as according to calorie supply or self-sufficiency in staple foods. For international comparisons the calorie supply is most commonly used. *Asahi Shimbun*, op. cit., pp. 135–6.
34 'China Replacing U.S. as Top Exporter to Japan', *The Nikkei Weekly*, 16 December 2002, p. 1.
35 Ibid., pp. 1, 23.
36 MOFA, Japan, *Diplomatic Bluebook 2004*, pp. 46–7. Online available www.mofa.go.jp/policy/other/bluebook/2004/chap2-a.pdf (accessed 28 December 2004).
37 G. Friedman and M. Lebard, *The Coming War with Japan*, New York: St Martin's Press, 1991, p. 182.
38 M. MccGwire, *Australia as a Regional Seapower: An External View*, SDSC Working Paper no. 11, Canberra: Australian National University, 1979, p. 16.
39 'MITI: Iraq Conflict Won't Affect Japan Fuel Prices', *Asahi Evening News*, 18 December 1998, p. 1.
40 METI, op. cit., p. 19.
41 For several years after China became a net importer of oil, it continued to export light oil from its Daqing field for use in Japanese power plants. Foreign Press Center, Japan, op. cit., p. 59.
42 'Japan, Iran Seal Azadegan Oil Deal', *Nikkei Weekly*, 23 February 2004, p. 3.
43 'Editorial: Challenges in Moscow', *Asahi Online*, 11 January 2003. Available www.asahi.com/english/op-ed/K2003011100246.html (accessed 11 January 2003).
44 'Japan Expects to Win Pipeline Route', *Financial Times*, 24 March 2004, p. 7.
45 'Japan, Iran seal Azadegan oil deal', *Nikkei Weekly*, op. cit., p. 3.
46 *Asahi Shimbun*, op. cit., p. 121.
47 METI, op. cit., p. 28.
48 M. Sachanta, 'Strategic Aim is to Diversify Sources of National Energy', *Financial Times*, 19 March 2004, p. 5.
49 J. Joonsoo, 'Critical Non-energy Import Dependencies in North-east Asia', in S. Bateman and S. Bates (eds), *Shipping and Regional Security*, Canberra Papers on Strategy and Defence, no. 129, Canberra: Australian National University Press, 1998, p. 83.
50 Foreign Press Center, Japan, op. cit., p. 41.
51 *Asahi Shimbun*, op. cit., p. 116.
52 Foreign Press Center, Japan, op. cit., p. 48.
53 MOFA, Japan, op. cit., pp. 46–7.
54 JSA, op. cit., p. 30.
55 'K'-line online company history. Online. Available www.kline.co.jp/profile/e_milestones3. htm (accessed 9 April 1999).
56 Gross tonnage is a measurement of space used for cargo and passenger vessels arrived at by dividing the volume of a ship in cubic feet by 100; only vessels above 1,000 GRT are included in the total given.
57 United States Federal Research Division, *Japan: A Country Study*, Washington, DC: Library of Congress/Department of the Army, 1992, p. 240.
58 United Nations Conference on Trade and Development, *Review of Maritime Transport, 2002*, New York and Geneva: United Nations, 2002, p. 127.
59 Tanker capacity is measured in deadweight tons (DWT), which refers to the weight of cargo and fuel carried, measured in metric tons.
60 Interview with Captain Osuka Yoshihiro, Asst General Manager, Marine Safety and Environmental Team, 'K'-Line, Tokyo, 28 February 2002.
61 Marisec.org., 'Shipping and World Trade'. Online. Available www.marisec.org/shippingfacts/keyfactsbenowners.htm (accessed 30 October 2004).
62 Comprehensive National Security Study Group, *Report on Comprehensive National Security* (unpublished government translation), 2 July 1980, p. 58.

63 Based on costs reported for the year 2000: JSA, *The Current State of Japanese Shipping*, March 2004, p. 19. Online. Available www.jsanet.or.jp/e/shipping-e/pdf/currentstate_e2004.pdf (accessed 18 November 2004).

64 Ibid., p. 7.

65 L. Wells II, *The Sea and Japan's Strategic Interests 1975–1985*, unpublished PhD thesis, 1975: Johns Hopkins University, Xerox University Microfilms, Ann Arbor, MI, p. 325.

66 The Great Circle Route highlights the distortions of the Mercator Projection in depicting relative distances beyond the Equator.

67 Comprehensive National Security Study Group, *Report on Comprehensive National Security* (unpublished government Translation), 2 July 1980, p. 11.

68 J. Noer and D. Gregory, *Chokepoints: Maritime Economic Concerns in Southeast Asia*, Washington, DC: National Defense University Press/Center for Naval Analyses, 1996, pp. 23–6.

69 K. Ouchi, 'Making the Straits Safer: A User's View of Alternative Routes', paper given at the International Conference on the Strait of Malacca: Meeting the Challenges of the 21st Century, Malaysian Institute of Maritime Affairs, 14–15 June 1994, p. 1.

70 H. J. Kenny, *An Analysis of Possible Threats to Shipping in Key Southeast Asian Sea Lanes*, Alexandria, Virginia: Center for Naval Analyses Occasional Paper, February 1996, p. 2; and H. Djalal, *Indonesia and the Law of the Sea*, Jakarta: Centre for Strategic and International Studies, 1995, p. 355.

71 'Energy Security and Sealane Disruption', *Australian Energy News*, Issue 24, June 2002. Online. Available www.industry.gov.au/resources/netetenergy/aen/aen24/6enrgy.html (accessed 16 December 2002).

72 'India Begins Patrolling Malacca Straits', *The Hindu*, 20 April 2002. Online. Available www.hinduonnet.com/thehindu/2002/04/20/stories/2002042002901100.htm (accessed 16 May 2002).

73 United Nations estimate, cited by Singaporean Defence Minister David Lim; Reuters News Service, 'Singapore Hosts 16-nation Naval Exercises', 12 June 2001.

74 'Maritime Security: Separating Fact from Hype', 30 June 2004, ICC Commercial Crime Services. Online. Available www.iccwbo.org/ccs/news_archives/2004/CCS_conference.asp (accessed 5 September 2004).

75 Cited in M. Atsumi, *Taiwan's Energy Security Issues: Domestic Energy Policies and Transporting Energy by Sea*, Tokyo: Institute for International Policy Studies, IIPS Policy Paper 300E, November 2003, p. 11. Online. Available www.iips.org/bp300e.pdf (accessed 27 November 2004).

76 Noer and Gregory, op. cit., pp. 56–8.

77 'Energy Security and Sealane Disruption', op. cit.

78 Energy Information Administration, US Department of Energy, 'World Oil Transit Chokepoints', November 2002, pp. 2–5. Online. Available www.eia.doe.gov/emeu/cabs/choke.html (accessed 16 December 2002).

79 The draft of the Straits of Malacca is deep enough to accommodate even the largest 500,000 DWT ULCCs making the outward-bound journey to the Middle East with ballast (Chia Lin Sien, in Hamzah (ed.), *The Straits of Malacca: International Co-operation in Trade, Funding and Navigational Safety*, Kuala Lumpur: Maritime Institute of Malaysia/Pelanduk Publications, 1997, p. 104).

80 Noer and Gregory, op. cit., p. 10.

81 Ibid., Appendix A, p. 68.

82 Ouchi, op. cit., p. 19.

83 Ibid., p. 4.

84 J. McBeth, 'Troubled Waters', *Far Eastern Economic Review*, 29 December 1994 and 5 January 1995, p. 19; and H. Djalal, *Indonesia and the Law of the Sea*, Centre for Strategic and International Studies, Jakarta, 1995, p. 357.

85 R. Swinnerton, 'A Description of Regional Shipping Routes: Navigational and Operational Considerations', *Maritime Studies*, no. 87, March/April 1996, pp. 10–22.
86 D. P. Djalal, *The Geopolitics of Indonesia's Maritime Territorial Policy*, Jakarta: Centre for Strategic and International Studies, 1996, p. 130.
87 Noer and Gregory, op. cit., p. 12.
88 Chia Lin Sien, op. cit., pp. 104–19.
89 Noer and Gregory, op. cit., p. 61.
90 According to Swinnerton (op. cit., pp. 17–19) significant fuel, operating and crewing cost savings are generated when a 550,000 ton tanker passing through Lombok is compared with the 2.75 journeys it would require for a 200,000 tanker to move an equivalent cargo though the Malacca Strait, notwithstanding the limited number of VLCCs and extra capital and terminal costs involved.
91 Chia Lin Sien, op. cit., pp. 116–19.
92 Atsumi, op. cit., p. 11.
93 K. Akimoto, 'Re-routing Options and Consequences: Safeguarding Seaborne Trade in Straits and Archipelagic Regimes', Conference Paper given at the Thirteenth International Conference on Sea Lines of Communications, Canberra, April 2001.
94 McBeth, op. cit., p. 19.
95 Interview with Captain Osuka Yoshihiro Asst General Manager, Marine Safety and Environmental Team, 'K'-Line (Kawasaki Kisen Kaisha), Tokyo, 28 February 2002.
96 Noer and Gregory, op. cit., p. 56.
97 S. Kawamura, 'Shipping and Seaborne Trade – Regional Security Interests', *The Kawamura Papers*, Chiba: The Kawamura Institute, November 1998, p. 108.
98 Interview with Admiral Soenardi, Republic of Indonesia Navy, Jakarta, March 2000.
99 B. R. Victor, 'Denial of Passage Rights in the Indonesian Archipelago – Australian Implications', *Journal of the Australian Naval Institute*, February 1994, p. 45.
100 Shilling, op. cit., p. 226.
101 H. J. Donohue, 'Protection of Sea Lines of Communications – Potential for Regional Co-operation in the Western Pacific' *Journal of the Australian Naval Institute*, May 1990, pp. 57–64.
102 Japanese estimates from the 1980s claim that shipping distances would increase by up to 78 per cent if tankers were forced to sail around Australia (T. Akaha, 'Japan's Response to Threats of Shipping Disruptions in Southeast Asia and the Middle East', *Pacific Affairs*, 1986; 59(2): 266).
103 Akimoto, op. cit.
104 JSA, *Annual Report 2002*: 'Port-Related International Problems'. Online. Available www.jsanet.or.jp/e/annualr-e/pdf/j_shipping2002.pdf (accessed 30 October 2004).
105 'Japanese Companies Mull Alternate Distribution Routes to Avoid Middle East Fracas', *The Nikkei Weekly*, 10 February 2003. Online. Available www.nni.nikkei.co.jp/AC/TNW/Search/Nni20030210FR7IRAQI.htm (accessed 16 February 2003). Itochu Corporation undertook a 'detailed study' into the consequences of re-routing and increased shipping insurance premiums in the Middle East in advance of the Iraq War.

2 Sea lines in strategy

1 A. T. Mahan, *The Influence of Seapower Upon History, 1660–1783*, First American Century Series Edition, New York: Hill and Wang, 1957, reprint of the 1890 edition, p. 9.
2 J. S. Corbett, *Some Principles of Maritime Strategy*, Annapolis: Naval Institute Press Classics of Sea Power Series, 1988, reprint of the 1911 edition, pp. 315–23.
3 Ibid., p. 94.

4 Ibid., p. 95.
5 P. Dibb, *Review of Australia's Defence Capabilities*, Canberra: Australian Government Publishing Service, 1986.
6 JDA, *Defense of Japan 1997*, Tokyo: JDA/*Japan Times*, 1997, p. 105.
7 Luck was on Japan's side: although bad weather frustrated the Mongols' two invasion attempts in the late thirteenth century, Japan was able to launch a brief but highly destructive invasion of Korea across the strait via Pusan, under Hideyoshi, in 1592–98.
8 S. Satō, 'Clarifying the Right of Collective Self-Defense', *Asia–Pacific Review*, 1996; 3(2): 98–9.
9 B. Buzan, 'Japan's Defence Problematique', *The Pacific Review*, 1995; 8(1): 26.
10 N. Friedman, *The U.S. Maritime Strategy*, London: Jane's, 1988, p. 62.
11 E. J. Grove, 'The Security of Shipping: The Global Perspective', in S. Bateman and S. Bates (eds), *Shipping and Regional Security*, Canberra Papers on Strategy and Defence no. 129, SDSC, Canberra: Australian National University, 1998, p. 2.
12 M. MccGwire, 'The Geopolitical Importance of Strategic Waterways in the Asian-Pacific Regional', *Orbis*, 1975; 19(3): 1059–60.
13 C. S. Gray, *The Leverage of Sea Power: The Strategic Advantages of Navies in War*, New York: The Free Press, 1992, pp. 17–18.
14 Corbett, op. cit., p. 95.
15 Mahan, op. cit., p. 23 [My ellipsis].
16 Ibid., p. 9.
17 Corbett, op. cit., pp. 315–23.
18 Ibid., Preface, p. xxix, p. 94.
19 R. Castex, *Strategic Theories: Selections translated by Eugenia C. Kiesling*, Annapolis: Naval Institute Press Classics of Seapower Series, 1994, p. 36. Castex, though a lesser influence on naval theory is included within the scope of this study because unlike Mahan and Corbett, whose focus lay more in the pursuit of 'sea command', he wrote during the inter-war period from a national perspective more attuned to a 'sea denial' strategy.
20 Preface by Eric J. Grove in Corbett, op. cit., p. xxxv.
21 D. Wettern, 'Ships, Not Lines, Must be Defended', *Pacific Defence Reporter*, 1989 Annual Reference Edition, p. 93.
22 Mahan, op. cit., pp. 27–8, 481n.
23 Corbett, op. cit., pp. 100–1.
24 Ibid., p. 269.
25 Ibid., pp. 261–5.
26 Ibid., pp. 270–5.
27 Castex, op. cit., p. 39.
28 B. Liddell Hart, *History of the First World War*, Trowbridge & Escher: Redwood Burn, 1977. First published as *The Real War 1914–1918*, 1930, pp. 400–3.
29 Castex, op. cit., p. 30.
30 Ibid., pp. 360–3, 372–7.
31 Ibid., pp. 367–70.
32 M. Poirier, 'Sea Control and Regional Warfare', *U.S. Naval Institute Proceedings*, July 1993, p. 64.
33 J. Winton, *Convoy: The Defence of Sea Trade 1890–1990*, London: Michael Joseph, 1983, p. 319.
34 B. Brodie, *A Layman's Guide to Naval Strategy*, Princeton, NJ: Princeton University Press, 1943, p. 84.
35 Ibid., p. 59.
36 Ibid., p. 85.
37 Ibid., pp. 82–103.
38 There are four categories of evasive routing: unescorted convoy, random independent routing, stream routing and wave routing (H. J. Donohue 'Protection of Sea Lines of

Communications – Potential for Regional Co-operation in the Western Pacific', *Journal of the Australian Naval Institute*, May 1990, pp. 57–64).

39 J. A. Boutilier, 'Air Defence of Merchant Ships', *Journal of the Australian Naval Institute*, 1989; 15(3): 41.

40 Liddell Hart, op. cit., p. 402.

41 Cited in E. J. Grove (ed.), *The Defeat of the Enemy Attack on Shipping, 1939–1945*; A Revised Edition of the (1957) Naval Staff History Volumes 1A (Text and Appendices) and 1B (Plans and Tables), Aldershot: The Navy Records Society/Ashgate Publishing Limited, 1997, pp. 13, 32.

42 D. W. Waters' confidential 1957 staff history *The Defeat of the Enemy Attack on Shipping, 1939–1945*, edited by Eric Grove, was released by the Navy Records Society in 1997.

43 Grove, op. cit., p. 49.

44 D. Wettern, 'Ships, Not Lines, Must be Defended', *Pacific Defence Reporter*, 1989 Annual Reference Edition, p. 93.

45 Grove, op. cit., p. 49.

46 Boutilier, op. cit. p. 42.

47 G. Priestnall, 'ANZUS and the Radford-Collins Agreement: Australia's Naval Mission', *Journal of the Australian Naval Institute*, January/March 1997, pp. 49–52.

48 Donohue, op. cit.

49 Testimony of Adm Metzel to the Senate Committee on Armed Services, for Department of Defence (DoD) Authorizations for FY 1980, 96th Congress, Washington, DC: US Government Printing Office, p. 2934.

50 R. Komer, *Maritime Strategy or Coalition Defense?*, Lanham: University Press of America/Abt Books, 1984, pp. 61–3.

51 J. P. Keddell, *The Politics of Defense in Japan: Managing Internal and External Pressures*, Armonk, New York: M.E. Sharpe, 1994, p. 131.

52 Admiral J. D. Watkins, *The Maritime Strategy*, Annapolis: The US Naval Institute, US DoD, February 1986, p. 482 [My ellipsis].

53 D. Ball, 'Escalation and the Use of Nuclear Weapons', Chapter 6, '*Provocative Plans: A Critique of US Strategy for Maritime Conflict in the North Pacific*', Canberra Papers on Strategy and Defence no. 79, Canberra: Australian National University Press, 1991, pp. 81–93.

54 For example, W. L. Owen, 'Is the Convoy System Old Hat?', *Pacific Defence Reporter*, September 1985.

55 'Convoy or Defended Lanes', *Journal of the Australian Naval Institute*, August 1989, p. 56.

56 Ibid., pp. 57–8.

57 See D. Ball and J. T. Richelson, *The Ties That Bind: Intelligence Cooperation between the UKUSA Countries*, Sydney: Allen and Unwin, 1985.

58 D. Wettern, 'Ships, Not Lines, Must be Defended', *Pacific Defence Reporter*, 1989 Annual Reference Edition, p. 90.

59 S. Kanemaru, Foreword in M. J. Kennedy and M. J. O'Connor (eds), *Safely By Sea*, Lanham, MD: University Press of America, 1990, pp. x–xi.

60 K. Booth, 'The New World Order' and the Future of Naval Power', *Journal of the Australian Naval Institute*, November 1991, pp. 17–27.

61 See Z. Dian, 'Sea Lane Security', *Asian Defence Journal*, July 1985, p. 3.

62 G. Adhikari, 'The End of the Unipolar Myth', *International Herald Tribune*, 27 September 2004, p. 6.

63 P. Dibb, *Force Modernisation in Asia: Towards 2000 and Beyond*, SDSC Working Paper no. 306, Strategic and Defence Studies Centre, Canberra: Australian National University, 1997.

64 E. J. Grove, 'Navies in Future Conflicts', in A. Bergin and H. Smith (eds), *Naval Power in the Pacific: Toward the Year 2000*, Boulder and London: Lynne Rienner, 1993, pp. 169–70.

65 D. Lague, 'We All Live for Another Submarine', *Far Eastern Economic Review*, 15 August 2002, pp. 12–14.
66 M. Poirier, 'Sea Control and Regional Warfare', *U.S. Naval Institute Proceedings*, July 1993, p. 65.
67 J. Noer and D. Gregory, *Chokepoints: Maritime Economic Concerns in South-east Asia*, Washington, DC: National Defense University Press/Center for Naval Analyses, 1996, p. 1.
68 Ibid., p. 6.
69 From under 6 trillion ton-miles in 1965, to 23 trillion in 2002; Marisec.org., 'Shipping and World Trade'. Online. Available www.marisec.org/shippingfacts/worldtradevolume.htm (accessed 30 October 2004).
70 See K. E. Calder, 'Asia's Empty Tank', *Foreign Affairs*, 1996; 75(2): 55–69; and Brian Cooper, 'The Coming Conflict – the Battle of the SLOCs', *Asia–Pacific Defence Reporter*, January 2000, pp. 9–12.
71 'Energy Security and Sealane Disruption', *Australian Energy News*, Issue 24, June 2002. Online. Available www.industry.gov.au/resources/netetenergy/aen/aen24/6enrgy.html (accessed 16 December 2002); and interview with Gary Eng, Team Leader, Asia Pacific Energy Research Centre (APERC), Tokyo, 5 March 2002.
72 See G. Klintworth, 'Asia–Pacific: More Security, Less Uncertainty, New Opportunities', *The Pacific Review*, 1992; 5(3): 222; and K. Snitwongse, 'Structural Changes in Asia–Pacific International Relations: Impact on South-East Asia', *Hitotsubashi Journal of Law and Politics, Special Issue*, 1994, pp. 35–46.
73 Poirier, op. cit., p. 64; and Kawamura, in Bateman and Bates (eds), *Shipping and Regional Security*, Canberra Papers on Strategy and Defence no. 129, Canberra: Australian National University Press, 1998, pp. 18–20.
74 D. Coulter, 'The Economics of SLOC protection; an Overvalued Mission', paper presented at the Eleventh International Conference on the Sea Lanes of Communication (SLOC) Studies, Tokyo, 17–18 November 1997.
75 MccGwire, op. cit., p. 1061.
76 A. Granitsas, 'In Evergreen's Wake', *Far Eastern Economic Review*, 2002; 24: 50–2.
77 Marisec.org., 'Shipping and World Trade'. Online. Available www.marisec.org/shippingfacts/worldtradelowcosts.htm (accessed 30 October 2004).
78 United Nations Conference on Trade and Development, *Review of Maritime Transport, 2002*, New York and Geneva: United Nations, 2002, p. 45.
79 V. Mallet, 'China's rise revives an ailing industry', *Financial Times*, 14 December 2004, p. 17.
80 JSA/Asian Shipowners' Forum, Note of Understanding, 9 April 2004. Online. Available www.jsanet.or.jp/e/text/20040412.html (accessed 30 October 2004).
81 R. Wright, ClarkSea index data cited in 'The Shipping Forecast: Booming Trade puts Global Transport Links under Strain', *Financial Times*, 14 December 2004, p. 17.
82 See also MccGwire, op. cit., pp. 1059–62.
83 Ibid., pp. 1072–3.
84 D. Coulter, 'Hub Ports and Focal Points: New Entrants in the Maritime Security Lexicon', in A. L. Griffiths, R. H. Thomas and P. T. Haydon (eds), *The Changing Strategic Importance of International Shipping*, Centre for foreign Policy Studies, Halifax, Nova Scotia: Dalhousie University, 1998, pp. 135–45.
85 United Nations Conference on Trade and Development, op. cit., p. 72.
86 P. Day, 'Asian Shipping Industry Is Hit By Higher Costs After Attacks', *Wall Street Journal*, 26 September 2001.
87 B. A. Hamzah (ed.), *The Straits of Malacca: International Co-operation in Trade, Funding and Navigational Safety*, Kuala Lumpur: Maritime Institute of Malaysia/Pelanduk Publications, 1997, p. 126.
88 H. Djalal, *Indonesia and the Law of the Sea*, Jakarta: Centre for Strategic and International Studies, 1995, p. 84.

89 D. P. Djalal, *The Geopolitics of Indonesia's Maritime Territorial Policy*, Jakarta: Centre for Strategic and International Studies, 1996.
90 See Djalal, *Indonesia and the Law of the Sea*, op. cit.
91 I. Shearer, 'Current Law of the Sea Issues', in S. Bateman and R. Babbage (eds), *Maritime Change: Issues for Asia*, St Leonards: Allen and Unwin, 1993, p. 58.
92 The issue of marine resource ownership and deep-sea mining rights, contained in Article XI of UNCLOS, in fact proved to be a far more intractable issue to resolve during the third convention, owing mainly to opposition from the United States, but for which UNCLOS might otherwise have been implemented several years earlier.
93 See I. T. Laxton, 'Creeping Jurisdiction in Southeast Asia: Its Effect on Naval Mobility', *Journal of the Australian Naval Institute*, May 1988, p. 6; and Shearer, op. cit., p. 62; and L. Paul, in Sam Bateman (ed.), *Maritime Cooperation in the Asia–Pacific Region: Current Situation and Prospects*, Canberra Papers on Strategy and Defence no. 132, Canberra: Australian National University Press, 1999, p. 126.
94 The study found that the diversion of 5,800 nm would require an additional transit time of 15 days, assuming an average speed of 15 knots, and an extra fuel cost of $2.9 million: 'UNLOS Dept. of Defence Position Summary '94: National Security and the United Nations Convention on the Law of the Sea'. Online. Available www.prosea.org/articles-news/unesco/UNLOS_Dept_of_Defense_Position_Summary_94.html (accessed 4 June 1997).
95 Traces of TNT and parts of an inflatable speed-boat were found within the *Limburg*'s hull.
96 International Chamber of Commerce Commercial Crime Services, International Maritime Bureau (IMB), 'Make tanker lanes into no-go areas for other shipping says IMB', 14 October 2002. Online. Available www.iccwbo.org/home/news_archives/2002/stories/limburg.asp (accessed 9 August 2003).
97 United Nations Conference on Trade and Development, op. cit., 2002, pp. 75–6.
98 'Maritime States Seek Accord on terrorism at Sea', *Financial Times*, 29 May 2002, p. 10.
99 Marisec.org, 'Key Issues 2004: Delivering Maritime Security'. Online. Available www.marisec.org/ics-isfkeyissues2004/maritimesecuritytext.htm (accessed 30 October 2004).
100 IMB, *Piracy and Armed Robbery Against Ships: Annual Report 2001*, Barking: ICC IMB, January 2002, p. 22.
101 J. Brandon, 'Protect Asia's Shipping', Pacific Forum CSIS, PacNet 21A, 24 May 2002. Online. Available www.csis.org/pacfor/pac0221A.htm (accessed 5 November 2004).
102 J. Szep, 'Islamic militants trained for sea attacks', Reuters News Services, 21 January 2003.
103 ARF Statement on Cooperation Against Piracy and Other Threats to Maritime Security. Online. Available www.aseansec.org/14838.htm (accessed 31 August 2004).
104 'Shipping in South-east Asia: Going for the Jugular', *The Economist*, 12 June 2004, pp. 54–61 and 'Singapore to Increase Defence Spending to Counter Terrorism', BBC Monitoring, 15 June 2004.
105 IMB, Annual Report 2001, op. cit., pp. 17, 20.
106 'Armed Piracy Increasing in Aceh', International Chamber of Commerce Commercial Crime Services, IMB. Online. Available www.iccwbo.org/ccs/news_archives/2004/ache_2004.asp (accessed 15 September 2004).
107 'Pirates seize Malaysian boats near Philippines', Reuters News Service, 15 June 2001.
108 IMB, *Piracy and Armed Robbery Against Ships: Annual Report 2003*, Barking: ICC IMB, January 2004, Table 7, p. 10.
109 N. Tanaka and H. Takase, in Hamzah and Ogawa (eds), op. cit., pp. 166–7.

110 International Maritime Organization (IMO), *Reports on Acts of Piracy and Armed Robbery Against Ships: Annual Report – 2003*, MSC.4/Circ.50, 27 April 2004.

111 Ibid.

112 J. Abhyankar, 'An Overview of Piracy Problems: A Global Update', paper presented to Society of International Law, Singapore (SILS) Piracy Seminar, 22 October 1999, Orchard Hotel, Singapore. Online. Available www.sils.org/seminar/1999-piracy-02.htm (accessed 11 November 2000).

113 International Chamber of Commerce Commercial Crime Services, IMB, 'High Sea Terrorism Alert in Piracy Report', 29 January 2002. Online. Available www.iccwbo.org/home/news_archives/2003/stories/ piracy%20_report_2002.asp (accessed 20 February 2004); and 'Seafarers Warned on Indonesia Pirates, Somali Armed Gangs', Dow Jones Newswires, 23 October 2002.

114 J. Abhyankar, in Hamzah and Ogawa (eds), op. cit., p. 11.

115 See S. P. Menefee, 'Crossing the Line? Maritime Violence, Piracy, Definitions and International Law', in Hamzah and Ogawa (eds), op. cit., p. 66.

116 IMO draft Code of Practice for the Investigation of the Crimes of Piracy and Armed Robbery Against Ships (MSC/Circ.984) (Article 2.2) cited in IMO MSC.4/Circ.12, *Reports on Acts of Piracy and Armed Robbery Against Ships: Fourth Quarterly Report*, 31 December 2001.

117 IMB, Annual Report 2003, op. cit.

118 Even when apprehended, pirates may not face criminal proceedings. In the celebrated case of the *Petro Ranger*, a tanker intercepted by Indonesian pirates in the South China Sea and taken to the Chinese island of Hainan, Chinese authorities repatriated the crew's abductors to Indonesia without trial.

119 J. Abhyankar, 'Piracy and Ship Robbery: A Growing Menace', in Hamzah and Ogawa (eds), op. cit., pp. 10–59.

120 S. Weeks, 'Law and Order at Sea: Pacific Cooperation in Dealing with Piracy, Drugs and Illegal Migration', in S. Bateman and S. Bates (eds), *Calming the Waters: Initiatives for Asia Pacific Cooperation*, Canberra Papers on Strategy and Defence no. 114, Canberra: Australian National University Press, 1996, pp. 43–56.

121 Crew sizes of 30 or less are the norm onboard large container ships and tankers.

122 International Chamber of Commerce Commercial Crime Services, IMB, 'New Brand of Piracy Threatens Oil Tankers in Malacca Straits'. Online. Available www.iccwbo.org/ccs/news_archives/2003/piracy_ms.asp (accessed 28 November 2004).

123 Abhyankar, in Hamzah and Ogawa (eds), op. cit., pp. 10–59.

124 Interview with IMB Director Captain Pottengal Mukundan, Barking, 16 September 2004.

125 Weeks, op. cit., p. 46.

126 International Chamber of Commerce Commercial Crime Services, IMB, 'Maritime Security: Separating Fact from Hype', 30 June 2004. Online. Available www.iccwbo.org/ccs/news_archives/2004/CCS_conference.asp (accessed 28 November 2004).

127 The estimate is by James Warren of the School of Asian Studies at Murdoch University; 'Asia Piracy Costs $25 Billion a Year, Says Expert', Reuters News Service, 10 December 2002.

128 Poirier, op. cit., p. 64.

129 M. S. Navias and E. R. Hooton, *Tanker Wars: The Assault On Merchant Shipping During the Iran–Iraq Conflict, 1980–1988*, London: Tauris Academic Studies, 1996.

130 P. M. Cronin and N. Yamaguchi, 'Japan's Future Regional Security Role', *Strategic Review*, Summer 1992, pp. 20–1.

131 See, for example, H. J. Kenny, *An Analysis of Possible Threats to Shipping in Key South-east Asian Sea Lanes, Alexandria*, Virginia: Center for Naval Analyses Occasional Paper, February 1996.

132 B. Opall, 'U.S. Warns Claimants in South China Sea', *Defense News*, 15–21 May 1995, p. 3.

133 Quoted from 'US Congressman Raps Washington', *Asahi Evening News*, 28 December 1998, p. 3.
134 Noer with Gregory, op. cit., p. 56.
135 A. Friedberg, 'Ripe for Rivalry: Prospects for Peace in a Multipolar Asia', *International Security*, 1993–94; 18(3): 18–32.

3 Japan's pre-1945 SLOC security

1 S. Giffard, *Japan Among the Powers, 1890–1990*, New Haven and London: Yale University Press, 1994, p. 42.
2 T. Nakamura, *Lectures on Modern Japanese Economic History 1926–1994*, LTCB International Library Foundation, 1994, p. 17.
3 W. G. Beasley, *The Rise of Modern Japan*, Tokyo: Charles E. Tuttle Company, 1990, pp. 111–14.
4 These three phases have been adapted from W. G. Beasley, *Japanese Imperialism 1894–1945*, Oxford: Clarendon Press, 1987.
5 N. Choucri, R. C. North and S. Yamakage, *The Challenge of Japan Before World War II and After: A Study of National Growth and Expansion*, London: Routledge, 1992, p. 30.
6 Ibid., p. 40.
7 Beasley, op. cit., p. 148.
8 Choucri *et al.*, op. cit., p. 29.
9 Beasley, op. cit., p. 198.
10 Choucri *et al.*, op. cit., p. 28.
11 Beasley, op. cit., pp. 112–13.
12 Choucri *et al.*, op. cit., pp. 37–8.
13 I. Satō, 'The Naval Policy of Japan', *Brassey's Naval and Shipping Annual 1927*, London: William Cowes and Sons, pp. 71–80.
14 Nakamura, op. cit., pp. 6, 16–17.
15 Beasley, op. cit., p. 188.
16 Giffard, op. cit., pp. 115–16.
17 Beasley, op. cit., p. 189.
18 The importance of other bulk commodities to Japan's war economy is frequently overshadowed by dependence on oil imports. Iron ore requirements, for instance, expanded from less than 500,000 tons in 1940 to 1,718,000 tons in 1943, virtually all of which had to be brought in by sea.
19 Ibid., p. 201.
20 Giffard, op. cit., p. 42.
21 M. P. Parillo, *The Japanese Merchant Marine in World War II*, Annapolis: Naval Institute Press, 1993, pp. 50–2.
22 Nakamura, op. cit., p. 71.
23 J. E. Auer, *The Postwar Rearmament of Japanese Maritime Forces, 1945–71*, New York: Praeger, 1973, p. 14.
24 D. C. Evans and M. R. Peattie, *Kaigun: Strategy, Tactics and Technology in the Imperial Japanese Navy, 1887–1941*, Annapolis: Naval Institute Press, 1997, pp. 395–8.
25 D. W. Waters, 'Japan – Defeat through Blockade – 1941–45', *The Naval Review*, 1998; 76(3): 246–7.
26 Parillo, op. cit., p. 75.
27 Evans and Peattie, op. cit., pp. 319, 361.
28 Parillo, op. cit., pp. 15, 239; Table A.5, 'Control of Japanese Merchant Marine Tonnage during World War II'. The Imperial Army also designed, built and operated its own fleet of transport submarines throughout the war to resupply outlying garrisons.
29 Parillo, op. cit., pp. 34–8.

30 Nakamura, op. cit., pp. 109–10.
31 Ibid.
32 Waters, op. cit., p. 247.
33 Evans and Peattie, op. cit., p. 5.
34 When Satsuma's coastal artillery at Kagoshima dueled with a British naval squadron in August 1863, Tōgō Heihachirō, the victor at Tsushima in May 1905, was present as a gunner (E. P. Hoyt, *Three Military Leaders: Togo, Yamamoto, Yamashita*, Tokyo: Kodansha International, 1993, pp. 21–4).
35 I. Nish (ed.), *Anglo-Japanese Naval Relations*, papers by Kiyoshi Ikeda, Ian Gow, John Chapman, Chit-chung Ong, International Studies 1985/3, London School of Economics and Political Science, London, 1985.
36 Evans and Peattie, op. cit., pp. 163–4.
37 Although the United States Naval Academy closed its doors to Japanese students in the 1890s, this did not prevent Mahan from exerting a powerful influence on young officers such as Akiyama Saneyuki, who made an unsuccessful bid to lure Mahan to teach strategy in Japan (ibid., p. 71).
38 This resembled capability-led planning on the model of Great Britain's two-power standard, which had dictated the Royal Navy's force structure since 1889 (ibid., pp. 57–60).
39 J. S. Corbett, *Some Principles of Maritime Strategy*, Annapolis: Naval Institute Press Classics of Sea Power Series, 1988, p. 309n. Corbett was commissioned to write a confidential history of the Russo-Japanese War for the War Staff at the Admiralty.
40 M. Nomura, *Kaisenshi ni Manabu* ('Learning from the History of War at Sea'), Tokyo: Bungei Shunjū, 1994, p. 75.
41 Evans and Peattie, op. cit., pp. 107–9.
42 In 1901, Japan possessed a larger fleet than that of the United States, but by 1907 the United States had a superiority of eleven battleships (ibid., pp. 146–9).
43 Hector Bywater, writing in 1927, cites from the account of Franklin Roosevelt, as the former Assistant Secretary of the Navy, about 'ten nervous days in the summer of 1908, [when] the United States hovered on the edge of an ultimatum from Japan' over American plans to modernise its defences in the Philippines (H. C. Bywater, *Navies and Nations: A Review of Naval Developments since the Great War*, London: Constable and Company, 1927, p. 152).
44 Evans and Peattie, op. cit., p. 186.
45 M. R. Peattie, 'Akiyama Saneyuki and the Emergence of Modern Japanese Naval Doctrine', *Proceedings*, January 1977, pp. 61–9.
46 'Combined Fleet' (*rengō kantai*) was the name given to Imperial Navy's major battle force.
47 Evans and Peattie, op. cit., p. 129.
48 Parillo, op. cit., p. 26.
49 Most famously in *Teikoku kokubō shi ron* ['On Imperial Defence History'].
50 Evans and Peattie, op. cit., pp. 135–41.
51 Capital ships refers to battleships, heavy cruisers and, later, aircraft carriers.
52 Evans and Peattie, op. cit., p. 235.
53 Hostility between the Navy and Army was of a different order to the inter-service rivalry experienced in all large militaries. In the 1930s for example, the Navy fortified the Ministry in Kasumigaseki against the possibility of Army assault while Admiral Yamamoto Isoroku, the future chief of the Combined Fleet, was flanked by Navy bodyguards to deter assassination by the Army unit assigned to protect him. The jealously guarded autonomy of both services bred not only confusion and duplication of effort but prevented a centralized command structure. Incredibly, the Navy concealed preparations for the Pearl Harbor attack from General Tōjō until November 1941 and later masked the full extent of its losses at Midway from the premier (Parillo, op. cit.,

pp. 19–24; and E. P. Hoyt, *The Militarists: The Rise of Japanese Militarism Since WWII*, New York: Donald I. Fine, 1985, p. 101).

54 The Imperial Army dragged out its intervention into the rear of the Russian Civil War until 1925 when the last Japanese troops were withdrawn from northern Sakhalin, the southern half of which had been ceded to Japan by the Treaty of Portsmouth, in 1905.

55 Evans and Peattie, op. cit., p. 169.

56 E. J. Grove (ed.), *The Defeat of the Enemy Attack on Shipping, 1939–1945;* A Revised Edition of the (1957) Naval Staff History, Volumes 1A (Text and Appendices) and 1B (Plans and Tables), Aldershot: The Navy Records Society/Ashgate Publishing Limited, 1997, pp. 3–4.

57 Evans and Peattie, op. cit., p. 200.

58 Ballard cited in Bywater, op. cit., pp. 204–5.

59 An exceptional prewar exercise, conducted in October 1940, involved Japanese submarines patrolling Tsushima Strait, the Bungo Channel (between Shikoku and Kyūshū) and the approach to Tokyo Bay, against hypothetical submarine attacks on Japanese commerce. Despite the success of the simulated attacks, the high command was too perturbed by the apparent susceptibility of their submarines to radio direction-finding to develop this further as an operational concept (Evans and Peattie, op. cit., p. 430).

60 R. Goralski and R. W. Freeburg, *Oil & War: How the Deadly Struggle for Fuel in WWII Meant Victory or Defeat*, New York: William Morrow and Company, Inc., 1987, pp. 186–9, 199.

61 Evans and Peattie, op. cit., pp. 217–19. In the course of the war, only two campaigns were launched by Japanese submarines against Allied shipping; in the Indian Ocean in July 1942, and against ships sailing between Australia and the United States in spring 1943 (E. J. Grove (ed.), op. cit., p. 156).

62 Evans and Peattie, op. cit., pp. 201–5.

63 Hoyt, *The Militarists*, op. cit., p. 106.

64 Evans and Peattie, op. cit., pp. 475–6.

65 Displacement tonnage is used for the total weight of a ship and its contents, primarily for warships.

66 Parillo, op. cit., p. 16.

67 In February, an abortive army revolt in Tokyo paved the way for a purge of moderate politicians and later in the year the army bypassed the *gaimushō* to conclude the anti-Comintern Pact with Italy and Germany, preparing the ground for the Axis pact.

68 Hoyt, *The Militarists*, op. cit., pp. 92–3.

69 The Navy's Operational Plan for 1939 postulated *simultaneous* operations against four enemies including the Soviet Union (Evans and Peattie, op. cit., p. 466).

70 'Bunker' is fuel used for boiler-firing in ships. Bunker oil and heavy oil are the same thing. Japanese experiments with oil-fired boilers date back to the 1880s.

71 Figure for the *Mutsu* from Parillo, op. cit., pp. 41–2.

72 Evans and Peattie, op. cit., pp. 408–9; and Goralski and Freeburg, op. cit., pp. 93–4.

73 Goralski and Freeburg, op. cit., Appendix 14, 'Sources of Petroleum in Japan Proper, 1938–1945', p. 348.

74 Ibid., p. 100. On a speculative note, had Japan's attempts in the 1920s to purchase Sakhalin outright from the Soviet Union proved successful, history might have been different.

75 Ibid., p. 95.

76 Parillo, op. cit., p. 40.

77 Bywater, op. cit., pp. 200, 211. More unfortunately for Bywater – otherwise a prescient analyst – he also declared that Pearl Harbor was 'secure from all save spasmodic or casual attack' and that 'a Japanese expedition against Hawaii is never likely to take place'.

78 Evans and Peattie, op. cit., p. 406.

79 Nakamura, op. cit., p. 72.
80 Evans and Peattie, op. cit., p. 408, and Parillo, op. cit., p. 43.
81 Evans and Peattie, op. cit., p. 407. According to Nakamura (op. cit., p. 106), the reason Japan did not declare war on China in 1937 was in order to maintain commercial access to the US market out of concern over the terms of the Neutrality Act, which barred US exports to any belligerent nation.
82 Goralski and Freeburg, op. cit., pp. 95–100.
83 J. Toland, *The Rising Sun: The Decline and Fall of the Japanese Empire*, New York: Bantam Books, 1970, pp. 94–6; Japan had moved into northern Indochina in September 1940, but the United States had stopped short of including oil in its trade sanctions for fear of precipitating war.
84 Parillo, op. cit., p. 31.
85 Goralski and Freeburg, op. cit., 1987, p. 102.
86 Evans and Peattie, op. cit., p. 475.
87 Although Japan's designs on Southeast Asia originated with the Navy, the Army's preference was for an attack on Malaya rather than the Philippines, which the Navy felt should have priority in order to secure its lines of communication. This difference was resolved with a compromise to initiate simultaneous attacks on 8 December (Evans and Peattie, op. cit., p. 468).
88 Parillo, op. cit., pp. 43–4.
89 Nakamura, op. cit., p. 110. Prewar Navy estimates for East Indies production, cited by Evans and Peattie (op. cit., pp. 594–5, n. 58) were much higher, at 2 million tons in 1942, 6 million in 1943 and 10 million for 1944.
90 Parillo, op. cit., p. 28.
91 Evans and Peattie, op. cit., pp. 406–11, 503.
92 Ibid., p. 410.
93 Ibid., pp. 396–7.
94 Goralski and Freeburg, op. cit., p. 340, Appendix 4, 'World Tanker Fleet, 1940–1945'.
95 Parillo, op. cit., p. 48.
96 Goralski and Freeburg, op. cit., pp. 141–5.
97 Ibid., p. 150. After two years this was increased to 78 per cent (Parillo, op. cit., p. 45).
98 Goralski and Freeburg, op. cit., p. 192.
99 Ibid., pp. 152, 190. As with everything else, the Army and Navy ran their refining operations independently. In Southeast Asia, the Army kept all Burmese oil for itself leaving the Navy a single refinery in Balikpapan, Borneo.
100 Goralski and Freeburg, op. cit., pp. 191–2. Nakamura (op. cit., p. 113) cites anecdotal evidence that oil was being dumped in Sumatra for lack of available tankers.
101 The Joint Army–Navy Assessment Committee, *Japanese Naval and Merchant Shipping Losses During World War II By All Causes*, Washington, DC: Navy Department, February 1947, vii, Table II 'Japanese Naval and Merchant Shipping Sunk During World War II By United States Forces'.
102 Clay Blair describes a total of ten other operational roles for which US submarines were used (*Silent Victory: The U.S. Submarine War Against Japan*, Philadelphia and New York: J.B. Lippincott Company, 1975, pp. 357–8).
103 Goralski and Freeburg, op. cit., p. 192.
104 Blair, op. cit., p. 360.
105 The ship in question is possibly the *Gifu Maru*, torpedoed 2 November 1942 in Davao Gulf, Mindanao.
106 Blair, op. cit., pp. 509–10.
107 Goralski and Freeburg, op. cit., p. 196.
108 Parillo, op. cit., p. 238, Table A.4, 'Japanese Tanker Tonnage During World War II'.
109 Ibid., p. 247, Table A.11, 'Oil Production in Subjugated Areas and Imports to Japan during World War II'.
110 Ibid., p. 215.

111 Blair, citing post-war credited records, gives a higher total of 2.7 million tons (op. cit., p. 816).
112 Parillo, op. cit., Table A.5, 'Control of Japanese Merchant Marine Tonnage during World War II', p. 239; and Table A.9, 'Japanese Shipping Losses During World War II', p. 243. Nakamura's figure for Japanese ship losses in 1944 is higher, at 4.1 million tons (op. cit., p. 114).
113 Cited in Parillo, op. cit., p. 115.
114 Goralski and Freeburg, op. cit., pp. 196–7.
115 Parillo, op. cit., p. 247, Table A.11, 'Oil Production in Subjugated Areas and Imports to Japan during World War II'.
116 Goralski and Freeburg (op. cit., p. 319) thus explain the Imperial Navy's decision to fight the US Navy for control of the Philippines rather than pull back the fleet for a defence of home waters, quoting from the Chief of the Combined Fleet Admiral Toyoda Soemu: 'Should we lose in the Philippines operations, even though the fleet should be left, the shipping lane to the south would be completely cut off so that the fleet, if it should come back to Japanese waters, could not obtain its fuel supply. If it should remain in southern waters, it could not receive supplies of ammunition and arms. There would be no sense in saving the fleet at the expense of the loss of the Philippines.'
117 Small by comparison with the *Yamato*'s fuel capacity, the diversion of four thousand tons was profligate nonetheless, denying the Navy's escort forces of more than half their average monthly fuel allocation in 1945. The diversion of fuel away from commerce protection to permit the futile sortie of the *Yamato* epitomises the navy's obsession with 'big ships and big guns' to the bitter end (Parillo, op. cit., p. 30).
118 Cited in Blair, op. cit., p. 879.
119 J. Winton, *Convoy: The Defence of Sea Trade 1890–1990*, London: Michael Joseph, 1983, p. 314.
120 Goralski and Freeburg, op. cit., pp. 246–7.
121 Nomura, op. cit., p. 278.
122 Satō, op. cit., p. 26.
123 After the price of oil from the Dutch East Indies rose in the second half of the 1920s, Japan relied increasingly on cheaper oil from California, greatly lessening its dependence on Southeast Asia (Evans and Peattie, op. cit., p. 567, n. 68).
124 Satō, op. cit., p. 77.
125 Evans and Peattie, op. cit., p. 435.
126 Bywater, op. cit., pp. 206–7.
127 Cited in Parillo, op. cit., p. 38.
128 Nomura, op. cit., p. 278.
129 Evans and Peattie, op. cit., pp. 437–8.
130 Nomura, op. cit., p. 280.
131 Ibid., p. 281.
132 Evans and Peattie, op. cit., pp. 431, 435–41.
133 Goralski and Freeburg, op. cit., p. 311.
134 Nomura, op. cit., p. 282.
135 Parillo, op. cit., pp. 95–6.
136 Post-war interrogation of Vice Adm Hara, Rear Adm Sumikawa and Rear Adm Kojima, quoted in ibid., p. 15.
137 These were, in order of construction, *Senshū*, *Kunashiri*, *Ishigaki* and *Hachijō* (Nomura, op. cit., pp. 279–80).
138 Evans and Peattie, op. cit., p. 383.
139 D. W. Waters, *The Naval Review*, 1988; 76(3): 247.
140 Evans and Peattie, op. cit., pp. 440–1.
141 A total of three sub-chasers, for example, was assigned to screen oil tankers sailing from the navy refinery at Balikpapan through the Makassar Straits until May 1943.

142 Winton, op. cit., p. 313.
143 Ibid., pp. 310–12; and Parillo, op. cit., p. 67.
144 Goralski and Freeburg, op. cit., p. 194.
145 Blair, op. cit., p. 387.
146 Parillo, op. cit., pp. 69–70.
147 Winton, op. cit., pp. 313–16.
148 Japanese press reports cited by Bywater (op. cit., p. 221) suggest that an earlier version of this plan may have existed as far back as 1922, to defend sea communications along an outer line from Kamchatka to Taiwan and an inner line between Japan and Korea. It is possible this may have been misinformation.
149 Individual sailings were two-and-a-half times more likely to be sunk according to Winton (op. cit., p. 318).
150 Parillo, op. cit., p. 73.
151 Evans and Peattie, op. cit., p. 415. Night-fighting was a skill for which the Imperial Navy had equipped and trained with exceptional diligence.
152 Blair, op. cit., p. 18.
153 Parillo, op. cit., p. 71.
154 Winton, op. cit., p. 319.
155 Goralski and Freeburg, op. cit., pp. 189–90.
156 C. S. Gray, *The Leverage of Sea Power: The Strategic Advantages of Navies in War*, New York: The Free Press, 1992, p. 21.
157 Quoted in Parillo, op. cit., p. 46.
158 Waters, op. cit., pp. 246–7.

4 Japan's sea lane security in the era of defence constraints, 1945–77

1 P. Katzenstein and N. Okawara, *Japan's National Security: Structures, Norms and Policy Responses in a Changing World*, Ithaca, NY: Cornell East Asia Series, 1993, p. 99.
2 Ibid., pp. 7–8.
3 J. A. A. Stockwin, *Governing Japan*, Oxford: Blackwell, 1999, p. 46.
4 Cited in K. Murata, 'The US–Japan Alliance and the US–Korean Alliance: Their Origins, Dilemmas and Structures', *Comparative Strategy*, 1995; 14: 187.
5 K. Pyle, *The Japanese Question: Power and Purpose in a New Era*, Washington, DC: The AEI Press, 1996, p. 26.
6 J. W. Dower, *Empire and Aftermath: Yoshida Shigeru and the Japanese Experience, 1878–1954*, Cambridge, MA: Harvard East Asian Studies Monographs, 1979, pp. 401–3, 413.
7 Y. Soeya, 'Japan Normative Constraints Versus Structural Imperatives', in M. Alagappa (ed.), *Asian Security Practice: Material and Ideational Influences*, Stanford, CA: Stanford University Press, 1998, p. 203.
8 M. Weinstein, *Japan's Postwar Defence Policy*, Columbia University Press, New York, 1971, pp. 19–20.
9 M. Kōsaka, 'Japan's Major Interests and Policies in Asia and the Pacific', *Orbis*, 1975; 24(3): 793–808.
10 M. Weinstein, 'The Evolution of the Japan Self-Defense Forces', in J. H. Buck (ed.) *The Modern Japanese Military System*, Beverly Hills, CA: Sage publications, 1975, p. 42.
11 Kōsaka, op. cit., p. 794.
12 R. Drifte, *The Security Factor in Japan's Foreign Policy, 1945–1952*, Ripe: Saltire Press, 1983, p. 111.
13 Both Treaties came into effect on 28 April 1952, when the Occupation formally ended.
14 Under the 1951 Security Treaty US Forces retained an internal security function within their remit. When the Treaty was revised in 1960 this provision was removed.
15 Pyle, op. cit., p. 29.

16 J. W. Dower, *Embracing Defeat: Japan in the Aftermath of World War II*, London: Penguin Books, 1999, pp. 369, 394–8. The original version of Article Nine was drafted by Colonel Charles Kades, head of the Government Section's effort to draw up the Constitution, who believed that Japan should retain a right to limited re-armament 'for preserving its own security'.

17 S. Satō, 'Clarifying the Right of Collective Self-Defense', *Asia–Pacific Review*, 1996; 3(2): 95.

18 The Basic Policy is based on four principles:

(a) to support the activities of the United Nations and promote international cooperation, thereby contributing to the realization of world peace;
(b) to promote the public welfare and enhance the people's love for their country, thereby establishing the sound basis essential to Japan's security;
(c) to develop incrementally the effective defence capabilities necessary for self-defence, in accordance with the nation's resources and the prevailing domestic situation;
(d) to deal with external aggression on the basis of the Japan–US Security Arrangements, pending the effective capability of the United Nations in the future to deter and repel such aggression.

(JDA, *Defense of Japan 2000*, Tokyo: JDA/*Japan Times*, p. 246.)

19 M. J. Green, *Arming Japan: Defense Production, Alliance Politics and the Postwar Search for Autonomy*, New York: Columbia University Press, 1995, p. 42.

20 JDA, *Defense of Japan 1995*, Tokyo: JDA/*Japan Times*, p. 63.

21 Kōsaka, op. cit., p. 798.

22 R. Oga, *Shiirēn no Himitsu*, Tokyo: Shobunsha, 1983, p. 172.

23 J. E. Auer, 'Japan's Maritime Self-Defense Force: An Appropriate Maritime Strategy?', *Naval War College Review*, 1971; 24(4): 12.

24 Katzenstein and Okawara, op. cit, p. 77.

25 G. Friedman and M. Lebard, *The Coming War with Japan*, New York: St Martin's Press, 1991, p. 297.

26 Treaty text quoted from *Defense of Japan 1995*, Tokyo: JDA/*Japan Times*, p. 241 [My emphasis].

27 H. Sekino, 'Japan and Her Maritime Defense', *U.S. Naval Institute Proceedings*, 1971; 97(819): 119.

28 Drifte, op. cit., p. 104.

29 Ibid., p. 103.

30 Interview with Captain Otsuka Umio, MSDF, Agenda Coordinator, Western Pacific Naval Symposium, Plans and Programme Division, Maritime Staff Office, JDA, Tokyo, 1 March 2002.

31 J. E. Auer, *The Postwar Rearmament of Japanese Maritime Forces, 1945–71*, New York: Praeger, 1973, pp. 49–52.

32 Ibid., pp. 63–4.

33 S. Taoka, 'Possible Involvement in Mine Sweeping and Danger of Handling Over Carte Blanche – Pitfalls of US–Japan Guidelines', *Aera*, 23 June 1997, pp. 27–8; FBIS-EAS-97-119, 23 June 1997.

34 Auer, op. cit., p. 80 [My ellipsis].

35 Hoshina attained the rank of Vice Admiral in the Imperial Navy and, under instruction from Naval Minister Yōnai Mitsumasa, at the war's end played a key role in safe-guarding its traditions and technology to pass on to Japan's postwar maritime security institutions. Hoshina was elected to the Diet in 1955 and served four terms, becoming the first chairman of the LDP's national defence division (*Tokyo Shimbun*, 22 June 2004, p. 26).

36 Auer, op. cit., p. 72.

37 Ibid., p. 82.

38 Ibid., pp. 94–5.
39 Ibid., p. 154.
40 During fiscal years 1955–57, defence expenditure averaged 13.3 per cent of government general account outlays. After falling steadily, by fiscal 1977, defence accounted for just under 6 per cent of government expenditure (JDA, *Defense of Japan, 1977*, Tokyo: JDA/*Japan Times*, p. 166).
41 Javed S. Maswood, *Japanese Defence: the Search for Political Power*, Institute of Southeast Asian Studies, Singapore: Allen and Unwin, 1990, p. 31.
42 Auer, op. cit., p. 159.
43 *Waga Kuni ni okeru Bōeiryoku Seibi no Keika* ('Trends in Japan's defence equipment build-up'), 1982, p. 45. This report was commissioned internally within the JDA as an account of history of postwar defence planning.
44 Cited in T. Maeda, *The Hidden Army: The Untold Story of Japan's Military Forces*, Edition Q Inc., Chicago, IL, 1995, p. 231.
45 Auer, op. cit., p. 165.
46 Sekino, op. cit., p. 115.
47 Cited in ibid., p. 111.
48 M. Gotō, 'Japan in Asia', *Japan Quarterly*, 1996; 26(4): 390–1.
49 The importance of individual decision-makers' contribution to Japan's post-war defence policy is one of the central contentions of Katahara Eichi's unpublished doctoral thesis (*The Politics of Japanese Defence Policy Making, 1975–1989*, unpublished PhD thesis, Griffith University, Brisbane, 1990). This applies not only to Nakasone in the 1945–77 period, but to the troika formed by Kubo Takuya, Sakata Michita and Miki Takeo, as explored later in this chapter.
50 *Asahi Shimbun*, 18 May 1969, Daily Summary of the Japanese Press, US Embassy, Tokyo, May 1969 [My emphasis].
51 E. Katahara, *The Politics of Japanese Defence Policy Making, 1975–1989*, unpublished PhD thesis, Griffith University, April 1990, p. 132.
52 O. Kaihara, '*Jissai Mondai to shite Fukanō*' ('Such a Mission is far beyond Japan's Power': On the Sea-Lane Defense Problem in Dispute no. 2), *Sekai no Kansen*, December 1982, p. 130; and Maeda, op. cit., pp. 230–4.
53 J. P. Keddell, *The Politics of Defense in Japan: Managing Internal and External Pressures*, Armonk, NY: M.E. Sharpe, 1994, p. 48.
54 *Mainichi Shimbun*, 21 May 1969, 'To Strengthen Autonomous Defense; Keidanren To Decide at Its General Meeting of 23rd', Daily Summary of the Japanese Press, May 1969.
55 Green, op. cit., pp. 53–9.
56 Maeda, op. cit., p. 142.
57 Gotō, op. cit., pp. 390–1.
58 B. S. Gupta, T. T. Poulose, H. Bhatia, *The Malacca Straits and the Indian Ocean: A Study of the Strategic and Legal Aspects of a Controversial Sea-lane*, New Delhi: Macmillan, 1974, p. 62.
59 Ibid., pp. 42–3.
60 The idea to compare and contrast Sekino and Kaihara is adapted from Auer's *The Postwar Rearmament of Japanese Maritime Forces*, op. cit. The analysis presented here also draws from original material.
61 Sekino, op. cit., pp. 98–121.
62 Ibid., p. 109.
63 Against nuclear threats, Sekino believed the US nuclear umbrella would deter the Soviet Union from attacking Japan, although he also thought that a 'local retaliatory force' might be required to deter China at some point in the future.
64 Ibid., p. 102.
65 Cited in J. E. Auer, 'Japan's Maritime Self-Defense Force', op. cit., p. 9.
66 Sekino, op. cit., pp. 107–8.
67 Ibid., p. 105.

68 Japan's strategic advantage as a natural barrier to passage from the Sea of Japan was equally evident to US Cold War planners who have sought Japanese help in monitoring the Tsushima, Tsugaru and particularly the Sōya straits since the 1960s. Japan began laying acoustic monitoring equipment in the Tsugaru Strait in 1968, while sound surveillance sonar system (SOSUS) sets were also installed in the Tsushima and Sōya Straits (N. Usui, 'Japan Plans to Bolster Already Formidable ASW Capability', *Defense News*, 24 June 1991, p. 14).
69 Ibid., p. 120 [My ellipsis].
70 Ibid., p. 103.
71 Ibid., p. 121.
72 R. Nishijima, 'Participation of Maritime Self-Defense Forces in RIMPAC', *Asia Pacific Community*, 1980; 7: 43–53.
73 O. Kaihara, '*Jissai Mondai to Shite Fukanō*' ('Such a Mission is Far Beyond Japan's Power': On the Sea-Lane Defense Problem in Dispute no. 2), *Sekai no Kansen* December 1982, pp. 129–30; and Auer, *The Postwar Rearmament*, op. cit., pp. 134–9.
74 Kaihara, op. cit., pp. 130–1.
75 Ibid., p. 133.
76 Tokyo's tacit acceptance of the use of Kadena air base for B-52 bombing missions over Indochina after reversion was part of the price for securing the return of Okinawa and the affirmation of the US security guarantee to Japan inherent in the Communiqué.
77 Yaacov Y. I. Vertzberger, *Coastal States, Regional Powers, Superpowers and the Malacca–Singapore Straits*, Institute of East Asian Studies Research Paper, Berkeley: University of California, 1984, p. 64.
78 *Yomiuri Shimbun*, 17 May 1969.
79 Green, *Arming Japan*, op. cit., pp. 59–62.
80 *Asahi Shimbun*, 23 May 1969, 'Finance Ministry Is Guarded Against Possible Increase in Defense Power in Course of Okinawa Reversion Negotiations', Daily Summary of the Japanese Press, US Embassy, Tokyo, May 1969.
81 Katahara, op. cit., p. 133.
82 *Asahi Shimbun*, 28 August 1975, p. 2; and *Nihon Keizai Shimbun*, 5 June 1978, p. 1.
83 Katahara, op. cit., pp. 135–7.
84 JDA, op. cit., p. 57.
85 L. Wells, 'The Sea and Japan's Strategic Interests 1975–1985', unpublished PhD thesis, Johns Hopkins University Xerox University Microfilms, Ann Arbor, MI, 1975, p. 203, n. 15.
86 Interview with Itō Kenichi, Mitsubishi Electric Corp, Tokyo, 8 March 1999.
87 JDA, op. cit., p. 53; and *Defense of Japan 1995*, p. 73.
88 Each flotilla is typically composed of eight escort destroyers equipped with ASW helicopters (N. D. Levin, M. Lorell and A. Alexander, *The Wary Warriors: Future Directions in Japanese Security Policies*, Santa Monica, CA: Rand, 1993, p. 51).
89 *Tokyo Shimbun*, 2 March 1974, Daily Summary of the Japanese Press, March 1974, US Embassy, Tokyo, p. 14.
90 Interview with Itō Kenichi, Mitsubishi Electric Corp, Tokyo, 8 March 1999.
91 JDA, *Waga Kuni ni okeru Bōeiryoku Seibi no Keika*, 1982, p. 88.
92 Interview with Hoshuyama Noboru, former JDA Director, Defense Facilities Administration Agency, Adviser, Kyōei Life Insurance, Tokyo, 11 March 1999.
93 Of all the weapons systems acquired by the SDF after the *Taikō*, the P-3C – approved in December 1978 – demonstrated that a quantum leap in capability could be achieved within the equipment ceilings outlined in 1976. In contrast to the far more limited P-2J, each P-3C could patrol an area equivalent to Shikoku island and monitor all convergence zones under ideal conditions.
94 P. J. Woolley and M. S. Woolley, 'Japan's Sea Lane Defense Revisited', *Strategic Review*, 1996; 24(4): 50.
95 Although the E-2C was designed as a naval platform to give US carrier battle groups an organic AEW capability, the ASDF fought for and gained control over the

programme. This followed the undetected incursion of a defecting Soviet MiG-25, on 6 September 1976, which landed at Hakodate, Hokkaidō, exposing shortcomings in Japan's air defence readiness (JDA, *Defense of Japan 1977*, Tokyo: JDA/Japan Times, pp. 126–40).

96 Of the MSDF's five bases only Maizuru gives direct access to the Sea of Japan.

97 Wells, op. cit., p. 201.

98 JDA, op. cit., p. 14.

99 Ibid., pp. 12–29.

100 Ibid., p. 66.

101 Mihara was replying to a question on Japan's ability to protect shipping in the Malacca Straits, an exercise that the JDA chief stressed was still beyond both the MSDF's constitutional mandate and level of capability ('Japan Shipping Defenseless in Malacca Strait', *The Japan Times*, 16 November 1977, p. 4).

102 Op. cit., pp. 100–1.

103 S. Etō, 'Japanese Perception of National Threats', in Charles Morrison (ed.), *Threats to Security in East Asia–Pacific*, Lexington, MA: Pacific Forum/Lexington Books, 1983, p. 54.

104 T. Sakanaka, *Alternative Force Structure of Japan's Self Defence Force*, unpublished draft provided by the author, June 1977, pp. 30–40.

105 Allowing for crew rotation, repairs and the Soviet priority accorded to protecting the nuclear-powered, ballistic missile submarine (SSBN) fleet, Japan estimated in the late 1970s that only around 20 attack submarines would be assigned to the SLOC interdiction mission in the Western Pacific (Nishijima, op. cit., pp. 49–50).

106 Sakanaka, op. cit., pp. 39–40.

107 D. C. Hellmann, 'Japan and America in East Asia in the Wake of the Cold War', in A. Clesse, T. Inoguchi, E. B. Keehn and J. A. A. Stockwin (eds), *The Vitality of Japan: Sources of National Strength and Weakness*, Oxford: St Antony's Press, 1997, p. 184.

5 Sea lane defence and alliance cooperation, 1977–90

1 Sekai Keizai Jouhou Service, *Japanese–American Relations and Comprehensive Security*, Tokyo: Research Institute for Peace and Security, 1986, p. 15; and A. Watanabe (ed.), *Sengo Nihon no Shushōtachi* (Japan's Postwar Prime Ministers), Tokyo: Chuo Kōronsha, 1995, p. 327.

2 R. Komer, *Maritime Strategy or Coalition Defense?*, Lanham, MD: University Press of America/Abt Books, 1984, p. 16.

3 J. E. Auer, 'Japan's Maritime Self-Defense Force: An Appropriate Maritime Strategy?', *Naval War College Review*, 1971; 24(4): 16.

4 'An Interview with CINCPAC, Admiral Robert L. J. Long', *Sea Power*, 1983; 26(8).

5 Geoffrey Jukes, *Russia's Military and the Northern Territories Issue*, SDSC Working Paper no. 227, Strategic and Defence Studies Centre, Canberra: Australian National University, 1993, pp. 7–9.

6 The Soviet Pacific Fleet was assigned responsibility for 35 per cent of the Soviet strategic submarine force and the second most important strategic mission in the Soviet Navy. However, the Pacific Fleet acquired new models only 2–3 years after these had been introduced into the Northern Fleet. (Interview with Capt. Nakanishi Kenji, Research Department, Maritime Staff College, 4 March 2002.)

7 From the 1960s onwards, US carrier battle groups transiting the Pacific were regularly intercepted by pairs of Tu-95 bombers, in an area referred to as the 'Bear Box', extending approximately 1,000 nm east of Japan.

8 CINCPAC Admiral Robert L. J. Long, Address to the Navy League, 28 October 1982, USIS Official Text, 3 December 1982.

9 Cited in 'An Interview with CINCPAC, Admiral Robert L. J. Long', op. cit.

10 Statement by Commander-in-Chief, Pacific Admiral Maurice Weisner, *Asahi Shimbun*, 28 August 1978.

11 H. Lee, 'US Stresses Allies Roles in Sea Lane Security', *USICA Backgrounder*, 9 November 1982 [My ellipsis].
12 Fred Ikle, US Under-Secretary of Defense for Policy; statement before the Senate Foreign Relations Committee, 10 June 1982; USICA Official Text, 15 June 1982.
13 Report of the Secretary of Defense to the Congress FY 1983 Budget, 8 February 1982, II-30.
14 Quoted in B. Sen Gupta, T. T. Poulose and H. Bhatia, *The Malacca Straits and the Indian Ocean: A Study of the Strategic and Legal Aspects of a Controversial Sea-lane*, New Delhi: Macmillan, 1974, pp. 63–4.
15 *Asahi Shimbun*, 27 August 1975.
16 *Asahi Shimbun*, 2 April 1975, p. 3 [My ellipsis].
17 *Yomiuri Shimbun*, 29 August 1975.
18 *Asahi Shimbun*, 24 August 1975.
19 *Mainichi Shimbun*, 27 August 1975, p. 1.
20 J. Tsunoda 'Japanese Security Problems and Perspectives in the Late 1970s', *Orbis*, 1975; 24(3): 884–5.
21 *Asahi Shimbun*, 29 August 1975.
22 *Yomiuri Shimbun*, 2 April 1975.
23 *Yomiuri Shimbun*, 3 April 1975, p. 2.
24 *Tokyo Shimbun*, 16 November 1978, p. 2.
25 *Yomiuri Shimbun*, 16 November 1978, p. 2.
26 *Nihon Keizai Shimbun*, 3 July 1978.
27 *Yomiuri Shimbun*, 2 July 1978.
28 R. Nishijima, 'Participation of Maritime Self-Defense Forces in RIMPAC', *Asia Pacific Community*, 1980; 7: 46–7.
29 T. Maeda, *The Hidden Army: The Untold Story of Japan's Military Forces*, Chicago, IL: Edition Q, Inc., 1995, p. 234.
30 Testimony of Admiral James L. Holloway before the US Congress, Hearings before the Senate Foreign Relations Committee, East–West Relations: Focus on the Pacific, 97th Congress, 2nd Session, 16 June 1982, pp. 53–4.
31 Komer, op. cit., p. 87.
32 H. C. Hinton, 'The United States and Extended Security Commitments: East Asia', *The Annals of the American Academy of Political and Social Science*, 1981; 457: 99.
33 P. Keal, *Japan's Role in United States Strategy in the Pacific*, Working Paper no. 106, Strategic and Defence Studies Centre, Canberra: Australian National University, 1986.
34 J. F. Lehman Jr, *Command of the Sea*, New York: Charles Scribner's Sons, 1988, p. 404.
35 See, for example, Michael Armacost's account of US attempts to sell the AWACs aircraft to Japan: *Friends or Rivals? The Insider's Account of U.S.–Japan Relations*, New York: Columbia University Press, 1996, p. 89.
36 'Japan's Budget for Arms Seen as Inadequate', *New York Times*, 31 December 1980, p. 1.
37 Interview with Ambassador Okazaki Hisahiko, Okazaki Institute, Tokyo, 12 March 1999.
38 *Asahi Shimbun*, 5 October 1980, p. 2 [My ellipsis].
39 R. Armitage and K. D. Jackson, 'U.S. Strategic Interests in East Asia and the Pacific', *Asian Pacific Defense Forum*, 1988; 12(4): 39–40.
40 Sekai Keizai Jouhou Service, op. cit., p. 11.
41 N. Agawa, *Umi no Yūjō*, Tokyo: Chuō Kōronsha, 2001, pp. 210–20.
42 Sekai Keizai Jouhou Service, op. cit., p. 17.
43 Agawa, op. cit., pp. 217–18.
44 L. Niksch, 'Defence Burden-Sharing in the Pacific: US Expectations and Japanese Responses', *Asian Affairs*, 1981: July/August: 333–4.
45 Interview with Ambassador Okazaki Hisahiko, Okazaki Institute, Tokyo, 12 March 1999.

46 Agawa, op. cit., pp. 220–5.
47 Yoshida would become MSDF Chief of Staff in the 1990s.
48 Nishijima, op. cit., pp. 43–53.
49 Interview with Ambassador Okazaki Hisahiko, Okazaki Institute, Tokyo, 12 March 1999. JDA Director General Omura Jōji stated before a Diet committee in 1980 that the Soviet military build-up constituted a 'latent threat' (T. Matsumae, *The Limits of Defense: Japan as an Unsinkable Aircraft-Carrier*, Tōkai University Press, 1988, pp. 125–6).
50 'LDP, DSP Agree Japan Needs Improved Defense Capabilities', *The Japan Times*, 25 October 1980, p. 1.
51 'SDF Could Legally Protect Sea Lanes, Ships if Capable: Suzuki', *The Japan Times*, 11 November 1980, p. 1.
52 Sekai Keizai Jouhou Service, op. cit., pp. 11–12.
53 E. Katahara, *The Politics of Japanese Defence Policy Making, 1975–1989*, unpublished PhD thesis, Griffith University, April 1990, p. 215.
54 Commander US Forces, Japan, Charles Donnelly, quoted by Lee, op. cit.
55 Sekai Keizai Jouhou Service, op. cit., p. 15.
56 P. Woolley, *Japan's Navy: Politics and Paradox, 1971–2000*, Boulder, CO: Lynne Reiner, 2000, p. 70; and A. George, *The Nakasone Challenge: Historical Constraints and New Initiatives in Japan's Defence Policy*, Legislative Research Service, The Parliament of the Commonwealth of Australia, Discussion Paper no. 2, 1987, p. 11.
57 Report of the Secretary of Defense to the Congress FY 1983 Budget, 8 February 1982, II-30.
58 J. P. Keddell, *The Politics of Defense in Japan: Managing Internal and External Pressures*, Armonk, New York: M.E. Sharpe, 1994, p. 68.
59 Comprehensive National Security Study Group, *Report on Comprehensive National Security*, Japanese government translation, GE:118489, 2 July 1980, p. 7.
60 The party only endorsed the development of a 'water's edge' anti-invasion capability for the SDF (Keddell, op. cit., pp. 15–18, 92–100).
61 Deng Xiaoping's pragmatic acceptance of the Security Treaty as part of China's normalization with Japan further undercut the Socialists' position (J. E. Dornan and D. S. Dornan, 'Japan: Domestic Factors', in J. M. Roherty (ed.), *Defense Policy Formation: Towards Comparative Analysis*, University of South California, 1980, pp. 203–18.
62 Interview with Ambassador Okazaki Hisahiko, Okazaki Institute, Tokyo, 12 March 1999.
63 S. Nishimura, *Transformation of the U.S.–Japan Defense Posture: The New Soviet Challenge*, International Institute for Global Peace (IIGP) Policy Paper 65E, Tokyo: International Institute for Global Peace, October 1991.
64 See, for example, Summaries of Selected Japanese Magazines 1985, American Embassy, Tokyo, Political Section Office of Translation Services; Maruyama Hiroyuki, *Shokun*, 'Be Guarded Against Soviet Pacific Fleet', November 1985, pp. 41–3; and Nakamura Kenichi, 'Extrication from Soviet Threat Argument', *Sekai*, April 1985, pp. 20–6.
65 Chapman *et al.*, op. cit., p. 69; and Matsumae, op. cit., p. 108.
66 R. Oga, *Shiirēn no Himitsu*, Tokyo: Shobunsha, 1983, pp. 164–204.
67 Ryōhei Oga graduated from military training November 1942 and participated in the Japanese withdrawal from the Aleutian island of Kiska before retraining and serving out the remainder of the war as a submariner. In August 1945, his mother and sister were both killed at Nagasaki. In 1950, he commanded an MSA minesweeping unit sent to Korean waters.
68 Agawa, op. cit., p. 216.
69 See, for example, H. Asanuma, 'Jōhō no Tōtaru Shisutemu ga Fukaketsu' ('Total System of Intelligence is Indispensable'), On the Sea-Lane Defense Problem in Dispute no. 1, *Sekai no Kansen*, December 1982, pp. 126–9.

70 Oga, op. cit., p. 171.
71 K. Uchida, 'Naval Competition and Security in East Asia', in Jonathan Alford (ed.), *Sea Power and Influence: Old Issues and New Challenges*, Farnborough: International Institute for Strategic Studies, 1980, p. 107.
72 JDA, *Defense of Japan 1983*, Tokyo: JDA/*Japan Times*, Tokyo, 1983, pp. 73–7.
73 'The 1983 Japanese White Paper: An Assessment', *Asian Defence Journal*, December 1983, p. 54.
74 O. Kaihara, '*Jissai Mondai to shite Fukanō*' ('Such a Mission is Far Beyond Japan's Power'), On the Sea-Lane Defense Problem in Dispute no. 2, *Sekai no Kansen*, December 1982, pp. 130–3; and 'U.S. and Japan: Defense Tensions', *Wall Street Journal*, 12 January 1982, p. 28.
75 'Shiirēn: Nichibei Kyōdō Kenkyū', *Yomiuri Shimbun*, 6 January 1987, p. 1.
76 This assumed that the Soviet Union would commit around 200 surface combatants, 40 submarines and 950 aircraft (including 150 *Backfire* bombers) and the equivalent of two to three air and seaborne divisions. SDF forces available in 1986 included 14 submarines, 53 destroyers and 79 fixed-wing ASW aircraft and 280 ASDF combat aircraft ('Study Predicts Soviets Could Seize Sea-Lanes', *The Daily Yomiuri*, 6 January 1987, p. 1).
77 See also Matsumae Tatsurō, op. cit., pp. 139–40.
78 'Rearming Japan', *Christian Science Monitor*, 4 April 1983, pp. 13–15.
79 George, op. cit., pp. 24–6.
80 'Japan's Choice: A Strategy for World Peace and Prosperity': Nakasone's Speech at the International Institute for Strategic Studies, 11 June 1984, Press Release no. 1149, Embassy of Japan, Canberra, 18 June 1984. See also Norman D. Levin, *Japan's Changing Defense Posture*, Rand Note N-2739-OSD, June 1988, pp. 21–3.
81 'Shouldering Arms – and a Bigger Budget Burden', *Far Eastern Economic Review*, 3 February 1983, p. 46 [My ellipses]. Nakasone's interview is intriguing not only in that he referred to the Strait of Taiwan rather than the Bashi channel as the southern extent of Japan's sea lane defence area, but he also specified four straits to be defended within Japan's immediate environs. In addition to Sōya, Tsugarū and Tsushima, Nakasone was probably referring to the Osumi strait near Shimonseki, separating Kyūshū and southern Honshū.
82 'Policy Speech by Prime Minister Yasuhiro Nakasone to the 98th session of the National Diet', 24 January 1983, Press Release no. 1122, Embassy of Japan, Canberra, p. 8.
83 S. Satō, 'Clarifying the Right of Collective Self-Defense', *Asia–Pacific Review*, 1996; 3(2): 91–107.
84 T. Akaha, 'Japan's Response to Threats of Shipping Disruptions in Southeast Asia and the Middle East', *Pacific Affairs*, 1986; 59(2): 270–1.
85 Interview with Capt. Nakanishi Kenji, Research Department, Maritime Staff College, 4 March 2002.
86 K. Chūma, 'The 1986–90 Defense Plan: Does It Go Too Far?', *Japan Quarterly*, 1986; 33(1): 13–18.
87 JDA, 'The Mid-term Defense Program (FY 1986–1990)', *Defense Bulletin*, 1985; 9(1), Public Information Division.
88 JDA, *Defense of Japan 1985*, Tokyo: JDA/*Japan Times*, p. 149.
89 Interview with Capt. Nakanishi Kenji, Research Department, Maritime Staff College, 4 March 2002.
90 M. J. Green, 'Despite Aegis, Japan Still Will Depend on U.S. Navy', *Defense News*, 13 August 1990, p. 8.
91 Acquisition of F-15s was one area where the MTDP fell short of its procurement targets: a total of 187 aircraft was not acquired until the 1991–95 MTDP.
92 A 1989 article by Japan's defence attaché to Washington, Matsukane Hisamoto, reveals the extent to which sea lane defence served as a rationale to justify the force

structure and operational concepts of all three Self Defense Forces (SDFs); 'Japan and Security of the Sea Lanes', *Global Affairs*, 1989; Spring: 61–3.

93 Keddell, op. cit., p. 127.

94 Katahara, op. cit., pp. 280–2.

95 Keddell, op. cit., pp. 100, 131.

96 S. J. Maswood, *Japanese Defence: The Search for Political Power*, Institute of Southeast Asian Studies, Singapore: Allen and Unwin, 1990, pp. 46–7.

97 The respective figures are 1.013 per cent of GNP and 6.51 per cent of the general account (Keddell, op. cit., p. 149).

98 Levin *et al.*, op. cit., p. 53; and N. Usui, 'Japanese Navy Stresses Updates ASW Capability', *Defense News*, 9 September 1991, p. 9.

99 Armacost, op. cit., pp. 88–90; and interview with Adm. Kawamura Sumihiko, Okazaki Institute, March 1999.

100 *Yomiuri Shimbun*, 8 October 1980, p. 1.

101 Akaha, op. cit., pp. 255–77.

102 Globalsecurity.org, 'Operation Earnest Will', Global Security.org. Online. Available www.globalsecurity.org/military/ops/earnest_will.htm (accessed 17 October 2004).

103 'Iran attacks Japanese-leased oil-tankers', *The Japan Times*, 19 September 1987, p. 1.

104 Interview with Japan's former ambassador to Washington, Murata Ryōhei, Nippon Foundation, Tokyo, 6 March 2002; and S. Sudo, *Southeast Asia in Japanese Security Policy*, Singapore: Institute of Southeast Asian Studies, 1991, p. 39.

6 Japan's sea lane diplomacy in Southeast Asia since the 1970s

1 Comprehensive National Security Study Group, *Report on Comprehensive National Security*, Japanese government translation, GE:118489, 2 July 1980, p. 54.

2 MOFA, Japan, 'Strategy and Approaches of Japan's Energy Diplomacy', December 2002. Online. Available www.mofa.go.jp/policy/energy/diplomacy.html (accessed 8 March 2003).

3 See, for example, J. L. Batongbacal, 'Archipelagic Sealanes and Transit Passage Through Straits: Shared Responsibilities Is [*sic*] Essential to Implementation', paper presented at the Thirteenth International Conference on Sea Lines of Communications, Canberra, April 2001, p. 6.

4 T. Akaha, *Japan in Global Ocean Politics*, Honolulu: University of Hawaii Press and Law of the Sea Institute, 1985, pp. 77–9.

5 See, for example, local press coverage of JDA Director General Kawara Tsutomu's 1988 visit to Indonesia: 'Kawara Ends his Indonesia Trip Satisfactorily', *Jakarta Post*, 2 July 1988, p. 1; and JDA Director General Mihara Asao's 1977 testimony before the House of Councillors Cabinet Committee 'Japan Shipping Defenseless in Malacca Strait', *The Japan Times*, 16 November 1977, p. 4.

6 C. Kamchoo, 'Japan's Role in South-east Asian Security: *Plus ça Change*', *Pacific Affairs*, 1991; 64: 9–10.

7 Japan's ODA programme has laid special emphasis on building up the infrastructure of local economies through an allocation to public-works projects double the average of developed country donors.

8 MOFA, Japan, *Diplomatic Bluebook 1998*, Tokyo: Urban Connections, 1998, p. 97.

9 S. Chan, 'Humanitarianism, Mercantilism, or Comprehensive Security? Disbursement Patterns of Japanese Foreign Aid', *Asian Affairs*, 1992; 19(1): 10–14.

10 D. Kruger and M. Hiebert, 'Battered but Still on Top', *Far Eastern Economic Review*, 24 January 2002, pp. 24–5.

11 R. Cronin, 'Japan's Expanding Role and Influence in the Asia Pacific Region: Implications for US Interests', *Current Politics and Economics of Japan*, 1993; 3(2/3): 121.

12 National Institute for Defense Studies, 'Southeast Asia: Toward a New Unity', Tokyo: National Institute for Defense Studies, *East Asian Strategic Review 2003*, 2003, pp. 205–30.
13 See Prime Minister Koizumi Junichirō's speech delivered in Singapore, 14 January 2002: 'Japan and ASEAN in East Asia – A Sincere and Open Partnership'; MOFA, Japan. Online. Available www.mofa.go.jp/region/asia-paci/pmv0201/speech.html (accessed 8 March 2003).
14 Marisec.org., 'Shipping and World Trade'. Online. Available www.marisec.org/shippingfacts/safenregconventions.htm (accessed 30 October 2004).
15 M. Leifer, *International Straits of the World: Malacca, Singapore and Indonesia*, The Netherlands: Sijthoff and Noordhoff, 1978, p. 175.
16 G. L. Curtis (ed.), *Japan's Foreign Policy: After the Cold War: Coping with Change*, Armonk, New York: M.E. Sharpe, 1993, pp. 4–5.
17 Akaha, op. cit., p. 116.
18 T. Iguchi, 'Emerging Ocean Regime for International Security Cooperation', *Ocean Governance and OPK: The Thirteenth International Symposium Proceedings*, Tokyo: National Institute for Defense Studies, 1998, p. 4.
19 K. Uchida, 'Naval Competition and Security in East Asia', in J. Alford (ed.), *Sea Power and Influence: Old Issues and New Challenges*, Farnborough: International Institute for Strategic Studies, 1980, pp. 105–6.
20 M. Yamamoto, 'Sealane in the Asia–Pacific Region Today and their Vulnerabilities', paper presented to the Eleventh International Conference on the Sea Lanes of Communication (SLOC) Studies, Tokyo, 17–18 November 1997, pp. 1–6.
21 Interview with Masahiro Akiyama, Chairman, Ship and Ocean Foundation, Nippon Foundation, Tokyo, 4 March 2002.
22 D. P. Djalal, *The Geopolitics of Indonesia's Maritime Territorial Policy*, Jakarta: Centre for Strategic and International Studies, 1996, pp. 115–24.
23 K. L. Koh, *Straits in International Navigation: Contemporary Issues*, London: Oceana Publications, 1982, pp. 56–8.
24 J. Morgan, 'Strait and Narrow', *Far Eastern Economic Review*, 4 December 1971, p. 46.
25 Koh, op. cit., p. 77.
26 Current contributors include oil firms, marine insurers, the JSA and individual shipping companies such as 'K'-line. (Interview with Capt. Osuka Yoshihiro, Assistant General Manager, Marine Safety and Environmental Team, 'K'-line, 28 February 2002.)
27 Leifer, op cit., 1978, p. 40.
28 Djalal, op. cit., p. 116.
29 Koh, op. cit., p. 60.
30 Hasjim Djalal notes that Japan has employed a similar tactic of using private organizations to conclude bilateral fisheries agreements with Indonesia over access to the Banda Sea (*Indonesia and the Law of the Sea*, Jakarta: Centre for Strategic and International Studies, 1995, p. 154).
31 Leifer, op cit., pp. 42–3.
32 B. Sen Gupta, T. T. Poulose and H. Bhatia, *The Malacca Straits and the Indian Ocean: A Study of the Strategic and Legal Aspects of a Controversial Sea-lane*, New Delhi: Macmillan, 1974, pp. 58–9.
33 Leifer, op. cit., p. 45.
34 Morgan, op. cit., p. 46.
35 Sen Gupta *et al.*, op. cit., p. 57.
36 'What's in it for Them?', *Far Eastern Economic Review*, 11 December 1971, p. 2.
37 Cited in Koh, op. cit., p. 61.
38 Ibid., p. 62 [My ellipsis].
39 In a contemporary essay, Hasjim Djalal wrote that 'the right to be compensated for works undertaken to facilitate passage' should not be confused with an intention by

Indonesia to establish tolls (*Indonesia and the Law of the Sea*, Jakarta: Centre for Strategic and International Studies, 1995, p. 327).

40 'What's in it for Them?', op. cit., p. 2.

41 According to Hasjim Djalal, 'cooperation between the three states and Japan . . . has been very successful, although it is not clear whether it is well-known outside Japan and the three coastal states' [My ellipsis] (*Indonesia and the Law of the Sea*, Jakarta: Centre for Strategic and International Studies, 1995, pp. 360–1).

42 Koh, op. cit., p. 77.

43 Djalal, *The Geopolitics*, op. cit., p. 129.

44 Koh, op. cit., pp. 80–3.

45 In an effort to improve safety standards for ships, after 1978 Japan granted 'scrap-and-build' subsidies to domestic shipbuilders to encourage the modernization of its tanker fleet.

46 As noted in Chapter 1, 'K'-line is among those shipping firms that have sought to negotiate a 0.5 m reduction to the under-keel clearance limit. (Interview with Capt. Osuka Yoshihiro, Assistant General Manager, Marine Safety and Environmental Team, 'K'-line, 28 February 2002.)

47 Singapore's recommended underkeel clearance was 2.5 m less than Indonesia's estimated minimum clearance, despite the fact that the Singapore Strait is statistically the most dangerous waterway in the Straits of Malacca. Some commentators have speculated that Indonesia was attempting to further its development agenda by making it more economical for large tankers to divert via Lombok, where Jakarta had plans to construct oil storage and docking facilities (Koh, op. cit., pp. 85–95).

48 Ouchi, op. cit., p. 4.

49 *Far Eastern Economic Review*, 26 February 1973, pp. 14–15.

50 A. Ono, 'Japan's Contribution to Safety and Pollution Mitigation in the Straits of Malacca', in Hamzah (ed.), *The Straits of Malacca: International Co-operation in Trade, Funding and Navigational Safety*, Kuala Lumpur: Maritime Institute of Malaysia/Pelanduk Publications, 1997, pp. 241–6.

51 JSA, Annual Report 2002: 'Measures for Safe Passage through the Malacca-Singapore Straits'. Online. Available www.jsanet.or.jp/e/annualr-e/pdf/j_shipping2002.pdf (accessed 30 October 2004).

52 Teh Kong Leong, 'The Revolving Fund – a Unique Facility', paper given at the 'International Conference on the Strait of Malacca: Meeting the Challenges of 21st Century', Malaysian Institute of Maritime Affairs, Kuala Lumpur, 14–15 June, 1994, p. 2.

53 Chia Lin Sien, 'The Strait of Malacca as a Tanker Pipeline: Some Considerations for Northeast Asian Users', paper given at the International Conference on the Strait of Malacca: Meeting the Challenges of 21st Century, Malaysian Institute of Maritime Affairs, Kuala Lumpur, 14–15 June 1994, pp. 14–17.

54 The Singapore Conference on the Straits of Malacca and Singapore – Issues, Perspectives and Post-Conference Developments. Online. Available www.sils.org/seminar/1996-straits-overview.htm (accessed 19 April 2000).

55 Ono, op. cit., p. 242.

56 Koh, op. cit., pp. 90–1.

57 In October 1990, shipping radars were installed in the Singapore Strait, with data feeding into the vessel traffic information system.

58 Ono, op. cit., pp. 242–3.

59 JSA, Annual Report 2002: 'Measures for Safe Passage through the Malacca-Singapore Straits'. Online. Available www.jsanet.or.jp/e/annualr-e/pdf/j_shipping2002.pdf (accessed 30 October 2004).

60 *Tokyo Shimbun*, 31 May 2004.

61 Akaha, op. cit., pp. 119–23.

62 Quoted in ibid., p. 127 [My ellipsis].

63 'Shipping in South-east Asia: Going for the Jugular', *The Economist*, 12 June 2004, pp. 54–61.
64 R. Swinnerton, 'A Description of Regional Shipping Routes: Navigational and Operational Considerations', *Maritime Studies*, 1996; 87: 10–22.
65 'Kra Canal Project'. Online. Available www.kracanal.or.th/problemeng1. htm (accessed 4 March 2001).
66 'The Kra Canal: Thailand's $25 billion question', *Asia Times*. Online. Available www.atimes.com/editor/A10Ba01.html (accessed 15 September 2002).
67 Supradit Kanwanich, 'Kra Canal Project: To dig or not to dig' *Bangkok Post*, 23 January 2000.
68 Y. I. Vertzberger, *Coastal States, Regional Powers, Superpowers and the Malacca-Singapore Straits*, Institute of East Asian Studies Research Paper, Berkeley: University of California, 1984, pp. 78–82.
69 'Hong Kong Firm Gets Study Deal', *Bangkok Post*, 21 January 2003. Online. Available www.bangkokpost.com/210103_News/21Jan2003_news06.html (accessed 5 August 2003).
70 Djalal, *The Geopolitics*, op. cit., p. 102.
71 Ibid., p. 29.
72 Maj. Gen. Subijakto, 'Indonesia's Perception of SLOC in Southeast Asia', *Journal of the Australian Naval Institute*, November 1989, pp. 27–31.
73 Minister of Foreign Affairs Press Release Concerning Indonesia's Archipelagic Sea Lanes, no. 28/PR/VI/98, 15 June 1998. Online. Available www.deplu.go.id/english2/pr28-98.htm (accessed 10 June 1999).
74 According to Hasjim Djalal, 'The sad history of our people during the colonial domination had indicated to us that whenever the waters between the islands were regarded as a separating factor, the whole Indonesian nation disintegrated. In fact, this was used as a means by previous dominating powers to subdue the nation. We have learned the lesson that the unity of Indonesia as a nation can only be preserved by the archipelagic concept' (*Indonesia and the Law of the Sea*, op. cit., p. 318).
75 Chia Lin Sien, in Hamzah (ed.), op. cit., p. 104.
76 Djalal, *Indonesia and the Law of the Sea*, op. cit. pp. 326–7.
77 D. Coulter, 'The Economics of SLOC Protection; an Overvalued Mission', Eleventh International Conference on the Sea Lanes of Communication (SLOC) Studies, Tokyo, 17–18 November, 1997, p. 4.
78 Djalal, *Indonesia and the Law of the Sea*, op. cit., pp. 360–1.
79 J. McBeth, 'Troubled Waters', *Far Eastern Economic Review*, 29 December 1994 and 5 January 1995, p. 18.
80 *Defender* 1988/89; 5(4); and N. Chanda, 'Troubled Waters', *Far Eastern Economic Review*, 10 November 1988, p. 18.
81 Djalal, *The Geopolitics*, op. cit., p. 130.
82 Interview with Umemoto Kazuyoshi, Director, First International Organizations Division, Economic Affairs Bureau, MOFA, February 1999.
83 Interview with Capt. Osuka Yoshihiro, Assistant General Manager, Marine Safety and Environmental Team, 'K'-line.
84 International Maritime Organisation, Maritime Safety Committee, MSC 67/7/2, 67th Session, 30 August 1996.
85 F. Chan, 'Jakarta to Open Three Sea Lanes for International Passage', *Shipping News*, 17 June 1998.
86 'Water of Strife', *Far Eastern Economic Review*, 29 February 1996, p. 30.
87 Swinnerton, op. cit., p. 21.
88 Djalal, *Indonesia and the Law of the Sea*, op. cit., pp. 239–40.
89 R. Skelton, 'Jakarta shipping plan sparks anger', *Sydney Morning Herald*, 5 June 1996, p. 15.

90 K. Ouchi, 'Making the Straits Safer: A User's View of Alternative Routes', paper given at the International Conference on the Strait of Malacca: Meeting the Challenges of the 21st Century, Malaysian Institute of Maritime Affairs, 14–15 June 1994.
91 'Jakarta Challenges US Warship', *The Australian*, 29 October 2000, p. 7.
92 'Indonesian Navy Fires at Dredgers off Singapore', *Reuters News Service*, 1 June 2002.
93 This includes the government of South Korea, which expressed its concern to Tokyo in July 1999 that MOX fuel might be delivered to Japanese ports via the Korea [Tsushima] Strait ('ROK Expresses Concern Over Plutonium Shipment', *Yonhap News Agency*, 12 July 1999).
94 See, for example, Ji Guoxing, 'SLOC Security in the Asia Pacific', Center Occasional Paper, Asia–Pacific Center for Security Studies, Honolulu, February 2000. Online. Available www.apcss.org/Paper_SLOC_Occasional.htm (accessed 12 July 2001).
95 Subsequent shipments have been transported aboard purpose-built PNTL vessels including the *Pacific Swan* (1979), the *Pacific Teal* (1982) and the *Pacific Pintail* (1987). These vessels incorporate such safety features as double hulling, twin engines, radiation-monitoring systems, fire-fighting systems and advanced navigation and communication equipment, in accordance with IMO and International Atomic Energy Agency standards. They are also armed with naval guns and manned by a UK-trained security crew.
96 Interview with Lt. Gen. Shikata Toshiyuki, Tokyo, 7 March 1999.
97 G. Hewison, 'Shipping and Regional Security', in S. Bateman (ed.), *Maritime Cooperation in the Asia–Pacific Region: Current Situation and Prospects*, Canberra Papers on Strategy and Defence, no. 132, Canberra: Australian National University Press, 1999, pp. 145–6.
98 The MOX shipments have also received a Japan Coast Guard (JCG) surface escort (*Sekai Nippō*, '*Shiirēn: Nihon Yūji no Shinario*', 25 February, 1999, p. 1).
99 While Article 26(2) makes provision for 'payment only for specific services rendered to the ship', Article 26(1) states that 'No charge may be levied upon foreign ships by reason only of their passage through the territorial seas'.

7 Japan's post-Cold War SLOC security: piracy and terrorism at sea

1 Fleet Air Force P-3Cs conduct patrols under the coordination of ASW operation centres at Hachinohe, Atsugi, Kanoya and Naha (N. Usui, 'Japanese Navy Stresses Updates ASW Capability', *Defense News*, 9 September 1991, p. 6).
2 N. D. Levin, M. Lorell and A. Alexander, *The Wary Warriors: Future Directions in Japanese Security Policies*, Santa Monica: Rand, 1993, pp. 62–3.
3 L. Peng, 'Japan and the Spratlys Dispute: Aspirations and Limitations', *Asian Survey*, 1996; 36: 1009 n.
4 A. Stephens, 'Japanese Aerospace Power', *Asia–Pacific Defence Reporter*, January 2000, p. 17.
5 Levin *et al.*, op. cit., pp. 49–56.
6 JDA, *Defense of Japan 2000*, Tokyo: JDA/*Japan Times*, p. 345.
7 Ibid., p. 78.
8 *Shiirēn bōei to kaikyō fūsa* ['Sealane defence and straits blockade'], *Seiron*, July 1983, pp. 66–7; and interview with Adm. Sakonjo Naotoshi, MSDF (Retd), Research Institute for Peace and Security, Tokyo, 12 February 1999.
9 JDA, *Defense of Japan 1995*, Tokyo: JDA/*Japan Times*, pp. 45–9.
10 See, for example, Satō Seizaburō, 'Security in the Asia–Pacific Region: Threats, Risks and Opportunities, *Asia–Pacific Review*, 1994; 1(1); and S. Nishimura, *Transformation of the U.S.–Japan Defense Posture: The New Soviet Challenge*, Tokyo: International Institute for Global Peace (IIGP) Policy Paper 65E, October 1991.

11 C. Purrington, 'Tokyo's Policy Response During the Gulf War', *Pacific Affairs*, 1992; 65: 167.
12 I. Gow, 'Civil–Military Relations in Contemporary Japan – Civilian Control of Whose Military?', *The Japan Society*, 2001; 136: 9.
13 The 1991 dispatch of MSDF minesweepers to the Gulf was supported by the Keidanren, the Japan Oil League, the JSA, the Japan Seamen's Union and the Arabia Oil Company (Purrington, op. cit., p. 172).
14 'Japan's Role in the International Community' (Draft Report), February 1992, *Japan Echo*, Summer 1992, pp. 49–58.
15 The five 'Basic Guidelines' adopted as part of the 1993 PKO Law set out as a precondition for Japan's participation in UN peacekeeping: (1) a cease-fire in place; (2) the consent of all parties to Japan's participation; (3) strict impartiality on the part of the peace-keeping force; (4) the ability of Japan to withdraw its contingent; and (5) restrictions on the use of weapons to the 'minimum necessary' (JDA, *Defense of Japan 1995*, Tokyo: JDA/*Japan Times*, p. 99).
16 N. Usui, 'Hosokawa Accelerates Review', *Defense News*, 10–16 January 1994, p. 4.
17 JDA, op. cit., p. 143; and M. Mochizuki, *Japan: Domestic Change and Foreign Policy*, Santa Monica, CA: National Defense Research Institute/RAND, 1995, p. 72.
18 N. Usui, 'Japanese will Follow U.N. Action on Korea', *Defense News*, 25 April–1 May 1994, p. 18; and 'Japan to seek broader regional power', *Defense News*, 9–15 May 1994, pp. 4, 44.
19 Advisory Group on Defense Issues, *The Modality of the Security and Defense Capability of Japan*, Japanese government translation, GM:3338-, 12 August 1994, pp. 7–10, 17–18.
20 As of June 2000, Japan had institutionalized security and/or defence consultations with the following states and organizations: NATO, France, Germany, the United Kingdom, China, Russia, South Korea, Indonesia, Malaysia, Singapore, Thailand, Australia and Canada. JDA officials have also held regular defence talks with the Philippines and Vietnam since 1999, and India since 2000 (JDA, *Defense of Japan 2000*, Tokyo: JDA/*Japan Times*, pp. 177–8).
21 Advisory Group on Defense Issues, op. cit., p. 18.
22 Ibid., p. 22.
23 A. Lim, 'Japanese Peacekeeping Operations', *Military Review*, April 1994.
24 The SPY-1 radar at the heart of the Aegis system is capable of tracking and targeting up to 100 aerial targets simultaneously; the MSDF DDG *Myōko* tracked the North Korean *Taepodong* missile launch over Japan in August 1998 from the Sea of Japan. Similarly, the March 1996 Chinese short-range ballistic missile tests in the Taiwan Strait were tracked by the US Navy DDG USS *Bunker Hill* (Y. Funabashi, *Alliance Adrift*, Council on Foreign Relations, New York, 1999, p. 360; and *Bungei Shunjū*, November 1998, pp. 150–7).
25 N. Usui, 'Japan's Sub Upgrade Proceeds Despite Cuts', *Defense News*, 23–29 January 1995, p. 6.
26 'MSDF seeking to use its submarine capability after Cold War', *Asahi Shimbun*, 19 March 2004.
27 Article by Rear Admiral Yamazaki Makoto, Director, Logistics Department, Maritime Staff Office, *Gekkan Jadi*, November 1996, pp. 7–17 (FBIS-JST-97-001, 14 January 1997); and D. Lague, 'We All Live for Another Submarine', *Far Eastern Economic Review*, 15 August 2002, p. 14.
28 Two of the satellites are optical and two will use radar imagery, both with a reported optimal resolution of one metre. The first pair was initially deployed to concentrate on North Korea and the Middle East, with a second pair scheduled for launch in August. However, a failed second launch has since held up the programme (*Daily Yomiuri*, 4 March 2003. Online. Available www.yomiuri.co.jp/newse/20030304wo41.htm (accessed 4 March 2003); and *Daily Yomiuri*, 6 March 2003.

Online. Available www.yomiuri.co.jp/newse/20030304wo71.htm (accessed 6 March 2003).

29 'Defense Reduction in Dispute', *Daily Yomiuri Online*, 26 October 2004. Online. Available www.yomiuri.co.jp/index-e.htm (accessed 26 October 2004).

30 For an in-depth consideration of Japan's involvement in BMD see C. W. Hughes, Japan's Re-emergence as a 'Normal' Military Power, International Institute of Strategic Studies Adelphi Paper 368–9, Oxford: International Institute of Strategic Studies/Oxford University Press, 2004, pp. 108–14.

31 'Panel Proposes Cutbacks in Destroyers, Tanks; 1 Trillion Yen Budget for Missile Defense: Interim Report on NDPO Revision', *Mainichi Shimbun*, 2 August 2004, p. 1. Although JDA commentators have been at pains to point out that *Osumi* is not suited for fixed-wing operations owing to the thinness of its deck construction, *Jane's* noted that its flight deck appears 'unfinished, as though a ski-jump may be added in due course' (*Jane's Fighting Ships 1999–2000*, Coulsdon: Jane's Information Group, 1999, p. 386).

32 J. Noer with D. Gregory, *Chokepoints: Maritime Economic Concerns in Southeast Asia*, Washington, DC: University Press/Center for Naval Analyses, 1996, p. 6.

33 Mochizuki, op. cit., p. 70; and N. Holloway and S. Moffett, 'Cracks in the Armour', *Far Eastern Economic Review*, 2 May 1996, pp. 14–16.

34 'Japan Urged to Defend Longer Sea Lanes in Wartime', *Jiji Press* newswire, 30 May 1996.

35 M. Mochizuki, 'Toward a New Japan–U.S. Alliance', *Japan Quarterly*, July–September 1996, pp. 15–16.

36 'Guidelines for US–Japan Defense Cooperation', *Defense of Japan 2000*, Tokyo: JDA/*Japan Times*, pp. 284–21.

37 JDA, *Defense of Japan 2003*, Tokyo: JDA/Inter Group Corporation, 2003, pp. 145–52.

38 K. Akimoto, 'OPK (Ocean-Peace Keeping): Multilateral Naval Cooperation for Ocean Stabilization', *Ocean Governance and OPK: The Thirteenth International Symposium Proceedings*, Tokyo: National Institute for Defense Studies, 1998, pp. 16–23.

39 K. Akimoto, 'Mission and Contribution of the Japan Maritime Self Defense Force in the Post-Cold War and EEZ Era', paper given to the International Conference sponsored by the Korean Institute for Maritime Strategy, 11 December 1998, p. 3.

40 S. Kawamura, 'SLOC Security – A Japanese Perspective', in S. Bateman and S. Bates (eds), *The Seas Unite: Maritime Cooperation in the Asia Pacific Region*, Canberra Papers on Strategy and Defence, no. 118, Canberra: Australian National University Press, 1996, pp. 165–7 [My ellipses].

41 S. Kawamura, *The Kawamura Papers*, Chiba: The Kawamura Institute, November 1998, p. 101.

42 S. Kondō, 'The Maritime Priorities of Japan', in S. Bateman and R. Babbage (eds), *Maritime Change: Issues for Asia*, St Leonards: Allen and Unwin, 1993, p. 147.

43 K. Nakamura, 'Strategic Influence of JMSDF', *U.S. Naval Institute Proceedings*, March 1994, p. 82.

44 C. Hayashizaki, 'Retired Admiral on Post-Cold War MSDF Strategy', *Securitarian*, November 1996, pp. 15–19; and M. Yoshida, 'Resources, Maritime Transport and SLOC Security', in M. J. Kennedy and M. J. O'Connor (eds), *Safely By Sea*, Lanham, MD: University Press of America, 1990, p. 36. See also K. Katsutoshi, 'Japan's Military Role: Alliance Recommendations for the Twenty-First Century', *Naval War College Review*, 1998; 51(4): 18.

45 *Asahi Shimbun*, 5 June 2004, p. 1; and 'Govt may Export Decommissioned Ships', *Daily Yomiuri*, 22 December 2004, Online. Available www.yomiuri.co.jp/index-e.htm (accessed 22 December 2004).

46 M. Yamamoto, 'Sealane in the Asia–Pacific Region Today and their Vulnerabilities', paper presented to the Eleventh International Conference on the Sea Lanes of Communication (SLOC) Studies, Tokyo, 17–18 November, 1997, pp. 1–6.

47 *Mainichi Shimbun*, 14 April 1998, p. 3.

48 Y. Soeya, 'Japan: Normative Constraints Versus Structural Imperatives', in M. Alagappa (ed.), *Asian Security Practice: Material and Ideational Influences*, Stanford, CA: Stanford University Press, 1998, p. 199.
49 'Outlook for Asian Energy and its Global Implications', *Middle East Economic Survey*, 2002; 45(51/52) D9. Transcript of a paper delivered by Masuda Tatsuo at the 8th International Energy Forum, Osaka, 21–23 September 2002.
50 MOFA, Japan, 'Strategy and Approaches of Japan's Energy Diplomacy', December 2002. Online. Available www.mofa.go.jp/policy/ energy/diplomacy.html (accessed 8 March 2003).
51 Okazaki's role in decision-making concerning sea lane defence in the 1980s is explored in Chapter 5.
52 H. Okazaki, 'In Anticipation of an Animated Discussion', 27 January 1998. Online. Available www.glocomnet.or.jp/okazaki-inst/sealane.okazaki.e.html (accessed 12 February 2000).
53 Interview with Ambassador Okazaki Hisahiko, Okazaki Institute, Tokyo, 12 March 1999.
54 National Institute for Defense Studies, 'Maritime Security Environment in East Asia', *East Asian Strategic Review 2000*, Tokyo: National Institute for Defense Studies, 2000, p. 95.
55 JDA, *Defense of Japan 1997*, Tokyo: JDA/*Japan Times*, p. 106.
56 Ibid., p. 109.
57 JDA, *Defense of Japan 2003*, op. cit., p. 180.
58 *National Defense Program Guideline for FY 2005 and After*, unofficial Japanese government translation, December 2004, p. 3.
59 M. J. Green, *Japan's Reluctant Realism: Foreign Policy Challenges in an Era of Uncertainty*, London: Palgrave, 2003.
60 According to the Nippon Foundation, the IMO estimates that 86 per cent of incidents occur beyond the high seas.
61 IMB, *Piracy and Armed Robbery Against Ships: Annual Report 2003*, Barking: ICC/IMB, January 2004, Table 12, p. 13.
62 Ibid., Table 13, p. 14.
63 MOFA, Japan, *Diplomatic Bluebook 2003*, pp. 175–7. Online. Available www.mofa.go.jp/policy/other/bluebook/2003/ (accessed 30 October 2004). See also Japanese Shipowners' Association, *Kaizoku kyōi ni kansuru chōsa kekka ni tsuite* ('results of an investigation into the piracy threat'), Online. Available www.jsanet.or.jp/d2-3.html (accessed 30 October 2004).
64 The annual totals of piracy incidents involving Japanese ships, as reported to the IMO, is as follows (global totals in parentheses): 1995: 8 (132); 1996: 11 (228); 1997: 18 (252); 1998: 19 (210); 1999: 39 (309); 2000: 31 (471); 2001: 10 (370).
65 The Nippon Foundation database should not be regarded as scientifically based, being based on the cooperation and selectivity of response among individual shipping firms. While minor thefts committed in port are included more serious incidents reported elsewhere were not listed in the database. Nippon Foundation. Online. Available www.db01.nippon-foundation.or.jp/cgi-bin/zaidan/search_e.cgi (accessed 23 March 2001).
66 T. Akaha, 'Japan's Response to Threats of Shipping Disruptions in Southeast Asia and the Middle East', *Pacific Affairs*, 1986; 59(2): 255–7.
67 'Ajia no umi to kaizoku no kyōi' ['Asia's Seas and the Piracy Threat'], *Gaikō Foramu*, 2001; 156: 38–41.
68 K. Ishida, 'Piracy seen Increasing in Strait of Malacca', *Daily Yomiuri*, 29 December 1998, p. 2.
69 S. Kawamura, 'Regional Cooperation against Piracy and Armed Robbery', in A. Hamzah and A. Ogawa (eds), *Combating Piracy*, Kuala Lumpur: The Okazaki Institute, 2001, pp. 142–3.

70 N. Tanaka and H. Takase, 'Piracy and Ship's Safety: A View from the Shipping Industry', in ibid., pp. 160–1.
71 J. Abhyankar, 'Piracy and Ship Robbery: A Growing Menace', in ibid., pp. 38–9.
72 ICC Commercial Crime Services, 'Indian coastguards arrest hijacked freighter off Goa'. Online. Available www.iccwbo.org/ccs/news_archives/1999/indian_coastguards_arrest_hijacked_freighter.asp (accessed 16 November 1999).
73 IMB statement quoted in 'Piracy watchdog calls for secure sea lanes for ships', Reuters News Service, 24 October 2002 [My ellipsis].
74 Energy Information Administration, US Department of Energy, 'World Oil Transit Chokepoints', pp. 2–5. Online. Available www.eia.doe.gov/emeu/cabs/choke.html (accessed 30 November 2002).
75 Noer with Gregory, op. cit., Appendix A, Table 30, p. 69.
76 IMB, op. cit., Table 5, Status of ships during actual attacks, January to December 2003, p. 9.
77 MOFA, Japan op. cit.; see also: MOFA Policy statement from September 2001: 'The Issue of Piracy in Asia'. Online. Available www.mofa.go.jp/policy/piracy/asia2000.html (accessed 1 September 2004).
78 ICC Commercial Crime Services, 'Japanese Insurer Offers Piracy Cover', 25 July 1999. Online. Available www.iccwbo.org/ccs/institutional/introduction. asp (accessed 3 December 2001).
79 The majority of Japanese ships targeted were fishing vessels. The Japanese total is for the period January 1992–February 1993, from Table 8:1 in S. Kawamura, 'Maritime Transport and Communications', in S. Bateman and S. Bates (eds), *Calming the Waters: Initiatives for Asia Pacific Cooperation*, Canberra Papers on Strategy and Defence, no. 114, Canberra: Australian National University Press, 1996, p. 98.
80 'Gunboat Diplomacy', *Far Eastern Economic Review*, 16 June 1994, pp. 22–6.
81 S. Hiramatsu, 'China's Naval Advance: Objectives and Capabilities', *Japan Review of International Affairs*, 1994; 8(2): 128–32.
82 JDA, *Defense of Japan 1999*, Tokyo: JDA/*Japan Times*, p. 41; and JDA, *Defense of Japan 2000*, Tokyo: JDA/*Japan Times*, p. 50.
83 National Institute for Defense Studies, op. cit., p. 95.
84 S. Weeks, 'Law and Order at Sea: Pacific Cooperation in Dealing with Piracy, Drugs and Illegal Migration', in Bateman and Bates (eds), op. cit., p. 51.
85 Interview with Gotō Shinichi, CGSI-III (Commander), Deputy Director, International Affairs and Crisis Management Division, and Hideki Mochinaga, Senior Planning Officer, Policy and Legal Affairs Division, Administration Dept, JCG, 6 March 2002.
86 N. Chanda, 'Foot in the Water', *Far Eastern Economic Review*, 9 March 2000, pp. 28–9.
87 M. J. Valencia, 'Piracy and International Politics', in Hamzah and Ogawa (eds), op. cit., p. 81.
88 'China Goes it Alone at Asian Anti-Piracy Conference', Agence France Presse International; 28 April 2000; and M. J. Valencia, 'Piracy and International Politics', in ibid., p. 81.
89 Statement issued at Asia Anti-Piracy Challenges 2000 conference, 27–29 April 2000; and Press Release no. 21, Embassy of Japan in India. Online. Available www.japan-emb.org.in/pressreleases/Press_ReleasesMenu.htm (accessed 2 December 2000).
90 ASEAN-Plus-Three groups South Korea, Japan and China together with ASEAN's ten members.
91 Speech by Prime Minister Koizumi Junichirō, 'Japan and ASEAN in East Asia – A Sincere and Open Partnership', given in Singapore, 14 January 2002; MOFA, Japan. Online. Available www.mofa.go.jp/region/asia-paci/ pmv0201/speech.html (accessed 17 February 2003).
92 *Jane's Fighting Ships 1999–2000*, Coulsdon: Jane's Information Group, 1999, pp. 394–403.

93 Maritime Safety Agency, *Annual Report on Maritime Safety 1998*, Tokyo: Maritime Safety Agency, pp. 7–8.
94 JCG, 'Japan Coast Guard', Tokyo: JCG Policy Evaluation and Public Relations Office, 2002, pp. 4, 22.
95 J. Abhyankar, 'Piracy and Ship Robbery: A Growing Menace', in Hamzah and Ogawa (eds), op. cit., p. 54; and interview with Commander Gotō Shinichi, Deputy Director, International Affairs and Crisis Management Division, JCG, 6 March 2002.
96 MOFA, Japan, op. cit., p. 177.
97 The Japanese maritime surveillance version of the Falcon has a 3,460 nm range and a powerful belly-mounted search radar.
98 IMO, Maritime Safety Committee, 'Report of the Maritime Safety Committee on its Seventy-Eighth Session', Agenda Item 26, MSC 78/26, 28 May 2004, pp. 121–3; and 'Japan to Send Boat, Jets to Southeast Asia to fight Piracy', *The Japan Times*, 17 July 2002. Online. Available www.japantimes.co.jp/cgi bin/getarticle.pl5?nn20020717c3.htm (accessed 10 August 2004).
99 Kawamura, op. cit., pp. 147–50.
100 J. Burton and S. Donnan, 'Malacca Strait Pirates Will Sail into Choppier Waters', *Financial Times*, 21 July 2004.
101 'Singapore Seeks Joint Patrols of Malacca Straits, Involving Japan', *Kyodo*, 20 May 2004.
102 JDA, *Defense of Japan 2003*, Tokyo: JDA/*Japan Times*, p. 79.
103 Kawamura, op. cit., p. 151.
104 ICC Commercial Crime Services, 'ICC Report Sends Six Warships into Battle against Pirates', 12 February 2002. Online. Available www.iccwbo.org/home/news_archives/2002/piracy.asp (accessed 3 December 2001).
105 J. McBeth, 'The Army's Dirty Business', *Far Eastern Economic Review*, 7 November 2002, pp. 20–1; and T. Huxley, 'Disintegrating Indonesia: Implications for Regional Security', *Adelphi Paper 349*, London: International Institute for Strategic Studies, July 2002, p. 18.
106 'Shipping in South-east Asia: Going for the Jugular', *The Economist*, 12 June 2004, pp. 54–61.
107 'Patrol Boats Donated to Indonesia for Anti-Terrorism Work', BBC Monitoring/*Nihon Keizai Shimbun*, 31 May 2004.
108 'Govt may Export Decommissioned Ships', *Daily Yomiuri*, 22 December 2004. Online. Available www.yomiuri.co.jp/index-e.htm (accessed 22 December 2004).
109 'Indian, Japanese Coast Guard Vessels Hold Joint Exercise', *The People's Daily*, 9 November 2000. Online. Available 207.121.189.139/english/200011/09/eng20001109_54726.html (accessed 9 November 2000).
110 'Japanese Coast Guard Vessel to Visit India', Press Release no. 34, Embassy of Japan in India, 30 October 2000. Online. Available www.japan-emb.org.in/pressreleases/Press_ReleasesMenu.htm (accessed 2 December 2000).
111 Huxley, op. cit., p. 83.
112 'Coast Guard Adds to Arsenal to Fight High-seas Crime', *Nikkei Weekly*, 11 February 2002, p. 6.
113 E. Luce, 'Indian Navy Agrees to Protect US Shipping', *Financial Times*, 6 February 2002, p. 10.
114 'India begins Patrolling Malacca Straits', *The Hindu Online*, 20 April 2002. Online. Available www.hinduonnet.com/thehindu/2002/04/20/stories/2002042002901100.htm; and *Defense of Japan 2003*, op. cit., p. 81.
115 A. Almazan, 'Tougher Anti-Piracy Solutions Sought', *Shipping Times*, 28 February 2002.
116 S. Sudo, *Southeast Asia in Japanese Security Policy*, Singapore: Institute of Southeast Asian Studies, 1991, p. 39.
117 Testimony of Admiral Thomas B. Fargo, United States Navy Pacific Commander, US Pacific Command: House of Representatives Armed Services Committee.

Online. Available www.house.gov/hasc/openingstatementsandpressreleases/108thcongress/04-03-31fargo.html (accessed 31 August 2004).

118 J. Burton and S. Donnan, op. cit.

119 According to a defence assistant secretary and spokesman for The Philippines' Anti-Terrorism Task Force, consultations were held between the US and the Philippines to deploy anti-terror forces to the Straits of Malacca, but only Singapore supported the reported proposal to base a US Marine Corps contingent adjacent to the Straits ('Arroyo Reaffirms Philippines–US–Japan Alliance; Malacca Straits Discussed', BBC Monitoring, 8 April 2004).

120 N. Tanaka and H. Takase, 'Piracy and Ship's Safety: A View from the Shipping Industry', in Hamzah and Ogawa (eds), op. cit., p. 173; and Kawamura, ibid., p. 152.

121 JSA, *Annual Report 2002*, 'Problems of Crimes Committed on Foreign Vessels'. Online. Available www.jsanet.or.jp/e/annualr-e/pdf/j_shipping2002.pdf (accessed 30 October 2004).

122 Interview with Commander Gotō Shinichi, Deputy Director, International Affairs and Crisis Management Division, JCG, 6 March 2002.

123 J. Abhyankar, 'Piracy and Ship Robbery: A Growing Menace', in Hamzah and Ogawa (eds), op. cit., p. 56; and Tanaka and Takase ibid., pp. 166–8.

124 'Seafarers Warned On Indonesia Pirates, Somali Armed Gangs', Dow Jones Newswires, 23 October 2002.

125 IMO, Maritime Safety Committee, 'Piracy and Armed Robbery Against Ships: Regional Co-operation Agreement on Combatting Piracy and Armed Robbery Against Ships in Asia', Agenda Item 20, Submitted by Japan, MSC 78/INF.11, 5 March 2004, pp. 1–3.

126 IMO, Maritime Safety Committee, 'Report of the Maritime Safety Committee on its Seventy-Eighth Session', Agenda Item 26, MSC 78/26, 28 May 2004, pp. 121–3.

127 United Nations General Assembly (UNGA), 'Resolution Adopted by the General Assembly 58/240: Oceans and the Law of the Sea', Fifty-Eighth Session, Agenda item 52(a), A/RES/58/240, 5 March 2004, p. 8.

128 ARF Statement on Cooperation Against Piracy and Other Threats to Maritime Security. Online. Available www.aseansec.org/14838.htm (accessed 31 August 2004).

129 JSMEA News. Online. Available www.jsmea.or.jp/NEWS_E/sm2000/news_sm0011.html (accessed 10 May 2001).

130 The Yokohama-Hamburg route via Suez is 11,400 nm, compared to 6,600 nm via the NSR (International Northern Sea Route Programme, overview. Online. Available www.fni.no/insrop (accessed 10 May 2001).

131 N. Tanaka and H. Takase, 'Piracy and Ship's Safety: A View from the Shipping Industry', in Hamzah and Ogawa (eds), op. cit., pp. 165–6.

132 ICC Commercial Crime Services, 'Shipowners call for coordinated international sea patrols', 35th ICC World Congress, 8 June 2004. Online. Available www.iccworldcongress.net/mainpages/media/press/news.pp?news_id = 40 (accessed 1 September 2004).

133 JSA, *Annual Report 2002*, 'Issue on [*sic*] Piracy and Armed Robbery against Ships'. Online. Available www.jsanet.or.jp/e/annualr-e/pdf/j_shipping2002.pdf (accessed 30 October 2004).

134 Given the trend towards smaller crews and larger vessels, some ships now regard lighting the deck directly as counter-productive, since this advertises points of vulnerability to potential attackers. Increasingly, light is directed at the water around the vessel in order to help those on deck to detect approaching vessels.

135 Shiploc is a tracking system which relies on Global Positioning Satellite (GPS) technology and a concealed, battery-powered transmitter placed on board participating ships, giving shipowners the ability to track a vessels' movements in real time by regular 'polling' via the Internet (up to 15 times per day). It is relatively cheap, with an installation cost of $280 (Shiploc.com. Online. Available www.shiploc.com (accessed 17 June 2002)).

136 A Japanese shipping industry interviewee expressed some skepticism about the security value of Shiploc and other polling systems that rely on course deviation to trigger an alarm at the monitoring location, given that this provides a deterrent only to long-term seizures.
137 'Asia Sails Ahead in Implementing Maritime Anti-Terror Code', *Agence France-Presse*, 1 July 2004.
138 *Nihon Keizai Shimbun*, 18 November 1999, p. 11.
139 IMB, *Piracy and Armed Robbery Against Ships: Annual Report 2001*, op. cit., p. 23.
140 Tanaka and Tarase, in Hamzah and Ogawa (eds), op. cit., 2001, p. 173.
141 Kawamura, op. cit., p. 166.
142 K. Akimoto, 'OPK (Ocean-Peace Keeping [*sic*]): Multilateral Naval Cooperation for Ocean Stabilization', in Susumu Takai (ed.), *Ocean Governance and OPK: The Thirteenth International Symposium Proceedings*, National Institute for Defense Studies, Tokyo, 1998, p. 17; and 'Mission and Contribution of the Japan Maritime Self Defense Force in the Post-Cold War and EEZ Era', paper given to the International Conference sponsored by the Korean Institute for Maritime Strategy, 11 December 1998, p. 7.
143 Interview with Captain Otsuka Umio, MSDF, Agenda Coordinator, Western Pacific Naval Symposium, Plans and Program Division, Maritime Staff Office, JDA, Tokyo, 1 March 2002.
144 M. J. Valencia, 'Joining Up With Japan to Patrol Asian Waters', *International Herald Tribune*, 28 April 2000.
145 Speech by Ishiba Shigeru given in absentia at the International Institute for Strategic Studies Third Shangri-La Dialogue, 5 June 2004, Singapore [My ellipsis]. Online. Available www.iiss.org/showdocument.php?docID = 377 (accessed 5 August 2004).
146 'Three Japanese Navy Vessels Call at West Port', Bernama, 13 March 2001.
147 C. W. Hughes, 'Japan's Aum Shinrikyō, the Changing Nature of Terrorism, and the Post-Cold War Security Agenda', *Pacific Review*, 1998; 10(1): 56.
148 'Japan Patrol Boat Leaves for Antiterror Drill with South Korea', BBC Monitoring/*Kyodo*, 1 April 2004.
149 'Anti-terrorism Drills Held at Japan's Nagoya Port', BBC Monitoring/*Kyodo*, 12 February 2004.
150 'Remarks by Mr Yasuo Fukuda, Chief Cabinet Secretary, Regarding the Dispatch of Destroyers and Another Vessel for Information Gathering', The MOFA, 8 November 2001. Online. Available www.mofa.go.jp/region/n-america/us/terro0109/speech/ccs1108.html (accessed 12 December 2002).
151 See Second and Third Revisions to the Government of Japan's Basic Plan under the Anti-Terrorism Special Measures Law; JDA, *Defense of Japan 2003*, Tokyo: JDA/Inter Group Corporation, 2003, pp. 205–51.
152 'SDF Activities Continue in Arabian Sea', *Nikkei Net Interactive*, 28 February 2002. Online. Available www.nni.nikkei.co.jp/FR/FEAT/terro/terro00259.html (accessed 7 March 2003) and 'Japan Extends Arabian Sea Deployment of Maritime Force Until 1 May', BBC Monitoring/*Kyodo*, 26 March 2004.
153 'Japan Dispatches Two Destroyers to Arabian Sea on Support Mission', BBC Monitoring/*Kyodo*, 17 May 2000; 'Japan to Extend Troops Dispatch to Iraq for US Anti-Terror Operations', BBC Monitoring/*Kyodo*, 20 April 2004; and 'Japan to Spend 46 m Dollars on Extension of Naval Mission in Arabian Sea', BBC Monitoring/*Kyodo*, 26 April 2004.
154 'Aegis Warships a No-go', *Asahi Shimbun/International Herald Tribune*, 8 November 2002.
155 Satō Yōichirō, 'Japan's Naval Dispatch Plans Expand the Envelope', Pacific Forum CSIS, 24 January 2003.
156 'US Informs Japan Joint Missile Shield to be Deployed in '08', *Kyodo*, 10 November 2002.

157 Japan's Laws Permit It to Supply US Forces, Bloomberg News, 11 September 2002.
158 'MSDF to refuel ships of 8 more nations', *Daily Yomiuri*. Online. Available www.yomiuri.co.jp/newse/200030214wo41.htm (accessed 14 February 2003).
159 'Japan to refuel German, French, NZ ships in Arabian Sea', *Kyodo*, 28 February 2003.
160 JDA, op. cit., p. 252.
161 'Transport Ship Leaves Hiroshima to Supply Japanese Iraq Troops', BBC Monitoring/*Kyodo*, 14 February 2004.
162 N. Shimoyachi, 'Overseas Missions Straining MSDF to the Limit', *The Japan Times*, 20 February 2004. Online. Available www.japantimes.co.jp/ggi-bin/getarticle.pl5?nn20040220b1.htm (accessed 3 September 2004).
163 'Govt to address Iraq war concerns', *Daily Yomiuri Online*, 7 February 2003. Online. Available www.yomiuiri.co.jp/newse/20030207wo02.htm (accessed 30 September 2003).
164 *National Defense Program Guideline for FY 2005 and After*, unofficial translation, December 2004, p. 6.
165 A. Berkofsky, 'Japan's navy salvo catches politicians off guard', *Asia Times*, 16 May 2002. Online. Available www.atimes.com/japan-econ/DE16Dh01.html (accessed 11 October 2002).
166 'US asks Japan for high-tech Afghan back-up-media', Reuters News Service, 30 April 2002.
167 'Will Armitage Report 2 ask Japan to defend sea lanes up to 5,000 nautical miles', *Shukan Bunshun*, 8 July 2004, p. 46.
168 US Department of State, 'Biography of Torkel L. Patterson', 17 May 2004. Online. Available www.state.gov/p/sa/rls/32539.htm (accessed 2 November 2004).
169 National Institute for Defense Studies, 'Southeast Asia: Toward a New Unity', *East Asian Strategic Review 2003*, Tokyo: National Institute for Defense Studies, 2003, p. 213.

8 Japan's post-Cold War SLOC security: China, North Korea and regional conflict

1 MOFA, Japan, *Diplomatic Bluebook 2004*, pp. 46–7. Online. Available www.mofa.go.jp/policy/other/bluebook/2004/chap2-a.pdf (accessed 28 December 2004).
2 M. J. Green and B. L. Self, 'Japan's Changing China Policy: From Commercial Liberalism to Reluctant Realism', *Survival*, 1996; 38(2): 35–58.
3 J. Welfield, 'The American Japanese Alliance at the Turn of the Millennium', *Pacific Research*, May 1996, p. 10.
4 S. Konapalli, *China's Naval Power*, New Delhi: Knowledge World in association with Institute for Defence Studies and Analyses, 2001, pp. 5–12.
5 Liu retired in 1996 as Vice Chairman of the Central Military Commission, China's top military decision-making body (You Ji, *The Armed Forces of China*, Sydney: Allen and Unwin, 1999, Chapter 1, pp. 160–200).
6 'Outlook for Asian Energy and its Global Implications', *Middle East Economic Survey*, 45:51/52, December 23/30, 2002, D4. Transcript of a paper delivered by Masuda Tatsuo at the 8th International Energy Forum, Osaka, 21–23 September 2002.
7 'Asia's New Thirst', *Financial Times*, 24 May 2004, p. 16.
8 J. Kynge and D. Roberts 'Comment and Analysis: China', *Financial Times*, 5 February 2003, p. 15.
9 'Review of Maritime Transport, 2002', United Nations Conference on Trade and Development, New York and Geneva: United Nations, 2002, p. 69.
10 V. Mallet, 'China's rise revives an ailing industry', *Financial Times*, 14 December 2004, p. 17.
11 Liu Yi-chien, 'China's 21st Century Navy Prospects', *Ta Kung Pao*, FBIS China Daily Report, FBIS-CHI-1999-1011, 1 September 1999.
12 Konapalli, op. cit., p. 3.

13 Y. Hirama, 'The Growing Chinese Navy and its Influence on Triple-Relation [*sic*] – Japan, US and Korea', paper given at Conference on Post-Unification Security Cooperation Among the United States, Korea and Japan, Hawaii, 20–23 April 1998, pp. 8–9.
14 Liu Yi-chien, op. cit.
15 You Ji, op. cit., pp. 212–13.
16 J. W. Garver, *The Sino-American Alliance: Nationalist China and American Cold War Strategy in Asia*, Armonk, New York: M.E. Sharpe, 1997, pp. 15–16.
17 Huang Chung-jung, 'Taiwan foreign minister optimistic about development of ties with Japan', *Tzu Yu Shih Pao*/BBC Monitoring, 28 September 2002.
18 'Taiwan opposition leader urges Japan to consider regional collective security', BBC Monitoring/Central News Agency Website, 27 August 2004.
19 'Sea Power, the Great Enabler: Conversation with Admiral Liu Ho Chien', *Taiwan Defense Affairs*, 2001; 1(3): 193.
20 Li Yaqiang, 'What is Japan Doing Southward', *Jianchuan Zhishi* ('Naval and Merchant Ships'), 6 June 1997, FBIS China Daily Report FBIS-CHI-97-247, 4 September 1997 [My ellipses].
21 You Ji, op. cit., pp. 181–2.
22 J. Pomfret, 'China nears deal for 8 submarines', *International Herald Tribune*, 7 June 2002, p. 1. *Kilo* submarines have a range of 7,500 miles when snorkelling at 7 knots. Both the Song and obsolete Ming-classes have a submerged range of 3,800 km. China's Nuclear-powered *Han*-class attack submarines (SSN), with a displacement of 5,500 tons, have unlimited range, but would be less suited to the anti-shipping role.
23 The *Ming*-class submarine is basically a re-modelled *Romeo*-class submarine; the *Song*-class is an original design, developed with Israeli and French assistance.
24 'Chinese navy to reinforce submarine fleets to counter US force', *Sankei Shimbun*/BBC Monitoring, 8 September 2004.
25 As explored in Chapter 3, the Bashi Channel/Luzon Strait was the major killing ground for Japanese merchant ships during the Second World War.
26 J. Ruwitch, 'Chinese Navy Cruises Toward Modernization', *Reuters New Service*, 1 October 2002; and US DoD, *Annual Report on the Military Power of the People's Republic of China*, July 2002, p. 26. Online. Available www.globalsecurity.org/military/library/report/2002/d20020712china.pdf (accessed 2 November 2004).
27 JDA, *Defense of Japan 2003*, Tokyo: JDA/Inter Group Corporation, 2003, p. 66.
28 Ibid., pp. 20, 53.
29 D. Lague, 'We All Live for Another Submarine', *Far Eastern Economic Review*, 15 August 2002, p. 13.
30 P. L. Young, 'New Submarine Technology and the Asian Market in the Nineties', *Asian Defence Journal*, November 1990, p. 72.
31 Statement by Chinese Foreign Minister Qian Qichen addressing ASEAN Foreign Ministers in August 1995, FBIS China Daily Report, FBIS-CHI-99-025, 25 January 1999.
32 FBIS China Daily Report, FBIS-CHI-2000-1125, 25 November 2000 [My ellipsis].
33 Interview with Adm. Sakonjo Naotoshi, Research Institute for Peace and Security, Tokyo, 12 February 1999.
34 US DoD, *Annual Report on the Military Power of the People's Republic of China*, July 2002, p. 50. Online. Available www.globalsecurity.org/military/library/report/2002/d20020712china.pdf (accessed 2 November 2004).
35 Ibid., p. 46.
36 M. M. Tsai and Y. W. Chen, 'Submarines and Taiwan's Defense', *Taiwan Defense Affairs*, 2001; 1(3): 126–7, 135. Tsai was subsequently appointed as defence adviser to President Chen Shui-bian [My ellipsis].
37 The planned sale of eight conventional submarines, as part of a package of US arms transfers to Taiwan approved by President George W. Bush's administration, would do

much to raise Taiwan's ASW capability (D. Lague, 'We All Live for Another Submarine', *Far Eastern Economic Review*, 15 August 2002, pp. 12–14).

38 The Taiwanese Navy is assessed by the US Defense Department to be generally well-run and maintained, focused on counter-blockade and SLOC defence missions. However, there are doubts about its ability to perform overlapping missions simultaneously (US DoD, *Annual Report on the Military Power of the People's Republic of China*, July 2002, p. 55. Online. Available www.globalsecurity org/military/library/report/2002/d20020712china.pdf (accessed 2 November 2004).

39 Tsai and Chen, op. cit., pp. 122–77.

40 US DoD, *Annual Report on the Military Power of the People's Republic of China*, July 2002, pp. 23, 51. Online. Available www.globalsecurity.org/military/library/report/2002/d20020712china.pdf (accessed 2 November 2004).

41 You Ji, op. cit., pp. 202–4.

42 Tensions first rose between Japan and China over the Senkaku (called the Diaoyu in China) in 1972 and 1978. China's policy towards the territorial dispute with Japan was thereafter defined according to Deng Xiaoping's vague formula of deferring a solution for a 'wiser generation' of Japanese and Chinese leaders to conclude. However, tensions resurfaced in 1990 and 1996, linked to the activities of rightist groups in Japan seeking to assert sovereignty claims to the uninhabited islands, ceded by China under the Treaty of Shimonoseki in 1895. Most recently, in March 2004 seven Chinese activists landed on Uotsurishima in the Senkaku group, prompting Japanese Coast Guard vessels to mount a cordon around the island ('20 JCG ships sent to guard Senkaku Is', *Daily Yomiuri*, 29 March 2004. Online. Available www.yomiuri.co.jp/newse/20040329wo41.htm (accessed 29 March 2004).

43 Chen Lineng, 'The Japanese Self-defense [*sic*] Forces Are Marching Towards the 21st Century', *Guoji Zhanwang* (World Outlook), no. 2, pp. 18–20, 8 February 1996, in FBIS China Daily Report, FBIS-CHI-96-085, 1 May 1996 [My ellipses].

44 Interview with Zhang Zhaozhong, 'US, Japan Role in Cross-Strait War Viewed', *Ta Kung Pao*, FBIS-CHI-1999–0819, 18 August 1999.

45 Li Yaqiang, 'What is Japan Doing Southward?', *Jianchuan Zhishi* ('Naval and Merchant Ships') 6 June 1997, FBIS-CHI-97-247, 4 September 1997.

46 B. Garrett and B. Glasser, 'Chinese Apprehensions About Revitalization of the U.S.–Japan Alliance', *Asian Survey*, 1997; 37(4): 390–9.

47 'China Says No to Japanese Doctrine "Which Hides Its Head But Shows Its Tail" ', *Zhongguo Tongxun She* news agency, broadcast 1235 GMT, 18 January 1997, BBC Summary of World Broadcasts, Asia–Pacific, 21 January 1997.

48 Y. Soeya, 'The South China Sea: A Japanese Perspective', in C. Hernandez (ed.), *Security Implications of Conflict in the South China Sea: Perspectives from the Asia–Pacific*, Proceedings of the First International Conference on the South China Sea, Manila, 12–14 November, 1995, Quezon City: Pacific Forum/CSIS and Institute for Strategic and Development Studies, 1997, p. 129.

49 W. Mendl, *Japan's Asia Policy: Regional Security and Global Interests*, London and New York: Routledge, 1995, p. 82.

50 JDA, *Defense of Japan 2000*, Tokyo: JDA/*Japan Times*, 2000, p. 44.

51 *Annual Report on Maritime Safety 1998*, Tokyo: Maritime Safety Agency (MSA), Japan, p. 17.

52 Lam Peng, 'Japan and the Spratlys Dispute: Aspirations and Limitations', *Asian Survey*, 1996; 36: 996.

53 Ibid., pp. 1004–7.

54 Green and Self, op. cit., p. 37.

55 Y. Funabashi, *Alliance Adrift*, Council on Foreign Relations, New York, 1999, pp. 351–7.

56 BBC Summary of World Broadcasts, Japan, 6 March 1996, FE/2553 E/1 and FE/2559 E/1, 13 March 1996.

57 *Bungei Shunjū*, November 1998, pp. 150–7.
58 BBC Summary of World Broadcasts: Asia Pacific: Japan, 'Spokesman says China's Proposed Missile Launchings Near Taiwan "undesirable" ', FE/2553 E/1 [1].
59 M. Sasajima and K. Iizuka, 'Chi's visit marks improving defense ties', *Daily Yomiuri*, 29 January 1998, p. 2.
60 *The Modality of the Security and Defense Capability of Japan*, Japanese government translation GM:3338-, 12 August 1994, pp. 4–6.
61 JDA, *Defense of Japan 1996*, Tokyo: JDA/*Japan Times*, 1996, p. 45.
62 General Shikata Toshiyuki, 'Japan's Response to the Situations in Areas Surrounding Japan', Okazaki Institute. Online. Available www.glocomnet.or.jp/okazaki-inst/korea-pro-jap/shikata.kj3.eng.html (accessed 22 April 2001).
63 National Institute for Defense Studies, *East Asian Strategic Review 2000*, Tokyo: National Institute for Defense Studies, 2000, pp. 104–7.
64 Ibid., pp. 199–203.
65 'Japan to Protest China Survey near Okinotori', *The Japan Times*, 10 May 2004. Online. Available www.japantimes.co.jp/cgi-bin/getarticle.pl5?nn20040510a3.htm (accessed 14 August 2004).
66 'China reportedly set to infringe on EEZ', *The Japan Times*, 18 October 2004. Online. Available www.japantimes.co.jp/cgi-bin/getarticle.pl5?nn20041018a1.htm (accessed 18 October 2004).
67 N. Shimoyachi, 'Defense policy overhauled to meet new global threats', *The Japan Times*, 11 December 2004. Online. Available www.japantimes.co.jp/cgi-bin/getarticle.pl5?nn20041211a1.htm (accessed 22 December 2004).
68 Soeya, op. cit., p. 130; and N. Usui, 'Japan Spots Chinese Jets', *Defense News*, 28 August–3 September 1995, p. 10.
69 N. Usui, 'East Asian Nations Aim to Bolster Sub Fleets', *Defense News*, 19–25 August 1996, p. 8.
70 'Japan Mulling New Plan Against Submarine Invasion', Bernama-Kyodo/Asia Intelligence Wire, 4 October 1996.
71 *Sankei Shimbun*, 17 April 1999, p. 3.
72 'Japan Voices Concern at Chinese Naval Activities Around Japan', *Kyodo Weekly*, 23 June 2000. Online. Available home.kyodo.co.jp/JapanWeekly/20000623.html#WEEKLY_4 (accessed 25 July 2000); and M. Malik, 'Japan Wary of Assertive China', *Jane's Intelligence Review*, December 2000, pp. 22–5.
73 *Asahi Shimbun*, 5 June 2004, p. 1.
74 'Japan continues tracking submarine, defends steps taken for naval action', *Kyodo*, 11 November 2004.
75 'Japan still tracking mystery submarine; Chinese embassy has no comment', *Kyodo*, 11 November 2004.
76 S. Hiramatsu, 'China's Security Mind-set', *The Japan Times*, 15 September 1998, p. 18; and 'China's Naval Advance: Objectives and Capabilities', *Japan Review of International Affairs*, 1994; 8(2): 118.
77 M. J. O'Connor, 'Introduction', in M. J. Kennedy and M. J. O'Connor (eds), *Safely by Sea*, Lanham, MD: University Press of America, 1990, p. 56.
78 'China: A Function of the Japan–US Alliance', *Asia–Pacific Review*, 3(1): 1996, 45–50.
79 H. Okazaki, 'Can Taiwan's Freedom Be Preserved?' *Daily Yomiuri*, 1 June 1998.
80 Interview with Ambassador Okazaki Hisahiko, Okazaki Institute, Tokyo, 12 March 1999.
81 See Vice Admiral Yamamoto Makoto, 'Sealane in the Asia–Pacific Region Today and their Vulnerabilities', paper presented to the Eleventh International Conference on the Sea Lanes of Communication (SLOC) Studies, Tokyo, 17–18 November, 1997, p. 7.

82 According to a non-official 1989 MSDF assessment, 'although the PRC and North Korea do possess attack submarines, we estimate that they do not have sufficient capabilities to attack Japanese sea lanes in the foreseeable future' (T. Hozumi, 'Naval Control of Shipping', in M. J. Kennedy and M. J. O'Connor, *Safely By Sea*, Lanham, MD: University Press of America, 1990, p. 285).
83 Confidential interview with JDA Operations Bureau official, 5 March 2002.
84 Interview with Captain Nakanishi Kenji, Research Department, Maritime Staff College, 4 March 2002.
85 FY 1981 Arms Control Impact Statements, 96th Congress, 2nd Session p. 342. SURTASS is a US-made system that is designed to supplement SOSUS seabed hydrophone arrays with a mobile submarine detection capability deployed aboard purpose-built, twin-hulled vessels. The MSDF's two *Hibiki*-class vessels (commissioned in 1991 and 1992) are equipped with the UQQ-2 towed array. *Hibiki*-class vessels have a mission radius of 3,000 nm and the ability to deploy on station for 90 days. SURTASS data is relayed to shore stations via the Defense Satellite Communications System for processing and analysis and is shared with the United States. The *Hibiki* and its sister ship are reported to include five US technicians among their crew (N. Friedman, *The Naval Institute Guide to World Naval Weapons, 1997–99*, Annapolis: Naval Institute Press, 1997).
86 H. Izumi, 'Improvement of the National Defense Strategy and Defence Buildup Plans for Post-Cold War Japan', paper presented to the '93 International Defense Academic Seminar, Korea National War College, 2 November 1993, p. 59.
87 Interview with Ambassador Okazaki Hisahiko, Okazaki Institute, Tokyo, 12 March 1999.
88 S. Taoka, '21 Seiki Higashi Ajia no Senryaku Kankyō' ['East Asia's Strategic Environment in the Twenty-First Century'], *Sekai no Kansen*, December 1995, no. 504, pp. 70–5; and 'Commentator Debunks PRC Arms Buildup', *Ronza*, September 1996, pp. 66–71, in FBIS-EAS-96-162, pp. 15–21.
89 Interview with Adm. Hirama Yōichi, MSDF (Retd), National Defense Academy, Yokosuka, 16 March 1999.
90 Y. Hirama, 'The Growing Chinese Navy and its Influence on Triple-Relation [*sic*] – Japan, US and Korea', paper given at Conference on Post-Unification Security Cooperation Among the United States, Korea and Japan, Hawaii, 20–23 April 1998.
91 Lieutenant Commander Doshita Tetsurō, 'Regional Security Links Japan and US', *US Naval Institute Proceedings*, March 1995, pp. 51–4.
92 M. Mitsuhisa, *Defense Policy of Japan: Maritime Self-Defense Force (JMSDF) in the Early 21st Century*, MA Thesis, Naval Postgraduate School, Monterey: US Department of Commerce National Technical Information Service, March 1995, p. 80 [My italics].
93 JDA, *Defense of Japan 2000*, Tokyo: JDA/*Japan Times*, 2000, p. 271.
94 *Sankei Shimbun*, 18 December 2000.
95 Interview with Prof. Tadokoro Masayuki, National Defense Academy, Yokosuka, 7 March 2002.
96 JDA, *Mid-term Defense Program (Fiscal 2005–2009) (Summary)*, unofficial translation, December 2004.
97 D. Ball and E. Graham, *Japan's Airborne SIGINT Capabilities*, SDSC Working Paper no. 11, Canberra: Australian National University, 2000, p. 9.
98 A 1996 public affairs report by Master Sergeant Marvin D. Krause on the US Pacific Command's website, profiling 'Indonesia Air Show (IAS) '96', stated that 'A B1B Lancer bomber from McConnell AFB, Kansas landed at IAS '96 after flying nonstop from Kansas to Jakarta. Part of the bomber's mission involved air exercises over the Republic of Korea, then exercises with the Japanese over the South China Sea,

before refueling in the air and proceeding to Jakarta.' Online. Available www.pacom.mil/forum/airshow2.htm (accessed 14 January 1997).

99 Nishimura Yoshiaki, adviser to Kawasaki Heavy Industries and former commander, MSDF Fleet Submarine Force, quoted in *Bōei Gijutsu Jānaru* (Defence Technology Journal), September 1997, pp. 4–19, in FBIS-EAS-97-314, Daily Report, FBIS Translated Text [My ellipsis].

100 'Japan Joins in Multilateral Submarine Rescue Drill', *Weekly Kyodo News*, 2 October 2000.

101 'Singapore hosts 16-nation naval exercises', *Reuters News Service*, 12 June 2001.

102 'Singapore to seek Japanese, South Korean help on Malacca mines drill', *Kyodo*, 20 December 2004.

103 According to Okazaki Hisahiko, during the vacuum created by the withdrawal of US naval forces from South-east Asian waters to the Indian Ocean at the end of the 1970s, requests were in fact made to Japan by 'countries bordering the Strait of Malacca for equipment to prepare waterways and sweep mines, together with technological assistance'. (*Japan Echo*, vol. 20, Special Issue, p. 35.) Thai Prime Minister Chatichai Choonhavan also reportedly proposed joint naval cooperation with Japan in 1990 (C. Khamchoo, 'Japan's Role in Southeast Asian Security: "Plus ça change" ', *Pacific Affairs*, 1991; 64: 18).

104 Adm. Sakuma Makoto 'Former MSDF Staff Chief on Security Issues', *Securitarian*, 10 July 1996, pp. 23–8, in FBIS-EAS-96-156, 12 August 1996, pp. 4–9.

105 S. Kawamura, 'Former Admiral on South China Sea Balance', *Sekai no Kansen*, August 1996, pp. 70–7, in FBIS-EAS-96-155, 9 August 1996.

106 'Energy Security and Sealane Disruption', *Australian Energy News*, Issue 24, June 2002. Online. Available www.industry.gov.au/resources/netetenergy/aen/aen24/6enrgy.html (accessed 13 December 2002).

107 Interview with Adm. Kawamura Sumihiko, Okazaki Institute, 1 March 2002.

108 Interview with Capt. Otsuka Umio, MSDF, Agenda Coordinator, Western Pacific Naval Symposium, Plans and Program Division, Maritime Staff Office, JDA, Tokyo, 1 March 2002.

109 Interview with former JDA Administrative Vice-Minister Akiyama Masahiro, Ship and Ocean Foundation, Nippon Foundation, Tokyo, 4 March 2002.

110 ' "Confidential" documents show Japan to defend islands in China–Taiwan conflict', *Kyodo*, 14 May 2004.

111 'Protecting Japan Part II: Residents of remote isles live in fear of Taiwan Strait tensions', *Daily Yomiuri*, 10 March 2003. Online. Available www.yomiuri.co.jp/newse/20040310wo01.htm (accessed 10 March 2004).

112 Historically, the Liberal Democratic Party (LDP) was divided along a faultline between the pro-Taipei *Ajia mondai kenkyūkai ('A-ken'*: Asia problems research group) and the pro-Beijing *ajia-afurika mondai kenkyūkai ('AA- ken'*: Asia–Africa problems research group).

113 R. S. Ross, *Managing a Changing Relationship: China's Japan Policy in the 1990s*, U.S. Army War College, September 1996, p. 1.

114 S. V. Lawrence, 'Prickly Pair', *Far Eastern Economic Review*, 22 July 1999, p. 20.

115 *Sankei Shimbun*, 28 November 1995.

116 Y. Soeya, 'Japan: Normative Constraints Versus Structural Imperatives', in M. Alagappa (ed.), *Asian Security Practice: Material and Ideational Influences*, Stanford University Press, California, 1998, pp. 203–7.

117 S. Etō, 'China and Sino-Japanese Relations in the Coming Decades', *Japan Review of International Affairs*, 1996; 10(1): 24 [My ellipsis].

118 Y. Soeya, 'Islands of Contention', *Look Japan*, May 1995, p. 23.

119 K. Satō, 'The Japan Card', *Far Eastern Economic Review*, 13 April 1995, p. 32.

120 Y. Soeya, 'The South China Sea: A Japanese Perspective', in Carolina Hernandez (ed.), *Security Implications of Conflict in the South China Sea: Perspectives from the Asia–Pacific*, Proceedings of the First International Conference on the South China Sea, Manila, 12–14 November 1995, Quezon City: Pacific Forum/CSIS and Institute for Strategic and Development Studies, 1997, pp. 130–1.
121 M. Atsumi, *Taiwan's Energy Security Issues: Domestic Energy Policies and Transporting Energy by Sea*, Institute for International Policy Studies, IIPS Policy Paper 300E, November 2003, pp. 10–16 [My ellipses]. Online. Available www.iips.org/bp300e.pdf (accessed 27 November 2004).
122 'The sub that never was…Defense Ministry says', *Korea Herald*. Online. Available www.koreaherald.co.kr/SITE/data/html_dir/2004/10/15/200410150005.asp (accessed 15 October 2004).
123 Nishimura Yoshiaki, adviser to Kawasaki Heavy Industries and former commander, MSDF Fleet Submarine Force, quoted in *Bōei Gijutsu Jānaru* [Defence Technology Journal], September 1997, pp. 4–19.
124 JDA, *Defense of Japan 2003*, Tokyo: JDA/Inter Group Corporation, 2003, p. 51.
125 M. E. Manyin, *Japan-North Korea Relations: Selected Issues*, Congressional Research Service Report for Congress, 26 November 2003, pp. 10–11. Online. Available www.nautilus.org/DPRKBriefingBook/Japan/CRS.pdf (accessed 15 October 2004).
126 M. Okabe, 'North Korea's Japanese Connection', *Japan Echo*, October 2003, pp. 41–3.
127 'Discarded Electric Appliances Exported to North Korea', *Daily Yomiuri*, 13 February 2004. Online. Available www.yomiuri.co.jp/newse/20040213wo25.htm (accessed 13 February 2004).
128 A. Misawa, 'Japan Perspective: Grim Reality Returns to E. Asia', *Daily Yomiuri Online*, 5 May 2002. Online. Available www.yomiuri.co.jp/newse/20020705wo41.htm (accessed 6 May 2002).
129 'Japanese Action Hailed', *Times Digest*, *New York Times*,14 January 2002, p. 2.
130 'N. Korean Spy Ship Same as 1998 Drug-Deal Vessel', *Mainichi Daily News*, 6 December 2002. Online. Available mdn.mainichi.co.jp/news/archive/200212/06/20021206p2a00m0dm012001c.html (accessed 14 August 2004).
131 National Institute for Defense Studies, *East Asian Strategic Review 2003*, Tokyo: National Institute for Defense Studies, 2003, p. 304.
132 One of the major criticisms levelled at the JDA after the December 2001 incident related to a delay of several hours before the Agency passed on its knowledge about the 'spy ship' to the JCG, prompting calls for the JDA to share intelligence more promptly with other government bodies. As a result, P-3C bases at Kanoya and Naha have since been fitted with image transmission systems.
133 'Navy Will Deploy a Pair of Missile Patrol Boats on Japan Sea', *Japan Digest*, 4 February 2002, p. 10.
134 'Japanese Coast Guard Stresses Strict Inspection of North Korean Vessels', *Kyodo*, 11 May 2004.
135 National Institute for Defense Studies, *East Asian Strategic Review 2000*, Tokyo: National Institute for Defense Studies, 2000, pp. 103–4; and National Institute for Defense Studies, *East Asian Strategic Review 2003*, Tokyo: National Institute for Defense Studies, 2003, p. 305.
136 'Yomiuri Proposals for Territorial Security', *Daily Yomiuri*, 17 February 2000. Online. Available www. yomiuri.co.jp/teigen-e/pro-f.htm (accessed 17 February 2000).
137 'Faster SDF Response on Sea Urged', *Daily Yomiuri*, 12 April 2002.
138 'Japan Defence Agency considers law revision', *Reuters News Service*, 13 January 2002.
139 Confidential interview with JDA official, 5 March 2002.

140 'Japanese MPs Agree to Include Ban in Amended Bill', *Kyodo*, 21 May 2004; and 'Japanese Agency Carries "Gist" of N Korea Ship Ban Bill', *Kyodo*, 17 March 2004.
141 *Asahi Shimbun*, 18 February 2004, p. 1.
142 'Govt plans response to military attacks', *Daily Yomiuri*, 17 February 2004. Online. Available www.yomiuri.co.jp/newse/20040217wo-1.htm (accessed 17 February 2004).
143 *Asahi Shimbun*, 4 March 2004, p. 2.
144 'North Korea reportedly exported 580m dollars' worth of missiles', *Yonhap*, 13 May 2003.
145 Manyin, op. cit., p. 6.
146 See, for example, 'A Nuclear North Korea? Live with it', T. G. Carpenter, Cato Institute, 1 October 2003. Online. Available www.cato.org/research/articles/carpenter-031001.html (accessed 13 October 2004).
147 Kim Jong-son, 'Must end anti-republic international cooperation commotion', *Nodong Sinmun* commentary carried by North Korean Uriminjokkkiri web site: BBC Monitoring, 14 August 2004.
148 'Japan to Train ASEAN Nations to Intercept WMD at Sea', *Kyodo*, 2 May 2004.
149 'Japan to Host Multinational Drill to Prevent Smuggling of WMD – Paper', BBC Monitoring/*Asahi Shimbun*, 27 July 2004.
150 'Scud ship unloads in Yemen', *CNN*, 14 December 2002. Online. Available archives.cnn.com/2002/WORLD/meast/12/14/yemen.scuds/ (accessed 20 October 2004).
151 *Yomiuri Shinbun*, 4 August 2004, p. 2; and *Mainichi Shimbun*, 27 October 2004, p. 2.
152 The *Nodong*-1 has an estimated range of 1,300 kilometres, unlike the untested, long-range *Taepodong*-II. The recurrent fear of Japanese officials is that North Korea will test launch another *Nodong*-1, capable of reaching most of Japan, on the assumption that this would increase pressure on the United States to open bilateral negotiations without necessarily incurring a military response (T. Hidaka and T. Kawata, 'N. Korea next move test firing missile?', *Daily Yomiuri*, 1 March 2003. Online. Available www.yomiuri.co.jp/newse/20030301wo03.htm (accessed 2 March 2003).
153 'Govt devises N. Korea Missile Plan', *Daily Yomiuri*, 9 February 2003. Online. Available www.yomiuri.co.jp/newse/20030209wo41.htm (accessed 9 February 2003).
154 'Japanese officials to analyse information on North Korean missile activity', *Kyodo*, 23 September 2004.
155 'Japan could fire back if attacked: Nukaga', *The Japan Times*, 5 September 1998, p. 1.
156 JDA, *Defense of Japan 2003*, op. cit., p. 117 [My ellipsis and emphasis].
157 'ASDF to acquire JDAM bomb kits', *Daily Yomiuri*, 18 September 2003, p. 3.
158 'Pre-emptive strike ability said necessary for Japan', *The Japan Times*, 2 October 2004. Online. Available www.japantimes.co.jp/cgi-bin/getarticle. pl5?nn20041002a2.htm (accessed 2 October 2004).

Appendices

1 I. Shearer, 'Current Law of the Sea Issues', in S. Bateman and R. Babbage (eds), *Maritime Change: Issues for Asia*, Sydney: Allen and Unwin, 1993, p. 52.
2 See E. J. Molenaar, 'Navigational Rights and Freedoms: Grey Areas and Scope for Regional Agreement', in S. Bateman (ed.), *Maritime Cooperation in the Asia–Pacific Region: Current Situation and Prospects*, Canberra Papers on Strategy and Defence, No. 132, Canberra: Australian National University Press, 1999, pp. 97–121.

3 Shearer, op. cit., pp. 54–62.
4 L. Paul, 'Strategic, Legal and Political Initiatives for Cooperative Maintenance at Law and Order at Sea', in Bateman, op. cit., pp. 127–8.
5 Shearer, op. cit., p. 56.
6 Ibid., p. 55.
7 H. Djalal, *Indonesia and the Law of the Sea*, Jakarta: Centre for Strategic and International Studies, 1995, pp. 83–4.

Bibliography

Books and monographs

Agawa, Naoyuki, *Umi no Yūjō* ['Friendship of the Sea'], Tokyo: Chuō Kōronsha, 2001.

Akaha, Tsuneo, *Japan in Global Ocean Politics*, Honolulu, HI: University of Hawaii Press and Law of the Sea Institute, 1985.

Alagappa, Muthiah (ed.), *Asian Security Practice: Material and Ideational Influences*, Stanford, CA: Stanford University Press, 1998.

Armacost, Michael H., *Friends or Rivals? The Insider's Account of U.S.–Japan Relations*, New York: Columbia University Press, 1996.

Atsumi, Masahiro, *Taiwan's Energy Security Issues: Domestic Energy Policies and Transporting Energy by Sea*, IIPS Policy Paper 300E, Tokyo: Institute for International Policy Studies, November 2003. Online available www.iips.org/bp300e.pdf (accessed 27 November 2004).

Auer, James E., *The Postwar Rearmament of Japanese Maritime Forces, 1945–71*, New York: Praeger, 1973.

Ball, Desmond, *Escalation and the Use of Nuclear Weapons*, Canberra Papers on Strategy and Defence no. 79, Canberra: Australian National University Press, 1991.

Ball, Desmond and Graham, Euan, *Japan's Airborne SIGINT Capabilities*, SDSC Working Paper no. 11, Strategic and Defence Studies Centre Canberra: Australian National University Press, 2000.

Ball, Desmond and Richelson, Jeffrey T., *The Ties That Bind: Intelligence Cooperation between the UK–USA Countries*, Sydney: Allen and Unwin, 1985.

Barnett, Robert W., *Beyond War: Japan's Concept of Comprehensive National Security*, Washington, DC: Pergamon Brasseys, 1984.

Bateman, Sam (ed.), *Maritime Cooperation in the Asia-Pacific Region: Current Situation and Prospects*, Canberra Papers on Strategy and Defence no. 132, Strategic and Defence Studies Centre, Canberra: Australian National University Press, 1999.

Bateman, Sam and Bates, Stephen (eds), *Calming the Waters: Initiatives for Asia Pacific Maritime Cooperation*, Canberra Papers on Strategy and Defence no. 114, Strategic and Defence Studies Centre, Canberra: Australian National University Press, 1996.

——, *The Seas Unite: Maritime Cooperation in the Asia Pacific Region*, Canberra Papers on Strategy and Defence no. 118, Canberra: Australian National University Press, 1996.

——, *Shipping and Regional Security*, Canberra Papers on Strategy and Defence no. 129, Strategic and Defence Studies Centre, Canberra: Australian National University Press, 1998.

Beasley, William G., *Japanese Imperialism 1894–1945*, Oxford: Clarendon Press, 1987.

——, *The Rise of Modern Japan*, Tokyo: Charles E. Tuttle Company, 1990.

Blair, Clay Jr, *Silent Victory: The U.S. Submarine War Against Japan*, Philadelphia, PA and New York: J.B. Lippincott Company, 1975.

Brodie, Bernard, *A Layman's Guide to Naval Strategy*, Princeton, NJ: Princeton University Press, 1943.

Buck, James H. (ed.), *The Modern Japanese Military System*, Beverly Hills, CA: Sage Publications, 1975.

Bywater, Hector C., *Navies and Nations: A Review of Naval Developments since the Great War*, London: Constable and Company, 1927.

Castex, Raoul, *Strategic Theories: Selections Translated and Edited, with an Introduction, by Eugenia C. Kiesling*, Annapolis, MD: Naval Institute Press Classics of Seapower Series, 1994.

Center for Naval Analyses/Korea Institute for Defense Analyses, The National Institute for Defense Studies. *Trilateral Naval Cooperation: A Workshop Report*, Alexandria, VA: Center for Naval Analyses, 1997.

——, The Okazaki Institute, *Trilateral Naval Cooperation: Workshop II*, Alexandria, VA: Center for Naval Analyses, May 1998.

——, *Trilateral Naval Cooperation: Workshop III*, Alexandria, VA: Center for Naval Analyses, October 1999.

Chapman, John W. M., Drifte, Reinhard and Gow, Ian T. M., *Japan's Quest for Comprehensive Security: Defence, Diplomacy, Dependence*, London: Frances Pinter, 1983.

Choucri, Nazli, North, Robert C. and Yamakage, Susumu, *The Challenge of Japan Before World War II and After: A Study of National Growth and Expansion*, London: Routledge, 1992.

Clesse, Armand, Inoguchi, Takashi, Keehn, E. B. and Stockwin, J. A. A. (eds), *The Vitality of Japan: Sources of National Strength and Weakness*, London: Macmillan, 1997.

Corbett, Julian S., *Some Principles of Maritime Strategy*, Annapolis, MD: Naval Institute Press Classics of Sea Power Series, 1988, reprint of the 1911 edition.

Curtis, Gerald L. (ed.), *Japan's Foreign Policy: After the Cold War: Coping with Change*, Armonk, NY: M.E. Sharpe, 1993.

Dibb, Paul, *Force Modernisation in Asia: Towards 2000 and Beyond*, SDSC Working Paper no. 306, Strategic and Defence Studies Centre, Canberra: Australian National University Press, 1997.

Djalal, Dino Patti, *The Geopolitics of Indonesia's Maritime Territorial Policy*, Jakarta: Centre for Strategic and International Studies, 1996.

Djalal, Hasjim, *Indonesia and the Law of the Sea*, Jakarta: Centre for Strategic and International Studies, 1995.

Dower, John W., *Empire and Aftermath: Yoshida Shigeru and the Japanese Experience, 1878–1954*, Cambridge, MA: Harvard East Asian Studies Monographs, 1979.

——, *Embracing Defeat: Japan in the Aftermath of World War II*, London: Penguin Books, 1999.

Drifte, Reinhard, *The Security Factor in Japan's Foreign Policy, 1945–1952*, Ripe: Saltire Press, 1983.

——, *Japan's Foreign Policy*, London: Royal Institute of International Affairs/Routledge, 1990.

Evans, David C. and Peattie, Mark R., *Kaigun: Strategy, Tactics and Technology in the Imperial Japanese Navy, 1887–1941*, Annapolis, MD: Naval Institute Press, 1997.

Friedman, George and Lebard, Meredith, *The Coming War with Japan*, New York: St Martin's Press, 1991.

Friedman, Norman, *The U.S. Maritime Strategy*, London: Jane's, 1988.

——, *The Naval Institute Guide to World Naval Weapons, 1997–99*, Annapolis, MD: Naval Institute Press, 1997.

Funabashi, Yōichi, *Alliance Adrift*, New York: Council on Foreign Relations, 1999.

George, Aurelia, *The Nakasone Challenge: Historical Constraints and New Initiatives in Japan's Defence Policy*, Legislative Research Service, Canberra: The Parliament of the Commonwealth of Australia, Discussion Paper no. 2, 1987.

Giffard, Sydney, *Japan Among the Powers 1890–1990*, New Haven, CT and London: Yale University Press, 1994.

Goralski, Robert and Freeburg, Russell W., *Oil & War: How the Deadly Struggle for Fuel in WWII Meant Victory or Defeat*, New York: William Morrow and Company Inc., 1987.

Gray, Colin S., *The Leverage of Sea Power: The Strategic Advantages of Navies in War*, New York: The Free Press, 1992.

Green, Michael J., *Arming Japan: Defense Production, Alliance Politics and the Postwar Search for Autonomy*, New York: Columbia University Press, 1995.

——, *Japan's Reluctant Realism. Foreign Policy Challenges in an Era of Uncertainty*, London and New York: Palgrave, 2003.

Griffiths, Ann L., Thomas, Robert H. and Haydon, Peter T. (eds), *The Changing Strategic Importance of International Shipping*, Halifax, NS: Centre for Foreign Policy Studies, Dalhousie University, 1998.

Grove, Eric J. (ed.), *The Defeat of the Enemy Attack on Shipping, 1939–1945: A Revised Edition of the (1957) Naval Staff History Volumes 1A (Text and Appendices) and 1B (Plans and Tables)*, Aldershot: The Navy Records Society/Ashgate Publishing Limited, 1997.

Hamzah, Ahmad (ed.), *The Straits of Malacca: International Co-operation in Trade, Funding and Navigational Safety*, Kuala Lumpur: Maritime Institute of Malaysia/ Pelanduk Publications, 1997.

Hamzah, Ahmad and Ogawa, Akira (eds), *Combating Piracy*, Kuala Lumpur: The Okazaki Institute, 2001.

Hook, Glen, *Militarization and Demilitarization in Contemporary Japan*, London and New York: Routledge, 1996.

Hoyt, Edwin P., *The Militarists: The Rise of Japanese Militarism Since WWII*, New York: Donald I. Fine, 1985.

——, *Three Military Leaders: Togo, Yamamoto, Yamashita*, Tokyo: Kodansha International, 1993; Parts I and II.

Hughes, Christopher W., *Japan's Re-emergence as a 'Normal' Military Power*, International Institute of Strategic Studies Adelphi Paper 368–9, Oxford: International Institute of Strategic Studies/Oxford University Press, 2004.

Inoguchi, Takashi, *Japan's International Relations*, London: Pinter, 1991.

Japan Shipowners' Association, *Annual Report 2002*. Online available www.jsanet.or.jp/e/annualr-e/pdf/j_shipping2002.pdf (accessed 30 October 2004).

——, *The Current State of Japanese Shipping*, March 2004, Online available www.jsanet.or.jp/e/shipping-e/pdf/currentstate_e2004.pdf (accessed 18 November 2004).

Jukes, Geoffrey, *Russia's Military and the Northern Territories Issue*, SDSC Working Paper no. 227, Strategic and Defence Studies Centre, Canberra: Australian National University Press, 1993.

Kahn, Herman, *Japan: The Emerging Superstate*, Englewood Cliffs, NJ: Prentice Hall, 1970.

Katahara, Eichi, *The Politics of Japanese Defence Policy Making, 1975–1989*, unpublished PhD thesis, Griffith University, Brisbane, 1990.

Kataoka, Tetsuya, *Waiting for a 'Pearl Harbor': Japan Debates Defense*, Stanford, CA: Hoover Institution Press, 1980.

Katzenstein, Peter J., *Cultural Norms and National Security: Police and Military in Postwar Japan*, Ithaca, NY and London: Cornell University Press, 1996.

Katzenstein, Peter J. and Okawara, Nobuo, *Japan's National Security: Structures, Norms and Policy Responses in a Changing World*, Ithaca, NY: Cornell East Asia Series, 1993.

Kawamura, Sumihiko, Adm. MSDF (Retd), *The Kawamura Papers*, Chiba: The Kawamura Institute, November 1998.

Keal, Paul, *Japan's Role in United States Strategy in the Pacific*, Canberra Working Paper no. 106, Strategic and Defence Studies Centre, Canberra: Australian National University Press, 1986.

Keddell, Joseph P., Jr, *The Politics of Defense in Japan: Managing Internal and External Pressures*, Armonk, NY: M.E. Sharpe, 1994.

Kennedy, Malcolm J. and O'Connor, Michael J. (eds), *Safely By Sea*, Lanham, MD: University Press of America, 1990.

Kenny, Henry J., *An Analysis of Possible Threats to Shipping in Key Southeast Asian Sea Lanes*, Alexandria, VA: Center for Naval Analyses Occasional Paper, February 1996.

Kissinger, Henry, *The White House Years*, Sydney: Hodder and Stoughton, 1979.

Koh, Kheng Lian, *Straits in International Navigation: Contemporary Issues*, London: Oceana Publications, 1982.

Komer, Robert, *Maritime Strategy or Coalition Defense?*, Lanham, MD: University Press of America/Abt Books, 1984.

Konapalli, Srikanth, *China's Naval Power*, New Delhi: Knowledge World in association with Institute for Defence Studies and Analyses, 2001.

Lehman, John F., Jr, *Command of the Sea*, New York: Charles Scribner's Sons, 1988.

Leifer, Michael, *International Straits of the World: Malacca, Singapore and Indonesia*, the Netherlands: Sijthoff and Noordhoff, 1978.

Levin, Norman D., *Japan's Changing Defense Posture*, Rand Note N-2739-OSD, Santa Monica, CA: Rand, June 1988.

Levin, Norman D., Lorell, Mark and Alexander, Arthur, *The Wary Warriors: Future Directions in Japanese Security Policies*, Santa Monica, CA: Rand, 1993.

Liddell Hart, Basil, *History of the First World War*, Trowbridge & Escher: Redwood Burn, 1977. First published as *The Real War 1914–1918*, 1930.

MccGwire, Michael, *Australia as a Regional Seapower: an External View*, SDSC Working Paper no. 11, Strategic and Defence Studies Centre Canberra: SDSC, Australian National University Press, 1979.

McCormack, Gavan (ed.), *Peace and Regional Security in the Asia-Pacific: A Japanese Proposal*, Peace Research Centre, Working Paper, no. 158, Canberra: The Australian National University, September 1995.

Maeda, Tetsuo, *The Hidden Army: the Untold Story of Japan's Military Forces*, Chicago, IL: Edition Q, Inc., 1995.

Mahan, Alfred T., *The Influence of Seapower Upon History, 1660–1783*, First American Century Series Edition, New York: Hill and Wang, 1957, reprint of the 1890 edition.

Manyin, Mark E., *Japan–North Korea Relations. Selected Issues*, Congressional Research Service Report for Congress, Washington, DC: Congressional Research Service, Library of Congress, 26 November 2003. Online available www.nautilus.org/DPRKBriefingBook/Japan/CRS.pdf (accessed 15 October 2004).

Maswood, S. Javed, *Japanese Defence: the Search for Political Power*, Institute of Southeast Asian Studies, Singapore: Allen and Unwin, 1990.

Matsumae, Tatsurō, *The Limits of Defense: Japan as an Unsinkable Aircraft-Carrier*, Kanagawa: Tōkai University Press, 1988.

Mendl, Wolf, *Japan's Asia Policy: Regional Security and Global Interests*, London and New York: Routledge, 1995.

Mitsuhisa, Masahiko, *Defense Policy of Japan: Maritime Self-Defense Force (JMSDF) in the early 21st Century*, MA Thesis, Naval Postgraduate School, Monterey, CA: US Department of Commerce National Technical Information Service, March 1995.

Mochizuki, Mike, *Japan: Domestic Change and Foreign Policy*, Santa Monica, CA: National Defense Research Institute/Rand, 1995.

Murai, Shigeru, *Shiirēn: Umi no Bōeisen* ['Sea Lanes: Defence Lines of the Sea'], Tokyo: NHK, 1983.

Nakamura, Takafusa, *Lectures on Modern Japanese Economic History: 1926–1994*, originally published in 1986 under the title *Showa Keizai Shi* ['A History of the Showa Economy'], Tokyo: LTCB International Library Foundation, 1994.

Nariai, Osamu, *History of the Modern Japanese Economy*, Tokyo: Foreign Press Center, Japan, 1997.

Navias, Martin S. and Hooton, E. R., *Tanker wars: the assault on merchant shipping during the Iran–Iraq conflict, 1980–1988*, London: Tauris Academic Studies, 1996.

Nish, Ian (ed.), *Anglo-Japanese Naval Relations*: Papers by Kiyoshi Ikeda, Ian Gow, John Chapman, Chit-chung Ong, International Studies 1985/3, London: London School of Economics and Political Science, 1985.

Nishimura, Shigeki, *Transformation of the U.S.–Japan Defense Posture: The New Soviet Challenge*, International Institute for Global Peace (IIGP) Policy Paper 65E, Tokyo: International Institute for Global Peace, October 1991.

Noer, John H., with Gregory, David, *Chokepoints: Maritime Economic Concerns in Southeast Asia*, Washington, DC: National Defense University Press/Center for Naval Analyses, 1996.

Nomura, Minoru, *Kaisen Shi ni Manabu* ['Learning from the History of War at Sea'], Tokyo: Bungei Shunjū, 1994.

Oga, Ryōhei, *Shiirēn no Himitsu* ['Sea Lane Secrets'], Tokyo: Shōbunsha, 1983.

Okazaki Hisahiko, *A Grand Strategy for Japanese Defense*, Lanham, MD: Abt Books/ University Press of America, 1986.

Parillo, Mark P., *The Japanese Merchant Marine in World War II*, Annapolis, MD: Naval Institute Press, 1993.

Polomka, Peter, *Japan as Peacekeeper: Samurai State, or New Civilian Power?*, Canberra Papers on Strategy and Defence no. 97, Strategic and Defence Studies Centre, Canberra: Australian National University, 1992.

Purrington, Courtney Allen, *Governing an Alliance: The Political Economy of the Japan–U.S. Security Relationship*, unpublished PhD thesis, Ann Arbor, MI: Harvard University, Xerox University Microfilms, 1993.

Pyle, Kenneth B., *The Japanese Question: Power and Purpose in a New Era*, Washington, DC: The AEI Press, 1996.

Ross, Robert S., *Managing A Changing Relationship: China's Japan Policy in the 1990s*, Carlisle Barracks: U.S. Army War College, September 1996. Online available www.carlisle.army.mil/ssi/pdffiles/PUB87.pdf (accessed 12 July 2004).

Sakanaka, Tomohisa, *Alternative Force Structure of Japan's Self Defence Force*, unpublished draft report, June 1977.

Sekai Keizai Johou Service, *Japanese–American Relations and Comprehensive Security*, Tokyo: Research Institute for Peace and Security, 1986.

Sen Gupta, Bhabani, Poulose, T. T. and Bhatia, Hemlata, *The Malacca Straits and the Indian Ocean: A Study of the Strategic and Legal Aspects of a Controversial Sea-lane*, New Delhi: Macmillan, 1974.

Stockwin, J. A. A., *Governing Japan*, Oxford: Blackwell, 1999.

Sudo, Sueo, *Southeast Asia in Japanese Security Policy*, Singapore: Institute of Southeast Asian Studies, 1991.

Toland, John, *The Rising Sun: The Decline and Fall of the Japanese Empire*, New York: Bantam Books, 1970.

Tsurutani, Taketsugu, *Japanese Policy and East Asian Security*, New York: Praeger, 1981.

Valencia, Mark J., *Northeast Asia: Transnational Navigational Issues and Possible Cooperative Responses*, University of California, Institute on Global Conflict and Cooperation, IGCC Policy Paper 33. Online available www-igcc.ucsd.edu/publications/policy_papers/pp3303.html (accessed 2 May 2003).

Vertzberger, Yaacov Y. I., *Coastal States, Regional Powers, Superpowers and the Malacca-Singapore Straits*, Institute of East Asian Studies Research Paper, Berkeley, CA: University of California, 1984.

Watanabe, Akio (ed.), *Sengo Nihon no Shushōtachi* ['Japan's Postwar Prime Ministers'], Tokyo: Chuō Kōronsha, 1995.

Watkins, Admiral James D., *The Maritime Strategy*, Annapolis, MD: The US Naval Institute, US Department of Defense, February 1986.

Weinstein, Martin, *Japan's Postwar Defence Policy*, New York: Columbia University Press, 1971.

Welfield, John, *An Empire in Eclipse: Japan in the Postwar American Alliance System: A Study in the Interaction of Domestic Politics and Foreign Policy*, London and Atlantic Highlands, NJ: The Athlone Press, 1988.

Wells, Linton II, *The Sea and Japan's Strategic Interests 1975–1985*, unpublished PhD thesis, Ann Arbor, MI: Johns Hopkins University, Xerox University Microfilms, 1975.

Winton, John, *Convoy: The Defence of Sea Trade 1890–1990*, London: Michael Joseph, 1983.

Woolley, Peter J., *Japan's Navy: Politics and Paradox, 1971–2000*, Boulder, CO: Lynne Reiner, 2000.

You, Ji, *The Armed Forces of China*, Sydney: Allen and Unwin, 1999.

Book chapters, journal articles and conference papers

Abhyankar, Jayant, 'An Overview of Piracy Problems: A Global Update', Paper presented to Society of International Law, Singapore (SILS) Piracy Seminar, 22 October 1999, Orchard Hotel, Singapore. Online available www.sils.org/seminar/1999-piracy-02.htm (accessed 11 November 2000).

——, 'Piracy and Ship Robbery: A Growing Menace', in A. Hamzah and A. Ogawa (eds), *Combating Piracy*, Kuala Lumpur: The Okazaki Institute, 2001, pp. 10–59.

Akaha, Tsuneo, 'Japan's Response to Threats of Shipping Disruptions in Southeast Asia and the Middle East', *Pacific Affairs*, 1986; 59(2): 255–77.

Akaha, Tsuneo, 'Japan's Comprehensive Security Policy', *Asian Survey*, 1991; 31(4): 324–40.

Akimoto, Kazuhisa, 'OPK (Ocean-Peace Keeping [*sic*]): Multilateral Naval Cooperation for Ocean Stabilization', in Susumu Takai (ed.), *Ocean Governance and OPK: The Thirteenth International Symposium Proceedings*, Tokyo: National Institute for Defense Studies, 1998, pp. 16–23.

——, 'Mission and Contribution of the Japan Maritime Self Defense Force in the Post-Cold War and EEZ Era', paper given to the International Conference sponsored by the Korean Institute for Maritime Strategy, 11 December 1998.

——, 'Re-routing Options and Consequences: Safeguarding Seaborne Trade in Straits and Archipelagic Regimes', conference paper given at the Thirteenth International Conference on Sea Lines of Communications, Canberra, April 2001.

Asanuma, Hirosato, 'Jōhō no Tōtaru Shisutemu ga Fukaketsu' ('Total System of Intelligence is Indispensable'), On the Sea-Lane Defense Problem in Dispute no. 1, *Sekai no Kansen* ['Ships of the World'], December 1982, pp. 126–9.

Auer, James E., 'Japan's Maritime Self-Defense Force: An Appropriate Maritime Strategy?', *Naval War College Review*, 1971; 24(4): 3–20.

Berger, Thomas U., 'From Sword to Chrysanthemum: Japan's Culture of Anti-militarism', *International Security*, 1993; 17(4): 119–50.

Blouin, J., Vice-Admiral, USN, 'Convoy or Defended Lanes', *Journal of the Australian Naval Institute*, 1989; 15(3): 53–8.

Booth, Ken, 'The New World Order' and the Future of Naval Power', *Journal of the Australian Naval Institute*, 1991; 17(4): 17–27.

——, 'The Role of Navies in Peacetime: The Influence of Future History on Sea Power', in Anthony Bergin and Hugh Smith (eds), '*Naval Power in the Pacific: Toward the Year 2000*', Boulder, CO: Lynne Reiner, 1993, pp. 145–62.

Bouchard, Joseph F. and Hess, Douglas J., 'The Japanese Navy and Sea-Lanes Defense', *U.S. Naval Institute Proceedings*, 1984; 110(973): 89–96.

Boutilier, James A., 'Air Defence of Merchant Ships', *Journal of the Australian Naval Institute*, 1989; 15(3): 39–51.

Buzan, Barry, 'Japan's Defence Problematique', *The Pacific Review*, 1995; 8(1): 25–43.

Buzan, Barry and Segal, Gerald, 'Rethinking East Asian Security', *Survival*, 1994; 36(2): 3–21.

Chan, Steve, 'Humanitarianism, Mercantilism, or Comprehensive Security? Disbursement Patterns of Japanese Foreign Aid', *Asian Affairs*, 1992; 19(1): 10–14.

Chūma, Kiyofuku, 'The 1986–90 Defense Plan: Does It Go Too Far?', *Japan Quarterly*, 1986; 33(1): 13–18.

Coulter, Daniel, 'The Economics of SLOC Protection; an Overvalued Mission', paper given to the Eleventh International Conference on the Sea Lanes of Communication (SLOC) Studies, Tokyo, 17–18 November 1997.

——, 'Hub Ports and Focal Points: New Entrants in the Maritime Security Lexicon' in L. Ann Griffiths, H. Robert Thomas and T. Peter Haydon (eds), *The Changing Strategic Importance of International Shipping*, Centre for Foreign Policy Studies, Halifax, NS: Dalhousie University, 1998, pp. 135–45.

Cronin, Patrick M. and Yamaguchi, Noboru, 'Japan's Future Regional Security Role', *Strategic Review*, Summer 1992, pp. 16–22.

Cronin, Richard P., 'Japan's Expanding Role and Influence in the Asia Pacific Region: Implications for US Interests', *Current Politics and Economics of Japan*, 1993; 3(2/3): 105–66.

Cunanan, Carlito Y. Rear Adm. AFP., 'Foreign Access to National Bases: An Essential Aspect of the Regional Security of the Sea Lanes of Communication', *Journal of the Australian Naval Institute*, May 1989; 57–60.

Donohue, Hector J., 'Protection of Sea Lines of Communications – Potential for Regional Co-operation in the Western Pacific', *Journal of the Australian Naval Institute*, May 1990; 57–64.

Dornan, James E. and Dornan, Diane S., 'Japan: Domestic Factors', in James M. Roherty (ed.), *Defense Policy Formation: Towards Comparative Analysis*, University of South California, 1980, pp. 195–226.

Doshita, Tetsurō, Lt Cdr, MSDF, 'Regional Security Links Japan and US', *US Naval Institute Proceedings*, March 1995, pp. 51–4.

Etō, Shinkichi, 'Japanese Perception of National Threats', in Charles E. Morrison (ed.) *Threats to Security in East Asia-Pacific*, Lexington, MA: Pacific Forum/Lexington Books, 1983, pp. 53–64.

——, 'China and Sino-Japanese Relations in the Coming Decades', *Japan Review of International Affairs*, 1996; 10(1): 16–34.

Garrett, Banning and Glasser, Bonnie, 'Chinese Apprehensions About Revitalization of the U.S.–Japan Alliance', *Asian Survey*, 1997; 37(4): 383–402.

Gotō, Motoo, 'Japan in Asia', *Japan Quarterly*, 1969; 26(4): 390–1.

Gow, Ian, 'Civil–Military Relations in Contemporary Japan – Civilian Control of Whose Military?', *The Japan Society*, 2001; 136: 5–13.

Green, Michael J. and Murata, Kōji, *The 1978 Guidelines for the U.S.–Japan Defense Cooperation: Process and the Historical Impact*, Working Paper no. 17, September 2000. Online available www.hfni.gsehd.gwu.edu/~nsarchiv/japan/GreenMurataWP.htm (accessed 4 May 2001).

Green, Michael J. and Nagashima, Akihisa. 'Key Areas to Watch In Japan–U.S. Security Relations', *Japan Quarterly*, 1999; 46: 17–22.

Green, Michael J. and Self, Benjamin L., 'Japan's Changing China Policy: From Commercial Liberalism to Reluctant Realism', *Survival*, 1996; 38(2): 35–58.

Grove, Eric J., 'Navies in Future Conflicts', in Anthony Bergin and Hugh Smith (eds), '*Naval Power in the Pacific: Toward the Year 2000*', Boulder, CO and London: Lynne Reiner, 1993, pp. 163–73.

Guoxing, Ji, *SLOC Security in the Asia Pacific*, Center Occasional Paper, Asia-Pacific Center for Security Studies, Honolulu, HI: February 2000. Online available www.apcss.org/Paper_SLOC_Occasional.htm (accessed 13 June 2000).

Hamzah, Ahmad, B. 'The Security of Sealanes: The Search for an Equitable Straits Regime', *Asian Defence Journal*, June 1993; 6–12.

Harris, Stuart and Cooper, Richard N., 'The U.S.–Japan Alliance' in R. Blackwill and P. Dibb (eds), *America's Asian Alliances*, Cambridge, MA: MIT Press, 2000.

Hellmann, Donald C., 'Japan and America in East Asia in the Wake of the Cold War', in A. Clesse, T. Inoguchi, E. B. Keehn and J. A. A. Stockwin (eds), *The Vitality of Japan: Sources of National Strength and Weakness*, Oxford: St Antony's Press, 1997, pp. 180–93.

Hill, J. R., Rear Adm., Royal Navy, 'Maritime Strategy for Medium Powers', *Journal of the Australian Naval Institute*, May 1988; 37–45.

Hinton, Harold C., 'The United States and Extended Security Commitments: East Asia', The *Annals of the American Academy of Political and Social Science*, no. 457, September 1981, p. 99.

Hirama, Yōichi, Rear Adm., MSDF (Retd), 'Japanese Professor on China's Navy Strategy', *Sekai no Kansen*, August 1996, pp. 82–5.

——, 'The Growing Chinese Navy and its Influence on Triple-Relation [*sic*] – Japan, US and Korea', paper given at Conference on Post-Unification Security Cooperation Among the United States, Korea and Japan, Hawaii, 20–23 April 1998.

Hiramatsu, Shigeo, 'The Chinese Navy and the Revival of "Sinocentrism"', *Shin Bōei Ronshū* (*Journal of National Defence*), 1992; 20(3): 16–37.

——, 'China's Naval Advance: Objectives and Capabilities', *Japan Review of International Affairs*, 1994; 8(2): 118–32.

Hughes, Christopher W., 'The North Korean Nuclear Crisis and Japanese Security', *Survival*, 1996; 38(2): 389–415.

——, 'Japan's Aum Shinrikyō, the Changing Nature of Terrorism, and the Post-Cold War Security Agenda', *Pacific Review*, 1998; 10(1): 39–60.

International Institute of Strategic Studies, 'Japan's Naval Power: Responding to New Challenges', *Strategic Comments*, Vol. 6, October 2000.

Israeli, Raphael, 'The Three Lakes in Japan's Strategy in East and Southeast Asia', *Strategic Analysis*, 2000; 24(5): 987–1003.

Izumi, Hajime, 'Improvement of the National Defense Strategy and Defence Buildup Plans for Post-Cold War Japan', '93 International Defense Academic Seminar, Korea National War College, 2 November 1993, pp. 53–67.

Johnson, Chalmers, 'Go-Banken-Sama Go Home', *The Bulletin of the Atomic Scientists*, 1996; 52(4): 22–9.

Kaihara [sometimes Kaibara], Osamu, 'Jissai Mondai to shite Fukanō' ('Such a Mission is far beyond Japan's Power'), On the Sea-Lane Defense Problem in Dispute no. 2, *Sekai no Kansen* ['Ships of the World'], December 1982, pp. 130–3.

Katahara, Eichi, 'Japan's Concept of Comprehensive National Security in the Post-Cold War World' in Susan L. Shirk and Christopher P. Twomey (eds), *Power and Prosperity: Economics and Security Linkages in Asia-Pacific*', New Brunswick, NJ: Transaction, 1996.

Kawamura, Sumihiko, Adm., MSDF (Retd), 'SLOC Security – A Japanese Perspective', in Sam Bateman and Stephen Bates (eds), *The Seas Unite: Maritime Cooperation in the Asia Pacific Region*, Canberra Papers on Strategy and Defence no. 118, Canberra: Australian National University Press, 1996, pp. 165–7.

——, 'International Cooperation for SLOC Security', Twelfth International Conference on the Sea Lanes of Communication (SLOC) Studies, Seoul, 6–7 April 1999.

Kawano, Katsutoshi, Capt., MSDF, 'Japan's Military Role: Alliance Recommendations for the Twenty-First Century', *Naval War College Review*, 1998; 51(4): 9–21.

Khamchoo, Chaiwat, 'Japan's Role in Southeast Asian Security: "Plus ça change"', *Pacific Affairs*, 1991; 64(1): 7–22.

Kitaoka, Shinichi, 'The Case for a Stronger Security Treaty', *Japan Echo*, Summer 1996; 68–75.

Kojima, Tomoyuki, 'Sino-Japanese Relations: A Japanese Perspective', *Asia-Pacific Review*, 1996; 3(1): 73–105.

Kondō, Shigekatsu, 'The Maritime Priorities of Japan', in S. Bateman and R. Babbage (eds), *Maritime Change: Issues for Asia*, St Leonards: Allen and Unwin, 1993, pp. 141–9.

Kōsaka, Masataka, 'Japan's Major Interests and Policies in Asia and the Pacific', *Orbis*, 1975; 24(3): 793–808.

——, 'Diplomacy and Security in the Twenty-first Century', *Japan Echo*, Winter 1996; 60–9.

Lam, Peng Er 'Japan and the Spratlys Dispute: Aspirations and Limitations', *Asian Survey*, 1996; 36: 995–1010.

Laxton, I. T., Lt Cdr RAN, 'Creeping Jurisdiction in Southeast Asia: Its effect on Naval Mobility', *Journal of the Australian Naval Institute*, 1988; 14(2): 4–9.

Leong, Teh Kong, *The Revolving Fund – A Unique Facility*, paper given at the 'International Conference on the Strait of Malacca: Meeting the Challenges of 21st Century', Malaysian Institute of Maritime Affairs, Kuala Lumpur, 14–15 June 1994.

MccGwire, Michael, 'The Geopolitical Importance of Strategic Waterways in the Asian-Pacific Regional', *Orbis*, 1975; 19(3): 1058–76.

Malik, Mohan, 'Japan Wary of Assertive China', *Jane's Intelligence Review*, 2000; 12(12): 22–5.

Manning, Robert, 'Sino-Japanese Relations', *The Washington Quarterly*, 1994; 17(1): 45–58.

Martin, Edward L., Cdr, USN, 'The Evolving Missions and Forces of the JMSDF', *Naval War College Review*, 1995; 48(2): 39–67.

Matsukane, Hisamoto, 'Japan and Security of the Sea Lanes', *Global Affairs*, (Spring): 1989; 49–64.

Mochizuki, Mike, 'Toward a New Japan–U.S. Alliance', *Japan Quarterly*, 1996; 43: 4–16.

Mochizuki, Mike and O'Hanlon, Michael, 'A Liberal Vision for the US–Japanese Alliance', *Survival*, 1998; 40: 127–34.

Nakamura, K., Cdr, MSDF. 'Strategic Influence of JMSDF', *U.S. Naval Institute Proceedings*, March 1994, p. 82.

Nelsen, Harvey, 'Japan Eyes China', *Journal of Northeast Asian Studies*, 1995; 14(4): 81–90.

Niksch, Larry A., 'Defence Burden-Sharing in the Pacific: US Expectations and Japanese Responses', *Asian Affairs*, July/August, 1981; 333–4.

——, *Japan's Defense Policy*, Japan's Economic Challenge, Japan Economic Committee, October 1990. Online available www.gwjapan.com.ftp/pub/policy/jec/jec6-1.txt (accessed 16 November 2002).

Nishijima, Ryōichi, 'Participation of Maritime Self-Defense Forces in RIMPAC', *Asia Pacific Community*, 1980; 7: 43–53.

Nye, Joseph S., 'China's Re-emergence and the Future of the Asia-Pacific', *Survival*, 1997–98; 39(4): 65–79.

Oga, Ryōhei, *Kaijō Jietai ni okeru Hōseijō no Shomondai ni tsuite* ['On various legal questions concerning the Maritime Self Defense Force'], *Bōei Hōkenkyū* ['Defence Law Research'], 1982; 5: 64–73.

Okazaki Hisahiko, 'China: A Function of the Japan–US Alliance', *Asia-Pacific Review*, 1996; 3(1): 45–50.

——, 'In Anticipation of an Animated Discussion', 27 January 1998. Online available www.glocomnet.or.jp/okazaki-inst/sealane.okazaki.e.html (accessed 14 March 1999).

Ouchi, Kazuomi, 'Making the Straits Safer: A User's View of Alternative Routes', paper given at the 'International Conference on the Strait of Malacca: Meeting the Challenges of the 21st Century', Malaysian Institute of Maritime Affairs, Kuala Lumpur, 14–15 June 1994.

Park, Young-Kyu, 'Organizational Structures for SLOC Security in Northeast Asia', *Journal of the Australian Naval Institute*, 1990; 16(2): 36–5.

Peattie, Mark R., 'Akiyama Saneyuki and the Emergence of Modern Japanese Naval Doctrine', *U.S. Naval Institute Proceedings*, 1977; 103: 61–9.

Poirier, Michael Lt Cdr, USN, 'Sea Control and Regional Warfare', *U.S. Naval Institute Proceedings*, 1993; 119(7): 63–5.

Priestnall, Graham, 'ANZUS and the Radford-Collins Agreement: Australia's naval mission', *Journal of the Australian Naval Institute*, 1997; 23(1): 49–52.

Purrington, Courtney, 'Tokyo's Policy Response During the Gulf War', *Pacific Affairs*, 1992; 65: 161–81.

Sakhuja, Vijay, 'Maritime Order and Piracy', *Strategic Analysis*, 2000; 24(5): 923–39.

Sakurada, Daizō, 'Why We Need the US–Japan Security Treaty', *Asia-Pacific Review*, 1998; 5(1): 13–38.

Satō, Ichirō, 'The Naval Policy of Japan', *Brassey's Naval and Shipping Annual, 1927*, London: William Clowes and Sons, 1927, pp. 71–80.

Satō, Seizaburō, 'Clarifying the Right of Collective Self-Defense', *Asia-Pacific Review*, 1996; 3(2): 91–107.

Sekino, Hideo, Commander Imperial Japanese Navy (Retd), 'Japan and Her Maritime Defense', *U.S. Naval Institute Proceedings*, 1971; 97(819): 98–121.

Shearer, Ivan, 'Current Law of the Sea Issues', in S. Bateman and R. Babbage (eds), *Maritime Change: Issues for Asia*, Sydney: Allen and Unwin, 1993, pp. 47–69.

Shikata, Toshiyuki, 'Japan's Security Strategy: Meeting the Needs of a New Era', *Asia-Pacific Review*, 1996; 3(1): 51–72.

——, 'Redefinition of the Security Setup', *Japan Review of International Affairs*, 1996; 10(4): 291–313.

——, 'Japan's Response to the Situations in Areas Surrounding Japan', Okazaki Institute. Online available www.glocomnet.or.jp/okazaki-inst/korea-pro-jap/shikata.kj3.eng.html (accessed 22 April 2001).

Shilling, David, 'A Reassessment of Japan's Naval Defense Needs' *Asian Survey*, 1976; 16(3): 216–29.

Soeya, Yoshihide, 'Islands of Contention', *Look Japan*, May 1993.

——, 'The Japan–U.S. Alliance in a Changing Asia', *Japan Review of International Affairs*, 1996; 10(4): 265–75.

——, 'The South China Sea: A Japanese Perspective', in Carolina Hernandez (ed.), *Security Implications of Conflict in the South China Sea: Perspectives from the Asia-Pacific*, Proceedings of the First International Conference on the South China Sea, Manila, 12–14 November 1995, Quezon City: Pacific Forum/CSIS and Institute for Strategic and Development Studies, 1997, pp. 128–34.

——, 'Japan: Normative Constraints Versus Structural Imperatives', in Muthiah Alagappa (ed.), *Asian Security Practice: Material and Ideational Influences*, Stanford, CA: Stanford University Press, 1998, pp. 198–233.

Stockwin, J. A. A., 'Politics Japanese Style: Change or Continuity?', *Pacific Research*, May 1996; 3–5.

Subijakto, Maj Gen, 'Indonesia's Perception of SLOC in Southeast Asia', *Journal of the Australian Naval Institute*, 1989; 15(4): 27–31.

Swinnerton, Russ, 'A Description of Regional Shipping Routes: Navigational and Operational Considerations', *Maritime Studies*, 1996; 87: 10–22.

Tanaka, Akihiko, 'Japan's Security Policy in the 1990s', in Funabashi Yōichi (ed.) *Japan's International Agenda*, New York: New York University Press, 1994, pp. 28–56.

——, 'A Model for Japanese Security in the Twenty-first Century', *Japan Review of International Affairs*, 1996; 10(4): 276–90.

Taoka, Shunji, '21 Seiki Higashi Ajia no Senryaku Kankyō' ('East Asia's Strategic Environment in the 21st Century'), *Sekai no Kansen*, 1995; 504: 70–5.

Terashima, Hiroshi, 'The Role of NGOs in Dealing with Piracy at Sea', paper presented at Society of International Law, Singapore (SILS) Piracy Seminar', 22 October 1999,

Orchard Hotel, Singapore. Online available www.sils.org/seminar/1999-piracy-09.htm (accessed 19 April 2000).

——, 'Ajia no Umi to Kaizoku no Kyōi' ['Asia's Seas and the Piracy Threat'], *Gaikō Foramu*, 2001; 156: 38–41.

Till, Geoffrey, 'China and Japan: America's Search for Allies', *Armed Forces*, 1985; 4(9): 338–42.

Tsai, Michael, M. and Chen, York W., 'Submarines and Taiwan's Defense', *Taiwan Defense Affairs*, 2001; 1(3): 122–77.

Tsunoda, Jun, 'Japanese Security Problems and Perspectives in the Late 1970s', *Orbis*, 1975; 24(3): 874–86.

Tsurutani, Taketsugu, 'Japan: The Security Debate', in J. M. Roherty (ed.), *Defense Policy Formation: Towards Comparative Analysis*, Los Angeles, CA: University of South California, 1980, pp. 175–94.

Twomey, Christopher P., 'Japan, A Circumscribed Balancer', *Security Studies*, 2000; 9(4): 167–205.

Uchida, Kazutomi, Adm., MSDF (Retd), 'Naval Competition and Security in East Asia', in Jonathan Alford (ed.), *Sea Power and Influence: Old Issues and New Challenges*, Farnborough: International Institute for Strategic Studies, 1980, pp. 104–9.

Valencia, Mark J., 'Energy and Insecurity in Asia', *Survival*, 1997; 39(3): 85–106.

Victor, B. R., 'Denial of Passage Rights in the Indonesian Archipelago – Australian Implications', *Journal of the Australian Naval Institute*, 1994; 20(1): 41–50.

Waters, D. W., 'Japan – Defeat through Blockade – 1941–45', *The Naval Review*, 1988; 76(3): 246–7.

Weeks, Stanley, 'Law and Order at Sea: Pacific Cooperation in Dealing with Piracy, Drugs and Illegal Migration', in S. Bateman and S. Bates (eds), *Calming the Waters: Initiatives for Asia Pacific Cooperation*, Canberra Papers on Strategy and Defence no. 114, Strategic and Defence Studies Centre, Canberra: Australian National University Press, 1996, pp. 43–56.

Welfield, John, 'The American Japanese Alliance at the Turn of the Millennium', *Pacific Research*, May 1996; 6–11.

Wettern, Desmond, 'Ships, not lines, must be defended', *Pacific Defence Reporter*, 1989 Annual Reference Edition, pp. 90–3.

Woolley, Peter J. and Woolley, Mark S., 'Japan's Sea Lane Defense Revisited,' *Strategic Review*, 1996; 24(4): 49–58.

Yamaguchi, Noboru, 'Why the U.S. Marines Should Remain in Okinawa: a Military Perspective', in Ralph A. Cossa (ed.) *Restructuring the U.S.–Japan Alliance: Towards a More Equal Partnership*, Washington, DC: The CSIS Press, 1997, pp. 98–110.

Yamamoto, Makoto, Vice Adm., MSDF (Retd), 'Sealane in the Asia-Pacific Region Today and their Vulnerabilities', paper presented to the Eleventh International Conference on the Sea Lanes of Communication (SLOC) Studies, Tokyo, 17–18 November 1997.

Yoshida, Manabu, Adm., MSDF (Retd), Keynote Address, Eleventh International Conference on the Sea Lanes of Communication (SLOC) Studies, Tokyo, 17–18 November 1997.

Official documents and reference sources

Advisory Group on Defense Issues, *The Modality of the Security and Defense Capability of Japan*, Japanese government Translation GM:3338-, 12 August 1994.

Asahi Shimbun, *Japan Almanac 1999*, Tokyo: Asahi Shimbunsha, 1998.

Asia Pacific Energy Research Centre, *Emergency Oil Stocks and Energy Security in the APEC Region*, Tokyo: APERC, March 2000.

Australian Department of Industry, Tourism and Resources, Australian Energy News: 'Energy Security and Sealane Disruption', Issue 24, June 2002. Online available www.industry.gov.au/resources/netetenergy/aen/aen24/6enrgy.html (accessed 16 December 2002).

Australian Senate Standing Committee on Foreign Affairs, Defence and Trade, *Japan's Defence and Security in the 1990s*, Canberra: Senate Printing Unit, 1992.

BBC Monitoring Summary of World Broadcasts, Asia Pacific.

Comprehensive National Security Study Group, *Report on Comprehensive National Security*, Japanese government translation GE:118489, 2 July 1980.

Foreign Press Center, Japan. *Facts and Figures of Japan*, 1997 Edition, Tokyo: Foreign Press Center, Japan, 1997.

International Institute for Strategic Studies, *The Military Balance*, London: Brasseys, various editions.

International Maritime Bureau, *Piracy and Armed Robbery Against Ships, Annual Report 2001*, Barking: ICC International Maritime Bureau, January 2002.

——, *Piracy and Armed Robbery Against Ships. Annual Report 2003*, Barking: ICC International Maritime Bureau, January 2004.

International Maritime Organization. *Reports on Acts of Piracy and Armed Robbery Against Ships. Annual Report – 2003*, MSC.4/Circ.50, 27 April 2004.

Jane's, *Jane's Fighting Ships 1996–97*, Coulsden: Jane's Information Group, 1996.

——, *Jane's Fighting Ships 1999–2000*, Coulsden: Jane's Information Group, 1999.

Japan Defense Agency, *Defense of Japan*, Tokyo: Japan Defense Agency/Japan Times/Inter Group Corp., (successive issues 1976–2003).

——, *Waga Kuni ni okeru Bōeiryoku Seibi no Keika* ['Trends in Japan's Defence Equipment Build-up'], internal JDA report, 1982.

——, 'Shiirēn Bōei to sono Haikei' ['Sea lane defence and its background'], *Bōei Nenkan*, Tokyo: Japan Defense Agency, 1983, pp. 1–168.

——, *Mid-term Defense Program (Fiscal 2005–2009) (Summary)*, unofficial translation, December 2004.

——, *National Defense Program Guideline for FY 2005 and After*, unofficial translation, December 2004.

The Joint Army–Navy Assessment Committee, *Japanese Naval and Merchant Shipping Losses During World War II By All Causes*, Washington, DC: Navy Department, February 1947.

Ministry of Economy, Trade and Industry, Japan, *Energy in Japan*, Tokyo: Agency for Natural Resources and Energy, Ministry of Economy, Trade and Industry, September 2001.

Ministry of Foreign Affairs, Japan, *Diplomatic Bluebook*, Tokyo: Ministry of Foreign Affairs, Japan/Urban Connections, various issues (1988–2004).

National Institute for Defense Studies, *East Asian Strategic Review*, Tokyo: National Institute for Defense Studies, successive issues 1996/97–2003.

Special Study Group on Japan's Role in the International Community (Liberal Democratic Party), 'Japan's Role in the International Community' (Draft Report), February 1992, as published in *Japan Echo*, Summer 1992, pp. 49–58.

United Nations Conference on Trade and Development, *Review of Maritime Transport, 2002*, New York and Geneva: United Nations, 2002.

United States Department of Defense, *The United States Security Strategy for the East Asia-Pacific Region* (EASR 1995), Washington, DC: US Department of Defense, February 1995.

——, *The United States Security Strategy for the East Asia-Pacific Region* (EASR 1999), Washington, DC: US Department of Defense, November 1998.

——, *Annual Report on the Military Power of the People's Republic of China*, July 2002. Online available www.globalsecurity.org/military/library/report/2002/d20020712china.pdf (accessed 2 November 2004).

United States Embassy, Tokyo, Political Section, Translation Services Branch, *Daily Summary of the Japanese Press*, 1969–2004.

United States Federal Research Division, Library of Congress, *Japan: A Country Study*, Washington, DC: US Federal Research Division, Library of Congress/Department of the Army, 1992.

Online reference sources

Official

Japan Coast Guard. Online available www.kaiho.mlit.go.jp/e/index_e.htm (accessed 30 October 2004).

Japan Defense Agency. Online available www.jda.go.jp/e/index_.htm (accessed 30 October 2004).

Japanese Embassy in India. Online available www.japan-emb.org.in/pressreleases/Press_ReleasesMenu.htm (accessed 29 August 2004).

Ministry of Economy, Trade and Industry. Online available www.meti.go.jp/ (accessed 30 October 2004).

Ministry of Foreign Affairs, Japan. Online available www.mofa.go.jp/ index.html (accessed 30 October 2004).

Ministry of Internal Affairs and Communications Statistics Bureau. Online available www.stat.go.jp (accessed 30 October 2004).

US Department of Energy, Energy Information Administration. Online available www.eia.doe.gov (accessed 30 October 2004).

Non-official

BP Amoco Statistical Review of World Energy. Online available www.bp.com/centres/energy2002/oil/reserves.asp (accessed 6 May 2002).

The General Libraries, the University of Texas at Austin map collection. Online available www.lib.utexas.edu/maps/ (accessed 30 October 2004).

International Chamber of Commerce Commercial Crime Services, International Maritime Bureau. Online available www.iccwbo.org/ccs/institutional/introduction.asp (accessed 30 October 2004).

Japan Shipowners' Association. Online available www.jsanet.or.jp/index.html (accessed 30 October 2004).

Marisec.org. Online available www.marisec.org (accessed 30 October 2004).

The Nippon Foundation and Piracy Database. Online available www.nippon-foundation.or.jp/english/db01.nippon-foundation.or.jp/cgi-bin/zaidan/search_e.cgi (accessed 15 June 2000).

The Okazaki Institute. Online available www.glocomnet.or.jp/okazaki-inst/okazaki-eng.html (accessed 30 October 2004).

Reuters Business Briefing. Online available www.businessreuters.com (accessed 1 December 2002).

Interviews

Admiral Akimoto Kazumine, MSDF (Retd), National Institute for Defense Studies, 1 March 1999, and Ship and Ocean Institute, Tokyo, 4 March 2002.

Mr Akiyama Masahiro, (former JDA Vice Administrative Vice-Minister) Chairman, Ship and Ocean Foundation, Nippon Foundation, Tokyo, 4 March 2002.

Mr Arima Jun, Director for International Energy Strategy, Ministry for Economy, Trade and Industry, Tokyo, 28 February 2002.

Confidential interviews with JDA officials, 16 February 1999 and 5 March 2002.

Mr Gary Eng, Team Leader, Asia Pacific Energy Research Centre (APERC), Tokyo, 5 March 2002.

Commander Gotō Shinichi (CGSI-III), Deputy Director, International Affairs and Crisis Management Division, Japan Coast Guard, Tokyo, 7 March 2002.

Admiral Hirama Yōichi, MSDF (Retd), National Defense Academy, Yokosuka, 16 March 1999.

Mr Hoshuyama Noboru, (former Director, Defense Facilities Administration Agency) Adviser, Kyoei Life Insurance, Tokyo, 11 March 1999.

Ms Iimura Akiko, Deputy Director, International Division, Agency for Natural Resources and Energy, Ministry for Economy, Trade and Industry, Tokyo, 28 February 2002.

Mr Itō Kenichi, Mitsubishi Electric Corp, Tokyo, 8 March 1999.

Vice Admiral Kaneda Hideaki, MSDF (Retd), Senior Research Advisor for National Security, Mitsubishi Research Institute, Canberra, 4 April 2001.

Dr Katayama Yoshio, National Institute for Defense Studies, Tokyo, February, 1999.

Admiral Kawamura Sumihiko, MSDF (Retd), Okazaki Institute, Tokyo, March 1999 (various dates) and 1 March 2002.

Mr Manabe Ro, Japan Defense Agency, Tokyo, 9 March 1999.

Ambassador Murata Ryōhei (former Ambassador to the United States) Executive Director, Nippon Foundation, Tokyo, 6 March 2002.

Captain Nakanishi Kenji, MSDF, Research Department, Maritime Staff College, Tokyo, 4 March 2002.

Professor Nishihara Masashi, National Defense Academy, Yokosuka, March 1999.

Mr Nomura Eigo, Deputy Director, Equipment Coordination Division, Bureau of Finance and Equipment, Japan Defense Agency, Tokyo, 1 March 2002.

Ambassador Okazaki Hisahiko, Okazaki Institute, Tokyo, 1999, 12 March 1999.

Captain Osuka Yoshihiro, Asst General Manager, Marine Safety and Environmental Team, 'K'-Line (Kawasaki Kisen Kaisha), Tokyo, 28 February 2002.

Captain Otsuka Umio, MSDF, Agenda Coordinator, Western Pacific Naval Symposium, Plans and Program Division, Maritime Staff Office, Japan Defense Agency, Tokyo, 1 March 2002.

Captain Pottengal Mukundan, IMB Director, Barking, 16 September 2004.

Professor Sakanaka Tomohisa, President, Research Institute for Peace and Security, Tokyo, 12 February 1999.

Admiral Sakonjo Naotoshi, MSDF (Retd), Research Institute for Peace and Security, Tokyo, 12 February 1999 and 5 March 2002.

Mr Sam Jameson, Tokyo, 10 March 1999.
General Shikata Toshiyuki, GSDF (Retd), Tokyo, 7 March 1999.
Admiral Soenardi, Republic of Indonesia Navy, Jakarta, 11 March 2000.
Professor Tadokoro Masayuki, National Defense Academy, Yokosuka, 7 March 2002.
Mr Takamizawa Nobushige, Councillor, Cabinet National Security Affairs Office, Tokyo, 1 March 1999.
Mr Umemoto Kazuyoshi, Director, First International Organizations Division, Economic Affairs Bureau, Ministry of Foreign Affairs, February 1999.
Professor Watanabe Akio, Aoyama Gakuin University, Tokyo, 1999 (various) and as President, Research Institute for Peace and Security, Tokyo, 5 March 2002.
Mr Yoshizaki Tomonori, National Institute for Defense Studies, Tokyo, 4 March 2002.

Index